its Online T.E. (Open Dashboard)
"Instructional Teaching System" Click o

SCHOLAST

MW01691092

READ 180®

NEXT GENERATION

TEACHER IMPLEMENTATION GUIDE

p160 How to assign an "rskills test"

Book Cover Credits

ISBN-13: 978-0-545-34864-5
ISBN-10: 0-545-34864-1

5 6 7 8 9 10 14 20 19 18 17 16

Text pages printed on 10% PCW recycled paper.

Dear *READ 180* Next Generation Teacher,

Welcome to *READ 180* Next Generation! *READ 180* is a comprehensive, research-based intervention proven to accelerate the reading levels and test scores of struggling students in Grades 4–12. As the world's most effective system for raising student reading achievement, *READ 180* supports you with guiding your students to "do a 180" in their reading progress.

Have you ever seen a student "do a 180"? It's a complete turnaround. Understanding replaces confusion. Confidence replaces embarrassment. Motivation replaces frustration. Success replaces failure. *READ 180* is the answer to the number one problem in education: *older students reading below grade level*.

During today's training, you will learn about the components of *READ 180* and how they work together to prepare the next generation of learners for college and career success. Recognizing that raising reading achievement is everyone's responsibility, *READ 180* includes state-of-the-art tools to empower all partners in education.

- **Every Student Engaged** The Student Dashboard increases students' ownership, accountability, and motivation for learning by allowing them to track their own *READ 180* performance and reading progress.
- **Every Teacher Effective** The Teacher Dashboard is a comprehensive teaching management system that simplifies planning lessons, differentiating instruction, and monitoring student growth throughout the year.
- **Every Leader Empowered** The Leadership Dashboard provides unparalleled access to student performance data, helping school and district administrators manage their program implementation and provide follow-up support as needed.

This *Teacher Implementation Guide* and today's training will ensure that you have the resources and information you need to return to your classroom and begin effectively implementing all *READ 180* components with your students.

Thank you for joining us today and for helping to turn around the lives of struggling readers.

Sincerely,

Carol Chanter

Carol Chanter
Vice President, Implementation Services
Scholastic Education

Table of Contents

Getting Started Training: Part 1

Agenda

15 minutes	**Welcome and Introductions**
30 minutes	**Introducing *READ 180* Next Generation** • Building on a History of Success • Understanding the *READ 180* Instructional Model
90 minutes	**The Student Experience** • Experiencing the *READ 180* Instructional Model • Navigating the Instructional Software • Previewing the *READ 180* Library
	Break
90 minutes	**Implementing the Instructional Model** • Planning Whole- and Small-Group Instruction • Monitoring Instructional Software • Supporting Independent Reading
	Lunch
30 minutes	**Managing Learning With the Scholastic Achievement Manager** • Adding and Enrolling Students • Targeting *SRI* • Modifying *READ 180* Settings
30 minutes	**Teaching Effectively With the Teacher Dashboard**
	Break
30 minutes	**Preparing for Your First Three Weeks** • Communicating With Families • Setting Up the *READ 180* Classroom • Administering the *SRI*
15 minutes	**Final Questions & Evaluation**

Learning Outcomes

- Understand how *READ 180* Next Generation raises student reading achievement and increases college and career readiness.
- Experience the *READ 180* Instructional Model from the students' perspective.
- Use resources to effectively teach, manage, and assess each part of the Instructional Model.
- Manage classes and enrollment with the Scholastic Achievement Manager.
- Plan and teach daily *rBook* instruction effectively with the Teacher Dashboard.
- Prepare for your first three weeks with *READ 180* Next Generation.

Getting Started Training: Part 2

Agenda

10 minutes	**Welcome and Introductions**
30 minutes	**Structuring Engagement With Routines**
40 minutes	**Pacing an *rBook* Workshop**
	Break
40 minutes	**Planning and Teaching a Workshop With the Dashboard** • Planning Daily Lessons • Using the Interactive Teaching System (ITS) • Exploring Professional Development Resources
30 minutes	**Assessing Workshop Learning** • Wrapping Up With a Workshop Project • Administering Computer-Based *rSkills Tests*
30 minutes	**Evaluating the SAM Student Digital Portfolio** • Rating Success Zone Recordings • Scoring Student Writing
	Lunch
30 minutes	**Identifying SAM Reports to Monitor and Plan**
40 minutes	**Monitoring Student Progress With the Dashboard** • Understanding Data Snapshots • Customizing Notifications and Reports
40 minutes	**Planning Workshop CheckPoints With the Dashboard**
	Break
25 minutes	**Continuing Your Learning**
15 minutes	**Final Questions & Evaluation**

Learning Outcomes

- Implement key Instructional Routines effectively to structure student engagement.
- Pace and differentiate instruction throughout an *rBook* Workshop.
- Assess Workshop learning to identify student needs and target instruction.
- Use the Scholastic Achievement Manager to assess fluency, evaluate writing, and run key data-rich reports.
- Use the Teacher Dashboard to prepare lessons, monitor progress, and plan differentiation CheckPoints.
- Identify resources to support ongoing professional development.

Conversion Training

Agenda

10 minutes	**Welcome and Introductions**
25 minutes	**Introducing *READ 180* Next Generation**
60 minutes	**Using the Dashboard to Plan and Monitor Progress** • Planning Daily Instruction With ITS • Analyzing Data Snapshots • Customizing Notifications and Reports
	Break
75 minutes	**Enhancing Whole- and Small-Group Instruction** • Guiding Multiple Reads of Rigorous, Complex Texts • Strengthening Writing Practices • Facilitating Project-Based Learning • Differentiating Daily Small-Group Lessons
45 minutes	**Differentiating Effectively at CheckPoints** • Understanding New Support for CheckPoints • Forming Targeted Groups With the Groupinator™
	Lunch
60 minutes	**Building Student Accountability and Independence** • Tracking Progress on the Student Dashboard • Supporting Reading in the Writing Zone • Exploring Content-Area Connections With eReads
	Break
30 minutes	**Scoring With the SAM Student Digital Portfolio**
15 minutes	**Starting Your Year With *READ 180* Next Generation**
10 minutes	**Final Questions & Evaluation**

Learning Outcomes

- Understand the research-based enhancements to *READ 180* Next Generation.
- Plan daily data-driven lessons with the Teacher Dashboard.
- Enhance Whole- and Small-Group Instruction to build students' college and career readiness.
- Teach targeted lessons during CheckPoints for differentiated instruction.
- Guide students to develop reading and writing independence.
- Use the SAM Student Digital Portfolio to evaluate and track student work.
- Identify strategies for a successful start with *READ 180* Next Generation.

Follow-Up Training

Agenda

15 minutes	**Welcome and Introductions**
30 minutes	**Sharing Successes and Gathering Questions**
45 minutes	**Increasing Accountability in Your *READ 180* Classroom** • Monitoring Daily Independent Reading Progress • Maximizing Student Engagement in the Software
	Break
50 minutes	**Enhancing Reading Comprehension and Fluency** • Pacing Reading Instruction to Support All Learners • Identifying Resources to Differentiate Instruction
50 minutes	**Strengthening Student Writing** • Using Rubrics to Assess and Revise Writing • Targeting Instruction at Writing CheckPoints
	Lunch
60 minutes	**Building Expertise With SAM** • Adjusting Settings to Customize Learning • Running Key Reports and Identifying Resources
40 minutes	**Analyzing Data to Fine-Tune Differentiation** • Drilling Down Data to Diagnose Needs • Customizing Differentiation CheckPoints in the Groupinator
	Break
30 minutes	**Motivating *READ 180* Students**
10 minutes	**Final Questions & Evaluation**

Learning Outcomes

- Share motivational stories and identify challenges.
- Implement strategies to increase student engagement and accountability.
- Pace and differentiate instruction to support students with complex texts.
- Use rubrics to assess writing and target instruction at Writing CheckPoints.
- Deepen understanding of SAM features.
- Analyze report data to diagnose student learning needs and plan differentiation CheckPoints.
- Hold one-to-one conferences to reflect on progress and set learning goals.

READ 180 Contact Information

Know when and how to reach Scholastic contacts for answers to all of your *READ 180* implementation questions.

Contact	Can Help To...	Phone/Email
READ 180 Customer Service	• Activate software licenses • Answer questions about the status of materials	1-877-234-READ (7323) READ180custserv@scholastic.com
Product Maintenance and Support	• Answer questions about installation, specifications, or any technical program features (with a Product Maintenance and Support Plan)	1-800-283-5974 TechSupport@scholastic.com www.scholastic.com/read180ng/productsupport
Account Executive	• Order additional licenses • Purchase additional program or supplemental materials • Provide information about implementation and technical services	
Implementation Consultant/ Project Manager	• Provide *READ 180* implementation training • Support you with ongoing professional development services including *READ 180* seminars, interactive webinars, and In-Classroom Support	
"Ask Dee" on the *READ 180* Community Website	• Answer any questions related to teaching *READ 180*	www.read180.com/community

TEACHER IMPLEMENTATION GUIDE

Research and Program Overview

Reflecting on Your Struggling Readers

READ 180 **Next Generation was designed to address characteristic challenges for older struggling readers. Use the chart below to reflect on your students and their academic struggles.**

Challenge	Reflections
Lack of motivation or engagement	*Not feeling motivated to read prevents my students from…*
Below-grade level critical reading and comprehension skills	*My students struggle to understand what they have read when…*
Limited academic language and word-study skills	*I would describe my students' vocabulary for speaking, reading, and writing as...*
Slow or choppy fluency with connected text	*I notice that students who read passages word-by-word often struggle with...*
Difficulty with single or multi-paragraph writing	*One way weak writing skills affect my students' school performance is…*

Introducing *READ 180* Next Generation

***READ 180* Next Generation is a comprehensive system for raising reading achievement in older struggling readers.**

Comprehensive Research-Based System

READ 180 Next Generation is an intensive reading intervention program for students in Grades 4–12 who are reading below grade level. Designed to meet the needs of older struggling readers, *READ 180* provides individualized instruction through teacher-directed lessons, adaptive software, age-appropriate nonfiction and fiction texts, and data-driven differentiation.

As one of the most thoroughly tested and documented reading intervention programs in the country, *READ 180* has been proven to:

✓ Improve performance on state tests.

✓ Reduce the student dropout rate.

✓ Improve reading achievement for African American, Native American, and Latino students.

✓ Improve reading achievement for English language learners.

✓ Improve reading achievement for students receiving special education services.

✓ Increase teacher retention.

Three Stages of Instruction and Support

READ 180 accelerates learning and enables struggling readers to experience success in elementary, middle, and high school settings. Depending on the grade level you teach, your program materials will come from one of three Stages with age-appropriate content and leveled reading support.

Three Stages of Instruction and Support

	Elementary Stage A Grades 4–6	*Middle School* Stage B Grades 6–8	*High School* Stage C Grades 9 and up
Beginning Readers (BR)		***SYSTEM 44®***	
LEVEL 1 • Lexile® 200L–450L	**1.5 to 2.5**	**1.5 to 2.5**	**1.5 to 2.5**
LEVEL 2 • Lexile® 400L–700L	**2.5 to 4.0**	**2.5 to 4.0**	**2.5 to 4.0**
LEVEL 3 • Lexile® 600L–900L	**4.0 to 6.9**	**4.0 to 6.9**	**4.0 to 6.9**
LEVEL 4 • Lexile® 800L–1200L		**6.0 to 8.9**	**6.0 to 12.0**

READ 180 is intended to address the literacy needs of students who are reading with at least first grade proficiency. *System 44®*, a Scholastic intervention program for beginning readers, can be used to support students who need to build foundational phonics skills before entering *READ 180*.

Components of Successful Intervention

READ 180 incorporates the following features to successfully raise student reading achievement.

1. **Scientific Research Base**
   READ 180 is informed by an extensive body of scientific texts on best practices for teaching older struggling readers. Up-to-date research foundations are embedded throughout the program components to help you maximize instructional effectiveness and provide students with a highly engaging and empowering learning experience.

2. **Proven Results and Success**
   READ 180 is proven to work. More than a decade of validation through research and practice in over 20,000 classrooms across the country has affirmed the effectiveness of *READ 180* for raising reading achievement. Students who enter the program unable to read proficiently experience success and become readers. *READ 180* Next Generation builds on the history of success with technology-based teaching tools and more rigorous instructional content to accelerate student reading achievement.

3. **Purposeful Assessments**
   READ 180 gives you the power to track and analyze student performance at every step. The program includes a variety of assessment tools that help you accurately identify your students' most urgent needs. Then you, along with the adaptive Topic Software, can adjust instruction accordingly to target those needs with individualized lessons and practice.

4. **Unparalleled Access to Data**
   READ 180 gathers student performance data to help teachers effectively differentiate instruction. The Topic Software continually adjusts content and pacing to individualize the learning experience for students. The Teacher Dashboard supports you with planning and preparing differentiated instruction. The Scholastic Achievement Manager (SAM) allows you to run data-rich reports to stay alert to students' needs and monitor progress throughout the year.

5. **Comprehensive Instruction**
   The *READ 180* teaching system makes it easy to build essential reading and writing skills while also meeting individual student needs. You will implement a rich and engaging curriculum of skills instruction, target learning needs with resources for differentiation, and strengthen your teaching practices with point-of-use professional development.

6. **Simplified Planning and Differentiation**
   READ 180 offers state-of-the-art technology-based tools to simplify planning, teaching, and differentiating lessons. The Teacher Dashboard is your command station for planning effective daily instruction and data-driven differentiation. The Interactive Teaching System (ITS) provides anytime, anywhere access to instructional materials for your lessons.

7. **Embedded Professional Development**
   READ 180 incorporates various opportunities for you to continually strengthen your teaching skills. Use in-person and online implementation trainings and resources to build your program knowledge and enhance your teaching strategies. Explore embedded support in the *rBook Teacher's Edition,* Interactive Teaching System (ITS), and Teacher Dashboard for daily professional development right when you need it.

Exploring the System for Reading Achievement

READ 180 **incorporates features to increase student engagement, improve teacher effectiveness, and empower leaders to support change in their school or district.**

Working Together to Achieve Success

READ 180 acknowledges that raising reading achievement is everyone's responsibility. The program components encourage increased ownership for student learning and empower students, teachers, and school leaders to contribute to ongoing reading success.

LEARNING

Academic Writing Practice

Personalized Learning:

- Anytime, Anywhere Access to Content and Data
- Tools for Self-Directed Goal Setting and Planning
- Empowering Interface to Motivate Learning

Support for Structured Peer Feedback

Increased Text Complexity and Content Coverage

Anytime, Anywhere Access to Rigorous Reading

TEACHING

Direct Instruction of Higher Order Reading and Critical Thinking Skills and Strategies

Academic Writing Instruction

Online Feedback on Student Performance

Content Area Reading Connections

Connected Teaching:

- Anytime, Anywhere Access to Student Data and Professional Development Content
- Tools to Support Professional Networking
- Tools to Support Family Connections

LEADING

Increased Data Transparency for District and School Leaders

Outreach Materials for Family Engagement

Increased Visibility to Program Implementation

Connected Leading:

- Anytime, Anywhere Access to Data
- Administrative Tools to Plan and Manage Resources
- Administrative Tools to Monitor and Report Outcomes

Every Student Engaged

READ 180 engages students in learning and motivates them to achieve reading progress with:

- Adaptive Topic Software to build reading and writing proficiency.
- Rigorous literacy skills instruction and practice.
- Ownership and accountability for learning.
- High-interest, leveled fiction and nonfiction texts, including online texts for reading independence.
- Scaffolded reading support to build comprehension of increasingly complex texts.

Student Dashboard

Every Teacher Effective

READ 180 maximizes teacher effectiveness in raising reading achievement for older struggling readers with:

- Comprehensive curriculum for literacy intervention.
- State-of-the-art online lesson planning tools.
- Simplified differentiation support.
- Comprehensive assessments to monitor learning and target instruction.
- Unparalleled access to data.
- Just-in-time professional development.

Teacher Dashboard

Every Leader Empowered

READ 180 supports school and district leaders to achieve a high level of implementation fidelity and program success with:

- Access to critical student performance data at the class, grade, school, and district level.
- Support for managing implementation fidelity.
- Capacity-building of effective teachers.
- Flexible technology platforms for implementation.
- Opportunities to build relationships with families.

Leadership Dashboard

Components of Blended Learning

The research-based *READ 180* Model for Blended Learning structures direct instruction and scaffolded practice each day to maximize student reading growth. Scholastic provides flexible options to implement *READ 180* in 40–90 minutes. Work with your leadership team to determine how best to implement the model.

READ 180 Instructional Model

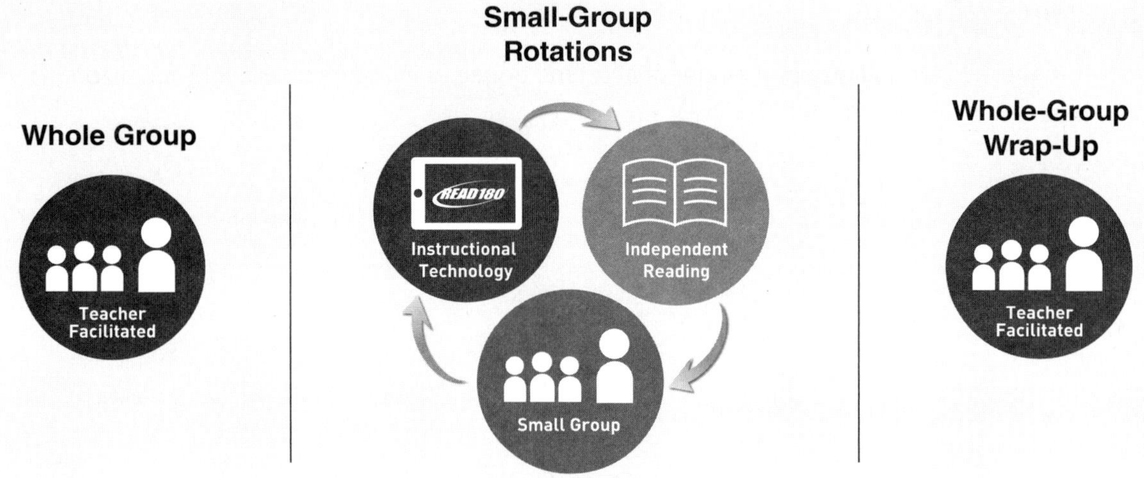

	Whole-Group Instruction	Small-Group Rotations	Whole-Group Wrap-Up
Overview	Explicit teacher-led instruction in reading, vocabulary, writing, and oral academic language for the whole class	Three groups of 5–7 students each rotate to engage in targeted teacher-directed instruction, Software practice, and independent reading	Brief end-of-class reflection and discussion about the day's learning for the whole class
Core Components	• *rBook* and *Teacher's Edition* • *rBook* Anchor Videos DVD	• *rBook* and *Teacher's Edition* • *Resources for Differentiated Instruction 1–4* • Topic Software • Paperbacks, Audiobooks, and eReads	• Wrap-Up prompts from the Interactive Teaching System
Assessment	• Workshop Wrap-Up Projects • Workshop Wrap-Up Tests • *rSkills* College & Career • *Scholastic Reading Inventory* College & Career	• Informal observations and assessment of classwork • Rubrics • *Scholastic Reading Counts!* • *rSkills* College & Career	• Informal observations and assessment of classwork

Structuring Class Time

The research is clear: students at risk of failure benefit from extra instructional time and smaller classes. Maximum *READ 180* results are achieved when schools implement the daily 90-minute Instructional Model and limit class size to 15–21 students.

Whole-Group Instruction Devote the first 20 minutes of class to explicit teacher-led instruction for all students. Use the *rBook Teacher's Edition* for lessons in reading, academic vocabulary, and writing.

Small-Group Instruction Work directly with one-third of your students at a time in Small-Group Instruction. After the allotted time, have the small groups rotate, so you have the opportunity to work closely with every student each day.

Instructional Software One small group of students at a time engages in independent, individualized skills practice using the Topic Software.

Modeled and Independent Reading One small group of 5–7 students at a time independently reads the Paperbacks, Audiobooks, and eReads. After 20 minutes, the small groups rotate.

Whole-Group Wrap-Up Bring the class back together at the end of the period. Use the Wrap-Up activities on the Interactive Teaching System (ITS) to guide student reflection and discussion.

Setting Up the Classroom

When students walk into *READ 180,* they immediately see something different. They realize this is a classroom designed for engagement—with technology, with text, with their teacher, and with each other.

Use the Model for Blended Learning to guide your *READ 180* classroom setup. Create distinct areas for each rotation to support productive independent work and make students excited to be there. See pages 90–91 for additional tips on making your classroom a welcoming place for learning, reading, and sharing.

Previewing the System Components

READ 180 **includes everything you need to motivate students to turn their lives around and successfully raise reading achievement.**

Student Materials

Direct Instruction and Practice

rBook
Interactive worktext for students to read, write, and react during daily Whole- and Small-Group Instruction

Instructional Software

Student Dashboard
Motivational software feature to track completed work and monitor reading progress

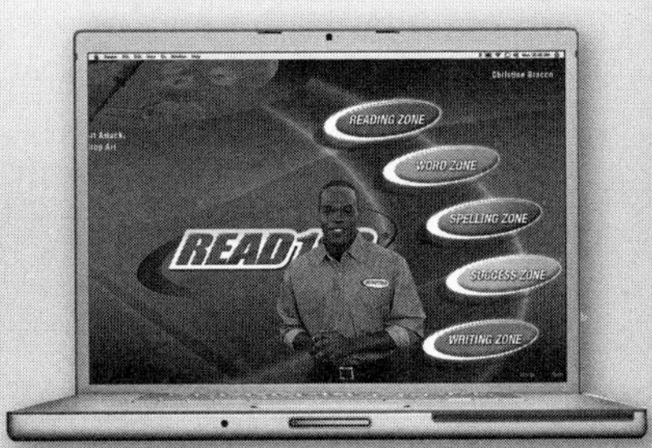

Topic Software
Adaptive technology for engaging, individualized instruction and practice

Modeled and Independent Reading

Audiobooks
Grade-level books on CD to model fluent reading and comprehension

Paperbacks
High-interest, leveled nonfiction and fiction texts for daily practice

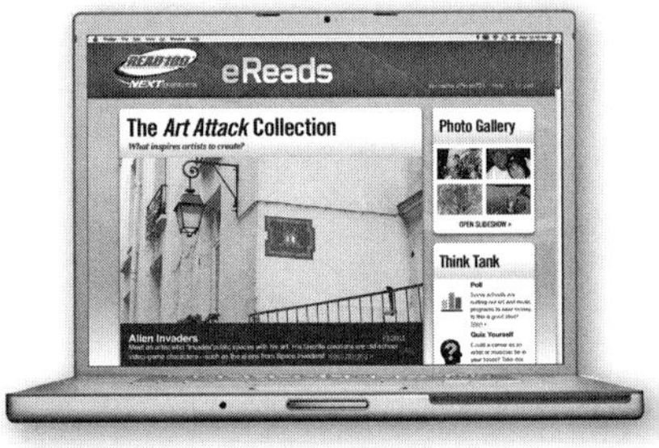

eReads
Informational online texts related to Software Topics

Assessment

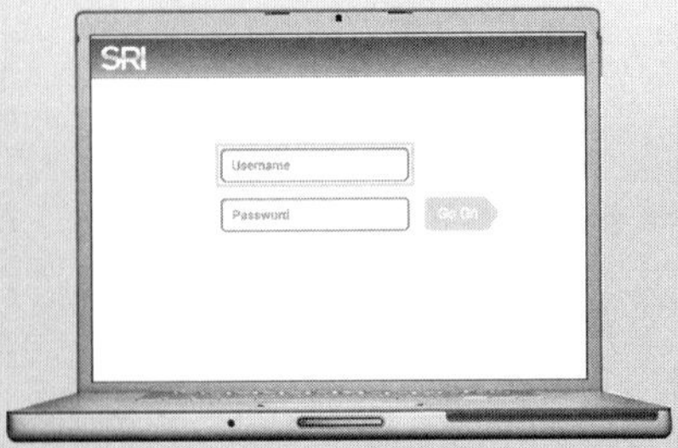

***Scholastic Reading Inventory (SRI)* College & Career**
Assessment of student reading proficiency for initial placement and progress monitoring

***rSkills* College & Career**
Curriculum-based tests to evaluate mastery of *rBook* Workshop skills

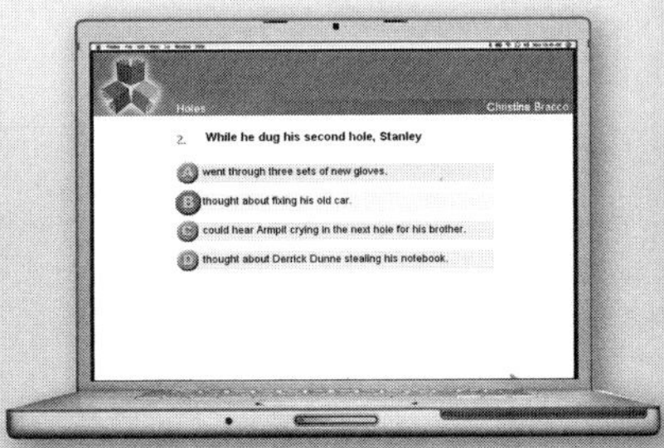

Scholastic Reading Counts! (SRC!)
Quizzes for the Paperbacks, Audiobooks, and eReads

Teacher Materials

Teacher-Led Instruction

rBook Teacher's Edition
Explicit lessons and routines for teaching Whole- and Small-Group Instruction

***rBook* Anchor Videos DVD**
Short videos to build background for readings

Teacher Dashboard
Comprehensive site for monitoring student performance and planning data-driven differentiated lessons

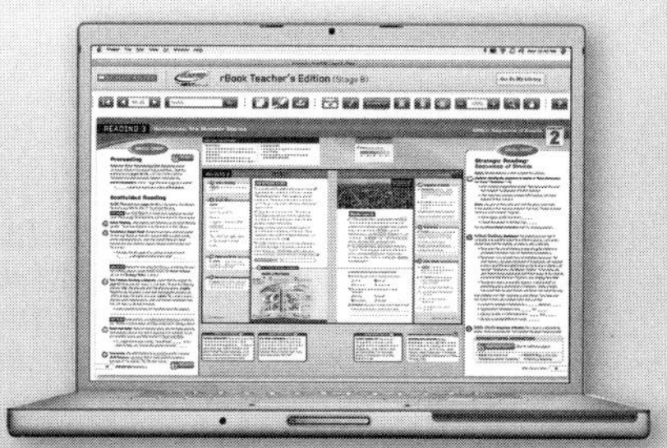

Interactive Teaching System (ITS)
Digital versions of the *rBook Teacher's Edition* and other instructional materials

Data-Driven Differentiation and Assessment

Resources for Differentiated Instruction (RDI) 1–4
Lessons to target reading and writing instruction and support English language learners

Placement, Assessment, and Reporting Guide
Comprehensive guide for assessing students and analyzing data to monitor progress

Scholastic Achievement Manager (SAM)
Tool for managing program enrollment, settings, reports, resources, and student work

Independent Reading Support

Teaching Resources
Support for monitoring independent student work in the small-group rotations and connecting *READ 180* instruction with content-area classes

Professional Development and Implementation

Getting Started: Your First Three Weeks
Lessons and resources for your first three weeks with *READ 180*

Implementation Videos
Support for implementing the Instructional Model and *READ 180* materials

Building on a History of Success

***READ 180* builds on two decades of scientific research, expert collaboration, and successful implementation with over one million students in over 20,000 classrooms nationwide.**

1985–1996 Early Research

1985–1996

Research by **Dr. Ted Hasselbring** of Peabody College, Vanderbilt University, leads to a breakthrough prototype for software that uses individual student performance data to differentiate reading instruction. This research was partially funded by a grant from the **Office of Special Education, U.S. Department of Education.**

1994–1996

Dr. Hasselbring joins forces with Dr. Janet Allen of the University of Central Florida, and Florida's Orange County public school system, to create the **Orange County Literacy Project** for its lowest-performing students. The project's instructional model, rooted in research-proven literacy practices, becomes the basis of the ***READ 180* Instructional Model.**

1997–1999 Field Testing

1997

Scholastic collaborates with Vanderbilt University and Orange County schools to replicate the best practices of their research in an intervention program. *READ 180* adopts the **Lexile Framework® for Reading, developed by MetaMetrics, Inc.,** as its leveling system. This framework provides a common metric for measuring text difficulty and student reading proficiency.

1998–1999

Council of the Great City Schools pilots *READ 180* in some of its largest urban school districts and enters into a research partnership to study the program efficacy.

Scholastic publishes ***READ 180,*** which is immediately implemented in hundreds of schools nationwide.

2003–2006 Validation and Implementation

2003–2006

READ 180 aligns with recommendations for reading intervention in national reports such as ***Reading Next*** (2004) and ***Writing Next*** (2006) by the Alliance for Excellent Education and the Carnegie Corporation. Studies in cities across the nation show that *READ 180* improves reading comprehension skills faster than other interventions.

2005

Through continued collaboration with Dr. Hasselbring and a new partnership with **Dr. Kevin Feldman** and **Dr. Kate Kinsella,** Scholastic launches ***READ 180* Enterprise Edition.** This new edition brings together five years of observing best practices and the knowledge of literacy experts to provide even more effective reading intervention.

2006

Dr. Bill Daggett and the **International Center for Leadership in Education** (ICLE) champion *READ 180* as the reading intervention program that most closely aligns with the center's recommendations on secondary school reform.

2006–2011

Continued and Sustained Improvement Based on Best Practices

2006

The **Council of Administrators of Special Education** (CASE) endorses *READ 180* for use with special education students.

ENDORSED BY CASE FOR USE WITH SPED

2007–2009

Scholastic works with **Dr. Kate Kinsella,** co-author of the *rBook,* and **Tonya Ward Singer** to publish the *LBook,* which supports the needs of English language learners in *READ 180*.

READ 180 student achievement results continue to be included in respected, third-party, peer-reviewed educational journals, such as ***Harvard Educational Review*** (2008), ***Reading Research Quarterly*** (2008), and ***Journal of Research on Educational Effectiveness*** (2009).

Scholastic and Dr. Hasselbring collaborate with

Dr. Marilyn Jager Adams to create ***System 44***, a reading intervention program for students who need to build foundational phonemic awareness and phonics skills.

Dr. Julie Washington, a leading authority on articulation and Standard Classroom English, lends her expertise to the development of instructional support for *READ 180* and *System 44* students who speak a community dialect and struggle with academic language.

2009–2010

Scholastic continues to develop new *READ 180* components—such as *READ 180* Stretch, Xtra Advance, and the Real Jobs Library—to add more rigorous reading to prepare students for college and careers.

Scholastic launches the first-ever 21st Century core English language arts program: **Expert 21.**

2010

The **Common Core State Standards Initiative** publishes standards that provide consistent and clear understanding of what students are expected to know and be able to do upon graduation. Scholastic begins developing ***READ 180* Next Generation** in alignment with the initiative.

COMMON CORE STATE STANDARDS INITIATIVE

2011

Scholastic launches ***READ 180* Next Generation,** the result of five years of intensive research and development. Informed by experience serving over one million students per day in over 20,000 classrooms, *READ 180* Next Generation reflects best practices from the most successful implementations across the country. A suite of new technology, data, content, and resources is designed to maximize student engagement, teacher effectiveness, and leader empowerment.

READ 180® NEXT GENERATION

Reviewing the Proven Results

Over a decade of research and hundreds of validation studies have proven that *READ 180* works to raise reading achievement for older struggling readers.

Research and Validation Studies

READ 180 has been providing high-quality adolescent literacy intervention, grounded in research and tested by classroom teachers, for over ten years. The program is currently being used by over one million students per day, in over 20,000 classrooms across all 50 states. Throughout its long history of use, *READ 180* has become one of the most research-tested and practice-validated reading intervention programs in the country.

The *Compendium of READ 180 Research* summarizes results from 30 representative research and validation studies conducted over the past decade. Several of the studies illustrate the positive impact on student achievement when *READ 180* is implemented "on model" daily for at least 90 minutes. Download your copy of the Compendium at **www.scholastic.com/research** to read about the proven effectiveness of *READ 180* in classrooms just like yours.

Compendium of READ 180 Research

Proven Results in School Districts

Continuous research and testing in elementary, middle, and high schools have proven that *READ 180* produces quantifiable gains in reading achievement for older struggling readers. Districts of all sizes have experienced gains so large that they have been the subject of hundreds of national and local news stories. With 106,000 students in metropolitan Houston, Cypress-Fairbanks ISD is one of many large districts that have shown results using *READ 180* to drastically raise student reading achievement.

DISTRICT SPOTLIGHT **Cypress-Fairbanks Independent School District, TX**

READ 180 Middle School Students Quadruple Passing Rates on the State Reading Test

Across all grades in this analysis, the percentage of *READ 180* students meeting expectations on the TAKS Reading increased from 2008 to 2009. Results were particularly impressive for middle school students, who demonstrated more than a four-fold increase on the TAKS. **To read the full report, visit read180.com/research.**

Cypress-Fairbanks Independent School District

Enrollment: 106,134
- 43% Hispanic
- 33% Caucasian
- 16% African American
- 8% Asian American
- >1% Native American

45% Economically Disadvantaged

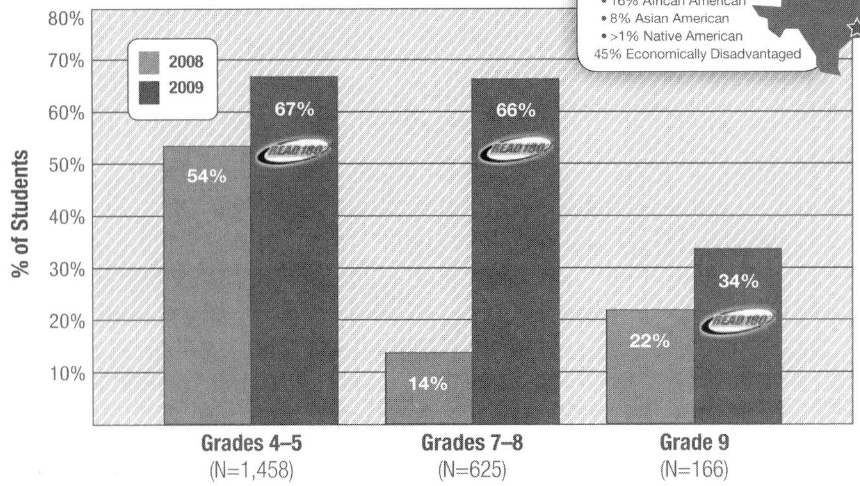

Success for Every Student

Research and validation studies have shown that *READ 180* produces reading gains for all types of student populations, including English language learners and students with special needs.

English Language Learners

READ 180 has been proven to raise the reading test scores of students learning English as a second language. See the *Compendium of READ 180 Research* for six representative research studies that prove program efficacy with English language learners nationwide.

Exciting, relevant nonfiction texts throughout *READ 180* engage English language learners and provide them with academic vocabulary and background knowledge for success across content areas. Special *READ 180* features support English language learners with achieving reading growth:

- Anchor Videos build background knowledge and mental models for reading.
- Topic Software provides opportunities for repeated oral reading practice, including making recordings for self-assessment.
- Oral language development and academic language strategies integrated in the teaching materials engage students with accountable response tasks.
- The *rBook* and Topic Software scaffold academic writing and revision.
- Multicultural content is relevant to students from diverse backgrounds.
- Audiobooks, eReads, and Topic Software allow students to read along with examples of modeled fluent reading.

***LBook:* Prepare, Support, Extend**
Use the *LBook* (available separately) to provide additional support for English language learners in your *READ 180* classroom. The explicit lessons build academic oral language skills to prepare, support, and extend *rBook* instruction.

Students in Special Education

Validation studies have demonstrated *READ 180* effectiveness with students who are classified for special education services. See the *Compendium of READ 180 Research* for ten representative studies that illustrate accelerated reading achievement for special education students across the country.

READ 180 was originally designed for students in special education and is built upon the principles of individualization and differentiation. Special *READ 180* features support students' individual learning needs:

- Age-appropriate, adaptive Topic Software and differentiated Small-Group Instruction allow students to move at their own pace and receive individualized instruction and support.
- Multimodal instructional and practice activities ensure that all students "see it, say it, hear it, read it, and write it."
- High-interest materials keep students motivated and engaged.
- Universal design features and 508 compliance enable students with certain physical disabilities to access the instructional content.

Teacher Tip

Visit www.scholastic.com/research to view and download *READ 180* research studies conducted in schools and districts similar to your own.

Supporting Response to Intervention

***READ 180* aligns to Response to Intervention (RTI), a national framework for instruction and intervention to address all students' academic needs.**

What Is RTI?

Response to Intervention (RTI) is a model used in schools across the nation to provide high-quality instruction and intervention that matches students' academic needs. The RTI model features three tiers of increasingly intensive educational support.

- **Tier 1** students experience success with the core grade-level curriculum.
- **Tier 2** students benefit from strategic supplemental instruction.
- **Tier 3** students need intensive intervention to meet academic goals.

Scholastic Solutions

Scholastic offers programs to address the needs of students on every tier of the RTI model for literacy instruction and intervention.

System 44 is a foundational intervention that meets the phonics and decoding needs of the lowest readers.

READ 180 provides scaffolded instruction and intervention support to build your students' skills for reading success.

Expert 21 is a core English language arts curriculum for proficient readers in Grades 6–9.

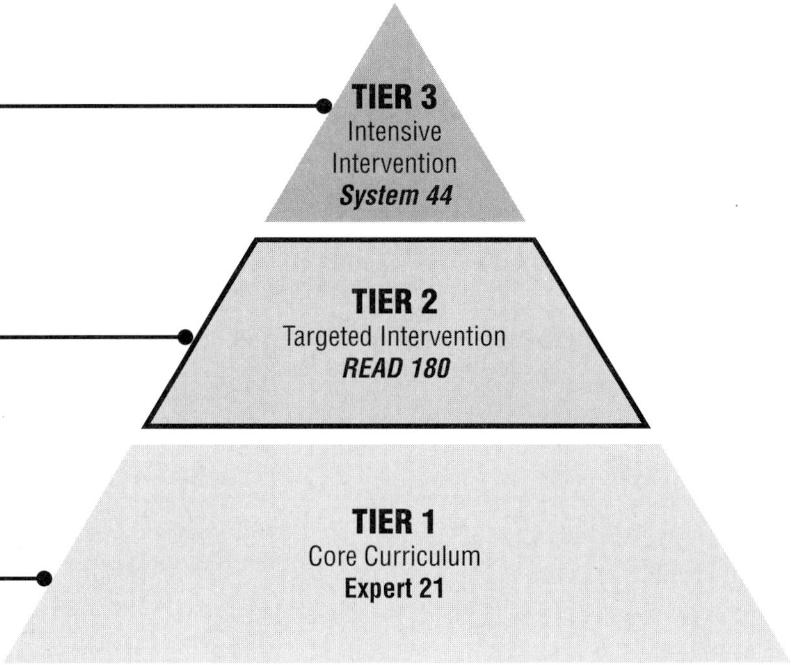

Role of Assessments

An essential component of RTI is initial and ongoing assessment to place students and evaluate the effectiveness of instructional strategies in use.

Universal Screening The RTI model recommends universal screening to place all students at the appropriate tier of instruction. The *Scholastic Reading Inventory (SRI)* and *Scholastic Phonics Inventory (SPI)* serve as universal screeners to inform student placement decisions.

Ongoing Progress Monitoring The RTI model emphasizes the importance of ongoing data collection to monitor student progress and determine whether interventions are working. *READ 180* integrates a variety of assessments to help you monitor progress and target instruction. Administer *SRI* to your *READ 180* students three times per year after initial placement to monitor overall reading growth.

Getting to Know the Authors

READ 180 **was developed with the expertise and experience of nationally recognized educational researchers and practitioners.**

Senior Program Author

Ted S. Hasselbring, Ed.D.

Dr. Ted Hasselbring is a Research Professor of Special Education and a Co-Director of the Learning Technology Center at Peabody College of Vanderbilt University. He has authored more than 100 articles and book chapters on learning and technology and serves on the editorial boards of six professional journals. He is also the author of other Scholastic technology-based educational programs, including *System 44* and *FASTT Math.*

Senior Program Developer

Laura Goin

Laura Goin is a designer of multimedia instructional software for students with learning difficulties. She researches and consults on the use of multimedia instructional technologies with disabled and nondisabled learners. She is also a former teacher of children with physical and mental disabilities and varying exceptionalities.

rBook Authors and Senior Advisors

Kate Kinsella, Ed.D.

Dr. Kate Kinsella is a faculty member in the Center for Teacher Efficacy at San Francisco State University. She consults nationally for state departments and school districts on K–12 reading instruction. She has extensively taught and developed curricula for English language learners and first-generation bilingual college students. She also co-authored the *LBook*.

Kevin Feldman, Ed.D.

Dr. Kevin Feldman is the Emeritus Director of Reading and Early Intervention with the Sonoma County Office of Education (SCOE). He consults nationally on literacy issues and develops, organizes, and monitors programs related to PreK–12, literacy, RTI, and prevention of reading difficulties. His career in education spans over forty years.

Professional Development Advisors

Marilyn Jager Adams, Ph.D.

Visiting Professor, Department of Cognitive, Linguistic, and Psychological Sciences, Brown University

Milton Chen, Ph.D.

Senior Fellow and Executive Director, Emeritus, The George Lucas Educational Foundation

Sharon M. Draper

Best-Selling Author, Educator, and 1997 National Teacher of the Year

Susan Gendron

Senior Fellow, International Center for Leadership in Education (ICLE), SMARTER Balanced Assessment Consortium

David Rose, Ed.D.

Founder and Chief Education Officer, Center for Applied Special Technology (CAST)

Julie A. Washington, Ph.D.

Professor, Department of Educational Psychology and Special Education, Georgia State University

English Language Learning Advisors

Tonya Ward Singer

Co-Author of the *LBook,* and Language Development and Literacy Consultant

Jo Gusman

Founder of New Horizons in Education, Inc., and a former classroom teacher

Cindi Sanchez

Implementation Manager, Scholastic Education

Unpacking the Underlying Research

Six research-based principles underlie all *READ 180* components for effectively raising the reading achievement of older struggling students.

Maximizing Engagement and Student Learning

Students experience greater motivation, confidence, and success when they are aware of their ongoing academic progress (Pressley, Gaskins, Solic, & Collins, 2006).

Research shows that students learn best when they can take ownership of their learning, feel engaged with the academic content, and track their own growth. *READ 180* features high-interest, age-appropriate, relevant topics to engage students in the *rBook*, Topic Software, and Library. The Student Dashboard allows students to monitor their Software progress and view overall *READ 180* performance.

Reflection

The motivational features in* READ 180 *will help my students by...

Developing Critical Readers and Writers

All students, especially English language learners and students with learning disabilities, benefit from explicit comprehension strategy instruction (National Institute of Child Health and Human Development, 2000).

Systematic instruction in comprehension strategies, critical reading, and writing skills is proven to support reading development. *READ 180* provides daily, direct Whole- and Small-Group Instruction with the *rBook Teacher's Edition* to teach literacy skills for long-term success. Additionally, the wide range of content-area and complex texts in *READ 180* support students with building college and career readiness.

Reflection

Critical reading, writing, and thinking are essential for 21st Century success because...

Structuring Effective Communication

Oral language development is an essential component of literacy development; well-developed listening and speaking skills are directly linked to reading and writing proficiency (August & Shanahan, 2006).

Research shows that purposeful, scaffolded instruction in academic language and vocabulary supports reading growth. *READ 180* lessons incorporate Instructional Routines to structure academic discussions during class. The *rBook*, Topic Software, and *READ 180* Library provide further support for vocabulary acquisition necessary for school success.

Reflection

Daily structured interactions will build my students' language skills by...

Harnessing Technology in Service of Learning

Computer-based instruction affords students the opportunity to receive individualized support, learn at their own pace, and receive immediate corrective feedback (Kamil, 2003).

Technology makes it easier to provide individualized instruction and build automaticity with literacy skills. The adaptive Topic Software individualizes content and pacing for students in a private, safe environment and supplies continuous data on their performance. Anchor Videos are also used as a tool across *READ 180* materials to build the background content knowledge essential for successful reading comprehension.

Reflection

The* READ 180 *Topic Software individualizes instruction by...

Differentiating Instruction

Differentiated instruction aims to optimize learning opportunities and outcomes for all students by tailoring instruction to meet their current level of knowledge and prerequisite skills (Bos & Vaughn, 2002).

Tailoring instruction to target individual strengths and challenges is proven to accelerate academic growth. The *READ 180* Instructional Model structures daily opportunities for providing targeted instruction and practice. The Groupinator™ on the Teacher Dashboard analyzes student performance data to streamline the process of grouping and planning for differentiation.

Reflection

One way* READ 180 *supports me with differentiating instruction is...

Using Assessment to Inform Instruction

Regular progress-monitoring is vital for tracking student growth and determining which students need additional help or intervention (National Joint Committee on Learning Disabilities, 2008).

Research shows that assessment is an integral component for student progress because it allows teachers to assess individual needs and target instruction accordingly. *READ 180* includes a variety of informal and formal assessments to provide a complete picture of each student's growth and challenges, engage students in monitoring their own progress, and supply teachers with clear, actionable data to guide instructional decision making.

Reflection

Using assessment data to inform instruction is important because...

Using Next Generation Technology for Teaching and Learning

READ 180 **harnesses the power of technology to support you with effectively teaching and engaging the next generation of learners.**

Digital Tools for Teachers

READ 180 offers technology tools to help plan, differentiate, scaffold, and manage daily instruction.

Teacher Dashboard

Launch the Teacher Dashboard to access a comprehensive "toolbox" of easy-to-use online resources for monitoring and supporting students' *READ 180* progress. Use the Teacher Dashboard to:

- Monitor student usage of and performance in each *READ 180* technology-based component.
- Identify and plan daily lessons for Whole- and Small-Group Instruction.
- Group students for differentiated instruction based on their performance data.
- Engage in daily professional development for continued learning.
- Schedule notifications and reports to stay alert on program usage and student progress.

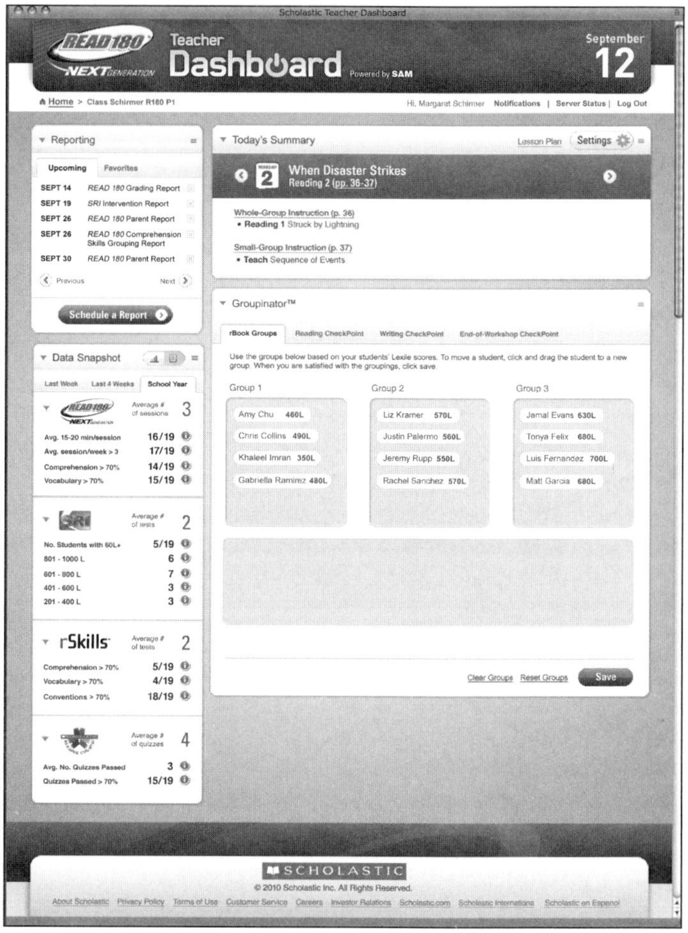

Teacher Dashboard Class Page

Interactive Teaching System (ITS)

Connect to ITS from the Teacher Dashboard for digital versions of instructional materials, including the *rBook Teacher's Edition, Resources for Differentiated Instruction 1–3*, *Getting Started: Your First Three Weeks With READ 180,* and downloadable SAM Resources.

ITS allows you to:

- Plan and prepare for Whole- and Small-Group Instruction anytime, anywhere.
- Access additional instructional content for beginning, ending, and differentiating each lesson.
- Display student resources using an interactive whiteboard or projector for scaffolding and engagement.

Scholastic Achievement Manager (SAM)

Log in to SAM for "behind-the-scenes" management and ongoing progress monitoring of your *READ 180* classes. SAM can help you to:

- Manage student rosters and adjust program settings.
- Run data-rich reports for class and student progress monitoring.
- Locate downloadable resources and leveled books for your classroom.
- Evaluate and store students' fluency and writing assignments.

Digital Resources for Students

Student technology in *READ 180* allows your struggling readers to track their ongoing reading growth and engage in individualized skill practice.

Student Dashboard

Students can explore their Dashboard each time they log in to the *READ 180* Topic Software. The motivational Student Dashboard allows students to:

- Monitor their performance and progress in the Topic Software, *Scholastic Reading Counts!* quizzes, and *Scholastic Reading Inventory*.
- Compete against themselves to improve upon their personal best on Software activities.
- Review Software Topics and independent reading books they have successfully completed.

Topic Software

The adaptive technology adjusts content and pacing based on performance to individualize instruction for each student. Students use the Topic Software to:

- Read leveled passages with scaffolded support in the Reading Zone.
- Build automaticity with high-utility vocabulary words in the Word Zone.
- Learn and practice spelling a customized word list in the Spelling Zone.
- Demonstrate comprehension and fluency in the Success Zone.
- Write an argument paragraph about the content-area topic in the Writing Zone.

eReads

The Web-based eReads are rigorous informational texts aligned to the Topic Software for students to build reading independence and explore content areas. Students can log in to the online eReads website to:

- Extend learning about Software Topics by reading related leveled texts in various nonfiction genres.
- Hear nonfiction articles read aloud for modeled fluency.
- Answer critical reading questions to self-monitor while reading.
- Engage in interactive polls and activities to share their opinions on the Topic.

Student Dashboard

Building College and Career Readiness

READ 180 **aligns with up-to-date research on preparing students with the literacy skills they need to be successful in college, the workplace, and the 21st Century world.**

Common Core State Standards

In 2010, the National Governors Association and the Council of Chief State School Officers sponsored a U.S. education initiative for standards-based educational reform. Known as the Common Core State Standards Initiative, the stated purpose was to "provide a consistent, clear understanding of what students are expected to learn, so teachers and parents know what they need to do to help them" (CCSS, 2010). Forty-two states have since adopted the Common Core State Standards as the curricular and instructional guidelines for their educational systems.

READ 180 Next Generation was developed with consideration to the Common Core State Standards. The program components deeply integrate the research-based guidelines outlined by the Common Core State Standards to bring struggling students up to grade-level proficiency for long-term college and career success.

Complex and Informational Texts

Research shows that reading a diverse array of high-quality classic and contemporary literature, as well as challenging informational texts in a range of subjects, helps students build knowledge, gain insights, explore possibilities, and broaden their perspectives (CCSS, 2010).

READ 180 offers multiple text types that build students' world knowledge and prepare them to comprehend across content areas. In fact, 77% of all readings in the program are nonfiction informational texts related to social studies, science, social sciences, and contemporary social issues. For example, the Web-based eReads are nonfiction texts in real-world genres such as news articles, editorials, and interviews. To support students with developing interdisciplinary literacy, *READ 180* uses the gradual release model to build independent mastery of increasingly complex texts over time.

eReads Poster, Stage B

Higher-Order Thinking

READ 180 supports students with developing higher-order thinking for successfully navigating the 21st Century world. The *rBook* Workshops, Topic Software, eReads, Paperbacks, and Audiobooks all incorporate opportunities for students to build proficiency with three key critical-thinking tasks:

- **Synthesize** Students learn to link new information with prior knowledge to produce original ideas, solve problems, or create a new product.
- **Evaluate** Students practice using formal, thoughtful criteria to make informed judgments about information, ideas, or solutions to problems.
- **Analyze** Students learn to examine a situation or issue by breaking it down into its component parts.

Learn more about these higher-order thinking skills and other strategies for reading comprehension in the Best Practices tab of the *rBook Teacher's Edition.*

Academic Language

Research and expert opinion support incorporating extended talk time and structured peer discussions into literacy instruction so students have multiple opportunities to practice academic language—especially important for English language learners and students who speak non-standard dialects of English (National Institute for Literacy, 2007).

READ 180 instruction integrates nine instructional "RED Routines" to build critical oral language and speaking skills with structured partner and class discussions. For example, use the Think (Write)-Pair-Share Routine to support students with exchanging ideas with a partner, using scaffolded sentence starters, and contributing to class discussion.

Teacher Tip

Every RED Routine uses sentence starters to reinforce academic language. Explicitly model completing the starters so students understand how to use academic and conversational English for effective collaboration.

Analytical Writing

The ability to write logical arguments based on sound reasoning and relevant evidence from the text is crucial for college and career literacy. *READ 180* reinforces students' analytical writing skills in every *rBook* Workshop, Topic Software Writing Zone, and Writing CheckPoint for differentiation.

READ 180 writing instruction is highly scaffolded to guide struggling students to gradually build mastery with these key types of writing:

- Informational/explanatory
- Argument
- Narrative
- Literary analysis
- Research paper

Additionally, opportunities to write short responses about readings are embedded in every *rBook* lesson to prepare students for the "on-demand" writing often expected on standardized tests.

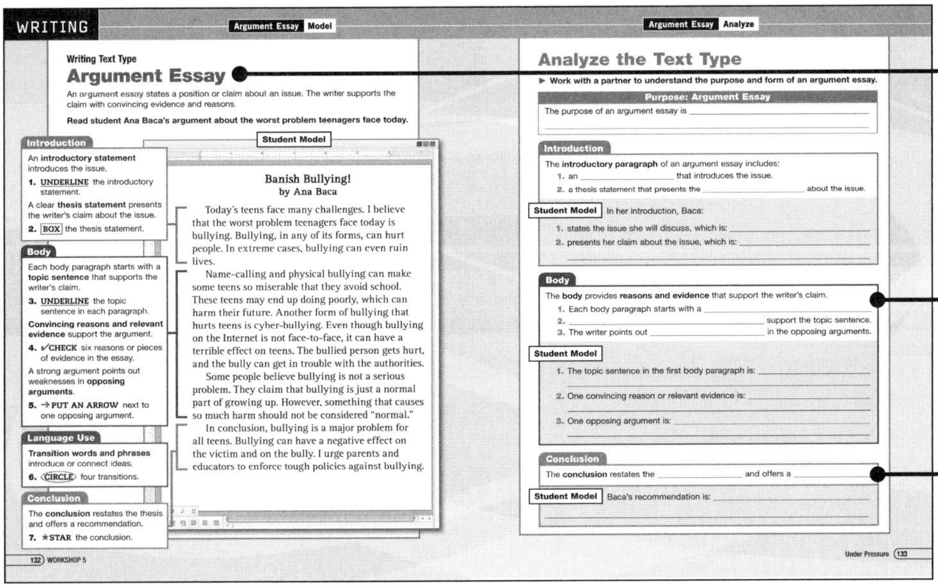

WRITING

Argument Essay Model

Writing Text Type

Argument Essay

An argument essay states a position or claim about an issue. The writer supports the claim with convincing evidence and reasons.

Read student Ana Baca's argument about the worst problem teenagers face today.

Introduction

An **introductory statement** introduces the issue.

1. UNDERLINE the introductory statement.

A clear **thesis statement** presents the writer's claim about the issue.

2. BOX the thesis statement.

Body

Each body paragraph starts with a **topic sentence** that supports the writer's claim.

3. UNDERLINE the topic sentence in each paragraph.

Convincing reasons and relevant evidence support the argument.

4. ✓CHECK six reasons or pieces of evidence in the essay.

A strong argument points out weaknesses in **opposing arguments**.

5. → PUT AN ARROW next to one opposing argument.

Language Use

Transition words and phrases introduce or connect ideas.

6. CIRCLE four transitions.

Conclusion

The **conclusion** restates the thesis and offers a recommendation.

7. ★STAR the conclusion.

Student Model

Banish Bullying!
by Ana Baca

Today's teens face many challenges. I believe that the worst problem teenagers face today is bullying. Bullying, in any of its forms, can hurt people. In extreme cases, bullying can even ruin lives.

Name-calling and physical bullying can make some teens so miserable that they avoid school. These teens may end up doing poorly, which can harm their future. Another form of bullying that hurts teens is cyber-bullying. Even though bullying on the Internet is not face-to-face, it can have a terrible effect on teens. The bullied person gets hurt, and the bully can get in trouble with the authorities.

Some people believe bullying is not a serious problem. They claim that bullying is just a normal part of growing up. However, something that causes so much harm should not be considered "normal."

In conclusion, bullying is a major problem for all teens. Bullying can have a negative effect on the victim and on the bully. I urge parents and educators to enforce tough policies against bullying.

132 WORKSHOP 5

Argument Essay Analyze

Analyze the Text Type

▶ **Work with a partner to understand the purpose and form of an argument essay.**

Purpose: Argument Essay

The purpose of an argument essay is ______

Introduction

The **introductory paragraph** of an argument essay includes:

1. an ______ that introduces the issue.
2. a thesis statement that presents the ______ about the issue.

Student Model In her introduction, Baca:

1. states the issue she will discuss, which is: ______
2. presents her claim about the issue, which is: ______

Body

The **body** provides **reasons and evidence** that support the writer's claim.

1. Each body paragraph starts with a ______
2. ______ support the topic sentence.
3. The writer points out ______ in the opposing arguments.

Student Model

1. The topic sentence in the first body paragraph is: ______
2. One convincing reason or relevant evidence is: ______
3. One opposing argument is: ______

Conclusion

The **conclusion** restates the ______ and offers a ______

Student Model Baca's recommendation is: ______

Under Pressure 133

***rBook*, Stage B**

Teach your students key features of each writing type by analyzing a model writing sample.

Guide students to support their argument with convincing evidence and strong reasons.

Build student mastery with single paragraphs in Workshops 1–3 before teaching multi-paragraph writing in Workshops 4–9.

Understanding Text Complexity

***READ 180* offers rigorous leveled texts of increasing complexity to support students with developing reading independence for success in college, career, and beyond.**

The Lexile Framework for Reading

The Lexile Framework for Reading, developed by MetaMetrics, Inc., measures texts and readers on the same scale. It is a reliable and extensively tested tool designed to bridge two critical aspects for targeted reading instruction—leveling text difficulty and assessing student reading proficiency. The result is two Lexile measures: one for the text and one for the student.

The developmental Lexile scale for text and readers ranges from 100L to above 1500L. Any score below 100L is reported as "BR," or Beginning Reader. Any score above 1500L is reported as 1500+. Lexile for a text is based on word choice frequency and sentence length.

When a student's Lexile matches the Lexile of a text, the student experiences 75% comprehension and feels confidence and control over the reading process. This means that the text is challenging enough for the student to grow as a reader but not overly frustrating.

Lexile Framework Poster

Lexile Measures in *READ 180*

READ 180 uses the Lexile Framework for Reading to assess students' baseline reading levels, match them to appropriate texts, and monitor their reading growth over time.

Scholastic Reading Inventory College & Career

Administer the *Scholastic Reading Inventory (SRI)* at the beginning of the year to determine a Lexile measure for each student and placement in the Topic Software. Re-administer the *SRI* three more times throughout the year to monitor student reading growth, as evidenced by increasing Lexile measures.

Leveled Texts

Support students with reading success by matching them to texts using their Lexile measures as determined by the *SRI*. The **Topic Software** and **eReads** automatically use student Lexile measures from the *SRI* to provide texts at the right level. You can also use *SRI* results to support students with selecting **Paperbacks** at the right level for success during Modeled and Independent Reading. All *READ 180* texts are divided into levels based on Lexile measures, with three levels for Stage A and four levels for Stages B and C.

READ 180 Level	Lexile Range
1	200L–450L
2	400L–700L
3	600L–900L
4 (Stages B & C only)	800L–1200L

The Importance of Text Complexity

Research indicates that the ability to read and comprehend complex texts is critical for success in school, college, and beyond (ACT, 2006; Adams, 2009). *READ 180* instruction guides students from highly scaffolded reading toward independent mastery of increasingly complex text to prepare them for the literacy demands they will encounter as citizens and workers in the 21st Century world.

Scholastic has created a three-part model for measuring text complexity, based on guidelines established by the Common Core State Standards Initiative (2010). The Text Complexity Triangle integrates three measures of text complexity: Quantitative, Qualitative, and Reader and Task.

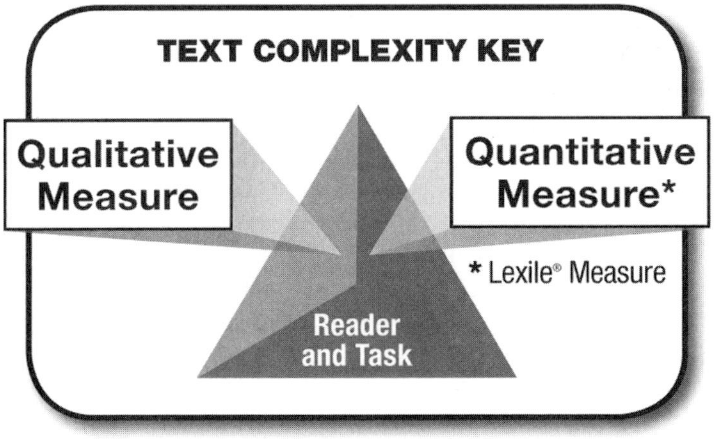

Quantitative (Lexile Measure) refers to the technical difficulty or readability of text, including factors such as sentence length, word frequency, and word length. Scholastic identifies this measure using the Lexile Framework for Reading. All *READ 180* texts are assigned a Lexile based on the level of difficulty.

Qualitative refers to the dimensions of text complexity that cannot be captured with a Lexile, such as levels of meaning or purpose, structure, language conventions, and knowledge demands. All *rBook* Workshop readings, Paperbacks, Audiobooks, and eReads are assigned one of five qualitative measures based on a scoring rubric: Simple, Moderate 1, Moderate 2, Complex 1, and Complex 2.

Reader and Task refers to your professional judgment about which texts and reading tasks are right for your students. A single text may be more or less challenging for different students, depending on their background knowledge, real-world experience, and amount of scaffolding provided. Carefully consider the reader's motivation and knowledge when choosing tasks to assign for reading a text.

Complex Texts in *READ 180*

Throughout *READ 180*, every text is marked with a Text Complexity Triangle icon to assist you with determining the reading difficulty and deciding how much scaffolding to provide. Look for the Text Complexity Triangle icon on each *rBook* Workshop reading to see how the passages vary in complexity. The *rBook* features a "staircase" of increasing complexity to build student confidence and independence with classic and contemporary literature as well as challenging informational texts.

To support students with accessing increasingly complex texts, every *rBook* Workshop uses a narrow reading approach: students read a series of passages with overlapping topics and recurring academic vocabulary to gradually build content knowledge, vocabulary, and confidence for reading success. Each Workshop also includes a "Stretch" text—available in *Resources for Differentiated Instruction 1* and on SAM—to use with students who are ready for more complex texts.

Increasing Ownership for Student Learning

***READ 180* incorporates features that empower all educational stakeholders—teachers, leaders, students, and parents—to contribute to raising reading achievement.**

Research Says

A strong base of evidence shows that achievement is positively impacted when schools, families, and communities partner to support student learning.
Mapp & Henderson, 2002

Teachers

Teachers can contribute to raising reading achievement by providing data-driven instruction targeted to meet individual needs. The Teacher Dashboard provides support for planning instruction, monitoring student learning, and maintaining high-quality program implementation for maximum effectiveness. By collecting, managing, and analyzing data for you, the Teacher Dashboard allows you to focus on high-quality instruction.

Teachers can also take increased ownership over the effectiveness of their program implementation to ensure maximum *READ 180* results. Download the research-based Classroom Implementation Review Checklist from SAM (Keyword: Implementation Review) to self-assess your implementation of the Instructional Model. Celebrate your successes and identify areas to help strengthen your implementation.

Reflection

One way I'll take ownership for raising reading achievement is...

Leaders

School and district leaders can contribute to reading growth by monitoring their *READ 180* implementation and providing follow-up support as needed. The Leadership Dashboard allows leaders to easily view data about student progress and program usage. It also provides access to professional development, technical, and peer support around best practices for achieving *READ 180* success. These tools and resources enhance leaders' ability to monitor fidelity of implementation and to identify and correct any problems.

Reflection

I'll work with my school leaders to ensure* READ 180 *success by...

Students

Students can maximize their success by working at their best during every class and pushing themselves to make continued reading growth. The Student Dashboard supports students in building executive function, monitoring their own effort and performance, and taking initiative for learning about selected topics in the Software and *READ 180* Library. Being able to contribute to their own learning path and track evidence of their progress builds students' motivation and academic resilience.

Reflection

I'll encourage students to take ownership for their reading growth by...

Parents

Parents can contribute to raising achievement by guiding reading practice at home and becoming involved and interested in the classroom. The *READ 180* Family Portal was developed for all kinds of families who may require different levels and types of support. Parents and caregivers can access the online portal to look up *READ 180* research and results, watch short videos about the program, read bilingual tips, and download fun reading resources and activities.

Reflection

One strategy I'll use to build a home-to-school connection that supports student learning is...

Engaging in Ongoing Professional Development

Scholastic offers comprehensive professional development resources to support you with implementing *READ 180* and raising student reading achievement.

Embedded Professional Development

All *READ 180* materials incorporate embedded professional development so you receive the research background, teaching routines, and instructional support that you need, right when you need it. Use these tools to build proficiency with *READ 180* and effective literacy intervention throughout the year:

- ***rBook Teacher's Edition:*** Research Foundations, Instructional Routines, and Best Practices
- **Teacher Dashboard:** Professional Development videos, presentations, and articles
- **SAM Resources:** Professional Articles and Scholastic Research Reports

In-Person Implementation Training

Attend up to three full days of in-person training targeted for *READ 180* teachers to learn how to implement the program effectively in your classroom. During Getting Started Training, you will get to know the program components, experience the Instructional Model, and learn tips for managing your classroom. During Follow-Up Training, you will take an in-depth look at writing instruction, practice analyzing SAM reports, and explore strategies for incorporating differentiation into your daily lessons.

Online Resources for Continued Learning

Scholastic offers interactive online resources to provide you with a deeper understanding of how to maximize *READ 180* success with your students.

Graduate-Level Online Course *READ 180* includes access to the graduate-level online course—*READ 180 Next Generation: Best Practices for Reading Intervention*—to build your program expertise.

Teaching With Technology Webinar Interact in a live online training, included with *READ 180,* to enhance your use of the Teacher Dashboard for planning, differentiating, and monitoring progress.

Training Zone The Training Zone, available at **www.scholastic.com/tz** with a Premium Maintenance and Support Plan, offers downloadable resources, video tutorials, model lessons, and interactive webinars to dive deep into key *READ 180* topics.

Scholastic U Access Scholastic U with a purchased subscription at **www.ScholasticU.com** for professional development to build teaching skills and strategies across all content areas.

Network for Professional Support

Register for the free *READ 180* Community website at **www.read180.com/community** to connect with other *READ 180* educators across the country. Download hundreds of classroom resources, join discussions on the message boards, and network with teachers for ongoing professional learning, advice, and support.

www.read180.com/community

TEACHER IMPLEMENTATION GUIDE

The Student Experience

Participating in the Student Experience

Use the following pages to engage in activities as you experience the *READ 180* Next Generation Instructional Model from a student's perspective.

Whole-Group Instruction

During Whole-Group Instruction, you will participate in a reading lesson from *rBook* Workshop 2: *When Disaster Strikes* (Stage B). Specifically, you will:

- Complete a Do Now prompt to get started.
- View the Anchor Video to build content knowledge before reading.
- Read and actively respond to a passage using Instructional Routines.
- Interact with the *rBook* and your peers using academic language.

Small-Group Instruction

During Small-Group Instruction, you will explore a strategic reading lesson that builds on whole-group learning and integrates scaffolds—or supports—for understanding. In this rotation, you will:

- Preview steps for teaching students to identify sequence of events, which is the Workshop focus skill.
- See how students use a graphic organizer to record the sequence of events in the passage.
- Learn about the differentiation strategies embedded in the lesson to scaffold and extend instruction.

Instructional Software

When your small group is in the Instructional Software area, you will experience the *READ 180* Topic Software using a software simulator with training tips. Specifically, you will:

- Explore the motivating features on the Student Dashboard.
- Watch a video and experience activities and assessments in each of the five Learning Zones.
- Engage in customized, adaptive instruction with immediate corrective feedback.

Modeled and Independent Reading

When your small group is in the Modeled and Independent Reading area, you will explore the *READ 180* Audiobooks, Paperbacks, and/or Web-based eReads. In this rotation, you will:

- Participate in a "Book Pass" to preview the leveled, high-interest Paperbacks.
- Hear an example of a Narrator and Reading Coach on the grade-level Audiobooks.
- Explore the range of engaging eReads Collections available for your *READ 180* Stage.

Whole-Group Wrap-Up

Last, you will have a chance to participate in Whole-Group Wrap-Up. You will write a response to a Wrap-Up prompt and participate in a group discussion to reflect on the Student Experience.

Engaging in a Lesson: Whole-Group Instruction

Participate in Whole-Group Instruction from a student's perspective to become familiar with the *READ 180* student materials, lesson activities, and integrated Instructional Routines.

Overview

During training, you will interact with the student *rBook* while participating in a reading lesson from Workshop 2: *When Disaster Strikes* (Stage B). This Workshop includes three informational texts that explore how the fury of natural disasters impacts people's lives. Sequence of events is the comprehension focus for Workshop 2, so students practice building this skill across the three readings.

You will read and analyze Reading 1, "Struck by Lightning," while your trainer models the lesson. This news article tells the story of a teenager who gets the shock of his life. Your trainer will first show an Anchor Video to build background before guiding you to read the passage using embedded Instructional Routines.

Key Features to Notice

Every Whole Group lesson includes instructional scaffolding, structured student engagement, and integrated routines. Look for the following key features of Whole-Group Instruction as you participate in the lesson.

Do Now The Interactive Teaching System (ITS) includes a Do Now prompt to start every Whole Group lesson. To display the daily prompt for your students, click its Do Now in the lesson in the digital *rBook Teacher's Edition*. Then direct students to respond in their notebooks upon entering the classroom.

Use the space below to complete the Do Now during the Student Experience:

____

____

____

____

Anchor Video The Anchor Videos DVD has a chapter for every *rBook* Workshop, with short clips that introduce the three Workshop passages. Each reading lesson in the *rBook Teacher's Edition* begins by showing the Anchor Videos DVD to support students with building background knowledge for reading success.

Multiple Readings The Scaffolded Reading Routines provide step-by-step support for guiding students to reread each Workshop passage multiple times to develop fluency, comprehension, and confidence with complex text.

Student Activities The margins of the *rBook* offer frequent opportunities for students to think about and engage with the Workshop passages. Step-by-step lessons in the *rBook Teacher's Edition* guide you to have students complete the activities independently or with a partner.

Integrated Routines Every *rBook* lesson includes integrated routines to help you provide consistent, effective instruction. Look for the following "RED Routines" during the Student Experience: Scaffolded Reading, Teaching Vocabulary, React and Write, Summarize, and Think (Write)-Pair-Share.

Using the *rBook*

During the model lesson, use this page from the student *rBook* to participate in Whole-Group Instruction.

READING 1

News Article

The Key Idea

WRITE What is this article mostly about?

VOCABULARY

Target Word

focus

fo•cus (verb)

Rate It: ① ② ③ ④

Meaning

to pay close

Example

An activity that is hard to focus on in a noisy place is

React and Write

WRITE Suppose that you saw lightning strike someone. What would you do?

Summarize

In one or two sentences, summarize what happened to Justin. Include the topic and important details.

Struck by Lightning

A teen's life changed in a flash!

September 6, 2001—Last month, 16-year-old Justin Norris headed to his after-school job at a fast-food restaurant. It seemed like an ordinary day. But it didn't stay that way for long. Justin was about to get the shock of his life!

Justin Norris survived being struck by lightning.

Justin started work inside the restaurant at the counter. After an hour, he moved to the drive-through window. He took orders from customers through a big menu board. Outside, a severe storm was building. "I heard loud thunder," Justin remembers.

At first, Justin ignored the thunder and **focused** on his work. But the thunder grew louder. Soon, Justin couldn't hear his customers through the speaker. He turned up the volume knob.

Then, a powerful bolt of lightning hit the outdoor menu board. A surge of electricity rushed in. It exceeded 15 million volts! The electricity shot through the board to the knob. Finally, it slammed into Justin's body and knocked him out. He was rushed to the hospital.

At the hospital, Justin had seizures. He couldn't remember names and numbers. The accident had wiped out his memory.

Now Justin is on the road to recovery. Currently, he still has memory loss. But Justin is happy. Why? He knows he's lucky to be alive. END

Words to Know! **exceeded** was greater than

rBook, Stage B

Reinforcing Strategies: Small-Group Instruction

Learn how Small-Group Instruction incorporates scaffolded instruction and targeted support that you will use with your students.

Overview

During training, you will continue exploring Reading 1 from *rBook* Workshop 2 (Stage B) to see how Small-Group Instruction reinforces the skills and strategies introduced during Whole-Group Instruction.

In this Small Group lesson, students first reread the news article, "Struck by Lightning," to continue building reading comprehension, fluency, and confidence. Then they complete a graphic organizer with text-based details about sequence of events, which is the comprehension focus for Workshop 2.

Key Features to Notice

Every Small Group lesson includes explicit modeling and instruction, embedded scaffolding, and strategies for differentiation. Look for the following key features of Small-Group Instruction as you preview the lesson.

Comprehension Focus Every *rBook* Workshop focuses on a different comprehension skill for reading success. The comprehension focus for Workshop 2 is sequence of events, so all of the reading lessons teach sequencing to build student mastery. Each of the nine *rBook* Workshops has a different comprehension focus, such as main idea and details, problem and solution, and make inferences.

Graphic Organizer After reading each Workshop passage, students complete a graphic organizer to practice the comprehension focus skill. This helps students visually organize their thoughts while reading so they can fully comprehend the text.

Critical Reading In many Small Group lessons, students practice higher-order thinking skills to develop college and career readiness. Follow the Critical Reading steps—indicated with a brain icon—in the *rBook Teacher's Edition* to guide your students to practice synthesizing, evaluating, and analyzing while reading.

Scaffolded Support Every Small Group lesson in the *rBook Teacher's Edition* offers strategies for differentiating instruction based on student readiness. When viewing the digital version of a lesson on the Interactive Teaching System (ITS), click its Scaffolded Support to see "Boost" and "Stretch" strategies. Boost your struggling students by providing scaffolds for lesson success, and Stretch your more advanced students to help them grow as readers.

Using the *rBook*

During the lesson, notice key features of the *rBook* page that students use for Small-Group Instruction.

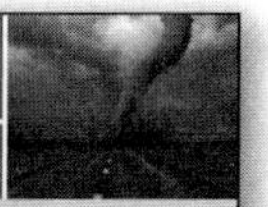

Earth Science

Comprehension Focus

Sequence of Events

Sequence is the order in which events happen. To find the sequence of events:

- Try to remember the order in which events take place.
- Look for times, dates, and signal words, such as *first*, *then*, *next*, *after*, and *finally*.
- When you know the order, check it again. Make sure it makes sense.

▶ **Complete this chart with the sequence of events that led to Justin being struck by lightning.**

At first

Justin ignored the thunder and focused on his work.

Soon

Then

Finally

When Disaster Strikes 37

***rBook*, Stage B**

Using Adaptive Technology: Instructional Software

Explore the *READ 180* Student Dashboard and Topic Software from a student's perspective to experience how the motivating features and adaptive technology raise reading achievement.

Using the Software Simulator

During training, you will use the *READ 180* Next Generation Software Simulator. The Simulator allows you to experience a sampling of instructional activities available on the Software in one session. You will see Training Tips with explanations or directions to guide your experience. As you explore the *READ 180* Student Dashboard and Topic Software using the Simulator, remember to:

- Take some time to explore each feature.
- Read the Training Tips when they appear. Click the **X** in the upper right corner of each tip to close it.
- Notice the motivating and adaptive features, such as exciting nonfiction content and individualized practice activities, that will support your students with reading growth over time.
- Think about which activities might be most engaging for your students and which ones might be most challenging.
- Make mistakes so you can experience how the Software provides immediate corrective feedback and customizes instruction.

Exploring the Instructional Software

You will work independently in the Instructional Software area during the Student Experience. Follow the steps below to experience the *READ 180* student Software using the Simulator. As you explore, turn to pages 43–45 to jot down your observations on the Student Dashboard and five Learning Zones.

1. Select **Student** as your role on the Simulator splash screen. Then choose your *READ 180* Stage and click **Go** to access the **Student Access** screen.
2. Click ***READ 180* Next Generation** on the **Student Access** screen, which shows all Scholastic technology programs on the selected server. Repeat on the next screen that appears. You may want to bookmark the second screen for your students.
3. Enter **cbracco180** as the **Username** and any word as the **Password.** Then click **Go On.**
4. Click each of the five tabs—**Home, My Topics, My Reads, My Reports,** and **My Personal Best**—to explore the motivational features of the Student Dashboard.
5. Click **Go On** at the top of the **My Dashboard** screen to access the Topic Software Zone Menu. Students are automatically prompted to move on.
6. Click the buttons on the Zone Menu in the following order to explore all learning activities: **Reading, Word, Spelling, Success,** and **Writing.** The Success Zone button will not appear until you have completed the Reading, Word, and Spelling Zones. The Writing Zone button will not appear until you have completed the Success Zone.
7. Follow the audio instructions and Training Tips to engage in learning activities in each Zone. After exploring all five Zones, click any of the buttons on the Zone Menu to revisit learning activities.
8. Click **Quit** on the Zone Menu to exit at the end of the Instructional Software rotation.

Student Dashboard

Reflection

A Student Dashboard feature that will motivate students is...

Features to Notice

- My Current Segment on the Home tab shows percent completion of each of the five Zones for the student's current Topic Software segment.
- Student-friendly reports on the Home and My Reports tabs allow students to monitor their own Software usage and reading progress.
- Virtual trophies in the My Personal Best tab highlight *READ 180* milestones.

Reading Zone

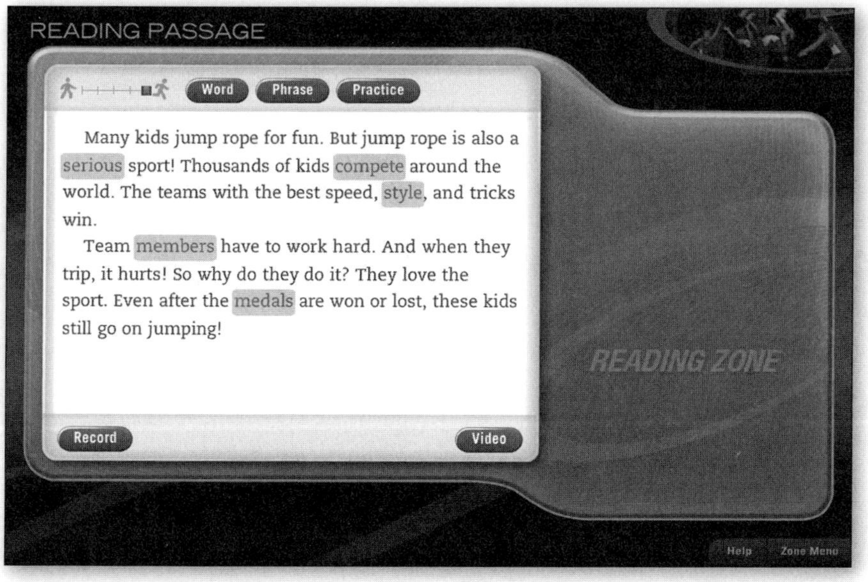

Reflection

The Reading Zone scaffolds a passage for students by...

Features to Notice

- Anchor Video builds background knowledge and content vocabulary.
- Reading Passage has audio-visual scaffolds and highlighted Power Words.
- Quick Check questions assess comprehension and vocabulary.

Word Zone

Reflection

The Word Zone individualizes instruction for students by...

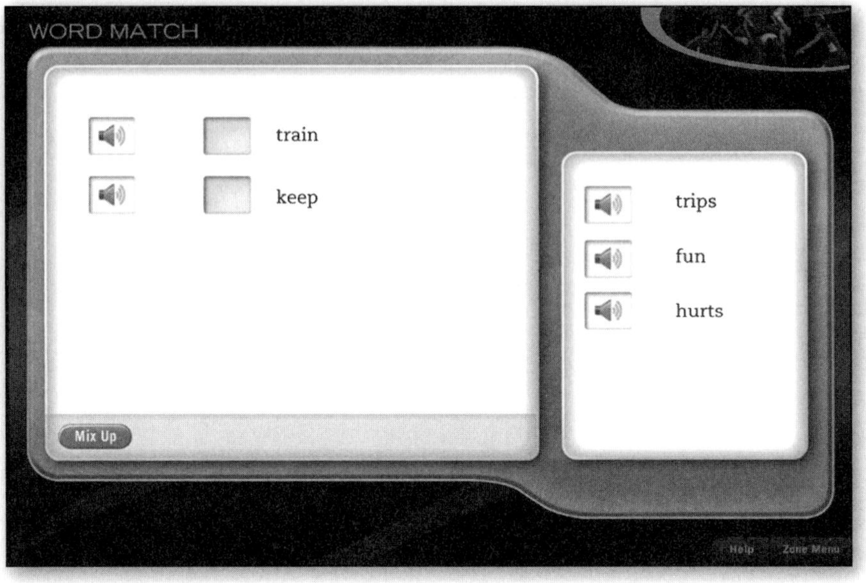

Features to Notice

- Word Assessment helps create a customized list of Study Words.
- Word Match asks students to listen to their recordings and match them to the right Study Words.
- Speed Challenge builds fluency and automaticity with the Study Words.

Spelling Zone

Reflection

Immediate Spelling Zone feedback helps students to...

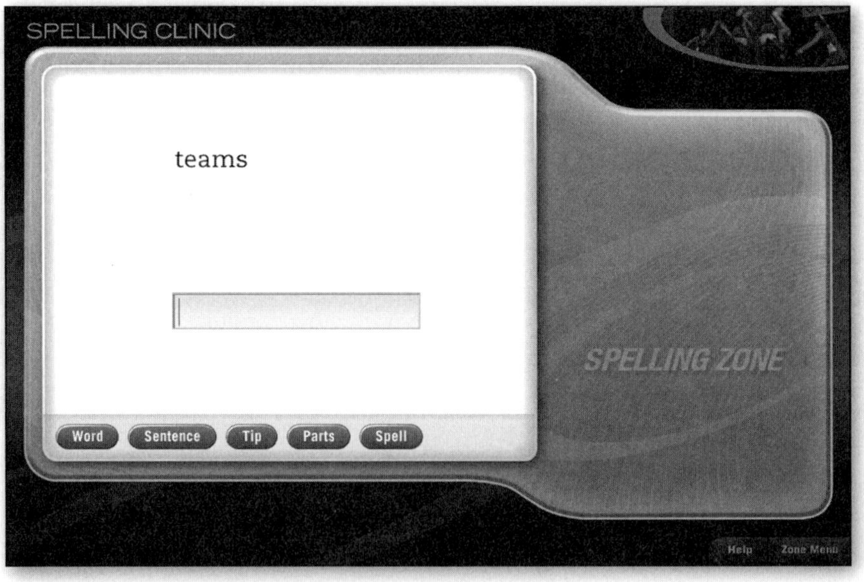

Features to Notice

- Spelling Assessment helps create a customized list of Study Words.
- Spelling Clinic provides explicit instruction in spelling and pronouncing each Study Word.
- Spelling Challenge offers immediate corrective feedback on any errors.

Success Zone

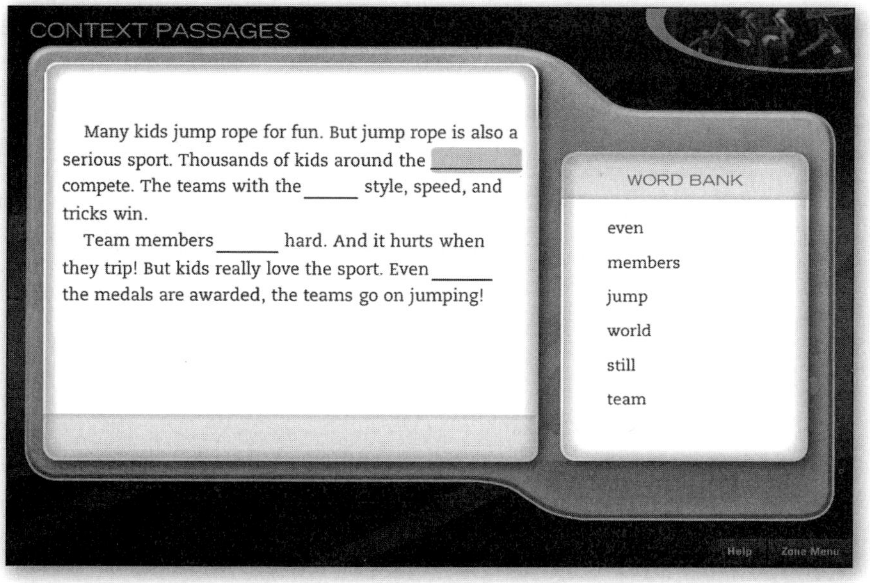

Reflection

The Success Zone assesses mastery of the passage by...

Features to Notice

- Discrepancy Passages test comprehension of the original passage.
- Context Passages allow students to practice identifying accurate vocabulary.
- Final Recording is accessible for grading in the SAM Student Digital Portfolio to assess student fluency.

Writing Zone

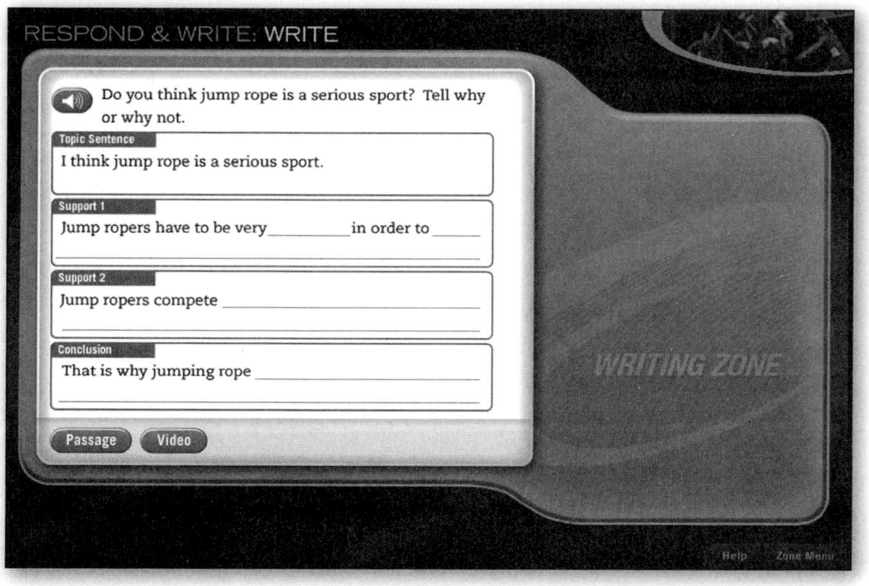

Reflection

One Writing Zone feature my students will really enjoy is...

Features to Notice

- Respond question directs students to choose their argument.
- Writing organizer scaffolds paragraph composition.
- Revising process encourages students to reread and improve their work.
- Publishing step allows students to submit a final draft that you can grade in the SAM Student Digital Portfolio.

Applying Skills: Modeled and Independent Reading

Explore the *READ 180* Paperbacks, Audiobooks, and/or eReads to preview the high-interest, age-appropriate texts available to students for daily independent reading.

Doing a Paperbacks Book Pass

During the Student Experience, follow the steps below to explore the Paperbacks with a Book Pass. See page 22 in *Getting Started: Your First Three Weeks With READ 180*, in your Teacher Bookshelf or online in the Interactive Teaching System (ITS), for a Book Pass lesson to use with your students.

1. Choose one group member with a watch to act as timekeeper, who will keep track of time while still participating in the activity.
2. Select a Paperback to preview. Look at the front and back covers. Then begin reading the first page.
3. After one to two minutes, when the timekeeper says "Stop," use the Reading Log on page 47 to jot down the title, Lexile, and your reaction to the book.
4. After one minute, when the timekeeper calls "Book Pass," pass the book to the person on your right. Repeat the whole process three to five times, previewing books and jotting down notes in your Reading Log.
5. Spend one to two minutes reflecting as a group on how to hold students accountable for independent work during Modeled and Independent Reading. Use a sticky note to jot down your accountability ideas.

Listening to the Audiobooks

Follow the steps below to listen to an Audiobook during the Student Experience:

1. Choose an Audiobook and CD to read.
2. Follow along in the book as you listen to the CD. You will hear two voices. One is the Narrator, who reads the book. The other is the Reading Coach, who models good reading habits and strategies.
3. When you finish reading, use the Reading Log on page 47 to jot down the title and your reaction to the book.
4. Remove the CD from the player and put it back in its case. Then return both the CD and book to their original place.

Exploring eReads

Follow the steps below to become familiar with eReads during the Student Experience.

1. Examine the eReads Poster and answer the questions below.

   There are a total of ____________ eReads Collections, with four informational articles each.

   The Collection that could best support a science project on changing climates is ____________.

   The eReads Collection that corresponds to Software Topic 13 is ____________.

   One "Your World + Beyond" Collection my students will connect to is ____________.

2. Use the Reading Log on page 47 to jot down the titles of two or three eReads Collections your students will especially enjoy, for reference when you return to your classroom.
3. Read one or two sample eReads, on the computer if available or as printed hard-copies. Use the following sentence starter to jot down your observations on the Reading Log: *One embedded eReads scaffold that will support my students with accessing complex informational text is ____________.*

Using a Reading Log

The Reading Log is a classroom management tool to promote student accountability for independent work during Modeled and Independent Reading. Use the log below to record notes on the Paperbacks, Audiobooks, and/or eReads that you explore during the Student Experience.

READ 180®
Modeled and Independent
Reading Log

Name ______________________________

Book Title ______________________________

My Lexile® ____________ Book Lexile® ____________

READ 180 Daily Reading Log

Day	Today's Response	Pages Read		Teacher Initials
		Starting Page	Ending Page	
Monday				
Tuesday				
Wednesday				
Thursday				
Friday				

Resource Links
SAM Keyword: Reading Log

READ 180 • Student Reading Log • **Modeled and Independent Reading**

Page 1 of 3

Modeled and Independent Reading Log
SAM Keyword: Reading Log

Wrapping Up the Student Experience

Participate in Whole-Group Wrap-Up during training to reflect on the Student Experience and the *READ 180* Instructional Model.

Whole-Group Wrap-Up

Whole-Group Wrap-Up occurs in the last ten minutes of every *READ 180* class for students to come together and reflect on the day's learning. Every *rBook* lesson includes a Whole-Group Wrap-Up prompt to guide reflection. To access the daily prompt, click its Wrap-Up in each lesson in the digital *rBook Teacher's Edition.* Guide students to respond in writing before contributing to a class discussion.

Use the space below to respond to the Whole-Group Wrap-Up prompt during the Student Experience:

____

____

Reflecting on Your Experience

Think about each part of the 90-minute *READ 180* Instructional Model that you experienced from a student's perspective. Record your reflections using the chart below.

Instructional Model	Reflections
Whole-Group Instruction	*One way Whole-Group Instruction supports and engages all students is…*
Small-Group Instruction	*In Small-Group Instruction, I can differentiate to meet individual needs by…*
Instructional Software	*Features of the Instructional Software that will motivate my students are…*
Modeled and Independent Reading	*The independent reading texts will keep my students engaged because…*
Whole-Group Wrap-Up	*It's important to leave time for Whole-Group Wrap-Up because…*

TEACHER IMPLEMENTATION GUIDE

Whole- and Small-Group Instruction

Overview: Whole- and Small-Group Instruction

Daily Whole- and Small-Group Instruction support students with building reading, academic vocabulary, writing, and oral language skills necessary for college, career, and beyond.

Understanding the Model for Blended Learning

The *READ 180* class begins with Whole-Group Instruction. Students then break into three small groups. Facilitate Small-Group Instruction with one group while the two other groups work independently in Instructional Software and Modeled and Independent Reading. Depending on the model your school is implementing, students spend 15–27 minutes in the first rotation. Then guide the groups to rotate. End class with Whole-Group Wrap-Up to reflect on the day's learning.

READ 180 Instructional Model

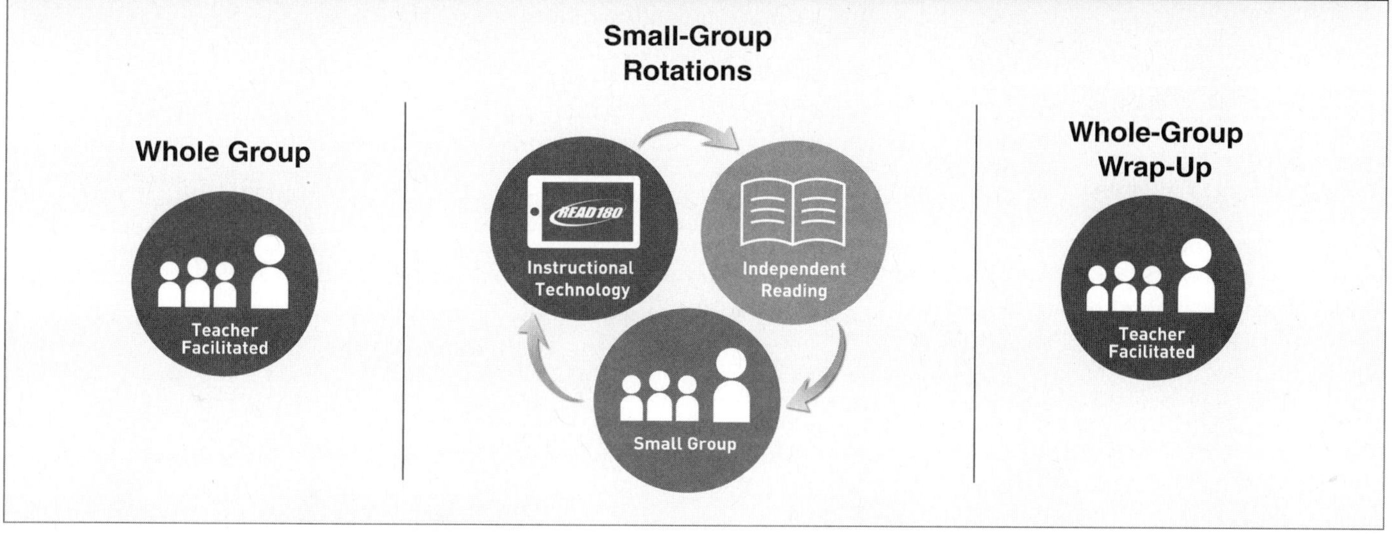

Building Your Knowledge

Use the K-W-L chart below to track your learning about **Whole- and Small-Group Instruction**. In the first column, reflect on what you already know from the Student Experience during training. Jot down any questions you have in the middle column. Use the last column to record notes as you learn more about Whole- and Small-Group Instruction.

K	W	L
I already know...	*I want to know . . .*	*I have learned . . .*

Understanding Whole- and Small-Group Instruction

Whole- and Small- Group lessons provide explicit, targeted, teacher-directed instruction to raise student reading achievement.

Research Says

Teacher-directed and scaffolded instruction helps students internalize and transfer comprehension strategies and critical reading skills to other texts.

Afflerbach et al., 2008

Purpose

Whole-Group Instruction builds reading, vocabulary, writing, and oral language skills through teacher-led lessons with embedded instructional routines. You may also occasionally choose to use this time to prepare students for tests, address district standards, discuss goals, or review procedures.

Small-Group Instruction allows you to work with a few students at a time and differentiate instruction based on their needs. When the students in Small-Group Instruction are working independently, you can also use this time to check in with students at the other two rotations or hold individual conferences.

Teacher Tip

See pages 18 and 42 in *Getting Started: Your First Three Weeks With READ 180*, available in your Teacher Bookshelf or on ITS, for model lessons that introduce Whole- and Small-Group Instruction to students.

Instructional Focus

To help students become better readers, writers, and speakers during Whole- and Small-Group Instruction:

- Show Anchor Videos to build background knowledge before reading.
- Read aloud *rBook* passages to model accuracy, fluency, and expression.
- Guide students to perform repeated readings of passages of increasing text complexity to build fluency and comprehension.
- Provide explicit instruction in academic vocabulary words and word parts.
- Scaffold practice with multi-paragraph writing in key writing types.
- Teach 21st Century literacy skills for college and career readiness.
- Assess mastery of Workshop skills with a Wrap-Up Project and Test before students take the computer-based *rSkills* College & Career.
- Incorporate Instructional Routines to actively involve students in their learning and strengthen speaking and listening skills.
- Differentiate daily lessons to scaffold or extend instruction for students at varying reading proficiency levels with different learning needs.
- Integrate CheckPoints to group students by need and target instruction at three points during each Workshop.

Teacher Materials

Use the *rBook Teacher's Edition* and *rBook* Anchor Videos DVD for daily Whole and Small Group lessons. Provide targeted support during differentiation CheckPoints using the three *RDI* books. Launch the Teacher Dashboard to preview and prepare for lessons, and connect to the Interactive Teaching System for digital versions of your teaching materials.

rBook Teacher's Edition

Anchor Videos DVD

Resources for Differentiated Instruction (RDI)

Teacher Dashboard

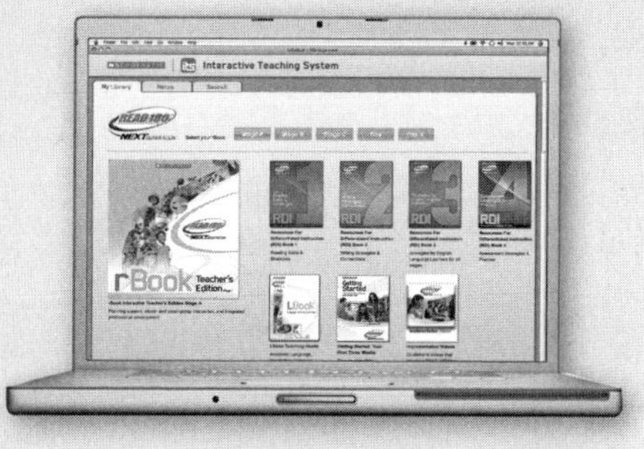

Interactive Teaching System (ITS)

Student Materials

Guide students to "read, write, and react" in the *rBook* during Whole- and Small-Group Instruction each day to develop reading, vocabulary, writing, and oral language skills.

rBook

Assessment Materials

Administer *rSkills Tests* after every *rBook* Workshop to assess student mastery of skills taught during Whole- and Small-Group Instruction. Log in to SAM to run reports and monitor progress throughout the year. Use the *Placement, Assessment, and Reporting Guide* for support with using all assessments and reports included in *READ 180*.

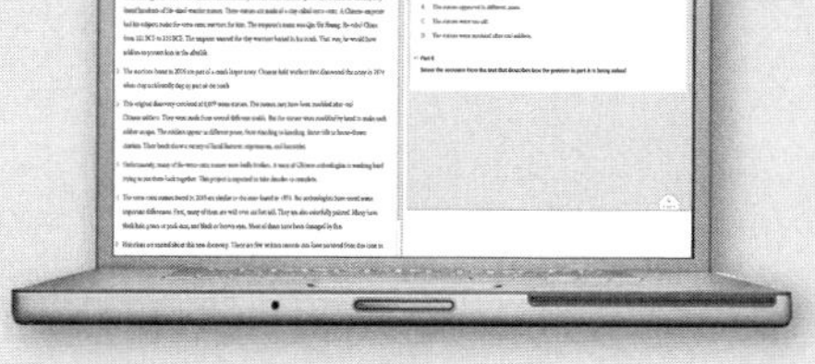

***rSkills* College & Career**

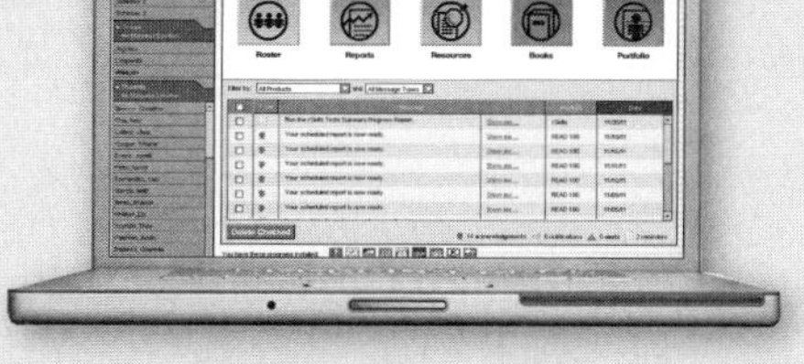

Scholastic Achievement Manager (SAM)

Placement, Assessment, and Reporting Guide

Integrating Instructional Routines

Lessons in the *rBook Teacher's Edition* incorporate nine research-based RED Routines to actively involve students in learning. As you practice the routines during training, reflect on how they will support your students' academic progress.

RED Routine 1: Teaching Vocabulary

Follow this engaging routine to teach students the academic and content-area vocabulary they need to understand *rBook* Workshop readings and content-area texts.

Reflection

This routine reinforces student understanding of new academic and content-area vocabulary by . . .

RED Routine 2: Scaffolded Reading

Support students to actively read each *rBook* passage multiple times using these five routines—Oral Cloze, Modeled Fluent Reading, Choral Reading, Partner Cloze, and Independent Reading—that build fluency and independence.

Reflection

One way Scaffolded Reading holds students accountable for actively reading is . . .

RED Routine 3: Think (Write)-Pair-Share

Think (Write)-Pair-Share is a structured engagement routine for daily academic discussion that creates a classroom of active and accountable learners.

Reflection

A great opportunity to incorporate Think (Write)-Pair-Share into my daily lessons is . . .

RED Routine 4: Idea Wave

This structured engagement routine offers a quick, effective, and low-risk way to add many voices to class discussions.

Reflection

One way this routine differs from traditional class discussions is . . .

RED Routine 5: Numbered Heads

Have students "put their heads together" for accountable group work and participation in collaborative discussions.

Reflection

Numbered Heads encourages all students to actively participate in group work by . . .

RED Routine 6: The Writing Process

The Writing Process provides students with a clear structure and sequence for developing and refining their academic writing skills.

Reflection

One way this routine prepares students for college and career readiness is . . .

RED Routine 7: Peer Feedback

This routine actively engages students in developing revision skills and collaborating with classmates to strengthen the overall quality of their writing.

Reflection

One way I can support my students with providing Peer Feedback is . . .

RED Routine 8: React and Write

React and Write is a teacher-mediated gradual release routine that supports students as they react to text through structured academic discussion and writing.

Reflection

It's important for students to practice using academic language in discussion and writing because . . .

RED Routine 9: Summarize

Guide students to identify what is essential in a text and process ideas deeply by expressing them in their own words.

Reflection

One place I can incorporate the Summarize Routine into my instruction is . . .

Integrating Instructional Routines

Incorporate at least one RED Routine into every Whole and Small Group lesson to provide consistent, effective instruction and actively involve students in learning.

Why Use Routines?

Research shows that using recursive instructional practices supports students with mastering new skills. Consistent, familiar routines allow students to focus on learning the lesson content, instead of learning the steps for a new activity. Use the RED Routines again and again throughout the year to:

- Provide consistent instruction and opportunities for student practice, even as the lesson content varies.
- Involve *all* students in actively learning and participating in the lesson, instead of just the two or three students who usually volunteer.
- Structure academic discussions with student partners, groups, or the whole class.
- Hold students accountable for actively completing group or independent work.
- Prepare students with the reading, writing, and academic language skills they need for college and career success.

When to Use Routines

Incorporate at least one RED Routine into every lesson to structure Whole- and Small-Group Instruction. Check out these resources to determine when to use each routine:

- See the daily Whole and Small Group lessons in the *rBook Teacher's Edition* for explicit tips on when to use each routine and how to tailor it for specific content.
- Check the Instructional Routines tab of the *rBook Teacher's Edition*. Here you'll find the research behind each routine, steps for facilitating it with students, and "When to Use" it during your instruction.

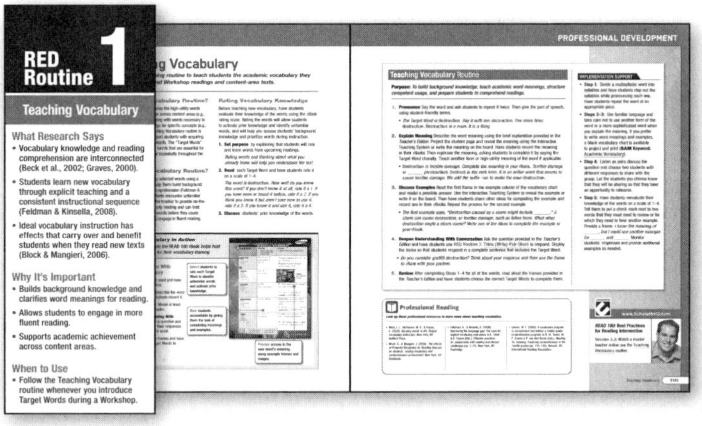

RED Routine 1

Teaching Vocabulary

What Research Says
- Vocabulary knowledge and reading comprehension are interconnected (Beck et al., 2002; Graves, 2000).
- Students learn new vocabulary through explicit teaching and a consistent instructional sequence (Feldman & Kinsella, 2008).
- Ideal vocabulary instruction has effects that carry over and benefit students when they read new texts (Block & Mangieri, 2006).

Why It's Important
- Builds background knowledge and clarifies word meanings for reading.
- Allows students to engage in more fluent reading.
- Supports academic achievement across content areas.

When to Use
- Follow the Teaching Vocabulary routine whenever you introduce Target Words during a Workshop.

PROFESSIONAL DEVELOPMENT

***rBook Teacher's Edition*, Instructional Routines Tab**

How to Use Routines

Follow these steps to prepare for incorporating a RED Routine into your daily instruction:

1. **Identify the Routine:** Read the Whole and Small Group lesson plans in the *rBook Teacher's Edition* to determine which routine(s) to use that day.
2. **Review the Routine:** Turn to the Instructional Routines tab in the *rBook Teacher's Edition* to review steps and read about the research behind the routine(s). When using the Interactive Teaching System (ITS), simply click the routine name in the Whole or Small Group lesson to link to relevant pages in the Instructional Routines tab.
3. **Watch the Routine:** In ITS, click the routine name in the Whole or Small Group lesson to see if there is an available video of a master teacher or *rBook* author modeling the routine. If so, click the video name to see the routine in action and learn tips for using it with your students.
4. **Use the Routine:** Follow the step-by-step directions in the Instructional Routines tab of your *rBook Teacher's Edition* to facilitate the routine during class. As you work through the *rBook*, notice how the routines are recursive in each Workshop. Spend time at the beginning of the year to explicitly teach, model, and practice the routines so they become automatic for students.

Exploring the *rBook Teacher's Edition*

Use the *rBook Teacher's Edition* to teach nine engaging, age-appropriate Workshops during the school year. Record notes below as you explore each part of an *rBook* Workshop in training.

Workshop Feature	Research-Based Reflections
Planning Guide	*One way the Planning Guide supports me with differentiated instruction is…*
Workshop Opener	*Pre-teaching vocabulary before reading supports comprehension because...*
Readings 1–3	*To support students with complex text, the passages include scaffolds such as...*
Vocabulary/ Word Study	*One strategy I'll use to build vocabulary in this part of the Workshop is…*
Writing and Conventions	*Scaffolds that support students' multi-paragraph writing include...*
21st Century Literacy	*A 21st Century literacy skill students practice in this part of the Workshop is…*
Wrap-Up Project and Test	*The Wrap-Up Project and Test help assess my students' learning by…*
CheckPoints for Differentiated Instruction	*The three CheckPoints help accelerate student reading success because…*

Navigating an *rBook* Workshop

Refer to the Planning Guide that precedes each Workshop in the *rBook Teacher's Edition* for support with pacing instruction and planning three differentiation CheckPoints.

Follow the suggested pacing to complete each *rBook* Workshop in about 4–6 weeks.

See how the Whole- and Small-Group Instruction objectives align with your state standards.

Incorporate strategies for differentiated support into daily lessons to meet individual student needs.

WORKSHOP 2: When Disaster Strikes

Using Data to Differentiate
CHECKPOINT 1

Planning Guide

Go to the Teacher Dashboard to customize and print daily lesson plans, view state standards, group students, and schedule reports. www.read180.com/teacherdashboard

READING CHECKPOINT (1–2 DAYS)

Focus on Comprehension Skills
Launch the Teacher Dashboard to group students for Small-Group Instruction.

- Review and reteach comprehension skills with **RDI Book 1** lessons.
- Apply the key skill with **Stretch Text:** "Search and Rescue Teams in Haiti Race Against Time."

See page 45C.

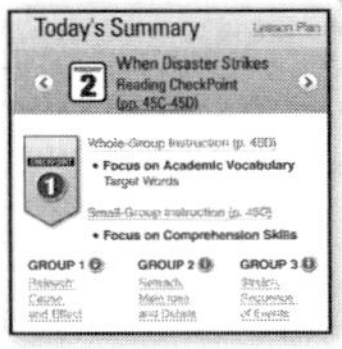

PACING SUGGESTION
2 DAYS → 5–6 DAYS →

WHOLE- AND SMALL-GROUP INSTRUCTION

Prereading	Reading 1	Reading 2	Reading 3
Build Background **Anchor Video,** p. 34G • **Video Story:** *Katrina Pet Rescue* DIFFERENTIATED INSTRUCTION **Scaffolded Support** • Oral Summary, p. 34H **Preview/Teach Vocabulary** ***When Disaster Strikes,*** p. 34 **Academic Vocabulary,** p. 35 DIFFERENTIATED INSTRUCTION **Scaffolded Support** • Generating Examples, p. 35 PROFESSIONAL DEVELOPMENT • **Special Needs:** Managing Rotations, p. 45B *Implement these strategies throughout the Workshop.*	**Teach** ***Struck by Lightning,*** p. 36 **Text:** News Article ✓**Key Skill:** Sequence of Events, p. 37 DIFFERENTIATED INSTRUCTION **Scaffolded Support** • Questioning, p. 37 **Meeting Individual Needs** • **Decoding/Syllabication:** Consonant + *-le, -al, -el,* p. 45A • **Fluency:** Using Correct Phrasing (Punctuation), p. 45A • **ELD:** Phrasal Verbs, p. 45B	**Practice** ***A Mountain on Fire,*** p. 38 **Text:** Magazine Article ✓**Key Skill:** Sequence of Events, pp. 39, 41 ✓Synthesize, p. 39 DIFFERENTIATED INSTRUCTION **Scaffolded Support** • Rereading, p. 39 • Self-Monitoring, p. 41 **Meeting Individual Needs** • **Fluency:** Using Correct Phrasing (Punctuation), p. 45A • **ELD:** Phrasal Verbs, p. 45B	**Apply** ***Hurricanes: The Monster Storms,*** p. 42 **Text:** Science Text ✓**Key Skill:** Sequence of Events, pp. 43, 45 ✓Main Idea and Details, p. 43 ✓Synthesize, pp. 43, 45 DIFFERENTIATED INSTRUCTION **Scaffolded Support** • Text Complexity, p. 43 • Questioning, p. 45 **Meeting Individual Needs** • **Decoding/Syllabication:** Consonant + *-le, -al, -el,* p. 45A • **Fluency:** Using Correct Phrasing (Punctuation), p. 45A • **ELD:** Phrasal Verbs, p. 45B

STANDARDS-BASED OBJECTIVES

Prereading	Reading 1	Reading 2	Reading 3
Reading • Preview texts to activate prior knowledge and make predictions. • Read a text three times to develop fluency and support comprehension. **Speaking and Listening** • Use active viewing and listening strategies to answer questions about a video and build knowledge about disasters. • View anchor video to activate and extend prior knowledge about natural disasters. • Collaborate to respond to questions using simple and compound sentences. **Language: Vocabulary** • Use new academic vocabulary and generate examples to reinforce meaning.	**Reading** • Read a news article three times to develop fluency and summarize an aspect of the text. • Organize information to find the sequence of events in a news article. **Critical Reading and Writing** • Respond to a news article in writing. **Speaking and Listening** • Discuss a text using complex sentences and formal English. **Language: Vocabulary** • Use new academic vocabulary in complete sentences and practice previously taught words. • Articulate an oral summary using present-tense reporting and citation verbs.	**Reading** • Read a magazine article three times to develop fluency. • Sequence events using text marking, signal words, and a graphic organizer. • Summarize the topic and important details of a section of a magazine article. **Critical Reading and Writing** • State a point of view and support it in writing. • Synthesize information from a magazine article. **Speaking and Listening** • Discuss a text using complex sentences and formal English. • Articulate and write a sequence of events using action verbs and signal words. **Language: Vocabulary** • Use new academic vocabulary and practice previously taught words.	**Reading** • Read a science text three times to develop fluency. • Sequence the events in a science text. • Summarize the topic and important details. • Review main idea and details. • Read and interpret a diagram. **Critical Reading and Writing** • State a point of view and support it. • Synthesize information from a science text. **Speaking and Listening** • Discuss a science text using complex sentences and formal English. **Language: Vocabulary** • Use new academic vocabulary and practice previously taught words. • Describe the features of a diagram using appropriate terms.

✓ = Assessed Skill

PROFESSIONAL DEVELOPMENT See Research Foundations, p. T75; Instructional Routines, p. T109; and Best Practices, p. T131.

34E **READ 180** Workshop 2

***rBook Teacher's Edition,* Stage B**

Notice the Planning Guide is color-coded to map onto pages in the *rBook* and *Teacher's Edition* for easy reference.

One question I have about differentiating is:

____

____

____

Using Data to Differentiate CHECKPOINT 2

WRITING CHECKPOINT (1–2 DAYS)

Focus on Revision Skills

Use the Narrative Rubric to assess student writing:

- Look for elements of the Narrative Rubric that score a 1 or 2.
- Provide support in each of these elements as students revise their narrative paragraphs.

See page 53.

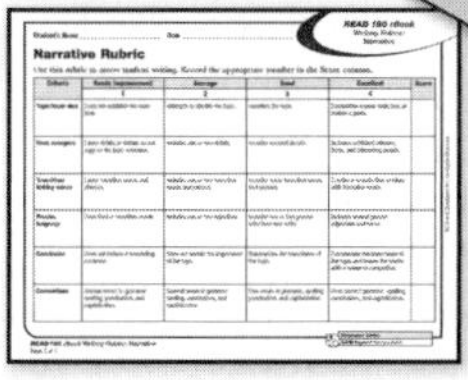

Using Data to Differentiate CHECKPOINT 3

END-OF-WORKSHOP CHECKPOINT (1–2 DAYS)

Review Workshop 2 Skills

Launch the Teacher Dashboard to group students for Small-Group Instruction. Reteach Workshop skills with **RDI Book 1** and **RDI Book 2** lessons:

- Sequence of Events
- Main Idea and Details
- Synthesize
- Prefixes
- Suffixes
- Sentence Fragments
- Capital Letters

See page 59B.

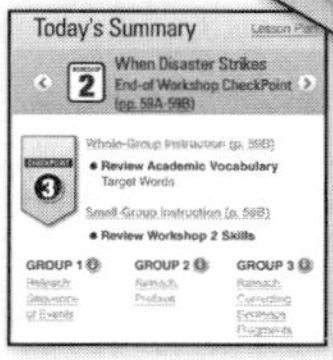

1–2 DAYS → 3 DAYS → 1 DAY → 3 DAYS →

Vocabulary/Word Study

Review and Extend

- Word Challenge, p. 46
- ✓Prefixes, p. 46
- ✓Suffixes, p. 47

DIFFERENTIATED INSTRUCTION
Scaffolded Support
- Generating Examples, p. 47

Target Words

- abandon
- cycle
- degree
- destruction
- focus
- increase
- major
- prevent
- recovery
- severe

Writing and Conventions

Writing

- ✓Narrative Paragraph, p. 48

DIFFERENTIATED INSTRUCTION
Scaffolded Support
- Choosing Language, p. 49
- Setting Goals, p. 51

Conventions

- ✓Correcting Sentence Fragments, p. 52
- ✓Using Capital Letters, p. 53

DIFFERENTIATED INSTRUCTION
Scaffolded Support
- Editing, p. 53

21st Century Literacy

College and Career Readiness

- **Technical Text:** Use a Weather Map, p. 54
- **Focus Skill:** Gather Information, p. 54
- **Career Path:** Storm Tracker, p. 55

DIFFERENTIATED INSTRUCTION
Scaffolded Support
- Questioning, p. 55

Informative Assessment

Wrap-Up Project

- **Proposal:** What is your disaster plan? p. 56
- **Focus Skill:** Evaluate Risk, p. 56
- **Focus Skill:** Ask Questions, p. 56

DIFFERENTIATED INSTRUCTION
Scaffolded Support
- Oral Summary, p. 57

Wrap-Up Test

- Comprehension, p. 58
- Vocabulary, p. 59
- Short Answer, p. 59

***rSkills* Assessment**

- Administer ***rSkills Test 2*** to assess skills from Workshop 2.

Click the blue hyperlinks in the Interactive Teaching System (ITS) to access relevant resources related to each lesson.

Speaking and Listening
- Participate in a group discussion to explain and elaborate on responses to academic vocabulary tasks.

Language: Vocabulary
- Review and use academic vocabulary in speaking and writing.
- Identify the meaning of common prefixes and suffixes.
- Determine the meanings of new words when a prefix or suffix is added to a known word.
- Express new word meanings using knowledge of prefixes.

Writing
- Analyze features of a narrative paragraph.
- Identify the purpose/audience for writing.
- Brainstorm ideas for writing a narrative text.
- Articulate an introductory statement that identifies the topic and point of view.
- Write a draft of a narrative text that includes sensory details in the correct sequence.
- Use a rubric to assess and revise writing.

Speaking and Listening
- Collaborate with a partner to discuss writing feedback using formal English.

Language: Conventions
- Identify and articulate transition words and vivid adjectives.
- Choose words that convey ideas precisely.
- Identify and correct sentence fragments; use correct capitalization.
- Edit a draft and proofread a writing sample for specific errors in conventions.

Reading
- Gather information from a weather map.
- Read a schedule and profile to learn about the career of a storm tracker.

Speaking and Listening
- Participate in a discussion using complex sentences and formal English.
- Use academic language to state and justify an opinion.

Writing
- Write an effective disaster plan with clear steps and memorable instructions.

Critical Reading and Writing
- Analyze features of a model proposal.
- Brainstorm risks of disaster.

Speaking and Listening
- Discuss and prioritize actions.
- Present using appropriate eye contact and verbal expression.
- Provide feedback to peers using frames.

Language: Vocabulary
- Show understanding of academic words.
- Review prefixes and suffixes.

Test Taking
- Practice answering fill-in-the-blanks.
- Show understanding of Workshop skills.
- Practice on-demand writing.

Visit the *READ 180* Community at www.read180.com/community for projects and other resources.

When Disaster Strikes 34F

Preteaching Academic Vocabulary

Begin each *rBook* Workshop by explicitly teaching academic vocabulary that students need to understand and discuss the Workshop readings.

Share the content and language goals to clarify lesson expectations and set a purpose for learning.

Show the *rBook* Anchor Videos DVD to help students build background for content-area reading.

Repeated reading of a passage helps students:

______

______

______

______

WORKSHOP 2 When Disaster Strikes

WHOLE GROUP

Preview

its Do Now

DVD **Activate Prior Knowledge** To preview the Workshop, replay the Anchor Video Introduction and Video Story. Then use the questions below to link key terms and ideas to each reading.

Reading 1: Have students view the photo as you read aloud the caption on page 36. *What can lightning damage? Lightning can damage ______.*

Reading 2: Read aloud the title and introductory text on page 38. *Why was this fire a disaster? This fire was a disaster because it ______.*

Reading 3: Read aloud the title, introductory text, and caption on pages 42–43. *Why are hurricanes often considered disasters? Since hurricanes can ______, they are often considered disasters.*

Scaffolded Reading

Build Fluency Read the introduction on **page 34** three times using RED Routine 2: Scaffolded Reading.

1ST READ Model fluent reading as you use Oral Cloze to read aloud the introduction. *Read along silently as I read aloud. When I leave out a word, chime in and read the word aloud.*

2ND READ Reread the introduction using Choral Reading. *Everyone read the introduction out loud along with me.*

3RD READ Have students reread the Workshop introduction using Partner Cloze. *Read the text silently and mark words to leave out. Next, read the text aloud while your partner fills in the words you leave out. Then switch roles.*

Ask students to respond to the question from the introduction:

- *I saw the dark side of nature when ______.*

Academic Vocabulary

Rate Vocabulary Knowledge Point out that the Target Words are from the Workshop readings and that students will see them in all types of reading.

- Read aloud each Target Word on the chart on **page 35** and have students rate their knowledge. (See **RED Routine 1:** Teaching Vocabulary.)

34 ***READ 180*** Workshop 2

its Wrap-Up

STUDENT OBJECTIVES

Content Goals

- Preview texts to activate prior knowledge about natural disasters and make predictions.
- Read a text three times to develop fluency and support comprehension.

Language Goals

- Use viewing strategies to answer questions about a video and build knowledge about disasters.
- Collaborate to respond to questions using complete sentences.
- Use new academic vocabulary and generate examples to reinforce meaning.

WORKSHOP 2 INFORMATIONAL TEXT	COMPREHENSION FOCUS Sequence of Events CRITICAL READING FOCUS Synthesize	Reading 1 Struck by Lightning | **News Article**
		Reading 2 A Mountain on Fire | **Magazine Article**
		Reading 3 Hurricanes: The Monster Storms | **Science Text**

***rBook* Teacher's Edition, Stage B**

Project this *rBook* page onto your board using ITS to guide students to accurately complete the graphic organizer.

SMALL GROUP

READ 180

Academic Vocabulary

Target Word ▶ Read the Target Words. Rate each one using the scale below.*	Meaning ▶ Read the Target Word meanings. Write in the missing words.	Examples ▶ Finish the Target Word examples below.
recovery (p. 36) *re•cov•er•y* *(noun)* ① ② ③ ④	the process of getting back to normal	• For quick **recovery** from the flu, you should rest. • **Recovery** from the earthquake will be long and difficult.
severe (p. 36) *se•vere* *(adjective)* ① ② ③ ④	very bad or serious	 A **severe** storm is headed our way.
prevent (p. 39) *pre•vent* *(verb)* ① ② ③ ④	to stop from happening	• The other team tried to **prevent** me from scoring a goal. • One injury I would like to **prevent** is breaking my arm.
destruction (p. 40) *de•struc•tion* *(noun)* ① ② ③ ④	terrible damage	• **Destruction** caused by a storm might include fallen trees. (flooded homes) • A pet dog caused **destruction** in my aunt's house.
major (p. 42) *ma•jor* *(adjective)* ① ② ③ ④	very large or important	• A **major** event during the school year is Student Council elections. • My 18th birthday will be a **major** one because I will be able to vote.

*Rating Scale ① = I don't know the word. ② = I've seen it or heard it. ③ = I think I know the word. ④ = I know it and use it.

When Disaster Strikes 35

DIFFERENTIATED INSTRUCTION

SPECIAL NEEDS: Managing Rotations For students who need support with self-regulation, circulate while students rotate, offering specific praise to reward smooth transition. For example, "Thank you for putting away the paperback and moving to the computer area quickly and quietly." See page 45B.

Academic Vocabulary

Unlock Meaning Refer to **RED Routine 1:** Teaching Vocabulary. Teach each word using Steps 1–4 and use Step 5 to review all words. Project the student page and reveal answers. A blank vocabulary chart is also available to project and print (**SAM Keyword:** Academic Vocabulary).

1. **Pronounce** Say the word and ask students to repeat it. Then give the part of speech.
2. **Explain Meaning** Provide the meaning and have students complete it in their *rBooks*. For *recovery* and *destruction*, teach another form of the words *(recover, destruct)*. For example: Destruct *is a verb, or an action word, that means "to cause terrible damage." We add the suffix* -ion *to make the noun* destruction. Then restate the meaning, asking students to complete it with the Target Word. For example: *Terrible damage is called ______. (destruction)*
3. **Discuss Examples** Read the first frame in the Example column and model a possible answer. Then have students share other ideas and record one in their *rBooks*. Repeat the process for the second example. Discuss this second example for the word *severe*:
   - *A student would be in **severe** trouble if ______.*
4. **Deepen Understanding With Conversation** Ask meaningful questions and have students use **RED Routine 3:** Think-Pair-Share and response frames to structure their answers.
   - *What would **prevent** a full **recovery** from a foot injury? ______ would **prevent** a full **recovery** from a foot injury.*
   - *What is a **severe** problem at our school? A **severe** problem at our school is ______.*
   - *Do you consider graffiti **destruction**? In my opinion, graffiti (is/is not) **destruction** because ______.*
   - *What is a **major** celebration in your culture? In my culture, ______ is a **major** celebration.*
5. **Review** Read each frame below, and have students choose the correct Target Word to complete it.
   - *Lightning is a natural thing that we cannot ______. (prevent)*
   - *Hurricane winds can cause terrible ______. (destruction)*
   - *The old damaged house needs ______ (major) repairs.*
   - *I missed the soccer game due to the ______ (severe) storm.*
   - *Lucy was back to school only a week after the accident; she made a quick ______. (recovery)*

DIFFERENTIATED INSTRUCTION

its Scaffolded Support Click for additional support.

- **Boost:** Generating Examples With Frames and Word Banks
- **Stretch:** Generating Examples With Supporting Sentences

When Disaster Strikes 35

Integrate RED Routines into your daily lessons using the steps in the Instructional Routines tab in the *rBook Teacher's Edition*.

Use embedded options for differentiation to meet specific needs and extend instruction in context.

Building Comprehension With Critical Reading

Every *rBook* Workshop has up to three different passages of increasing complexity with overlapping content and vocabulary to gradually build student reading independence.

Click the "Do Now" icon in ITS for a warm-up activity connected to the lesson that students can do at the start of class.

Follow the Scaffolded Reading Routines to hold students accountable for actively reading each passage multiple times.

READING 1 Struck by Lightning

WHOLE GROUP

Prereading

its Do Now

DVD **Activate Prior Knowledge/Set Purpose** Replay the Anchor Video for "Struck by Lightning." Read aloud the title and photo caption. Model how to ask questions: *Justin was struck by lightning. My question is: How did he survive?* Have partners ask how, what, or why questions and record them on the board.

Revisit Vocabulary Review Target Words on page 35 in context.

- *I (do/do not think) Justin had* ***severe*** *injuries because _____.*
- *I predict that Justin's* ***recovery*** *was ______.*

Scaffolded Reading

Build Fluency Read "Struck by Lightning" three times using RED Routine 2: Scaffolded Reading.

1ST READ Use Oral Cloze 1 to model fluent reading as you read the article aloud. *Read along silently, and be prepared to tell what the article is mostly about.*

The Key Idea Have students use this frame to share an important idea from the text: *This article is mostly about ______.* Then have them record the Key Idea in their *rBooks.*

Vocabulary: Target Word Pronounce the word *focus* and explain its meaning. (See RED Routine 1: Teaching Vocabulary.) Model a response for the example. Have students share additional ideas and record one in their *rBooks.* Then discuss this second example:

- *It is very important to* ***focus*** *while ______.* (verb + *-ing*)

Deepen understanding with conversation using this frame:

- *When I do homework, ______ makes it difficult to* ***focus.***

2ND READ Reread the article with Oral Cloze 2. Increase the pace and omit different words. Explain **Words to Know** and **Strategy Note 1**. Ask students to respond to their prereading questions.

3RD READ Reread the article using Choral Reading. *Everyone read the article out loud along with me.*

React and Write Read the question aloud. Use the frame below to have students discuss and record responses in a notebook. To use the complete routine, see RED Routine 8: React and Write.

- *If I saw lightning strike someone, I would ______ because ______. (Word Bank: help, run, scream)*

Summarize Guide students to use the frames and RED Routine 3: Think-Pair-Share to orally summarize what happened to Justin.

- *The news article (title) ______ describes how (topic) ______. (e.g., lightning struck Justin)*
- *The author explains that (important detail) ______. (e.g., Justin lost his memory)*

36 **READ 180** Workshop 2

its Wrap-Up

STUDENT OBJECTIVES

Content Goals

- Organize information to find the sequence of events in a news article.
- Read a news article three times to develop fluency and summarize an aspect of the text.
- Respond to a news article in writing.

Language Goals

- Discuss a text using complex sentences and formal English.
- Use new academic vocabulary in complete sentences and practice previously taught words.
- Articulate an oral summary using present-tense reporting and citation verbs.

READING 1 News Article

The Key Idea

WRITE What is this article mostly about?

Justin Norris's life changed after he was struck by lightning.

VOCABULARY
Target Word

focus

fo•cus (verb)

Rate It: ① ② ③ ④

Meaning

to pay close attention

Example

An activity that is hard to *focus* on in a noisy place is reading. (studying, sleeping)

React and Write

WRITE Suppose that you saw lightning strike someone. What would you do?

Summarize

In one or two sentences, summarize what happened to Justin. Include the topic and important details.

36 WORKSHOP 2

Struck by Lightning

A teen's life changed in a flash!

¶1 **September 6, 2001—** Last month, 16-year-old Justin Norris headed to his after-school job at a fast-food restaurant. It seemed like an ordinary day. But it didn't stay that way for long. Justin was about to get the shock of his life!

Justin Norris survived being struck by lightning.

¶2 Justin started work inside the restaurant at the counter. After an hour, he moved to the drive-through window. He took orders from customers through a big menu board. Outside, a severe storm was building. "I heard loud thunder," Justin remembers.

¶3 At first, Justin ignored the thunder and **focused** on his work. But the thunder grew louder. Soon, Justin couldn't hear his customers through the speaker. He turned up the [1] volume knob.

¶4 Then, a powerful bolt of lightning hit the outdoor menu board. A surge of electricity rushed in. It exceeded 15 million volts! The electricity shot through the board to the knob. Finally, it slammed into Justin's body and knocked him out. He was rushed to the hospital.

¶5 At the hospital, Justin had seizures. He couldn't remember names and numbers. The accident had wiped out his memory.

¶6 Now Justin is on the road to recovery. Currently, he still has memory loss. But Justin is (1) happy. Why? He knows he's lucky to be alive. END

Words to Know! **exceeded** was greater than

STRATEGY NOTE 1

MAKE INFERENCES *The article says Justin suffered loss of memory. I know that the brain is where memories are stored. So when lightning hit, it must have been transmitted through Justin's fingers to his brain.*

DIFFERENTIATED INSTRUCTION 1

ENGLISH-LANGUAGE DEVELOPMENT: Phrasal Verbs Teach students that some verbs are made up of two or three words. Discuss the meaning of the examples *turned up* and *knocked out* in the news article. See page 45B.

Use the Strategy Notes to model important reading strategies and best practices in context.

***rBook Teacher's Edition,* Stage B**

Check to see how the Workshop readings connect to core content areas your students are learning in other classes.

TEACH: Sequence of Events

WORKSHOP 2

SCAFFOLDING TRACKER

✓ **Skill:** Sequence of Events

Teach Practice Apply Review Reteach

Earth Science

Comprehension Focus

Sequence of Events

2 Sequence is the order in which events happen. To find the sequence of events:

- Try to remember the order in which events take place.
- Look for times, dates, and signal words, such as *first, then, next, after,* and *finally.*
- When you know the order, check it again. Make sure it makes sense.

▶ **Complete this chart with the sequence of events that led to Justin being struck by lightning.**

At first

Justin ignored the thunder and focused on his work.

Soon

Justin couldn't hear his customers.

He turned up the volume knob.

Then

A powerful bolt of lightning hit the menu board.

A surge of electricity rushed in.

Finally

The surge slammed into Justin.

He was knocked out.

An ambulance rushed him to the hospital.

When Disaster Strikes 37

SMALL GROUP

Strategic Reading: Sequence of Events

Teach/Model Read aloud the text at the top of **page 37**. Use **Strategy Note 2** to give a real-world example. Then tell students that you will show them how to follow these steps to find the sequence of events in "Struck by Lightning." Project the student page to model how to use the graphic organizer. A blank graphic organizer is also available to project and print (**SAM Keyword:** Sequence).

Think about the order in which events take place.

- **THINK ALOUD** *It's important to identify the order of events when you're reading to help you understand what happened.*

Thinking aloud to students helps them to:

____

____

____

____

Look for times, dates, and signal words that tell when the events took place. Reread paragraphs 1–2 aloud.

- **THINK ALOUD** *The date of the news article tells when it was written—September 6, 2001. The first paragraph tells when this story begins—*Last month. *Other signal words, such as* After an hour, *help me keep track of the sequence.*

1 **Identify signal words and phrases that tell the sequence.**

Reread paragraph 3. Ask students to circle signal words. *(at first, soon)*

- Read aloud the first event in the graphic organizer.
- **THINK ALOUD** *At first, Justin ignored the thunder. The word* soon *signals what happens next.*
- Guide students to enter the next event in the graphic organizer.

Use the **Differentiated Instruction** note with English learners.

Look for signal words and phrases that tell the next events.

Reread paragraphs 4–6 aloud, asking students to circle the signal words. *(then, finally, now, currently)*

- Guide students to complete the next sections of the graphic organizer, making sure to include only the most important events about when lightning struck Justin.

Make sure the sequence makes sense.

- **THINK ALOUD** *When you read the sequence of events, do you understand what happened?*
- Have students read the responses in their graphic organizers to a partner to ensure they make sense.

TEACHING WITH TECHNOLOGY 1

TEACH Display **pages 36–37** using the Interactive Teaching System. Use the Highlight tool to emphasize the signal words and phrases in the reading on **page 36**. Click the Select Answers icon to reveal sample responses for completing the graphic organizer on **page 37**.

STRATEGY NOTE 2

MAKE CONNECTIONS *Here's an example of sequence in our lives:* ***First,*** *you put on your socks.* ***Next,*** *you put on your shoes.* ***Last,*** *you tie your shoelaces.*

DIFFERENTIATED INSTRUCTION

its Scaffolded Support — Click for additional support.

- **Boost:** Questioning With Signal Words
- **Stretch:** Questioning With Frames

When Disaster Strikes 37

Click the "Scaffolded Support" icon in ITS to see strategies for scaffolding or extending each lesson based on student readiness.

Developing Word Knowledge

The *rBook* vocabulary/word study lessons review Workshop Target Words and teach high-utility word parts to support students with unlocking word meaning across content areas.

Knowing common word parts helps students to:

____

____

____

____

Follow the gradual release model (I do, We do, You do) to explicitly teach a skill before guiding student practice.

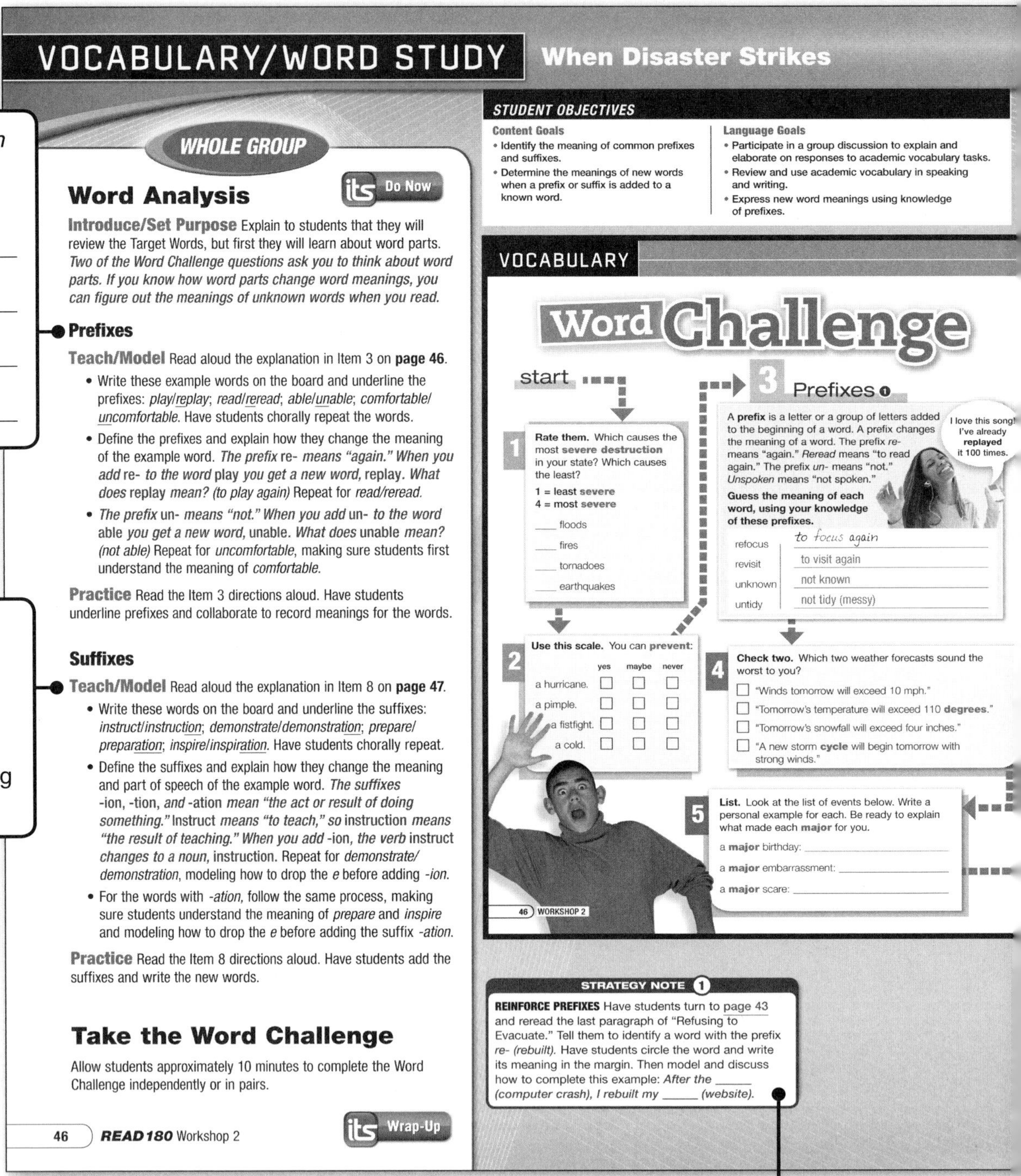

VOCABULARY/WORD STUDY **When Disaster Strikes**

WHOLE GROUP

Word Analysis

Do Now

Introduce/Set Purpose Explain to students that they will review the Target Words, but first they will learn about word parts. *Two of the Word Challenge questions ask you to think about word parts. If you know how word parts change word meanings, you can figure out the meanings of unknown words when you read.*

Prefixes

Teach/Model Read aloud the explanation in Item 3 on **page 46**.

- Write these example words on the board and underline the prefixes: *play/replay*; *read/reread*; *able/unable*; *comfortable/uncomfortable*. Have students chorally repeat the words.
- Define the prefixes and explain how they change the meaning of the example word. *The prefix* re- *means "again." When you add* re- *to the word* play *you get a new word,* replay. *What does* replay *mean? (to play again)* Repeat for *read/reread*.
- *The prefix* un- *means "not." When you add* un- *to the word* able *you get a new word,* unable. *What does* unable *mean? (not able)* Repeat for *uncomfortable*, making sure students first understand the meaning of *comfortable*.

Practice Read the Item 3 directions aloud. Have students underline prefixes and collaborate to record meanings for the words.

Suffixes

Teach/Model Read aloud the explanation in Item 8 on **page 47**.

- Write these words on the board and underline the suffixes: *instruct/instruction*; *demonstrate/demonstration*; *prepare/preparation*; *inspire/inspiration*. Have students chorally repeat.
- Define the suffixes and explain how they change the meaning and part of speech of the example word. *The suffixes* -ion, -tion, *and* -ation *mean "the act or result of doing something."* Instruct *means "to teach," so* instruction *means "the result of teaching." When you add* -ion, *the verb* instruct *changes to a noun,* instruction. Repeat for *demonstrate/demonstration*, modeling how to drop the *e* before adding *-ion*.
- For the words with *-ation*, follow the same process, making sure students understand the meaning of *prepare* and *inspire* and modeling how to drop the *e* before adding the suffix *-ation*.

Practice Read the Item 8 directions aloud. Have students add the suffixes and write the new words.

Take the Word Challenge

Allow students approximately 10 minutes to complete the Word Challenge independently or in pairs.

46 ***READ 180*** Workshop 2

Wrap-Up

STUDENT OBJECTIVES

Content Goals
- Identify the meaning of common prefixes and suffixes.
- Determine the meanings of new words when a prefix or suffix is added to a known word.

Language Goals
- Participate in a group discussion to explain and elaborate on responses to academic vocabulary tasks.
- Review and use academic vocabulary in speaking and writing.
- Express new word meanings using knowledge of prefixes.

VOCABULARY

Word Challenge

start

1 **Rate them.** Which causes the most **severe destruction** in your state? Which causes the least?
1 = least **severe**
4 = most **severe**
____ floods
____ fires
____ tornadoes
____ earthquakes

2 **Use this scale.** You can **prevent**:

	yes	maybe	never
a hurricane.	☐	☐	☐
a pimple.	☐	☐	☐
a fistfight.	☐	☐	☐
a cold.	☐	☐	☐

3 Prefixes ❶
A **prefix** is a letter or a group of letters added to the beginning of a word. A prefix changes the meaning of a word. The prefix *re-* means "again." *Reread* means "to read again." The prefix *un-* means "not." *Unspoken* means "not spoken."
Guess the meaning of each word, using your knowledge of these prefixes.
refocus ___to focus again___
revisit ___to visit again___
unknown ___not known___
untidy ___not tidy (messy)___

I love this song! I've already **replayed** it 100 times.

4 **Check two.** Which two weather forecasts sound the worst to you?
☐ "Winds tomorrow will exceed 10 mph."
☐ "Tomorrow's temperature will exceed 110 **degrees**."
☐ "Tomorrow's snowfall will exceed four inches."
☐ "A new storm **cycle** will begin tomorrow with strong winds."

5 **List.** Look at the list of events below. Write a personal example for each. Be ready to explain what made each **major** for you.
a **major** birthday: ______
a **major** embarrassment: ______
a **major** scare: ______

46 WORKSHOP 2

STRATEGY NOTE ①
REINFORCE PREFIXES Have students turn to page 43 and reread the last paragraph of "Refusing to Evacuate." Tell them to identify a word with the prefix *re- (rebuilt)*. Have students circle the word and write its meaning in the margin. Then model and discuss how to complete this example: *After the ______ (computer crash), I rebuilt my ______ (website).*

***rBook Teacher's Edition*, Stage B**

Revisit the Workshop readings to provide opportunities for students to apply word study skills in context.

Check here to see where the lesson's focus skill falls along the gradual release path for student mastery.

Model how to complete the response frames you assign so students understand how they are expected to answer.

SCAFFOLDING TRACKER

✓ **Skill:** Prefixes — Teach/Practice | Review/Reteach

✓ **Skill:** Suffixes — Teach/Practice | Review/Reteach

6 **Analyze.** Who causes accidents on the road? Put ***A*** for agree and ***D*** for disagree.

___ Mothers **increase** the risk of accidents.

___ Teen drivers **increase** the risk of accidents.

___ Sleepy drivers **increase** the risk of accidents.

___ Teachers **increase** the risk of accidents.

7 **Complete.** If I had to evacuate my home, . . .

I might **abandon**: ______

I would definitely **abandon**: ______

I would never **abandon**: ______

8 Suffixes ❷

A **suffix** is a letter or group of letters added to the end of a word. A suffix changes the meaning or part of speech of a word. The suffixes *-ion,-tion,* and *-ation* turn verbs into nouns. So, *evacuate* is a verb. *Evacuation* is a noun.

Turn these verbs into nouns by adding *-ion, -tion,* **or** *-ation.*

prevent:	prevention
construct:	construction
determine:	determination
adore:	adoration

construct + ion = construction

9 **Evaluate.** True or false, the best way to eat a worm is to chew it slowly and **focus** on how it tastes.

True **False**

Why? ______

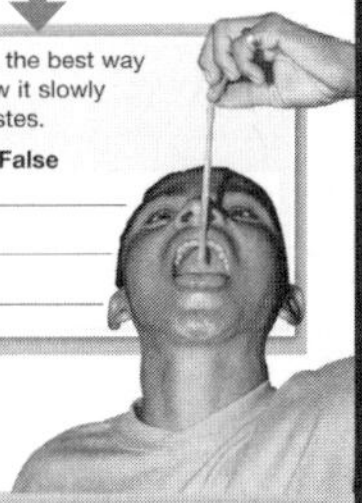

10 **Rate.** How long would your **recovery** be if you . . .

saw a scary movie? ______

had a fight with a friend? ______

broke a leg? ______

finish

When Disaster Strikes 47

STRATEGY NOTE ❷

REINFORCE SUFFIXES Have students turn to the Academic Vocabulary chart on page 35. Challenge them to find one verb that they can change to a noun by adding the suffix *-ion (prevent—prevention)* and one noun they can change to a verb by removing the suffix *-ion (destruction—destruct).* Model example sentences for each new word.

REVIEW AND EXTEND — WORKSHOP 2

SMALL GROUP

Revisit

Review Academic Vocabulary Discuss students' answers. Remind them that since there is not always a right or wrong answer, they need to explain responses. Use these steps for open-ended items (Items 1, 2, 4, 5, 6, 7, 9, 10):

1. Write a response frame on the board.
2. Provide a model answer using Target Words in your explanation.
3. Have students respond following your model.

For example, write this frame for Item 5:

- *A **major** birthday in my life was ______ because ______.*
- **THINK ALOUD** *A **major** birthday in my life was when I turned thirteen because I became a teenager.*

Use this frame for Item 6:

- *In my opinion, teen drivers (do/do not) **increase** the risk of accidents on the road because ______.*

Collaborate and Discuss Review answers to Items 3 and 8. Use the **Strategy Notes** to reinforce prefixes and suffixes in the context of the readings as time permits.

Then use these frames to model examples for words with the focus prefixes and suffixes. Have students use **RED Routine 3:** Think-Pair-Share and the frames to generate their own examples.

- *The class needed to **refocus** after ______.*
- *One place that I would like to **revisit** is ______ because ______.*
- *The reason why ______ is still **unknown**.*
- *The most **untidy** area at school is ______.*
- *There is no **prevention** for ______ because ______.*
- ***Construction** on a road may cause ______.*
- *Because of my **determination** to ______, I will ______.*
- *Many teens have an unhealthy **adoration** for ______.*

Return to Ratings To help students informally measure their vocabulary development, refer them to their initial word ratings, beginning on page 35. Have them take a minute or two to rate the Target Words again and share their progress.

DIFFERENTIATED INSTRUCTION

its Scaffolded Support — Click for additional support.

- **Boost:** Generating Examples With a Word Web
- **Stretch:** Generating Examples With Frames

When Disaster Strikes 47

Post response frames on the board or chart paper to encourage student accuracy with academic language.

Connecting Reading to Writing

Writing lessons in each Workshop scaffold practice with a key writing type. Students move from writing single paragraphs to building endurance with multi-paragraphs, beginning in Workshop 4.

Guide students to analyze a writing model for key features to include in their own paragraphs.

Locate more writing models to provide additional support with the key writing type.

Project the writing model from ITS onto an interactive whiteboard so students can use the whiteboard tools to annotate key features.

WRITING When Disaster Strikes

WHOLE GROUP

Narrative Paragraph

its Do Now

Connect Reading to Writing Read aloud the definition at the top of **page 48**. Discuss examples of narrative writing.

- *Narrative writing can tell a story about a real event or experience. For example, "A Mountain on Fire" tells the story of a real event—a fire in Colorado. Narrative writing can also tell the story of an imagined event or experience. If you write a story about visiting the moon, that is also narrative writing—about an imagined experience.*

Analyze a Model Read the student model aloud. Explain the features of a narrative text as students complete the activities.*

1. Examine the introductory statement. Reread the introductory statement aloud and explain its purpose.

- *The introductory statement identifies the topic. It also sets a point of view and lets us know who is telling the story.*
- Have students underline the introductory statement.

2–3. Identify detail sentences. Explain that a narrative text includes details—usually in time order—and sensory details.

- *Detail sentences tell the events in the order they happened. Sensory details help the reader see and feel what is happening. They make the writing more interesting.*
- Reread each detail sentence aloud and guide students to number the events from 1 to 5. Remind them that sequence signal words can help them identify the order of events.
- Have students check five sensory details.

4–5. Analyze language use. Remind students that transition words and phrases connect ideas and convey the sequence of events, telling the reader when there is a shift in time.

- **THINK ALOUD** *When I see the transition word* then, *I know that the next detail will tell what happened after Jaydon and his brother heard thunder.*
- Have students circle five transition words and phrases.
- Tell students that vivid adjectives such as *fierce* and *cracked* help make the event real for readers and help them picture it.
- Support students to double underline four vivid adjectives.

6. Examine the concluding sentence. Reread the last sentence aloud and explain how it ends the story and leaves the reader feeling satisfied.

- **THINK ALOUD** *After reading the concluding sentence, I felt relieved that the boys were okay, and I agree that they were lucky.*
- Have students put a star next to the concluding sentence.

* For additional models of narrative paragraphs, see **RDI Book 2**: pp. 17, 22, 27, 37, 42.

its Wrap-Up

48 ***READ 180*** Workshop 2

STUDENT OBJECTIVES

Content Goals
- Locate and mark the introductory statement, detail sentences, and concluding sentence in a narrative paragraph.
- Identify the purpose and audience for writing.
- Brainstorm ideas for writing a narrative paragraph using a graphic organizer.

Language Goals
- Identify and articulate transition words and phrases that connect details and convey sequence.
- Identify and articulate vivid adjectives that describe an event in a precise way.

WRITING — Narrative Paragraph Model

Writing Text Type

Narrative Paragraph

A narrative paragraph tells a story about a real or imagined event or experience.

▶ Read Jaydon Washington's narrative paragraph about a disaster in his town.

Introductory Statement
An **introductory statement** identifies the topic of the narrative and establishes a point of view.
1. UNDERLINE the introductory statement.

Detail Sentences
Detail sentences describe events in **time order**.
2. NUMBER the events 1–5 in time order.
Sensory details bring the setting, events, and people or characters to life for readers.
3. ✓ CHECK five sensory details.

Language Use
Transition words and phrases connect details.
4. CIRCLE five transition words and phrases.
The writer uses **vivid adjectives** to describe the experience in a lively way.
5. DOUBLE UNDERLINE four vivid adjectives.

Concluding Sentence
The **concluding sentence** completes the narrative in a satisfying way.
6. ★ STAR the concluding sentence.

Student Model

The Terrible Tornado
by Jaydon Washington

When I was 8, a fierce tornado nearly destroyed my hometown of Cincinnati, Ohio. 1 At first, my younger brother and I thought it was going to be a rainstorm. ✓ Dark, gray clouds blocked out the sun, and we heard a terrible rumble. ✓ 2 Then, the sky turned a frightening yellow-gray. ✓ 3 Soon, ✓ chunks of hail the size of softballs began pounding on our roof. The ✓ violent wind hollered and shook the trees. My mother rushed us into the basement, and we hid there for over an hour. 4 Later that evening, the news reported that the severe storm that passed over our area was actually a tornado! 5 The next day, we saw the destruction the tornado caused. ✓ Cracked branches and garbage cans were everywhere. ★ We realized how lucky we were!

48 WORKSHOP 2

rBook Teacher's Edition, **Stage B**

Graphic organizers support my students with brainstorming by:

____

____

____

Begin the Writing Process by guiding students to record ideas in response to a prompt.

NARRATIVE PARAGRAPH — WORKSHOP 2

SCAFFOLDING TRACKER

✓ **Skill:** Narrative Paragraph

Teach/Practice — Review/Reteach

Brainstorm

▶ Read the writing prompt in the middle of the idea web. Then use the boxes to help you brainstorm ideas.

Coldest Weather

Sample responses:
- a major snowstorm/ice storm prevented people from going out
- temperatures dropped below 10 degrees
- when the temperature hit a record low
- schools and businesses forced to close

Hottest Weather
- when temperatures reached 102 degrees
- weather so hot that people suffered heatstroke
- when temperature hit record high
- the heat advisory was in effect for a week

Writing Prompt: Tell about a time when you experienced severe weather.

Wettest Weather
- when it rained for several days
- floodwater covered cars
- when people were forced to abandon their homes
- when a major hurricane caused severe flooding

Wildest Weather
- weather so severe that people were forced to stay home
- when a major tornado hit and ripped houses apart
- severe and dangerous thunderstorms
- the government had to issue weather advisory

Choose Your Topic

▶ Select one of your ideas from the idea web. Then complete the sentences below.

I plan to write about Sample response: the time it rained for six days nonstop.

The weather was so severe that people were forced to abandon their homes.

SMALL GROUP

Generate Ideas

Unlock the Prompt Read the writing prompt aloud. Have students think about it and underline key words such as *severe weather.*

Identify the writing type. Ask students to identify the type of writing they will use to answer the prompt.

- *Is this prompt asking you to write a narrative about a real or imagined experience? How do you know? (The prompt is asking me to tell about a real experience. I know because I need to remember a time when I experienced severe weather.)*

Identify the audience/purpose. Tell students that the purpose for writing is the reason why they are writing, and their audience is the teacher and classmates.

- **THINK ALOUD** *My main purpose for writing is to tell a story about my experience with severe weather to entertain the audience—my teacher and classmates.*

Brainstorm Remind students that when they brainstorm, they think of many possibilities. Tell them that they will use some of their ideas to plan their narrative paragraphs. *You don't have to use every idea. You will have the chance to come back and pick your best ones.*

Record ideas for writing. Have students complete the idea web. Ask them to locate the headings above each box.

- **THINK ALOUD** *The labels on the web help me think of different types of weather I have experienced. For example, "Coldest Weather" reminds me of last year's record snowstorm.*

Discuss ideas for writing. Post these frames for partners or the group to share their ideas for writing.

- *The coldest weather I experienced was ______.*
- *I remember the hot weather that occurred when ______.*
- *We had extremely wet weather when ______.*
- *The wildest weather I remember was ______.*

Choose a Topic Guide students to select an idea from the web and complete the sentences at the bottom of **page 49**. *What weather event did you decide to write about? What do you remember about it?* Have students share their topics using **RED Routine 4:** Idea Wave.

DIFFERENTIATED INSTRUCTION

its **Scaffolded Support** Click for additional support.

• **Boost:** Choosing Language With Teacher Modeling	• **Stretch:** Choosing Language With a Partner

Support students with selecting just one topic to focus their writing.

Connecting Reading to Writing

The *rBook* writing lessons include scaffolded support to guide students through the organizing, writing, and revising steps of the Writing Process.

Build student mastery with single paragraphs in Workshops 1–3 before teaching multi-paragraph writing in Workshops 4–9.

Encourage students to use the precise Workshop Target Words in place of "tired" everyday words in their writing.

Focusing on one sentence at a time scaffolds writing by:

____

____

____

____

WRITING When Disaster Strikes

WHOLE GROUP

Organize and Write

its Do Now

Organize Reread the writing prompt in the middle of **page 50**. Guide students to complete the outline for their paragraphs.

Introductory Statement Have students record the topic—the specific severe weather experience—that they plan to write about. Remind them that the introductory statement in narrative writing includes the point of view of the person who is telling the story and his or her reaction to, or feelings about, the experience.

Detail Sentences Review the importance of writing detail sentences in time order. Then have students write two sensory details that will help the reader see and feel what is happening.

Concluding Sentence Remind students to write a concluding sentence that ends the narrative in a satisfying way, summing up the experience and making the reader feel a sense of closure.

Collaborate Have students use frames to discuss their notes.

- *The topic of my narrative paragraph is ______.*
- *One sensory detail that I will include is ______.*
- *My concluding sentence is satisfying because ______.*

Word Choices Explain that choosing precise words is an important part of writing an effective narrative paragraph.

- **THINK ALOUD** *We use everyday words like* cold *or* big *when we talk with friends. When we write, we use more formal or specific language. Your writing will be more powerful if you use precise words like* frigid *or* major.
- Read aloud an everyday word and a precise word from the chart on **page 50**. Give its meaning, and provide an example in the context of the writing prompt. Destruction *means "terrible damage" or "a very big mess." For one of my detail sentences, I could write: The destruction caused by the tornado included shattered windows.*
- Have students use RED Routine 3: Think-Pair-Share and a precise word from the chart to write a detail sentence for their paragraphs. Provide a frame: *The destruction caused by the ______ included ______.*
- Encourage students to use Target Words from the Workshop.

Draft Tell students that they will write a first draft of a narrative paragraph about the topic they selected.

Title Explain that the title should tell the topic of the paragraph.

- *The title of the model on page 48 is "The Terrible Tornado." It lets us know that the paragraph is about severe weather.*
- Direct students to write a title for their paragraph. Tell them that they can revise the title later.

First Draft Give students time to complete their drafts on a computer or separate piece of paper. Explain that the transition words and phrases are only suggestions; they can write their own.

50 ***READ 180*** Workshop 2

its Wrap-Up

STUDENT OBJECTIVES

Content Goals
- Write a draft of a narrative paragraph that includes sensory details in the correct sequence.
- Use a rubric to assess and revise a narrative paragraph.

Language Goals
- Articulate an introductory statement that identifies the topic and point of view.
- Collaborate with a partner to discuss writing feedback using formal English.
- Choose words that convey ideas precisely.

WRITING — Narrative Paragraph Write

Organize Ideas for Writing

▶ **Complete this outline with notes for your narrative paragraph.**

I. **Introductory Statement.** Identify the topic of your narrative.
Topic: ______________________
Point of View: ______________________

II. **Detail Sentences.** List two sensory details about the event or experience.
Detail 1: ______________________
Detail 2: ______________________

III. **Concluding Sentence.** Sum up the narrative in a satisfying way.
____
____

Write Your Draft

▶ **Write a draft of your narrative paragraph.**

Writing Prompt:
Tell about a time when you experienced severe weather.

WORD CHOICES	
Everyday	**Precise**
mess	destruction
said	reported
big	major

____
(narrative title)

▶ **Write your introductory statement.**

Introductory Statement
The most severe weather I experienced was ______________ (topic and point of view)
______________________.

▶ **Type your introductory statement on the computer or write it on paper. Then use these transition words and phrases to complete a draft of your paragraph.**

Detail Sentences

First, . . .	*Then, . . .*
After a while, . . .	*The next day, . . .*

Concluding Sentence

I/We felt . . .	*I/We thought . . .*

50 WORKSHOP 2

***rBook* Teacher's Edition, Stage B**

Build student proficiency with academic writing conventions by teaching grammar and mechanics in the next lesson.

Conventions Lesson, *rBook Teacher's Edition*, Stage B

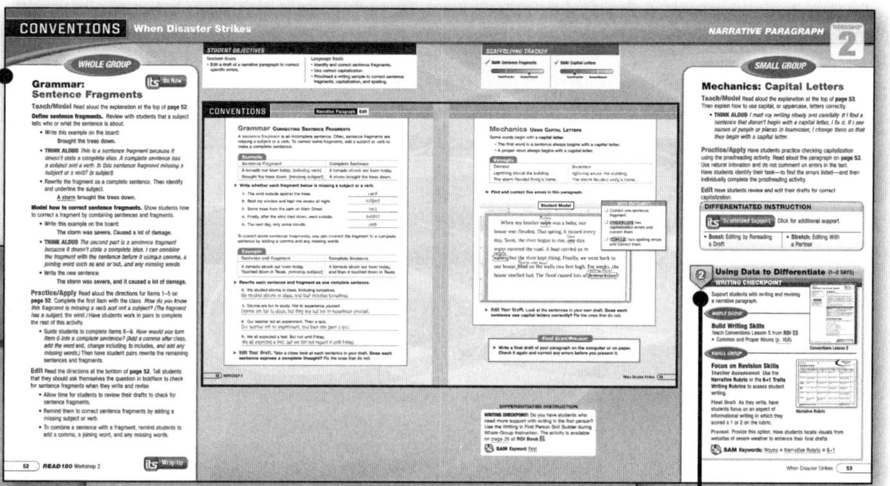

SCAFFOLDING TRACKER

✓ **Skill: Narrative Paragraph**

Teach/Practice | Review/Reteach

Narrative Paragraph **Revise**

Revise Your Paragraph

▶ **Evaluate: Rate your paragraph. Then have a writing partner rate it.**

Scoring Guide			
needs improvement	average	good	excellent
1	2	3	4

1. UNDERLINE the introductory statement. Does it identify the topic?
   Self 1 2 3 4
   Partner 1 2 3 4
2. NUMBER the events 1–5. Are they in time order?
   Self 1 2 3 4
   Partner 1 2 3 4
3. ✓CHECK the sensory details. Do they bring the story to life for readers?
   Self 1 2 3 4
   Partner 1 2 3 4
4. CIRCLE the transition words and phrases. Do they connect ideas?
   Self 1 2 3 4
   Partner 1 2 3 4
5. DOUBLE UNDERLINE the adjectives. Are they vivid?
   Self 1 2 3 4
   Partner 1 2 3 4
6. ★STAR the concluding sentence. Does it sum up the narrative in a satisfying way?
   Self 1 2 3 4
   Partner 1 2 3 4

▶ **Discuss: Give feedback on your partner's narrative paragraph.**

1. Start with positive comments about your partner's narrative paragraph.
   You did an effective job of ________
   ____
   The experience you described was ____
   ____
2. Give your partner suggestions for revision.
   I have a question about ________
   ____
   Your detail sentences ________
   ____
   The narrative paragraph needs ________
   ____
3. Answer any questions your partner has about your suggestions.
4. Ask your partner for feedback. Use the frames below to summarize your partner's feedback.
   You appreciated the way I . . .
   You had a question about . . .
   You suggested that . . .
   My paragraph needs . . .

▶ **Revise** Now revise your narrative paragraph.

When Disaster Strikes 51

Scoring Guide/Rubric Use the model paragraph (**SAM Keyword:** Revision W2) to demonstrate how to use a writing rubric for revision. Read aloud the narrative paragraph.

- **THINK ALOUD** *The paragraph is rated a 2 for sensory details because the writer doesn't describe what happened when the blizzard hit her town. What did the blizzard look like? What did it do to her home or her town? Let's brainstorm details that would help a reader see or feel what might have happened.*
- For items that rate a 3 or 4, discuss why the model is effective.
- Guide students to correct grammar and spelling errors and to replace everyday words with precise words.

Peer Assessment Follow the steps below to have partners self-assess and then assess each other's work using the scoring guide on **page 51** and **RED Routine 7:** Peer Feedback.

1. Direct students to read their own paragraphs and circle ratings in their *rBooks.*
2. Ask pairs to exchange paragraphs and *rBooks*, read their partner's paragraph, and circle ratings in their partner's *rBook.*

Discuss

Share Feedback Remind students to give their partners positive feedback before making suggestions for revision. Model an example.

- **THINK ALOUD** *You might say this to your partner: You did an effective job with identifying the topic in your introductory statement. However, your paragraph needs to tell the events in time order.*

3. Guide students to use the sentence starters to write positive comments and suggestions for revision in their partner's *rBook.*
4. Have pairs return drafts and have one partner discuss feedback.
5. Direct the second partner to ask questions and summarize the feedback using the sentence starters in the *rBook.*
6. Ask partners to switch roles.

Revise Provide time for students to revise their drafts and guide them to focus on areas with the lowest ratings.

- Guide students to circle everyday words in their drafts and replace with more precise words.

DIFFERENTIATED INSTRUCTION

its **Scaffolded Support** Click for additional support.

• **Boost:** Setting Goals for Revision With a Rubric	• **Stretch:** Setting Goals for Revision With a Checklist

When Disaster Strikes 51

Extend conventions instruction and differentiate to meet student needs during the Writing CheckPoint.

Teach students how to use sentence starters when collaborating with a partner (see page 73).

Ensure productive partner work by considering reading and writing proficiency levels when pairing students for discussions (see page 72).

Applying 21st Century Literacy Skills

Use the 21st Century literacy lessons in each *rBook* Workshop to prepare students for long-term success in college, career, and beyond.

Media literacy is crucial for the 21st Century because:

____

____

____

____

Teach students to analyze everyday functional documents necessary for success in the modern world.

21ST CENTURY LITERACY — When Disaster Strikes

WHOLE GROUP

Information and Media Literacy: Weather Map

its Do Now

Set Purpose Read aloud the headline, introduction, and directions on **page 54**. Then help students set a purpose for reading a weather map. *People use weather maps to understand the weather in a specific country or region. How can a weather map help us in our daily lives?* Provide a response frame.

- *Weather maps can help us ______. (e.g., plan how to dress for the day or what to pack when traveling)*

Teach/Model Tell students that they will read a weather map to gather information.

Read a Weather Map Model how to read the weather map.

- *The title of the weather map tells the type of information provided. Let's find the temperature of Kansas City.* Have students locate Kansas City on the map. *The first number under the city's name is the highest, or warmest, temperature of the day; the second number is the lowest, or coolest, temperature of the day.* Then have students locate the key. *The key explains the symbols that show information about the type of weather.*

Gather Information Explain that a weather map helps you compare and contrast temperatures and weather conditions in different locations.

- Have partners take turns reading city names and the temperatures. Then guide students to complete the text-marking activities.
- **THINK ALOUD** *First, I will look for cities with sunny weather. Both Minneapolis and San Francisco have the sunny symbol. Then I will see which of these two cities has the warmest weather. I know that 82 degrees is warmer than 75 degrees, so I will underline* Minneapolis.
- *Next, use the key to identify the symbol for storms. Where does that symbol appear on the weather map? Circle two areas.*
- *Compare highs and lows for all of the cities on the map and put a star next to the city with the coolest temperatures.*

Use the **Strategy Note** to illustrate how students can gather information.

Practice/Apply Read the directions and Questions 1–3 aloud and have students complete them. Use frames and **RED Routine 3: Think-Pair-Share** to structure responses to Question 3.

- *Based on the weather map, I (would/would not) want to visit ______ because ______.*
- *Even though it is ______, I ______. (Word Bank: cloudy, sunny, stormy, raining)*

54 ***READ 180*** Workshop 2

its Wrap-Up

STUDENT OBJECTIVES

Content Goals	Language Goals
• Gather information from a weather map. • Read a schedule and profile to learn about the career of a storm tracker.	• Participate in a discussion using complex sentences and formal English. • Use academic language to state and justify an opinion.

21ST CENTURY LITERACY — Information and Media Literacy

Focus Skill: Gather Information

Use a Weather Map

Severe storms or pleasant sunshine? Use a weather map to know the temperature and conditions outside.

► **Read this weather map of the mainland United States. Then, answer the questions below about gathering information.**

MARK IT

- **UNDERLINE** the city with the warmest sunny weather.
- **CIRCLE** two areas where thunderstorms are reported.
- ★**STAR** the city with the coolest temperatures.

Current Temperatures

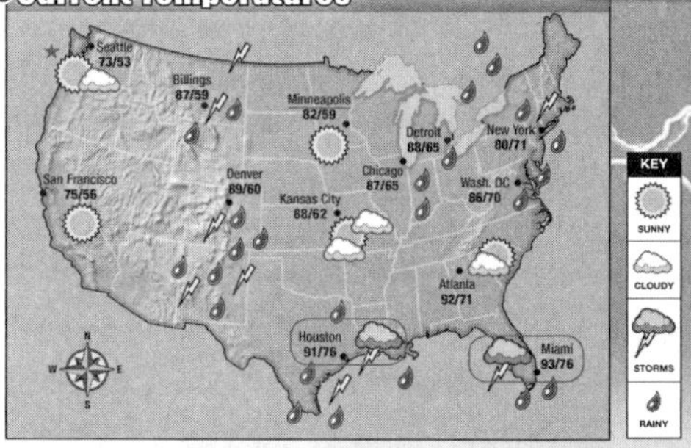

1. **Where are the most storms?**
   - (A) San Francisco
   - (B) in the East
   - (C) in the South
   - (D) Chicago

2. **Who might find this weather map useful?**
   - (A) a U.S. airline pilot
   - (B) a bus driver in Colorado
   - (C) a TV weather reporter
   - (D) all of the above

3. **Based on this weather map, would you rather be in Miami or Minneapolis? Explain.**
   Sample response: Based on this weather map, I would rather be in Minneapolis. I would not want to be in Miami because the temperature is 93 degrees with rain and thunderstorms. So, it is probably very hot, humid, and uncomfortable there.

54 WORKSHOP 2

STRATEGY NOTE 1

MAKE CONNECTIONS Discuss how students can gather information on a particular topic. *Imagine you are doing a science project on the deadliest natural disaster in Asia. What would you need to do to get the information you need?* Build participation by providing sentence frames: *First, I would need to _____, I would get the information by using _____ because _____.*

rBook Teacher's Edition, Stage B

Click the "Wrap-Up" icon in ITS to display a daily prompt for students to respond to at the end of the class period.

Introduce your students to a field expert and a type of document that he or she uses in daily work.

COLLEGE AND CAREER READINESS

WORKSHOP 2

Career Path — Science and Technology

Storm Tracker
Robin Tanamachi

This scientist tracks tornadoes to see how they form.

▶ **Read the work schedule and job information. Then answer the questions below about Robin Tanamachi's job.**

Thursday, March 19

9:00 AM – 10:00 AM	▸ Meet for a weather briefing about tornadoes that are expected in Wyoming.
11:00 AM – 3:00 PM	▸ Leave Oklahoma in a van with an engineer, Krystof, and our equipment: a radar unit to record data on the atmosphere, and weather balloons to collect information about changes in the atmosphere. ▸ We reach the storm area and set up our radar. Huge chunks of hail start pounding on us and our delicate radar dish. ▸ We move to a safer place, set up the radar, and watch the storm approach. A giant cloud wall heads our way. Looks good!
4:00 PM – 7:00 PM	▸ Watch the tornado funnel touch down. Record data on radar and track the storm all night.

ON THE JOB

EDUCATION
Bachelor's degree in Meteorology

RESPONSIBILITIES
- Records data on size, location, and other tornado details
- Analyzes data after each tornado-tracking mission
- Sets up, operates, and maintains technical equipment

SKILLS
- Working with a team
- Communicating data clearly to team leaders
- Operating scientific tools

SALARY
$29,000–$50,000

FAVORITE PART OF WORK
"I love being the first person to see new data. It makes me feel like an explorer!"

CAREER CONNECTION
Science, Technology, Engineering, and Mathematics
www.careerclusters.org

Related Jobs
- meteorologist
- science teacher
- science museum guide

1 What tools do Robin Tanamachi and the other scientists use to gather information about tornadoes?

Tanamachi and the other scientists use a radar unit and weather balloons to collect information about severe weather.

2 How risky do you think Tanamachi's job is? Mark the line.

1 — 2 — 3 — 4 — 5
Not very risky … Very risky

3 I think Tanamachi's job is/is not (circle one) risky because

Responses will vary.

When Disaster Strikes 55

SMALL GROUP

Career Path: Storm Tracker

Set Purpose Explain to students that storm trackers are scientists who use technology to track severe storms. Tell students that they will read about the job of one storm tracker, Robin Tanamachi. *As we read, be prepared to discuss what a storm tracker does on the job. Consider the ways Tanamachi gathers information about a storm.*

Teach/Model Read aloud the title and introduction. Explain that a work schedule summarizes the events of a workday. Tell students that the time of each event appears before the explanation of the event.

1 **Read and Clarify** Read aloud the schedule and the On the Job profile. Ask students to think about the risks of Tanamachi's job as they read along silently. Then have groups discuss details of her daily tasks and the type of background someone needs to do this job.

Check Understanding Ask students questions to check their understanding.

- *Why do you think Robin Tanamachi has to work with a team of scientists? (e.g., Since there are many jobs to do and equipment to run, many people are involved in tracking a tornado.)* **Make Inferences**
- *Why is it useful for scientists to try to find out how tornadoes form? (e.g., Scientists might be able to give people more advance warning if they know when a tornado is forming.)* **Synthesize**
- *What are some risks of Tanamachi's job? (e.g., getting struck by heavy flying objects during a tornado)* **Analyze**

Practice/Apply Review the Focus Skill **Gather Information**. Read aloud Questions 1–3 and provide thinking time for students to consider their answers and mark their *rBooks* independently.

- Have student pairs discuss each question.
- Build participation by providing response frames.
  1. *Robin Tanamachi and the other scientists use ______ and ______ to gather information.*
  2. *I rate the risk of Tanamachi's job a ______.*
  3. *Overall, I think Tanamachi's job is ______ because ______.*

DIFFERENTIATED INSTRUCTION

its Scaffolded Support — Click for additional support.

- **Boost:** Questioning With Text Marking
- **Stretch:** Questioning With Frames

When Disaster Strikes 55

TEACHING WITH TECHNOLOGY 1

EXTEND LEARNING To explore a career in meteorology, have students go to www.weather.gov and enter their zip code to view current weather conditions and temperatures for your area. Direct them to record the forecast for the next few days and compare it to the actual weather. For more information about careers in Science, Technology, Engineering, and Mathematics, go to www.careerclusters.org.

Direct students to visit related websites to explore career options while practicing media literacy skills.

Share key job facts to motivate students to consider a range of 21st Century career options.

Wrapping Up Workshop Learning

Guide students to complete a performance-based Wrap-Up Project and Test at the end of every *rBook* Workshop to apply skills and strategies they learned in Whole- and Small-Group Instruction.

Type the Keyword in SAM Resources to download and print student copies of the model Wrap-Up Project.

Guide students to collaborate, think critically, and problem solve.

Peer collaboration builds problem-solving skills by:

____

____

____

____

WRAP-UP PROJECT When Disaster Strikes

WHOLE GROUP

Introduce the Project

its Do Now

Set Purpose Read the question and introduction on **page 56**. Explain to students that they will think about what needs to be done during a disaster and create an emergency plan for themselves.

Analyze a Model Display the model disaster plan (**SAM Keyword:** Model W2) and distribute copies to students. Tell students that it is a sample of a disaster plan for teachers. The students' plan is for themselves. Read aloud the model disaster plan and then guide students to analyze its features and effectiveness.

- Ask students to number the three actions and star why they are important.
- Reread the three actions and discuss how they are clear and specific. *All three of the actions are simple sentences that tell me what I need to do in case of a disaster.*
- Have students discuss if the actions are easy to remember: *The actions (are/are not) easy to remember because ______.*
- Decide if the plan works for different emergencies: *This plan works for disasters such as ______ and ______.*

Brainstorm Risks Have students brainstorm possible disasters in your area using **RED Routine 4:** Idea Wave and a response frame: *A disaster that could hit our area is a(n) ______.*

Step 1: Ask students to list the two most likely disasters to record in their *rBooks*. Then model how to evaluate the risk of damage.

- **THINK ALOUD** *Let's evaluate the risks if an earthquake hits in our area. What damage could occur? There is a risk of a bridge collapsing. Also, there is a risk of help being delayed because emergency workers could not use the bridge.*
- Have students evaluate risks of damage from a disaster near your school: *There is a risk of ______ because ______.*

Ask Questions Explain that people have different questions during a disaster depending on their roles. *Since teachers and school officials are responsible for students' safety, they would want to know the best way to communicate with students so they can get them information and instructions quickly.*

Step 2: Have pairs work to record questions in their *rBooks*.

- Provide frames: *What is the ______ way to ______? Where is the ______ place to ______?*

Collaborate Tell students that their plans will include important actions. *One critical action is to follow instructions carefully.*

Step 3: Read aloud the directions for Step 3 on **page 56**. Have pairs work together to write and prioritize actions in their *rBooks*.

- Facilitate as students discuss actions with the group using response frames: *I wrote that students would need to ______. I think this action is critical because ______.*

56 ***READ 180*** Workshop 2 its Wrap-Up

STUDENT OBJECTIVES

Content Goals
- Analyze and discuss the features of a model proposal to determine its effectiveness.
- Brainstorm risks of disaster in a particular area.
- Collaborate to discuss and prioritize actions.
- Write an effective disaster plan with clear and specific steps and memorable instructions.

Language Goals
- Ask questions from the perspectives of different people affected by a disaster.
- Present a proposal using appropriate eye contact and verbal expression.
- Provide peer feedback and suggestions for improvement using frames.

WRAP-UP PROJECT Critical Thinking and Problem Solving

Focus Skills: Evaluate Risk | Ask Questions

What is your disaster plan?

A natural disaster could happen at any time. How would you respond if a major storm or earthquake hit while you were in school? Propose a plan **for what to do if a disaster strikes.**

1 **Brainstorm risks.** List two possible disasters that could hit your area.

A. Sample responses: hurricanes, wildfires, earthquakes, floods

B. ______

2 **Ask questions.** What questions might people have during an emergency? Consider the different groups at your school that would be affected.

Sample responses:

Groups Affected	Questions
Teachers and School Officials	• What's the best way to communicate the plan in the school building? • What's the fastest way to contact students' families? • Who is responsible for gathering emergency supplies?
Students	• Where's the safest place to stay? • How can I get in touch with my family?
Parents	• What is the school's evacuation plan? • How and where will I find my child?

3 **Collaborate.** Decide what would need to happen during a disaster. Add five more actions to the web. Then, circle the three best actions for students to take.

Sample responses:

What needs to be done?
- Follow instructions carefully.
- tell the teacher where you are
- find out more about the situation
- call for help/collect emergency supplies
- contact parents and guardians
- evacuate to a safe place

56 WORKSHOP 2

TEACHING WITH TECHNOLOGY 1

EXTEND LEARNING Have students design brochures on the computer to practice digital media skills. Using Microsoft® Word:

1. Select **Project Gallery** from the **File** menu.
2. Select **Brochures** from the **Business Forms** options.
3. Choose a brochure template.

Wrap-Up Project, *rBook Teacher's Edition*, Stage B

Administer the Wrap-Up Test to assess and review comprehension, vocabulary, and writing skills before students take the *rSkills Test*.

Wrap-Up Test, *rBook Teacher's Edition*, Stage B

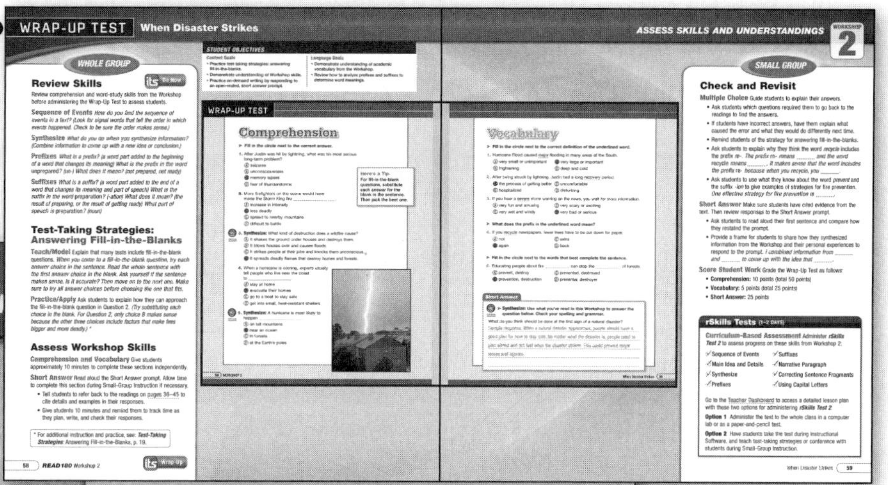

Proposal — Earth Science

4 Prepare your plan. Create a brochure or poster describing three actions students at your school should take in response to a disaster. Include or describe images for your brochure.

AN EFFECTIVE DISASTER PLAN
- ✓ shows clear and specific steps for safety.
- ✓ has instructions that are easy to remember (acronyms often help).
- ✓ can be used in different types of emergencies.

Title: Main Street Middle School Disaster Plan

Introduction: Responses will vary.

ACTION 1: *Follow instructions carefully.*

Why it is important: *This is important because we would hear important announcements about what to do and where to go to stay safe.*

ACTION 2: Evacuate to a safe place.

Why it is important: *This is important because* you have to move away from where you would risk getting injured.

ACTION 3: Let your teacher know where you are.

Why it is important: *This is important because* your teachers need to give specific and accurate information to parents or guardians.

Caption: Action 1: Follow instructions.

Caption: Action 2: Evacuate to a safe place.

When Disaster Strikes 57

Plan a Proposal Tell students they are going to use information from Steps 1–3 to outline their disaster plan posters or brochures.

Step 4: Read aloud the directions for Step 4 and go over the three criteria for an effective disaster plan on **page 57**. Tell students that you will look for these criteria when you assess their proposals. Refer to the model as students complete their disaster plan in their *rBooks*.

- **Title:** Point out that the title addresses teachers—the audience. Have students record a title for their plans in their *rBooks*.
- **Introduction:** Read aloud the model introduction. Explain that an effective introduction grabs attention, tells information you will find in the brochure, and tells why it's important. *This introduction makes me want to read the brochure. It tells me our lives might be at risk. The information will help me keep us all safe.* Have students write an introduction in their *rBooks*.
- **Actions:** Point out how the acronym in the model plan makes it easy for teachers to remember the actions. Read aloud Action 1 on **page 57** and have students record the remaining two actions that they circled on **page 56** in their *rBooks*.
- **Explanations:** Read aloud the explanation for Action 1 on **page 57**. Then guide students to complete the other two explanations.
- **Images:** View the images and read the captions in the model plan. Explain that the images should help students understand the actions to take during a disaster. Have students sketch ideas for two images and write captions in their *rBooks*.

1 Present Knowledge and Ideas Present the model disaster plan before students present their proposals to a partner.

- Model how to do an introduction. *Good morning. I am Ms. Cass. Today I'd like to talk about being prepared in case of an earthquake.* Have students take turns introducing themselves.
- Explain the importance of making eye contact. Read the model project while looking down. Then reread the model, making appropriate eye contact. Ask students to share what they noticed: *I noticed that you ______. This (was/was not) effective because ______.*
- Have students formally present their plans, either individually or in groups. Then have them provide peer feedback: *I appreciated how you ______. I agree that ______ because ______. One suggestion I have to improve your plan is ______.*
- Use the **Performance-Based Assessment** note to assess students' proposals.

DIFFERENTIATED INSTRUCTION

its Scaffolded Support — Click for additional support.

- **Boost:** Oral Summary With a Frame
- **Stretch:** Oral Summary With Two-Column Notes

When Disaster Strikes 57

PERFORMANCE-BASED ASSESSMENT

PROJECT EVALUATION Use the scoring guide for a Proposal to assess student work and give feedback. Make sure to include comments with specific examples from the projects so that students can consider your feedback and make improvements when they write proposals in Workshops 4 and 6.

SAM Keyword: Proposal Rubric

Download the scoring guide from SAM to evaluate students' Wrap-Up Projects and provide constructive feedback.

Build speaking and listening skills by having students present their proposals to each other.

Integrating Strategies for Effective Instruction

***READ 180* success depends on effective, engaging classroom instruction. Integrate these research-based best practices into your daily instruction to maximize student reading achievement.**

Research Says

Partner discussion enhances learning and motivation, especially for adolescents. Research shows that discussing books and sharing reading experiences with peers motivates students.
Pressley, 2006

Partnering Students

Students engage in a structured partner discussion at least once during every *rBook* lesson while participating in the Instructional RED Routines. Plan strategically for partnering to ensure that students feel comfortable working together and practicing academic language.

Assign "precision partners" by carefully considering students' reading and writing skills, English language development, behavior and social skills, personal interests, and attendance record. If assigning partners based on skill proficiency, then pair medium-level students with high and low students, instead of grouping the high and low students together.

Assign student responsibilities to maximize time on task during each partner interaction. Consider these ideas for assigning student roles and responsibilities:

- Assign each student in every pair a number: Partner 1 or Partner 2.
- Indicate which partner should begin the discussion.
- Alternate which partner speaks first throughout the lesson.
- Clarify for the partners any specific expectations, such as asking the second speaker to agree or disagree with the first speaker before sharing an idea of his or her own.

Reflection

A strategy I'll use to promote effective partnering is...

Manage partner interactions to ensure that all students work productively using academic language. Try these management tips:

- Keep partner interactions brief: 2 minutes or less.
- Develop a classroom setting arrangement—such as desks in groups of two or four—that allows for quick, frequent partner interactions.
- Teach your students the "4L's for Partner Work": **Look** at your partner; **lean** toward each other; use **low** voices to exchange ideas; and **listen** actively to what your partner has to say.
- Switch assigned partners at the beginning of each new Workshop.
- Develop a plan for supporting a lone student if his or her assigned partner is absent. For example, consider partnering two flexible and reliable "floaters" together for daily discussions. Whenever a student is absent, ask one floater to work with that student's partner. Have the other floater work with another pair who could benefit from an extra contributor.

Supporting Students With Standard Classroom English

All students—regardless of their linguistic, social, economic, or regional backgrounds—benefit from explicit instruction in Standard Classroom English (Labov, 2006). Standard Classroom English refers to the formal, academic language of school and the workplace.

Use the strategies below to teach Standard Classroom English in your classroom. See pages T88–T89 in the Research Foundations tab of the *rBook Teacher's Edition* for additional information and tips.

- Model Standard Classroom English at all times in your classroom by using academic vocabulary, grammar, and syntax and avoiding informal slang.
- Expose students to texts that incorporate academic vocabulary and syntax.
- Incorporate the suggested Differentiated Instruction strategies for decoding, fluency, and English-Language Development into your *rBook* lessons.
- Provide extra time and support for verbal responses to students who do not use Standard Classroom English at home.
- Give students corrective feedback on a respectful, case-by-case basis.
- Display and model completing sentence starters and response frames to support students with accurate use of academic language.

Research Says

Academic language proficiency is critical to achieving success in school, college, and beyond, and can be particularly important for English language learners and students whose home dialect differs from Standard Classroom English.

Dutro & Kinsella, 2010

Using Sentence Starters and Response Frames

Every *rBook* lesson and Instructional Routine includes sentence starters or response frames—printed in purple in the *Teacher's Edition*—to structure student practice with academic language. These frames also help scaffold responses for students who may be reluctant to participate or unsure of how to organize their thoughts before speaking.

Model Accurate Responses Model how to complete every response frame or sentence starter that you assign, so students understand how they are expected to respond. This helps generate appropriate student answers that promote accurate use of academic language.

Use these steps to model completing a response frame verbally and in writing for your students:

1. **Display** the frame in one color on your chalkboard or whiteboard. Write a model response in another color.
2. **Lead** students in chorally repeating the frame and your model response after you introduce it.
3. **Explain** what type of word or phrase students need to use to begin their response (e.g., past-tense verb or a verb + *-ing*). Point out how your model response begins with that type of word or phrase.
4. **Provide** a word bank with possible words or phrases to begin a response as an extra scaffold for generating responses.

Teacher Tip

Turn to the three red professional development tabs—Research Foundations, Instructional Routines, and Best Practices—in your *rBook Teacher's Edition* to learn additional strategies to inform and continually strengthen your daily instruction.

Monitoring Strategies for Effective Instruction

Routinely monitor student responses to your Whole and Small Group lessons to identify instructional strategies that are working and areas for growth.

Checking for Student Understanding

Integrate frequent, quick checks for student understanding throughout every lesson in Whole- and Small-Group Instruction. This helps you determine if students are absorbing what you are teaching and what questions they have.

Quick informal assessments allow you to check whether students are mastering the lesson content. They help you identify students who could benefit from additional support and those who might be ready for a challenge. Try the strategies below to integrate quick informal assessments into your lessons:

- Have students complete Exit Slips during Whole-Group Wrap-Up to demonstrate their learning at the end of each *READ 180* class. Make copies from page 246 or download and print from SAM (Keyword: Exit Slips).
- Ask all students to show a thumbs-up (to indicate "Yes") or thumbs-down (to indicate "No") in response to a question.
- Direct students to hold up a certain number of fingers in response to a question. For example, they could show one to four fingers to share their rating for each Target Word during the Teaching Vocabulary Routine. You may want to have students hold their hands close to their chests, to allow for more privacy in responding.
- Provide each student with an individual whiteboard and dry erase marker. Direct them to write a response to a question, then hold up their whiteboards. This allows you to see all responses at once from the front of the room.

Teacher Tip

An easy, cost-effective method for creating individual student whiteboards is slipping sheets of plain white paper into clear plastic sleeves.

Democratic participation means providing many students the opportunity to share during class discussions, instead of just the two or three who always volunteer. Asking "Does anyone have any questions?" or "Would anyone like to share?" may elicit responses only from your most confident or outgoing students. Instead, try these ideas to check in with a variety of students during a lesson:

- Write student names on popsicle sticks or index cards. Draw names randomly and call on those students to answer questions throughout the lesson.
- Nominate two or three students to jump-start a whole-group discussion, *before* asking if anyone else would like to volunteer to share.
- Guide "popcorn" participation by allowing the last student who contributed to select the next classmate to share.
- Ask students to nominate their partner to share an idea with the class after engaging in the Think (Write)-Pair-Share Routine. Ensure appropriate nominations by asking students to explain why they liked their partner's idea.

Reflecting on Your Instruction

The most effective *READ 180* teachers continually reflect on their instruction to identify strengths and challenges. Periodically complete the *rBook* Lesson Reflection on page 75 after teaching Whole- or Small-Group Instruction to assess your partnering strategies, checks for understanding, student engagement, and effectiveness of instruction.

You can also download the *READ 180* Classroom Implementation Review (SAM Keyword: Implementation Review) to monitor the fidelity of your program implementation, celebrate your successes, and identify areas for growth.

Date: ________ Class: __________ Lesson: ______________

rBook Lesson Reflection

Reflect on instructional practices that worked and strategies you want to try.

Which student response strategies did I use during the lesson to structure engagement and check for understanding?

Nonverbal Responses	Verbal Responses	Written Responses
❑ Focus visually (look at board, teacher, text) ❑ Track the text with a finger ❑ Mark the text (highlight, underline, circle, star) ❑ Signal (raise hand, thumbs-up/down)	❑ Read or repeat chorally ❑ Volunteer a response ❑ Answer when called on (not volunteers) ❑ Share with partner(s) ❑ Engage in small-group discussion ❑ Use a sentence starter or response frame	❑ Write a response using a sentence starter or response frame ❑ Take notes using an outline ❑ Use a graphic organizer ❑ Complete an answer blank ❑ Compose a paragraph in response to a prompt

What steps did I take to structure partner interaction?

❑ Assign a response frame that targets my students' reading, writing, or language proficiency level(s) and provides a structure for a specific type of response.
❑ Model how to complete the response frame verbally and in writing.
❑ Explain any target vocabulary and grammar in the response frame.
❑ Lead choral repetition of the response frame.
❑ Specify which partner will begin (Partner 1 or Partner 2).
❑ Monitor responses as partners share.
❑ Select two or three students to report before calling on volunteers.
❑ Remind students to use their "public voice" when sharing.
❑ Provide a word bank as an extra scaffold for generating responses.
❑ Assign a follow-up sentence starter or task to challenge "fast finishers."

Overall student engagement during the lesson *(circle one)*:

100% — 90% — 80% — 70% — 60% — 50% — 40% — 30% — 20% — 10%

Two successful instructional practices in this lesson:

____

____

Two ways I can strengthen my instruction:

____

____

Resource Links
SAM Keyword: Lesson Reflection

Lesson Planning With Your Dashboard

Follow these steps to use the Teacher Dashboard to select and prepare daily *rBook* lessons to teach during Whole- and Small-Group Instruction.

1. Check Today's Summary

Launch the Teacher Dashboard Home Page to check **Today's Summary** for each of your classes. This summary shows the current *rBook* Workshop, which lesson to teach that day, and a brief description of Whole- and Small-Group Instruction. A new lesson will automatically appear here each new weekday.

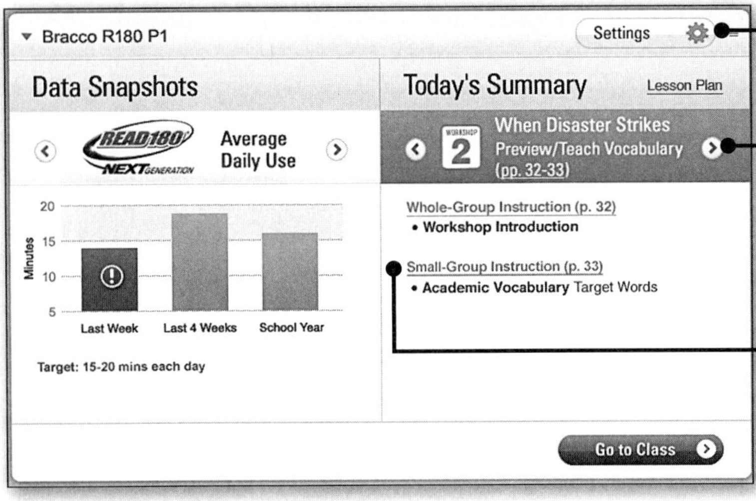

Click "Settings" to select the *rBook* your class is using and navigate to the current Workshop lesson.

Use the arrows to scroll through previous and future Workshop lessons.

Click the links to view digital versions of each *rBook Teacher's Edition* lesson in ITS.

Teacher Dashboard Home Page

2. Review Small Groups

Click **Go to Class** below **Today's Summary** on the Teacher Dashboard Home Page. This will open the Teacher Dashboard Class Page. Scroll to the bottom of the Class Page to see the **Groupinator**, which recommends small groups for daily rotations. The Groupinator uses software performance data to group students with similar learning needs.

Click the **rBook Groups** tab to see recommended groups for daily Whole- and Small-Group Instruction. The Groupinator uses results from the *Scholastic Reading Inventory (SRI)* to form three leveled groups for *rBook* lessons, so students are grouped by Lexile for daily instruction. Make any adjustments based on your classroom needs by dragging student names from one group to another.

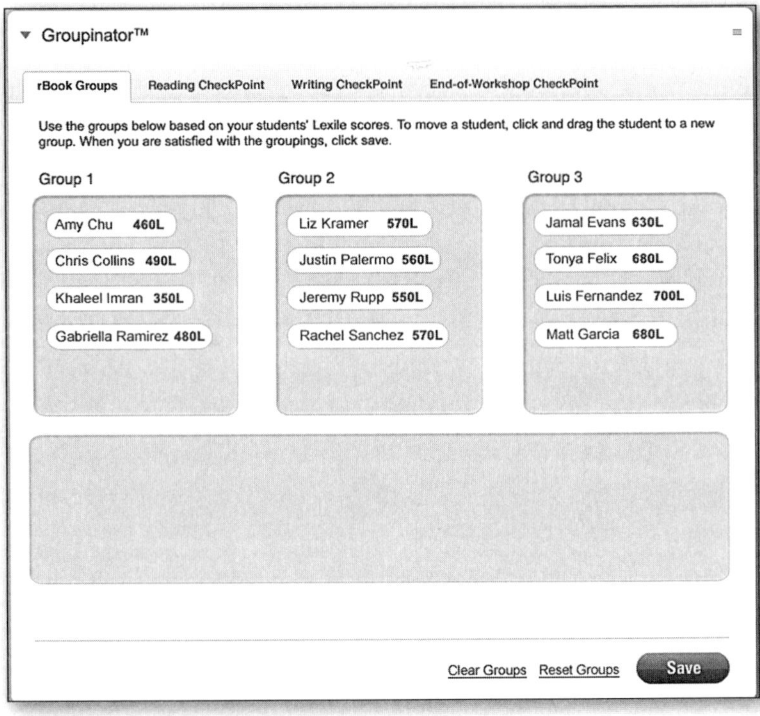

Groupinator, Teacher Dashboard Class Page

3. View and Print Your Lesson Plan

After reviewing what to teach and how to group students, click **Lesson Plan** in the **Today's Summary** header on the Teacher Dashboard Home or Class Page to see a printable lesson plan for that day. The lesson plan details exactly what to teach during each part of the Instructional Model. Customize it by adding notes in the blank fields. Then save it to your computer desktop and/or print it for reference while teaching Whole- and Small-Group Instruction.

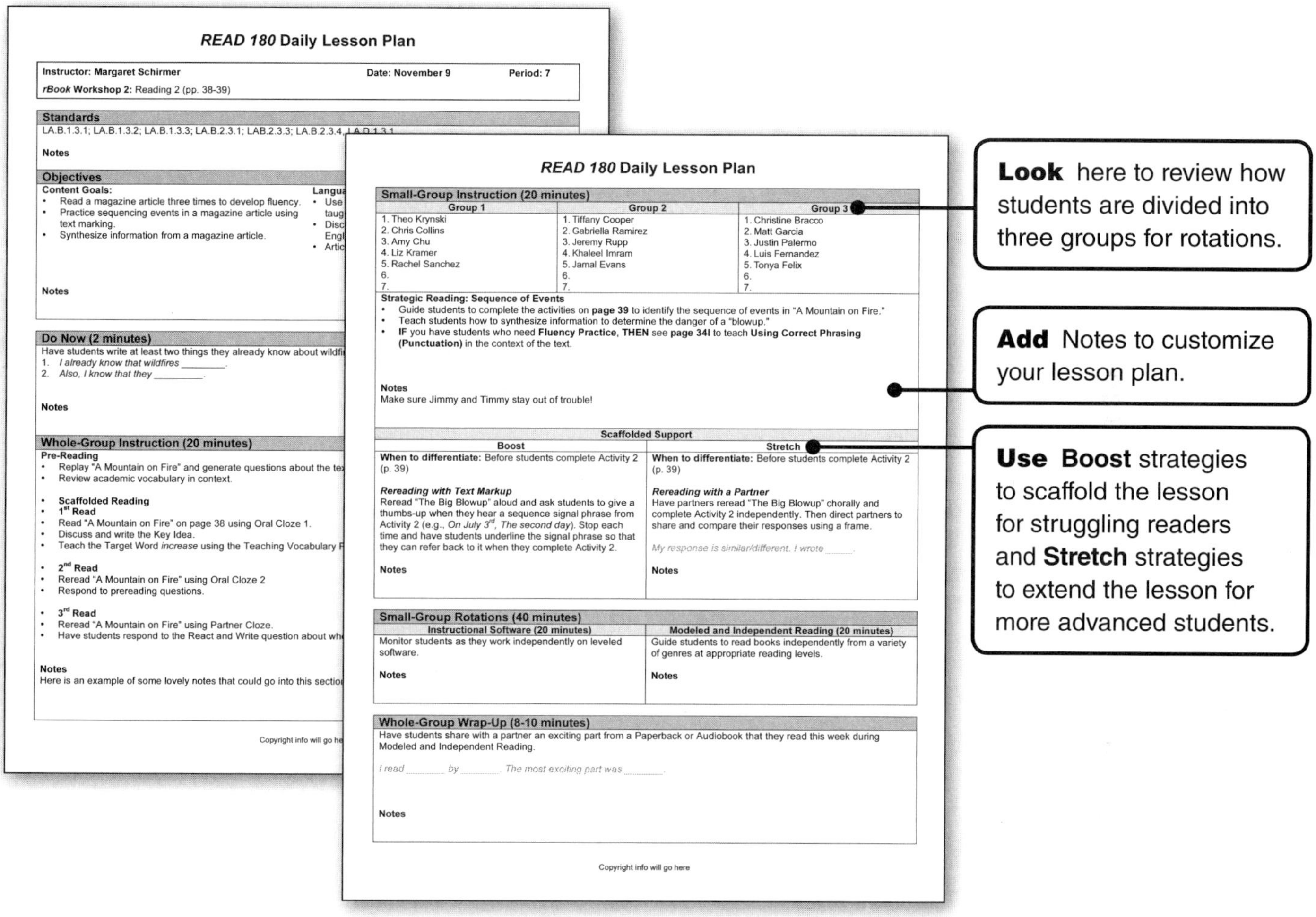
READ 180 Daily Lesson Plan

Instructor: Margaret Schirmer | Date: November 9 | Period: 7

rBook Workshop 2: Reading 2 (pp. 38-39)

Standards
LA.B.1.3.1; LA.B.1.3.2; LA.B.1.3.3; LA.B.2.3.1; LAB.2.3.3; LA.B.2.3.4, LA.D.1.3.1

Notes

Objectives
Content Goals:
- Read a magazine article three times to develop fluency.
- Practice sequencing events in a magazine article using text marking.
- Synthesize information from a magazine article.

Notes

Do Now (2 minutes)
Have students write at least two things they already know about wildfi
1. *I already know that wildfires* ________.
2. *Also, I know that they* ________.

Notes

Whole-Group Instruction (20 minutes)
Pre-Reading
- Replay "A Mountain on Fire" and generate questions about the te
- Review academic vocabulary in context.

- Scaffolded Reading
- 1st Read
- Read "A Mountain on Fire" on page 38 using Oral Cloze 1.
- Discuss and write the Key Idea.
- Teach the Target Word *increase* using the Teaching Vocabulary F

- 2nd Read
- Reread "A Mountain on Fire" using Oral Cloze 2
- Respond to prereading questions.

- 3rd Read
- Reread "A Mountain on Fire" using Partner Cloze.
- Have students respond to the React and Write question about wh

Notes
Here is an example of some lovely notes that could go into this sectio

Copyright info will go he

READ 180 Daily Lesson Plan

Small-Group Instruction (20 minutes)

Group 1	Group 2	Group 3
1. Theo Krynski	1. Tiffany Cooper	1. Christine Bracco
2. Chris Collins	2. Gabriella Ramirez	2. Matt Garcia
3. Amy Chu	3. Jeremy Rupp	3. Justin Palermo
4. Liz Kramer	4. Khaleel Imram	4. Luis Fernandez
5. Rachel Sanchez	5. Jamal Evans	5. Tonya Felix
6.	6.	6.
7.	7.	7.

Strategic Reading: Sequence of Events
- Guide students to complete the activities on **page 39** to identify the sequence of events in "A Mountain on Fire."
- Teach students how to synthesize information to determine the danger of a "blowup."
- **IF** you have students who need **Fluency Practice**, **THEN** see **page 34I** to teach **Using Correct Phrasing (Punctuation)** in the context of the text.

Notes
Make sure Jimmy and Timmy stay out of trouble!

Scaffolded Support

Boost	Stretch
When to differentiate: Before students complete Activity 2 (p. 39)	**When to differentiate:** Before students complete Activity 2 (p. 39)
Rereading with Text Markup Reread "The Big Blowup" aloud and ask students to give a thumbs-up when they hear a sequence signal phrase from Activity 2 (e.g., *On July 3rd*, *The second day*). Stop each time and have students underline the signal phrase so that they can refer back to it when they complete Activity 2.	***Rereading with a Partner*** Have partners reread "The Big Blowup" chorally and complete Activity 2 independently. Then direct partners to share and compare their responses using a frame. *My response is similar/different. I wrote* ____.
Notes	Notes

Small-Group Rotations (40 minutes)

Instructional Software (20 minutes)	Modeled and Independent Reading (20 minutes)
Monitor students as they work independently on leveled software.	Guide students to read books independently from a variety of genres at appropriate reading levels.
Notes	Notes

Whole-Group Wrap-Up (8-10 minutes)
Have students share with a partner an exciting part from a Paperback or Audiobook that they read this week during Modeled and Independent Reading.

I read ____ *by* ____. *The most exciting part was* ____.

Notes

Copyright info will go here

Sample *READ 180* Daily Lesson Plan

4. Use ITS to Prepare for Teaching the Lesson

Click **Whole-Group Instruction** and **Small-Group Instruction** under **Today's Summary** on the Teacher Dashboard Home or Class Page to view the corresponding *rBook Teacher's Edition* pages in the Interactive Teaching System (ITS). In ITS, click [its Do Now] and [its Wrap-Up] embedded in the *rBook Teacher's Edition* lessons to preview brief activities to begin and end the class period. Click [its Scaffolded Support] to see strategies to "Boost" or "Stretch" your students for success with the lesson. Use the ITS tools to highlight key steps and create "sticky notes" for reference while teaching.

5. Learn More With Professional Development

Check **Professional Development** on the right side of the Teacher Dashboard Home Page for a daily video or resource related to the lesson. Click to open the available resource and learn tips for using the day's lesson or routine with your students. A new video or resource will appear here for every Workshop lesson.

Differentiating Your Daily Instruction

Incorporate differentiated support into your daily *rBook* lessons using resources in the *rBook Teacher's Edition* and Interactive Teaching System (ITS).

Meeting Individual Needs

Every *rBook* Workshop includes embedded strategies for meeting individual student needs and extending instruction in the context of the reading lessons. Look for the yellow Differentiated Instruction pages after the three Workshop readings in your *rBook Teacher's Edition*.

Use these ideas to support students who need to build foundational phonics and decoding skills for reading success.

Guide students to build fluency skills by rereading the Workshop passages.

Target lessons to meet the needs of students who are learning English as a second language.

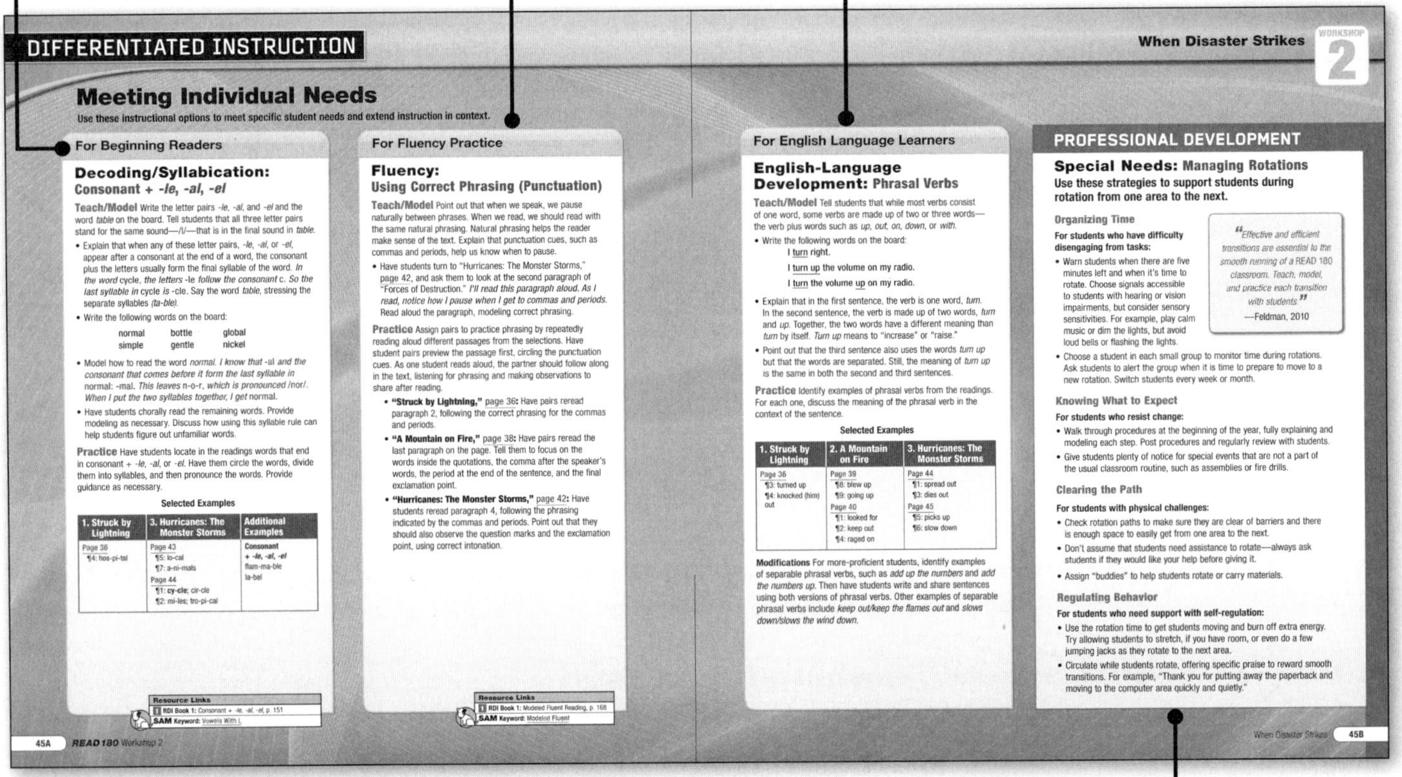

DIFFERENTIATED INSTRUCTION

Meeting Individual Needs

Use these instructional options to meet specific student needs and extend instruction in context.

For Beginning Readers

Decoding/Syllabication: Consonant + *-le, -al, -el*

Teach/Model Write the letter pairs *-le*, *-al*, and *-el* and the word *table* on the board. Tell students that all three letter pairs stand for the same sound—/l/—that is in the final sound in *table*.

- Explain that when any of these letter pairs, *-le*, *-al*, or *-el*, appear after a consonant at the end of a word, the consonant plus the letters usually form the final syllable of the word. *In the word* cycle, *the letters* -le *follow the consonant* c. *So the last syllable in* cycle *is* -cle. Say the word *table*, stressing the separate syllables *(ta-ble)*.
- Write the following words on the board:

normal	bottle	global
simple	gentle	nickel

- Model how to read the word *normal*. *I know that* -al *and the consonant that comes before it form the last syllable in* normal: -mal. *This leaves* n-o-r, *which is pronounced /nor/. When I put the two syllables together, I get* normal.
- Have students chorally read the remaining words. Provide modeling as necessary. Discuss how using this syllable rule can help students figure out unfamiliar words.

Practice Have students locate in the readings words that end in consonant + *-le*, *-al*, or *-el*. Have them circle the words, divide them into syllables, and then pronounce the words. Provide guidance as necessary.

Selected Examples

1. Struck by Lightning	3. Hurricanes: The Monster Storms	Additional Examples
Page 36 ¶4: hos-pi-tal	Page 43 ¶5: lo-cal ¶7: a-ni-mals Page 44 ¶1: cy-cle; cir-cle ¶2: mi-les; tro-pi-cal	Consonant + -le, -al, -el flam-ma-ble la-bel

Resource Links
RDI Book 1: Consonant + -le, -al, -el, p. 151
SAM Keyword: Vowels With L

For Fluency Practice

Fluency: Using Correct Phrasing (Punctuation)

Teach/Model Point out that when we speak, we pause naturally between phrases. When we read, we should read with the same natural phrasing. Natural phrasing helps the reader make sense of the text. Explain that punctuation cues, such as commas and periods, help us know when to pause.

- Have students turn to "Hurricanes: The Monster Storms," page 42, and ask them to look at the second paragraph of "Forces of Destruction." *I'll read this paragraph aloud. As I read, notice how I pause when I get to commas and periods.* Read aloud the paragraph, modeling correct phrasing.

Practice Assign pairs to practice phrasing by repeatedly reading aloud different passages from the selections. Have student pairs preview the passage first, circling the punctuation cues. As one student reads aloud, the partner should follow along in the text, listening for phrasing and making observations to share after reading.

- **"Struck by Lightning,"** page 36**:** Have pairs reread paragraph 2, following the correct phrasing for the commas and periods.
- **"A Mountain on Fire,"** page 38**:** Have pairs reread the last paragraph on the page. Tell them to focus on the words inside the quotations, the comma after the speaker's words, the period at the end of the sentence, and the final exclamation point.
- **"Hurricanes: The Monster Storms,"** page 42**:** Have students reread paragraph 4, following the phrasing indicated by the commas and periods. Point out that they should also observe the question marks and the exclamation point, using correct intonation.

Resource Links
RDI Book 1: Modeled Fluent Reading, p. 168
SAM Keyword: Modeled Fluent

45A READ 180 Workshop 2

When Disaster Strikes WORKSHOP 2

For English Language Learners

English-Language Development: Phrasal Verbs

Teach/Model Tell students that while most verbs consist of one word, some verbs are made up of two or three words—the verb plus words such as *up*, *out*, *on*, *down*, or *with*.

- Write the following words on the board:
  I turn right.
  I turn up the volume on my radio.
  I turn the volume up on my radio.
- Explain that in the first sentence, the verb is one word, *turn*. In the second sentence, the verb is made up of two words, *turn* and *up*. Together, the two words have a different meaning than *turn* by itself. *Turn up* means to "increase" or "raise."
- Point out that the third sentence also uses the words *turn up* but that the words are separated. Still, the meaning of *turn up* is the same in both the second and third sentences.

Practice Identify examples of phrasal verbs from the readings. For each one, discuss the meaning of the phrasal verb in the context of the sentence.

Selected Examples

1. Struck by Lightning	2. A Mountain on Fire	3. Hurricanes: The Monster Storms
Page 36 ¶3: turned up ¶4: knocked (him) out	Page 39 ¶8: blew up ¶9: going up Page 40 ¶1: looked for ¶2: keep out ¶4: raged on	Page 44 ¶1: spread out ¶3: dies out Page 45 ¶5: picks up ¶6: slow down

Modifications For more-proficient students, identify examples of separable phrasal verbs, such as *add up the numbers* and *add the numbers up*. Then have students write and share sentences using both versions of phrasal verbs. Other examples of separable phrasal verbs include *keep out/keep the flames out* and *slows down/slows the wind down*.

PROFESSIONAL DEVELOPMENT

Special Needs: Managing Rotations

Use these strategies to support students during rotation from one area to the next.

Organizing Time

For students who have difficulty disengaging from tasks:

- Warn students when there are five minutes left and when it's time to rotate. Choose signals accessible to students with hearing or vision impairments, but consider sensory sensitivities. For example, play calm music or dim the lights, but avoid loud bells or flashing the lights.
- Choose a student in each small group to monitor time during rotations. Ask students to alert the group when it is time to prepare to move to a new rotation. Switch students every week or month.

"Effective and efficient transitions are essential to the smooth running of a READ 180 *classroom. Teach, model, and practice each transition with students."*
—Feldman, 2010

Knowing What to Expect

For students who resist change:

- Walk through procedures at the beginning of the year, fully explaining and modeling each step. Post procedures and regularly review with students.
- Give students plenty of notice for special events that are not a part of the usual classroom routine, such as assemblies or fire drills.

Clearing the Path

For students with physical challenges:

- Check rotation paths to make sure they are clear of barriers and there is enough space to easily get from one area to the next.
- Don't assume that students need assistance to rotate—always ask students if they would like your help before giving it.
- Assign "buddies" to help students rotate or carry materials.

Regulating Behavior

For students who need support with self-regulation:

- Use the rotation time to get students moving and burn off extra energy. Try allowing students to stretch, if you have room, or even do a few jumping jacks as they rotate to the next area.
- Circulate while students rotate, offering specific praise to reward smooth transitions. For example, "Thank you for putting away the paperback and moving to the computer area quickly and quietly."

When Disaster Strikes 45B

***rBook Teacher's Edition*, Stage B**

Try these classroom strategies to support students with special learning needs.

Teacher Tip

Look for yellow Differentiated Instruction boxes at the bottom of reading lessons in the *rBook Teacher's Edition* to see when to integrate the strategies into your instruction to meet individual student needs.

Scaffolding Support With ITS

You may have a range of student proficiency levels in your *READ 180* classroom. Some students may need extra support to access *rBook* lessons while others may be ready for a challenge. The Interactive Teaching System (ITS) includes daily suggestions for differentiating Small-Group Instruction based on student readiness. Click its Scaffolded Support at the bottom right corner of every Small Group lesson in the *rBook Teacher's Edition*. This reveals "Boost" and "Stretch" strategies to scaffold or extend instruction as needed to meet student needs.

Scaffolded Support

Strategy: Self-Monitoring
When to Differentiate: After students complete Activity 3 (p. 43)

BOOST

Self-Monitoring With a Text Marking
Read aloud paragraphs 3–4 of "Hurricanes: The Monster Storms" and guide students to number the events in order from 1–4. Then have them check the order they wrote for Activity 3 to make sure it matches the numbers they marked in the text.

STRETCH

Self-Monitoring With a Partner
Have partners check the order of events for paragraphs 3–4 of "Hurricanes: The Monster Storms." Direct one partner to read the events in the order they marked while the other partner listens to see if it makes sense. Then switch roles and have students make any corrections.

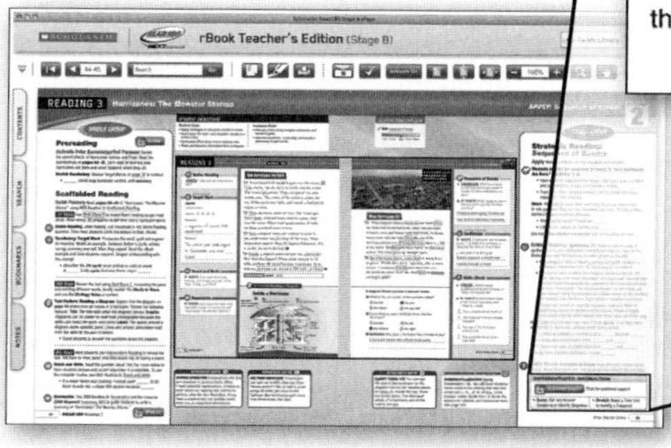

***rBook* Interactive Teacher's Edition, Stage B**

Boost strategies give struggling students the extra "boost" they need for success with *rBook* lessons. Consider using these strategies with your *READ 180* Level 1 students, or with any students who are struggling to master Workshop skills in Whole- and Small-Group Instruction.

Stretch strategies extend the lesson to "stretch" your more advanced students for continued reading growth. Consider using these strategies with your *READ 180* Level 3 and 4 students, or with any students who are ready for more of a challenge in Whole- and Small-Group Instruction.

Reflection

Some of my struggling students who will benefit from Boost support are...

Some of my more advanced learners who will benefit from Stretch extension are...

Targeting Needs at Differentiation CheckPoints

Every *rBook* Workshop includes three CheckPoints—Reading, Writing, and End-of-Workshop—that guide you to spend one to two days providing differentiated instruction to meet student needs.

1. Stop to differentiate three times per Workshop: after the readings, writing lessons, and *rSkills Test*.

2. Launch the Teacher Dashboard to see recommended student groups and targeted lessons for CheckPoint instruction.

3. Download the RDI tracking log from SAM (Keyword: RDI Tracking) to keep track of which lessons you have already used with each student.

CHECKPOINT 1

Reading CheckPoint

Using Data to Differentiate

The Reading CheckPoint provides an opportunity to review, reteach, and apply comprehension skills based on student performance on the *READ 180* Software.

Plan Instruction

Launch the Teacher Dashboard to group students for Small-Group Instruction.

Determine Small Groups

1. Click the ***Go to Class*** button to view Reading CheckPoint groups. Click the ***Save*** button to use these groups.
2. If you would like to adjust groups, use data from the *READ 180* Comprehension Skills Report to inform your decision. You may also wish to consider current classroom performance:

   APPLY: Did students **sequence events** using text marking, signal words, and graphic organizers?

   RETEACH: Did students struggle to identify or apply comprehension skills?

Organize Resources

3. Click on the links below to quickly access digital versions of **RDI** resources.

   APPLY: Assign the Stretch Text "Search and Rescue Teams in Haiti Race Against Time" to students who are ready to apply **sequence of events** to a more advanced text.

   RETEACH: Assign **RDI Book 1** lessons and resources to reteach comprehension skills to students who need more support.

Comprehension Skills	SAM Keywords
Read for Detail	Detail
Main Idea and Details	Main Idea
Sequence of Events	Sequence
Summarize	Summarize
Problem and Solution	Problem
Cause and Effect	Cause
Compare and Contrast	Compare
Make Inferences	Inferences
Draw Conclusions	Conclusions

To track **RDI** lessons assigned to students, download the RDI Assignment Tracking Log (**SAM Keyword:** RDI Tracking).

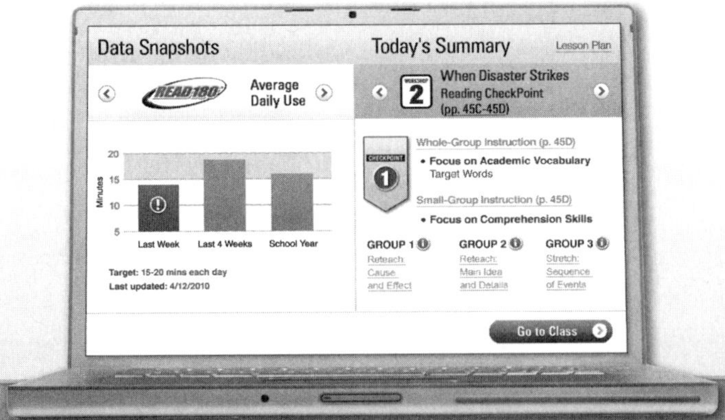

45C *READ 180* Workshop 2

***rBook Teacher's Edition*, Stage B**

Teach the recommended RDI lesson to all of your students during Whole-Group Instruction.

Notice the Teacher Dashboard Groupinator uses data to recommend groups and lessons for the Reading and End-of-Workshop CheckPoints.

Differentiate Instruction

WHOLE GROUP

Focus on Academic Vocabulary (its Do Now)

Teach/Model Remind students that they have learned the meanings of new Target Words. Explain that when we understand the meaning of words, we can use the words in different contexts. *We use words in many different contexts, or situations. For example, one situation that requires focus is taking a test in class.*

Guided Practice Distribute Example or Not? on page 256 of **RDI Book 1** (**SAM Keyword:** Example W2). Tell students that you will look at examples to determine which context shows the meaning of the Target Word. Model your thinking and guide students to complete the practice item.

THINK ALOUD *I know that* recovery *means "the process of getting back to normal." Example A shows the meaning of the word because it took two months for the quarterback's leg to heal. He has made a recovery. In Example B, the quarterback is out for the season, so he has not made a recovery.*

Apply Have students discuss the second item in pairs and complete the remaining items independently.

Workshop 2 Target Words	
abandon	increase
cycle	major
degree	prevent
destruction	recovery
focus	severe

(its Wrap-Up)

SMALL GROUP

Focus on Comprehension Skills

Teach **RDI** lessons associated with each assigned skill to differentiate instruction during Small Group. Note that the skills appearing in your grouping report may be any of nine comprehension skills. Monitor students and extend the lesson for another day if they need additional support with these skills.

Groupinator™

rBook Groups | Reading CheckPoint | Writing CheckPoint | End-of-Workshop CheckPoint

Use the groups below, based on your students' comprehension scores from the *READ 180* Topic Software, for small-group instruction.

- Use the drop down menu to select a different skill.
- To move a student, click and drag the student name into a new group.

When you have created groups, click Save

Group 1	Group 2	Group 3
Cause and Effect	Main Idea and Details	Stretch: Sequence of ...
Bracco, Christine	Collins, Chris	Chu, Amy
Cooper, Tiffany	Fernandez, Luis	Felix, Tonya
Evans, Jamal	Imran, Khaleel	Garcia, Matt
Kramer, Liz	Ramirez, Gabriella	Krynski, Theo
Palermo, Justin	Rupp, Jeremy	Sanchez, Rachel

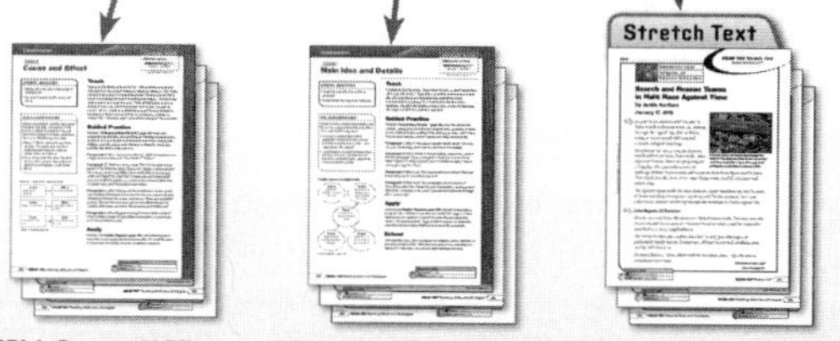

RDI 1: Cause and Effect | RDI 1: Main Idea and Details | RDI 1: Sequence of Events

CheckPoint Check-In

Focus on Sequence of Events

To monitor student progress on comprehension skills, download the Skills Checklist (**SAM Keyword:** Skills Checklist). Use the information from this checklist to determine when students are ready to move to the next lesson.

For example, students working on the current Workshop skill **Sequence of Events** will demonstrate proficiency when they successfully:

- ✓ Identify signal words related to sequence.
- ✓ Write a sequence of events in chronological order.
- ✓ Recognize when an event is out of order.

Use the Workshop Skills Checklist (SAM Keyword: Skills Checklist) to track student mastery of key reading strategies.

Use a suggested RDI lesson to reinforce skills for mastery or a Stretch Text to extend learning in Small-Group Instruction.

CheckPoint Planning With Your Dashboard

Integrate a Reading, Writing, and End-of-Workshop CheckPoint into every *rBook* Workshop to provide targeted instruction on the skills and strategies your students need most.

Understanding the CheckPoints

Each Workshop CheckPoint provides an opportunity to reteach, reinforce, or extend the skills your students need for reading success. Launch the Teacher Dashboard for support with grouping students and identifying targeted lessons on CheckPoint days.

1 Reading CheckPoint

- **Pacing** Stop for the Reading CheckPoint after teaching the three Workshop readings and before beginning the *rBook* vocabulary/word study lessons. Spend one to two days providing targeted instruction in reading comprehension.
- **Grouping** Check the Groupinator on the Teacher Dashboard Class Page to see suggested groups and lessons for Reading CheckPoint rotations based on Topic Software performance. The Groupinator analyzes student responses to the Quick Check questions in the Topic Software Reading Zone and uses this data to group students and select lessons for targeted skills instruction.
- **Teaching** Teach the recommended lessons from *Resources for Differentiated Instruction* (RDI) Book 1 to reteach reading skills, or use the Workshop Stretch Text to extend learning for students who are ready for a challenge. Check the Groupinator to see suggested lessons for each group. Run the *READ 180* Comprehension Skills Report to make any data-driven adjustments to Groupinator recommendations.

2 Writing CheckPoint

- **Pacing** Integrate the Writing CheckPoint after students have completed a rough draft of their Workshop paragraph or multi-paragraph essay. Spend one to two days guiding them to revise and present final drafts.
- **Grouping** Reflect on your informal observations about your students' writing to decide who may be struggling with similar skills and who is ready for a challenge. Use the Groupinator to drag student names into the three small groups for Writing CheckPoint rotations.
- **Teaching** Use the recommended scoring rubric to guide students to revise their writing drafts. Check the writing lessons in the *rBook Teacher's Edition* to see which scoring rubric to use depending on the Workshop writing type.

3 End-of-Workshop CheckPoint

- **Pacing** Schedule an End-of-Workshop CheckPoint after administering the Wrap-Up Test and *rSkills Test*. Spend one to two days reviewing, reteaching, or extending Workshop skills and strategies.
- **Grouping** Access the Groupinator on the Teacher Dashboard Class Page to request groups and review targeted lessons for End-of-Workshop CheckPoint rotations. The Groupinator analyzes *rSkills Test* results to group students who struggled with similar skills on the assessment.
- **Teaching** Use the RDI lessons recommended by the Groupinator to reteach and reinforce Workshop skills. Run the *rSkills Tests* Grading Report to make any data-driven adjustments to Groupinator recommendations. For students who demonstrated mastery on the *rSkills Test,* download a Workshop extension project from the *READ 180* Community at **www.read180.com/community.**

Planning for CheckPoints

Follow the steps below to use the Teacher Dashboard to plan and prepare lessons for Whole- and Small-Group Instruction during each of the three Workshop CheckPoints:

1. Launch the Teacher Dashboard from the **Educator Access** screen. Enter your SAM username and password.
2. Look at **Today's Summary** on the Teacher Dashboard Home Page. Ensure that it shows a yellow CheckPoint lesson for the day. If not, use the left and right arrows in **Today's Summary** to navigate to the CheckPoint lesson that you want.
3. Click **Go to Class** in **Today's Summary** to access the **Groupinator** on the Teacher Dashboard Class Page.
4. Notice the four tabs at the top of the Groupinator: ***rBook* Groups, Reading CheckPoint, Writing CheckPoint, End-of-Workshop CheckPoint**. You will automatically see the tab corresponding to the selected CheckPoint lesson. Click the tabs to navigate to other CheckPoints.
5. For the **Reading** and **End-of-Workshop CheckPoints**, the Groupinator will generate groups and suggest skills lessons based on student performance data. Review the three small groups and make adjustments if needed by clicking and dragging names from one group to another. Use the pull-down menus to select different skills to target based on report data and your own observations.
6. For the **Writing CheckPoint,** click and drag student names into the three groups. Use rubric assessment, report data, and anecdotal observations of student performance to inform your decisions.
7. Click **Save** to save the selection of targeted lessons and student groups.
8. Click the yellow links under each of the group names in **Today's Summary** on the Teacher Dashboard Home or Class Page to review the lesson steps to follow when teaching each group in Small-Group Instruction. Click **Lesson Plan** on the Teacher Dashboard Home Page for a printable lesson plan that includes the student groups.

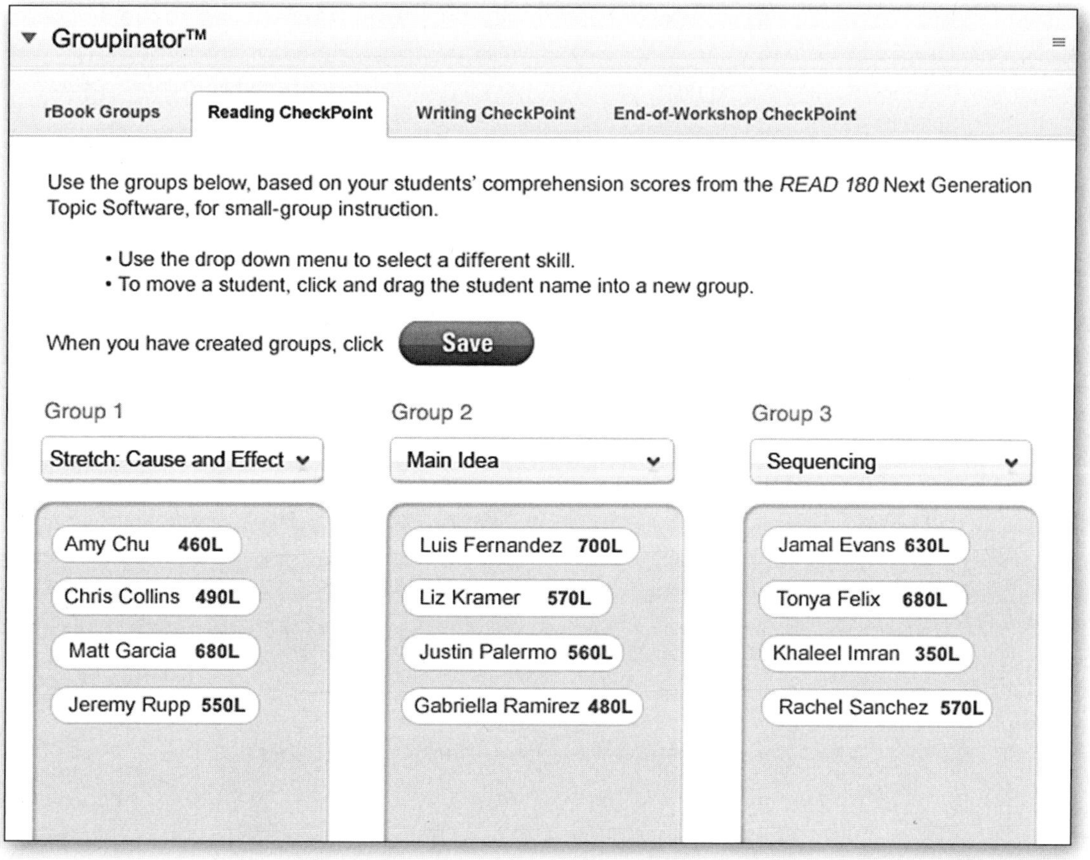

Groupinator, Teacher Dashboard

Assessing Workshop Learning

Every *rBook* Workshop concludes with three forms of assessment to help you determine student mastery of the skills and strategies you taught in Whole- and Small-Group Instruction.

Performance-Based Assessment

Each Workshop includes two performance-based assessments for students to demonstrate their learning and build crucial critical-thinking and problem-solving skills for success in college, career, and beyond.

Wrap-Up Project

At the end of every *rBook* Workshop, students work collaboratively to complete a Wrap-Up Project—a presentation, proposal, role play, or debate—during one class period. This project provides students the opportunity to reflect on the Workshop content and apply what they have learned to a real-world situation. Students practice critical thinking, problem solving, and 21st Century literacy skills for college and career readiness.

Introduce the Wrap-Up Project and get students started during Whole-Group Instruction. Then guide them to work in pairs or groups to complete the project during Small-Group Instruction. Assess students' critical thinking and project-based skills by downloading the Wrap-Up Project rubric from SAM using the SAM Keyword provided in the lesson.

Wrap-Up Test

Administer a Wrap-Up Test at the end of every *rBook* Workshop to assess your students' comprehension, vocabulary, and critical reading skills. The short assessment allows students to practice test-taking strategies and review Workshop skills in preparation for taking the *rSkills Test*. Each Wrap-Up Test includes 10 Workshop-specific multiple-choice questions and one short-answer writing prompt.

Review key skills and allow students to complete the Wrap-Up Test during Whole-Group Instruction. Guide students to share and explain their answers during Small-Group Instruction. Grade students' Wrap-Up Tests using the answers provided in the lesson in your *rBook Teacher's Edition.*

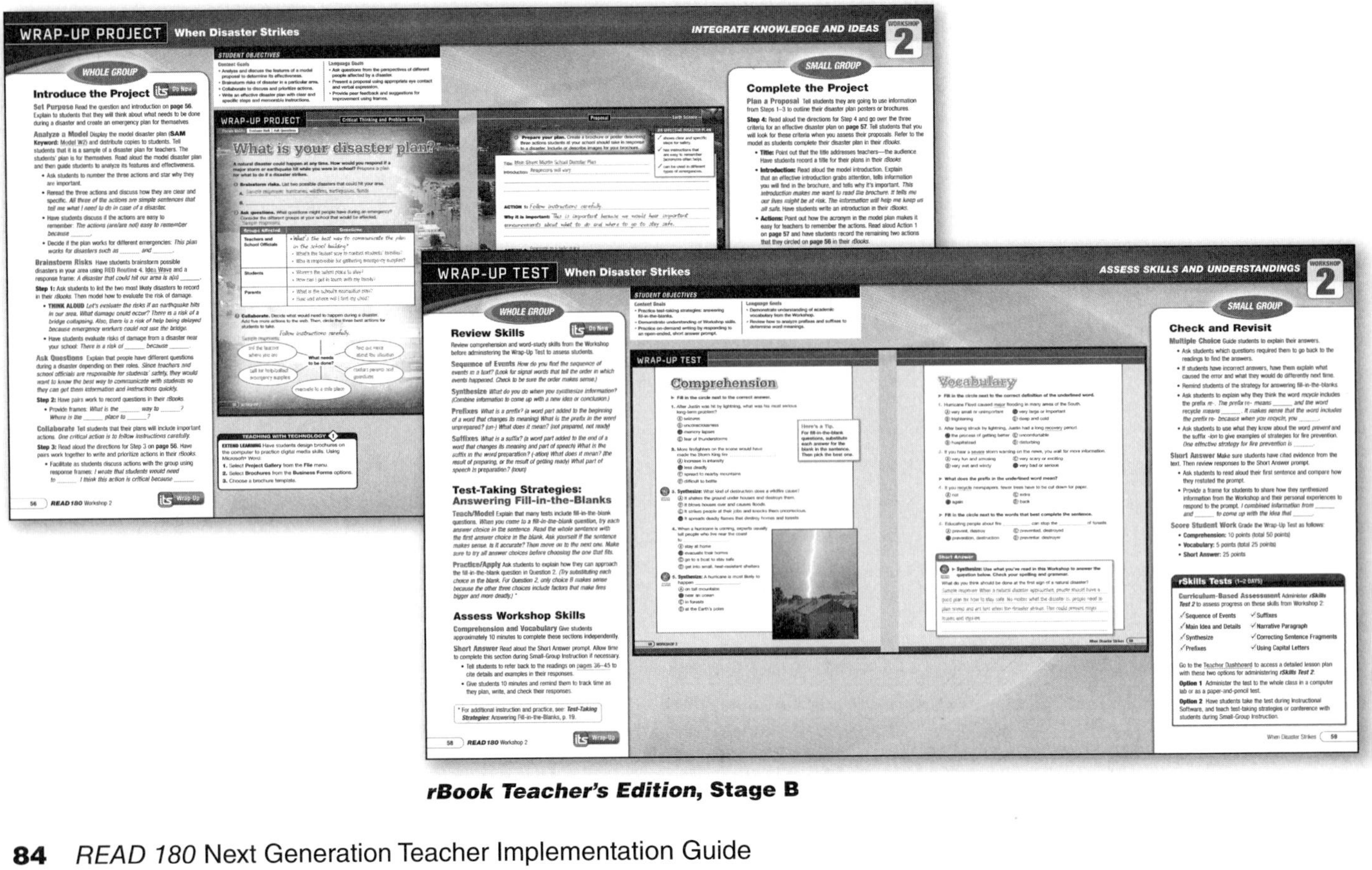

***rBook* Teacher's Edition, Stage B**

Curriculum-Based Assessment: *rSkills* College & Career

READ 180 Next Generation includes one *rSkills Test* for every *rBook* Workshop. These curriculum-based assessments determine whether students can successfully transfer and apply the reading, vocabulary, writing, and academic language skills that you taught during Whole- and Small-Group Instruction. Each test includes selected response questions, two optional constructed responses, and one extended constructed response prompt. Allow one to two days for students to complete each *rSkills Test* using the classroom computers or a computer lab, if available. You can also download and print copies from SAM to administer paper-based versions.

Assigning Leveled Tests

Each *rSkills Test* has two versions—one with below grade-level comprehension passages (Level a) and one with grade-level passages (Level b)—so that you can test students at their reading level to accurately assess their mastery of Workshop skills and strategies. Test Levels a and b assess the same skills and have the same item format. However, the two levels differ in Lexile range, passage length, and sentence complexity. Determine which *rSkills Test* to assign to students in SAM based on their *READ 180* Levels (1–4), software performance data, and your classroom needs.

Accessing *rSkills* College & Career Data

If students take *rSkills Tests* on the computer, you can access their results by running *rSkills* College & Career class and student reports in SAM. Use the SAM Student Digital Portfolio to read and evaluate students' responses to constructed response and extended constructed response *rSkills Tests* questions.

The Groupinator on the Teacher Dashboard also uses *rSkills* College & Career results to group students and identify skills to target during the End-of-Workshop CheckPoint.

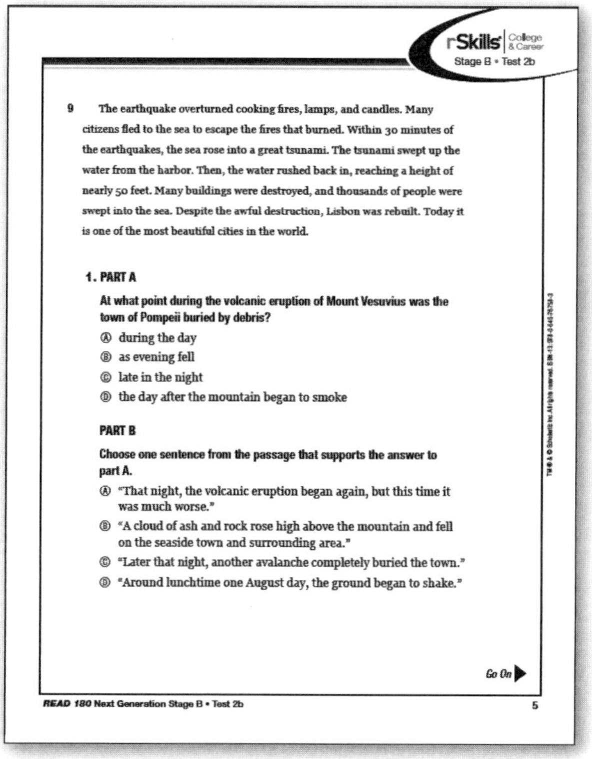

rSkills College & Career
Stage B • Test 2b

9 The earthquake overturned cooking fires, lamps, and candles. Many citizens fled to the sea to escape the fires that burned. Within 30 minutes of the earthquakes, the sea rose into a great tsunami. The tsunami swept up the water from the harbor. Then, the water rushed back in, reaching a height of nearly 50 feet. Many buildings were destroyed, and thousands of people were swept into the sea. Despite the awful destruction, Lisbon was rebuilt. Today it is one of the most beautiful cities in the world.

1. PART A

At what point during the volcanic eruption of Mount Vesuvius was the town of Pompeii buried by debris?

Ⓐ during the day
Ⓑ as evening fell
Ⓒ late in the night
Ⓓ the day after the mountain began to smoke

PART B

Choose one sentence from the passage that supports the answer to part A.

Ⓐ "That night, the volcanic eruption began again, but this time it was much worse."
Ⓑ "A cloud of ash and rock rose high above the mountain and fell on the seaside town and surrounding area."
Ⓒ "Later that night, another avalanche completely buried the town."
Ⓓ "Around lunchtime one August day, the ground began to shake."

Go On

READ 180 Next Generation Stage B • Test 2b 5

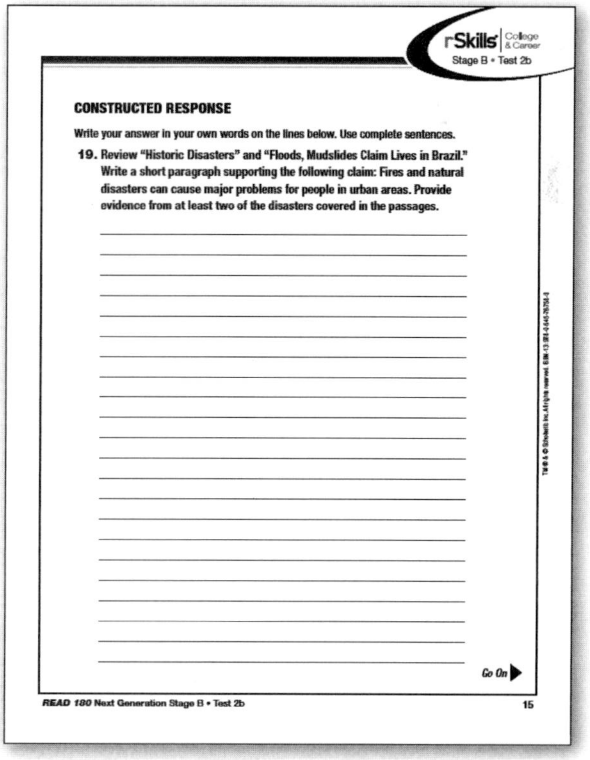

rSkills College & Career
Stage B • Test 2b

CONSTRUCTED RESPONSE

Write your answer in your own words on the lines below. Use complete sentences.

19. Review "Historic Disasters" and "Floods, Mudslides Claim Lives in Brazil." Write a short paragraph supporting the following claim: Fires and natural disasters can cause major problems for people in urban areas. Provide evidence from at least two of the disasters covered in the passages.

Go On

READ 180 Next Generation Stage B • Test 2b 15

***rSkills Test*, Level b (Stage B)**

Monitoring Whole- and Small-Group Progress

Launch the Teacher Dashboard for a quick glance at student performance on *rSkills* College & Career. Log on to the Scholastic Achievement Manager (SAM) for in-depth evaluation of test results.

Teacher Dashboard Data Snapshots: *rSkills* College & Career

The Teacher Dashboard offers snapshots of student performance on all *READ 180* technology-based components, including *rSkills Tests*. Check the *rSkills* Data Snapshot for a quick view of how your students did on the most recent test. Use the data to determine if your students are mastering the skills you are teaching in Whole- and Small-Group Instruction and provide follow-up instruction as needed.

Use the arrows to scroll through Data Snapshots for *READ 180, SRI, rSkills,* and *SRC!*

Follow up when student data does not meet the recommended benchmark (colored red for your attention).

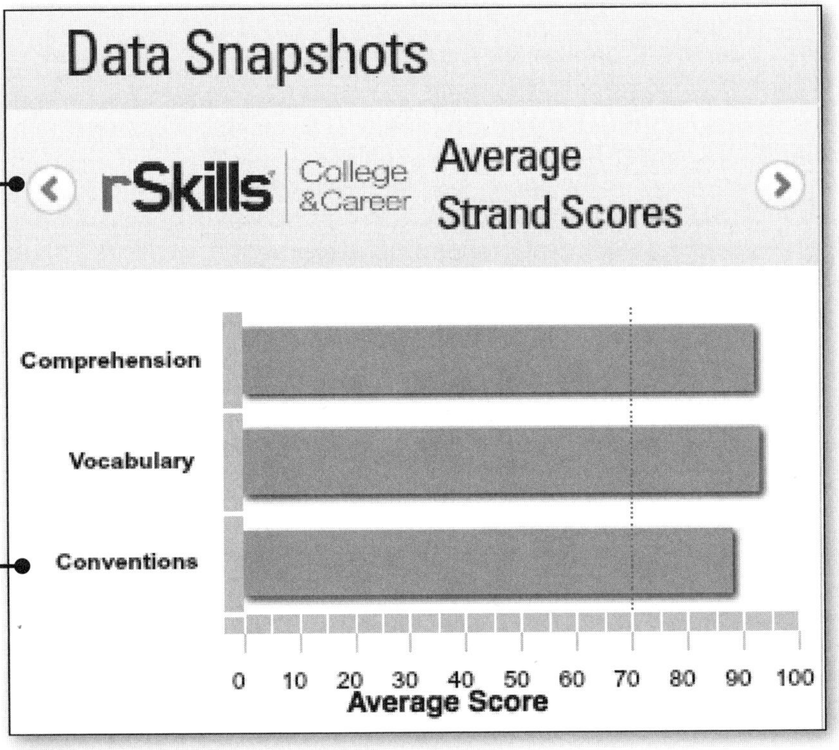

***rSkills* Data Snapshot, Teacher Dashboard**

Additional *rSkills Tests* Data

For more detailed information, go to the Teacher Dashboard Class Page to view the *rSkills* Data Snapshot in List View (see page 175). List View includes *rSkills* College & Career performance data in comprehension, vocabulary/word study, and conventions. Click the blue *i* icon for student names at each data point.

For further follow-up, run the following reports in SAM:

- ***rSkills* College & Career Grouping Report** Run this report at End-of-Workshop CheckPoints for a closer look at the data that powers the Groupinator.
- ***rSkills* College & Career Grading Report** Use this data to make data-driven adjustments to the Groupinator recommendations and inform grading decisions.

SAM Reports

The Scholastic Achievement Manager (SAM) serves as the learning management system for all *READ 180* technology-based components, including *rSkills* College & Career. SAM collects, organizes, and displays student software data in comprehensive reports, which you can run to evaluate the performance of your whole class or drill down on data for individual students. Run SAM reports every four to six weeks to monitor academic progress over time. Use the Teacher Dashboard Report Scheduler to receive SAM reports by email at a designated time (see pages 177–178).

SAM includes six *rSkills* College & Career reports to support you with monitoring student performance in Whole- and Small-Group Instruction. The following chart summarizes when and why to run the *rSkills* College & Career class and student reports. Look for additional information on each report on pages 174–187 in the *Placement, Assessment, and Reporting Guide*.

Teacher Tip

SAM will only show *rSkills* College & Career data for students who are enrolled in *rSkills* College & Career Next Generation and who completed the assessment on the computer. If any students took the paper-and-pencil version, download the answer key from SAM to manually evaluate their performance.

If You Want to...	Run This Report
Class Reports	
Review class scores for one *rSkills Test*	*rSkills* College & Career Grading Report
Group students for *rBook* End-of-Workshop CheckPoints	*rSkills* College & Career Grouping Report
Analyze overall performance on one *rSkills Test*	*rSkills* College & Career Summary Skills Report
Student Reports	
Monitor a student's *rSkills Test* results over time	*rSkills* College & Career Student Progress Report
Analyze results for a student on one *rSkills Test*	*rSkills* College & Career Student Skills Report
Review a student's answers on one *rSkills Test*	*rSkills* College & Career Student Test Printout

Assessing *rSkills* Writing

Use the Portfolio tab in the Scholastic Achievement Manager (SAM) to evaluate your students' written responses on *rSkills Tests* and monitor their writing development throughout the year.

SAM Student Digital Portfolio

The SAM Student Digital Portfolio collects and stores student responses to open response and writing prompts on the Topic Software and *rSkills Tests*. After administering each *rSkills Test*, go to the SAM Student Digital Portfolio to evaluate students' writing using the rubrics provided (see pages 165–166). Use this data to identify writing and conventions skills to reinforce during the End-of-Workshop CheckPoint and next Workshop writing assignment. Revisit students' stored assignments throughout the year to monitor how their writing is developing over time.

Check the SAM Portfolio Inbox to see which students have *rSkills Test* writing ready for grading.

Read the student's answer to the open response or writing prompt.

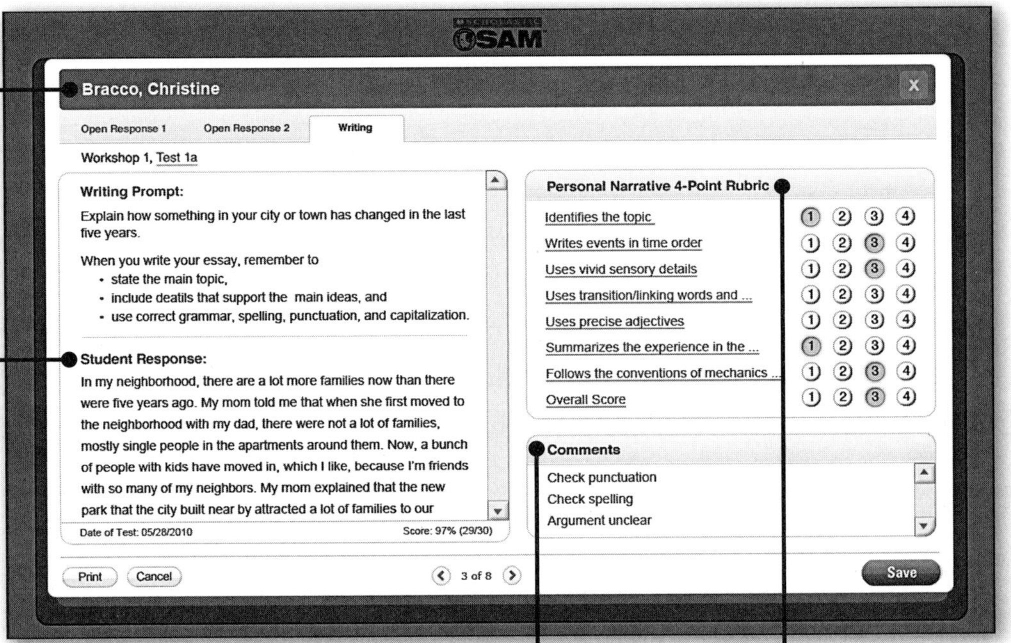

Student Digital Portfolio

Type in feedback to share with the student for writing improvement.

Use a 4- or 6-point rubric to rate each writing criterion.

Reflection

I'll take these next steps after each* rSkills Test *to monitor student learning in Whole- and Small-Group Instruction...

1.

2.

3.

Holding *rBook* Conferences

Hold one-to-one conferences to informally assess your students' overall level of engagement, understanding of *rBook* content, and mastery of skills in Whole- and Small-Group Instruction.

Why Conference?

Individual *rBook* conferences allow you to check in with students to determine if they are understanding what you are teaching in each *rBook* Workshop. Conferencing provides students the opportunity to discuss their own progress, encouraging them to take ownership for their learning. This is also a great time to set individual goals for using the *rBook* during Whole- and Small-Group Instruction.

When to Conference

Hold brief conferences with students during Small-Group Instruction. At the beginning of the rotation, get students started with an independent assignment, such as a Workshop project from the *READ 180* Community website at **www.read180.com/community.** Once they are comfortable working with minimal support, call on one student at a time to meet with you for a one to four minute conference. Set aside time to hold an *rBook* conference with each student once per Workshop, or once every four to six weeks.

How to Conference

Use this suggested procedure for holding a one-to-one *rBook* conference to monitor student progress in Whole- and Small-Group Instruction:

1. Direct the student to turn to the pages in the *rBook* Workshop that you will discuss.
2. Ask the student to share his or her reactions to the Workshop readings and lessons. Use React questions from the *rBook* for discussion ideas.
3. Ask the student to walk you through completed *rBook* pages in the Workshop. Use and share the Workshop Rubric (SAM Keyword: Workshop Rubric) to provide positive feedback and constructive criticism. Consider the following questions to guide your discussion: *Are all assigned activities complete? Does the student's work demonstrate thought and effort? Are answers legible and in complete sentences?*
4. Ask the student to point out any activities he or she found particularly difficult or confusing. Help the student set goals for growth (see page 247).
5. Share *rSkills Tests* results and SAM reports with the student to discuss his or her mastery of Workshop reading, vocabulary, and writing skills.
6. Wrap up by directing the student to the *rBook* Workshop Log in the back of the *rBook*. Guide the student to complete the questions to reflect on his or her Workshop work.

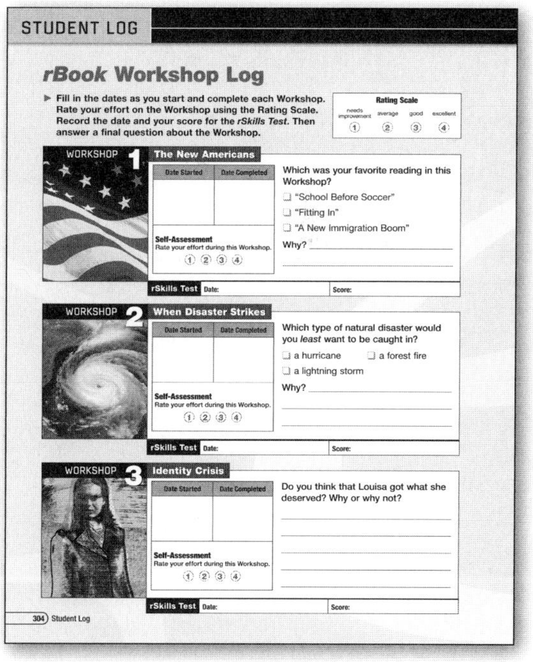
STUDENT LOG

***rBook* Workshop Log**

▶ Fill in the dates as you start and complete each Workshop. Rate your effort on the Workshop using the Rating Scale. Record the date and your score for the *rSkills Test*. Then answer a final question about the Workshop.

Rating Scale: needs improvement ① average ② good ③ excellent ④

WORKSHOP 1 The New Americans

Date Started	Date Completed

Self-Assessment
Rate your effort during this Workshop. ① ② ③ ④

Which was your favorite reading in this Workshop?
❑ "School Before Soccer"
❑ "Fitting In"
❑ "A New Immigration Boom"
Why? ______

rSkills Test Date: Score:

WORKSHOP 2 When Disaster Strikes

Date Started	Date Completed

Self-Assessment
Rate your effort during this Workshop. ① ② ③ ④

Which type of natural disaster would you *least* want to be caught in?
❑ a hurricane ❑ a forest fire
❑ a lightning storm
Why? ______

rSkills Test Date: Score:

WORKSHOP 3 Identity Crisis

Date Started	Date Completed

Self-Assessment
Rate your effort during this Workshop. ① ② ③ ④

Do you think that Louisa got what she deserved? Why or why not?

rSkills Test Date: Score:

304 Student Log

***rBook* Workshop Log, Stage B**

Setting Up the Next Generation Classroom

An effective *READ 180* classroom is a special place for reading, learning, and sharing ideas. When you set up your room, establish distinct areas for each part of the Instructional Model.

Creating a Positive Learning Environment

When setting up your room, consider these characteristics of an ideal *READ 180* classroom:

- Is large enough to easily accommodate distinct areas with appropriate furniture for each small-group rotation.
- Offers ample storage such as bookcases, cabinets, shelves, bins, and closets to organize materials.
- Has an interactive whiteboard or LCD projector for use with the Interactive Teaching System (ITS).
- Contains all required technology including computers with headphones and microphones; television, computer, or interactive whiteboard with DVD player; and CD players with headphones.
- Includes an additional computer in the Modeled and Independent Reading area for students to explore eReads and take *Scholastic Reading Counts! (SRC!)* quizzes during this rotation.
- Features at least two bulletin boards to track student Lexile growth and other reading successes.
- Has a bulletin board outside of the classroom to share student work with the school community.
- Includes posters with positive reading messages to remind students of the importance of becoming a successful reader for long-term success in college, career, and beyond.

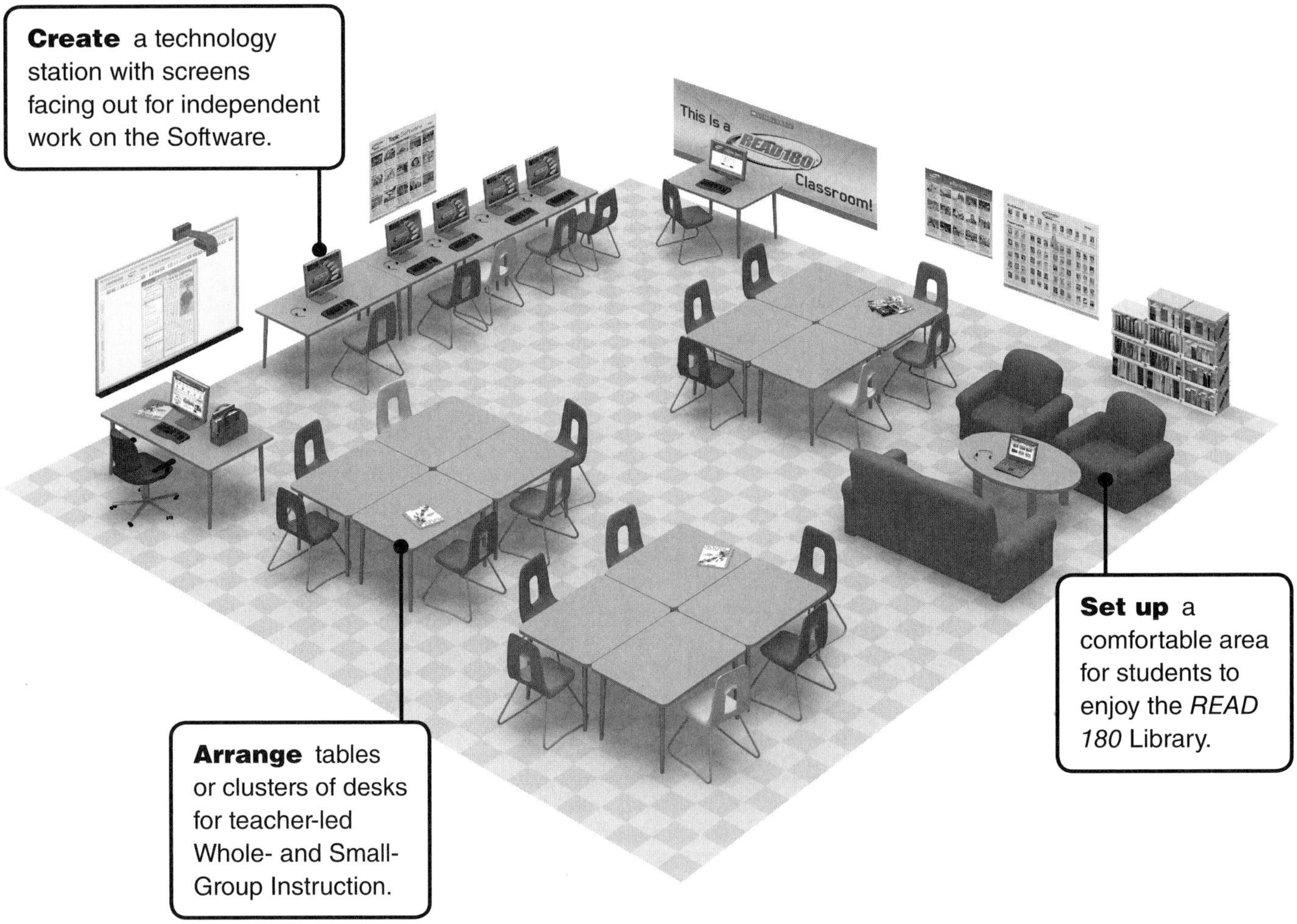

Tips for Setting Up Your Classroom

The classroom is a student's first impression of *READ 180*. Ensure that the space is inviting, print-rich, and organized to motivate students to grow as readers. Create a positive, productive environment where your *READ 180* students *want* to be learning each day. Consider these suggestions for setting up your classroom:

- Set up separate, distinct areas for each part of the Instructional Model: Whole- and Small-Group Instruction, Instructional Software, and Modeled and Independent Reading.
- Use the *READ 180* book crates as a room divider between two rotational areas.
- Create a different atmosphere for each classroom area. For example, place comfortable furniture in Modeled and Independent Reading to invite students to read. Position Instructional Software along one side of the room so you can easily see all computer screens. Hold Small-Group Instruction at a large group worktable to easily target your students' needs while keeping an eye on the other two rotations.
- Position your teacher's desk to the side of the room to keep the focus on the students.
- Hang the four *READ 180* posters around the room to support students with using the program materials.
- Create your own posters with procedures, routines, and sentence starters to use in each rotation area.
- Label baskets, crates, jars, tins, and boxes to store materials such as highlighters, pencils, and batteries.
- Organize and store student materials, like *rBooks* and writing notebooks, based on class period and assigned small groups.
- Develop a checkout system for the *READ 180* Paperbacks and Audiobooks.
- Organize reproducible files with copies of Reading Logs, QuickWrites, and Graphic Organizers.
- Create files to store hard copies of student assessments and sample work to share with parents.

Materials

Whole- and Small-Group Instruction

- ❑ One *READ 180* Teacher Bookshelf per teacher
- ❑ Teacher computer workstation, including printer
- ❑ LCD projector or interactive whiteboard
- ❑ TV and DVD player or interactive whiteboard
- ❑ 5–7 tables and enough chairs for all students
- ❑ 1 *rBook* per student
- ❑ Student files for assessments and classwork

Instructional Software

- ❑ 5–7 student computer workstations
- ❑ *READ 180* Topic Software Installation Kit
- ❑ Computer headsets with microphones (5–7, plus 2–3 replacement pairs)

Modeled and Independent Reading

- ❑ Comfortable furniture for reading area
- ❑ *READ 180* Paperbacks and Audiobooks
- ❑ Computer station for eReads
- ❑ CD players (5–7) with extra batteries
- ❑ CD headphones (5–7)
- ❑ Resealable plastic bags for book storage

Other Classroom Setup

- ❑ *READ 180* QuickStart Kit
- ❑ *READ 180* posters (4)
- ❑ Rotation labels/signs
- ❑ Rules and procedures posters
- ❑ Files for reproducible resources

Managing Whole- and Small-Group Instruction

Setting clear and consistent expectations for student behavior supports your classroom management and provides structure so students can focus on learning.

Establishing Procedures

Classroom procedures explicitly outline how students are expected to complete key tasks for learning. They help students understand how to respond and behave responsibly in various classroom situations, such as moving quickly from one rotation to the next or communicating respectfully with a partner.

Teaching procedures supports students with moving independently through the daily class schedule, maximizing their time on task and accelerating their learning. As one experienced *READ 180* educator said, "The *READ 180* classroom really belongs to the students. Once they figure everything out, they can basically run it themselves."

Identifying Procedures for Whole- and Small-Group Instruction

Establish classroom procedures for each part of the Instructional Model to help students understand your expectations for behavior and independent work. Think about what you want students to accomplish each day and how you want them to handle the *READ 180* materials. What procedures can you put in place so your students always know what to do next after they have completed a task or assignment? Add any procedures that are specific to your classroom to the suggested lists below:

Whole-Group Instruction

- Entering and exiting the classroom
- Completing the Do Now activity
- Participating in class and partner discussions using accountable academic language
- Using available interactive whiteboard tools with ITS
- Checking the Rotation Chart (page 241) for daily rotation grouping and order
- Completing the Whole-Group Wrap-Up activity
- ______________________________
- ______________________________
- ______________________________

Small-Group Instruction

- Coming prepared to Small-Group Instruction
- Obtaining and putting away *rBooks* and supplies
- Asking and answering questions
- Writing in the *rBook* with complete sentences
- Turning in completed work
- Working independently with minimal supervision as you hold one-to-one student conferences
- Transitioning to the next small-group rotation
- ______________________________
- ______________________________
- ______________________________

Research Says

Recursive routines, consistent classroom norms, and familiar instructional practices ensure that students understand expectations and spend more time on task.

Kinsella & Dutro, 2010

My *READ 180* Procedure for . . .

Choose one of the procedures from the Whole- or Small-Group Instruction list on page 92. During training, work with a partner, small group, or independently to draft a set of steps for students to follow for your selected procedure. For example, steps for entering the classroom might include:

1. Enter the room without talking.
2. Pick up your *rBook* and notebook from the class shelf.
3. Walk directly to your assigned seat.
4. Read the Do Now activity on the board.
5. Respond silently by writing in your notebook. Be prepared to share your response.

Procedure:
____
____
____
____
____

Teaching Procedures With a Step-by-Step Approach

The key to making classroom procedures automatic for students is practice, practice, practice. Spend time at the beginning of the year explicitly teaching, modeling, and guiding students to practice the steps for each classroom procedure. The investment of time and effort that you spend teaching classroom procedures during the first few weeks of school will pay off throughout the rest of the year.

Follow the simple steps below to help make each procedure automatic for students. See *Getting Started: Your First Three Weeks With READ 180* for additional tips and model lessons on teaching procedures in your classroom.

Step 1: Post the Procedure Create a classroom poster that outlines the procedure. Display the poster in the appropriate rotation area as a reminder for students throughout the year.

Step 2: Teach Simplify the procedure by breaking it into manageable steps. Introduce each step one at a time, while explaining what you want students to do. Emphasize the purpose of the procedure to increase student buy-in.

Step 3: Model Explicitly model how to accurately complete the procedure so students understand your expectations for each step.

Step 4: Practice Provide multiple opportunities for students to practice the procedure. Offer positive, constructive feedback to support them with accurately following the steps. Guide repeated practice as many times as needed.

Step 5: Revisit Use reminders, such as posters and verbal prompts, to reinforce the procedure throughout the school year. Acknowledge students with positive encouragement when they follow the steps correctly. Reteach the procedure and facilitate additional student practice if they do not follow it correctly.

Ending With Whole-Group Wrap-Up

Every *READ 180* class ends with Whole-Group Wrap-Up for students to reflect on and review the day's learning.

Research Says

When students develop positive relationships in the classroom, they feel safe and motivated to learn.
Jensen, 2005

Purpose

Whole-Group Wrap-Up brings the class together at the end of the day to reinforce the idea of the classroom as a community of learners. Students reconvene to review skills, reflect on their learning, share something they are working on independently, and celebrate their successes. You can also use this time to lead discussions about the Topic Software videos, facilitate Book Talks, review procedures, and assign any homework.

The digital *rBook Teacher's Edition* on the Interactive Teaching System (ITS) includes a suggested Whole-Group Wrap-Up activity for every day of instruction. Click its Wrap-Up icon at the bottom of Whole Group lessons in ITS to reveal a daily prompt or question for students to respond to in writing or class discussion.

Tech Tip

Use ITS with an interactive whiteboard or LCD projector to display the daily Wrap-Up prompts. Click in the ITS toolbar to project the *rBook* student page. Then click its and select Wrap-Up from the pull-down menu.

Instructional Focus

In addition to having students respond to daily Wrap-Up prompts, consider the following ideas for raising reading achievement during Whole-Group Wrap-Up:

- Review the skills you taught during Whole- and Small-Group Instruction.
- Guide students to discuss their independent reading and Software work using structured sentence starters. Create a poster with regularly used sentence starters for student reference.
- Ask students to present three-minute "Book Talks" with the class about their current Paperback, Audiobook, or eReads Collection.
- Recognize student successes such as completing a Topic Software segment or achieving a higher Lexile on the most recent *SRI* test.
- Lead a class discussion for students to share their progress on their *READ 180* goals (see page 250).
- Ask students to read aloud their final drafts of paragraphs or essays from the *rBook* and Topic Software Writing Zone, which you can print from the SAM Student Digital Portfolio.
- Direct students to complete the Exit Slips from page 246 (SAM Keyword: Exit Slips) or the Daily Reflection Journal from page 247 (SAM Keyword: Daily Reflection) to reflect on their learning.

Teacher Materials

Use the *rBook Teacher's Edition* to review key concepts and skills you have taught. Access the digital version of *rBook* lessons on ITS for suggested daily Wrap-Up activities. Use the summaries and questions in the *Teaching Resources* guides to help facilitate Book Talks and other class or partner discussions.

rBook Teacher's Edition

Interactive Teaching System (ITS)

Teaching Resources for Topic Software

Teaching Resources for Modeled and Independent Reading

Student Materials

Make copies of the reproducible Exit Slips and Daily Reflection Journal from pages 244 and 245, or download them from SAM (Keywords: Exit Slips and Daily Reflection). Distribute to students during Whole-Group Wrap-Up to guide reflection on the day's learning. Allow time for students to write down their reflections before sharing with the class.

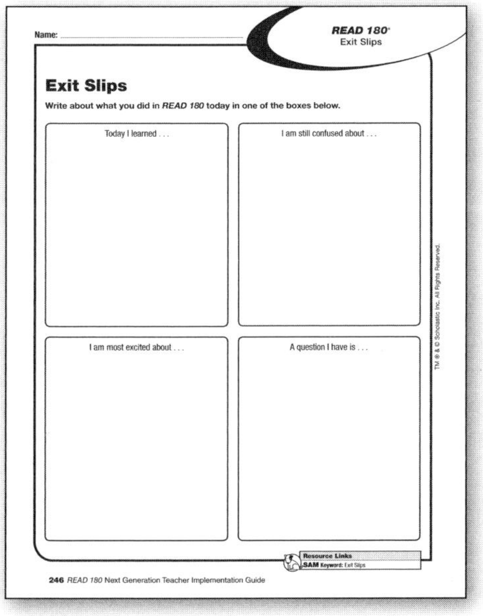

Name:

READ 180 Exit Slips

Exit Slips

Write about what you did in *READ 180* today in one of the boxes below.

Today I learned . . .	I am still confused about . . .
I am most excited about . . .	A question I have is . . .

TM ® & © Scholastic Inc. All Rights Reserved.

Resource Links
SAM Keyword: Exit Slips

246 *READ 180* Next Generation Teacher Implementation Guide

Exit Slips (SAM Keyword: Exit Slips)

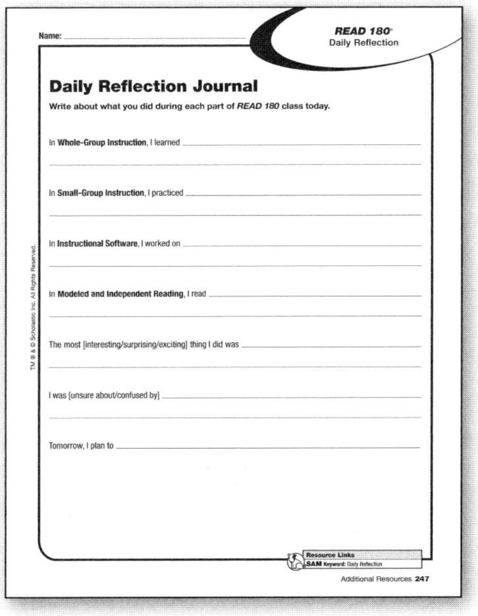

Name:

READ 180 Daily Reflection

Daily Reflection Journal

Write about what you did during each part of *READ 180* class today.

In **Whole-Group Instruction**, I learned

In **Small-Group Instruction**, I practiced

In **Instructional Software**, I worked on

In **Modeled and Independent Reading**, I read

The most [interesting/surprising/exciting] thing I did was

I was [unsure about/confused by]

Tomorrow, I plan to

TM ® & © Scholastic Inc. All Rights Reserved.

Resource Links
SAM Keyword: Daily Reflection

Additional Resources 247

Daily Reflection Journal (SAM Keyword: Daily Reflection)

Assigning *READ 180* Homework

Consider having students complete work outside of the *READ 180* class period to provide the extra practice they need to grow as readers.

Deciding Whether to Assign Homework

READ 180 is intended to support older struggling students who are reading below grade level. Depending on how far below grade level they are reading, your students may or may not be ready for completing independent work outside of class. Consider the following factors to decide whether to assign homework to your struggling readers:

- ***READ 180* Level:** Level 1 students may not be ready for completing independent work without teacher monitoring and support, while Level 3 and 4 students will likely benefit from the extra homework practice.
- **Support Needed:** Think about how much support your students typically need during independent activities in class. Do they often require extra scaffolding in Small-Group Instruction? Do they work productively in Modeled and Independent Reading? Students who usually need more intensive teacher support may not be ready for completing homework on their own.
- **Attention to Accuracy:** You may have students who tend to rush through their work, making careless mistakes along the way. Homework might serve only to reinforce their bad habits and academic errors. Instead, hold one-to-one conferences with these students to help them set goals to improve the overall quality of their work in class.

eReads for Homework

Students can access eReads through any computer with an Internet connection, so it is a great option for homework. The eReads library includes one Collection of four nonfiction passages aligned to each Topic on the *READ 180* Software. Each Collection comes in two levels: one for students at *READ 180* Levels 1 and 2, and one for students at Levels 3 and 4. After students complete a Software Topic, direct them to complete the four corresponding eReads for homework. An entire Collection should take students about a week to finish.

Hold students accountable by sending home copies of the eReads QuickWrites and H.O.T. Pages from *Teaching Resources for Modeled and Independent Reading*. Assess understanding of the text by having students take the *SRC!* quizzes for eReads in class.

Teaching Resources for Homework

Teaching Resources for Topic Software and *Teaching Resources for Modeled and Independent Reading* include various student resources that you can assign as independent homework:

- **QuickWrites** Assign these short writing prompts to assess student understanding of Topic Software segments, Paperbacks, Audiobooks, and eReads.
- **Topic Software Reading Passages** Make copies of the leveled passages for students to reread nightly at home for fluency practice and development.
- **Final Book Projects** Direct students to complete one of the six Modeled and Independent Reading projects after finishing books throughout the year.
- **New Vocabulary Log** Make copies of this Modeled and Independent Reading resource and encourage students to record new words they learn in other classes throughout their day.

Teacher Tip

Encourage students to extend their learning by visiting educational websites such as The Stacks (www.scholastic.com/kids/stacks), where students can access games and videos related to books they have read.

TEACHER IMPLEMENTATION GUIDE

Instructional Software

Overview: Instructional Technology

The Instructional Software rotation provides students with adaptive instruction, targeted practice, and immediate feedback to meet their individual learning needs.

Understanding the Model for Blended Learning

Instructional Software is one of the three small-group rotations that occur after Whole-Group Instruction. One small group of students works independently in Instructional Software while two other groups engage in Small-Group Instruction and Modeled and Independent Reading.

READ 180 Instructional Model

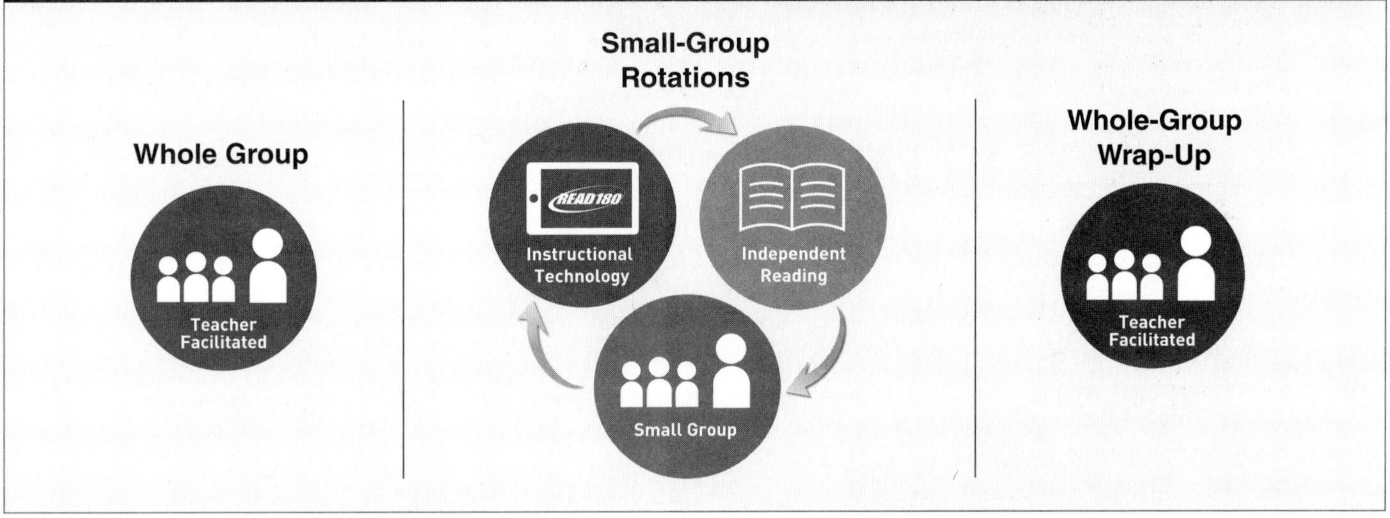

Building Your Knowledge

Track your learning about **Instructional Software** using the K-W-L chart below. Use the first column to reflect on what you already know about this rotation from the Student Experience during training. In the middle column, jot down any questions you have. In the last column, record notes as you learn more about Instructional Software.

K	W	L
I already know...	*I want to know ...*	*I have learned ...*

Understanding Instructional Software

Support your students as they work independently in Instructional Software each day to build comprehension, decoding, fluency, vocabulary, and writing skills.

Research Says

Computer-assisted instruction builds students' automaticity by allowing them to systematically practice new skills, with information presented in small individualized sets.

Hasselbring & Goin, 2004

Purpose

In the Instructional Software rotation, students use the *READ 180* Topic Software to engage in individualized instruction with adaptive technology. Adaptive technology is computer software that assesses each student's particular needs and adjusts content and pacing accordingly.

When logging in to the Topic Software, students first explore their Student Dashboard. The motivating Dashboard features enable students to track their own Software progress throughout the year. Next, students watch a Topic Software Anchor Video to develop background knowledge and content-area vocabulary before reading a leveled passage. The Reading, Word, Spelling, Success, and Writing Zones offer instructional activities related to the passage to develop comprehension, decoding, fluency, vocabulary, and writing skills.

Teacher Tip

Adjust *READ 180* Program Settings in SAM to support English language learners and students with special needs. See page 159 for steps to enable audio support, text captioning, button rollover, and alternate color scheme.

Instructional Focus

Help students strengthen their reading and writing skills in Instructional Software by guiding them to:

- Select one of 15 engaging Topics to spend about a month exploring four related segments (Level 1 students work sequentially through Topics).
- Watch an Anchor Video at the start of each segment to form a mental model before reading a related passage.
- Visit the **Reading Zone** every day and use scaffolds such as modeled reading, highlighted text, and word definitions to make meaning from text.
- Enter the **Word Zone** to develop fluency and automaticity with vocabulary words from the reading passage.
- Practice encoding—or spelling—a customized word list in the **Spelling Zone**.
- Demonstrate mastery of comprehension and vocabulary skills in the **Success Zone** before making a final recording of the passage.
- Write, revise, and publish a scaffolded paragraph in response to a high-interest prompt in the **Writing Zone**.
- Track and take ownership for their progress throughout the year with the motivational Student Dashboard.

Teacher Materials

Use *Teaching Resources for Topic Software* for Topic Overviews, Teaching Plans, QuickWrites, and copies of the leveled reading passages. Display the Topic Software Poster in your classroom to help students to select Topics. Work with your school's technical coordinator to install the Topic Software on your computers to make it run as efficiently as possible.

Teaching Resources for Topic Software

Topic Software Poster

Topic Software Installation Kit

Student Materials

Monitor students as they navigate the Student Dashboard to track their *READ 180* usage and progress throughout the year. Guide them to work independently on the Topic Software to build reading, vocabulary, and writing skills.

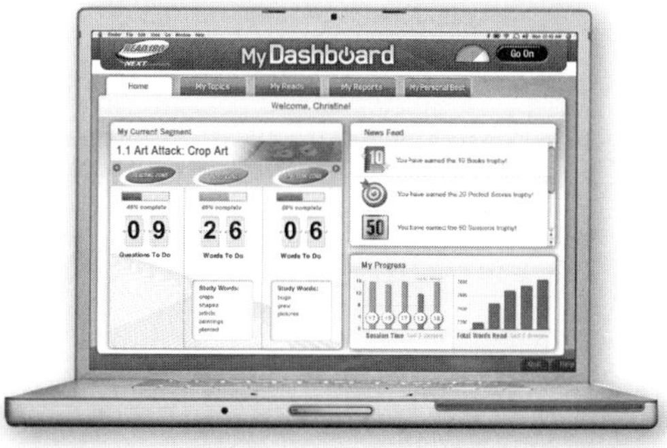

Student Dashboard

Topic Software

Assessment Materials

Run reports on the Scholastic Achievement Manager (SAM) to monitor Topic Software usage and performance. Check the Teacher Dashboard for a weekly snapshot of students' time on task during Instructional Software. Use the *Placement, Assessment, and Reporting Guide* for comprehensive support with monitoring Software progress.

Scholastic Achievement Manager (SAM)

Teacher Dashboard

Placement, Assessment, and Reporting Guide

Motivating Students With Their Dashboard

Encourage students to spend time exploring their Student Dashboard each time they log in to the Topic Software to track their *READ 180* progress throughout the year.

Tech Tip

Students have 45 seconds to explore their Dashboard when working on a Software segment. When they complete a segment, they have 1 minute. When they finish all four segments in a Topic, they have 3 minutes.

Increasing Ownership for Learning

The Student Dashboard empowers students to monitor and direct their own academic growth throughout the school year. Each time students log in to *READ 180,* they can explore personalized data on their Dashboard for a set amount of time: 45 seconds to 3 minutes, depending on their segment completion. Then they are taken to the Topic Software Zone Menu to begin the day's instructional activities. Staying up to date on their *READ 180* successes and progress encourages students to feel ownership for their learning. This results in increased motivation, more time on task, and improved personal effort during the daily Instructional Software rotation.

Student Dashboard Home Tab

After logging in to *READ 180* with their username and password, students arrive at the Student Dashboard, which opens on the Home Tab. Here they can view actionable data about their current Topic Software segment and overall *READ 180* progress. This private, personalized experience motivates students to take control over their learning.

Tell students to check here for a countdown of time for exploring their Dashboard each day.

Notice that the News Feed updates when students reach designated *READ 180* milestones.

Increase accountability for independent work by having students record their daily progress on the Software Log (page 242).

Student Dashboard Home Tab

Motivate students to continually track and increase their scores for average Software session time and total words read.

Exploring the Dashboard Tabs

In addition to the Home Tab, the Student Dashboard includes four other areas for students to keep track of their *READ 180* progress throughout the year: My Topics, My Reads, My Reports, and My Personal Best.

My Topics

- Shows all available Software Topics, with completed Topics and segments filled in and others grayed out.
- Offers a brief summary of each segment to support students with selecting Topics.

My Reads

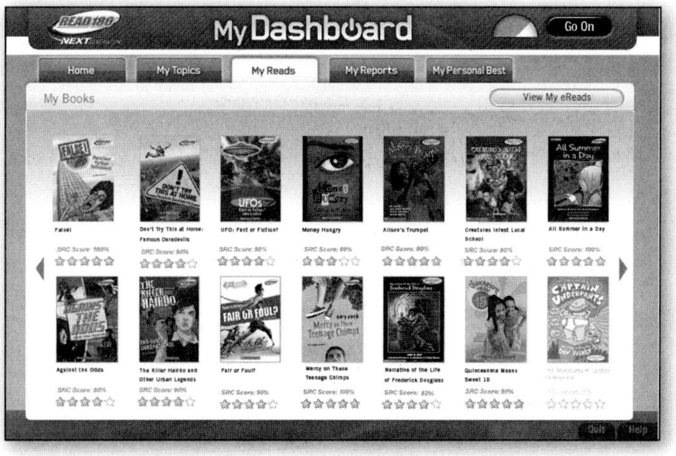

- Tracks the Paperbacks, Audiobooks, and eReads for which students have passed *SRC!* quizzes and shows texts they have yet to read.
- Displays results for *SRC!* quizzes passed.

My Reports

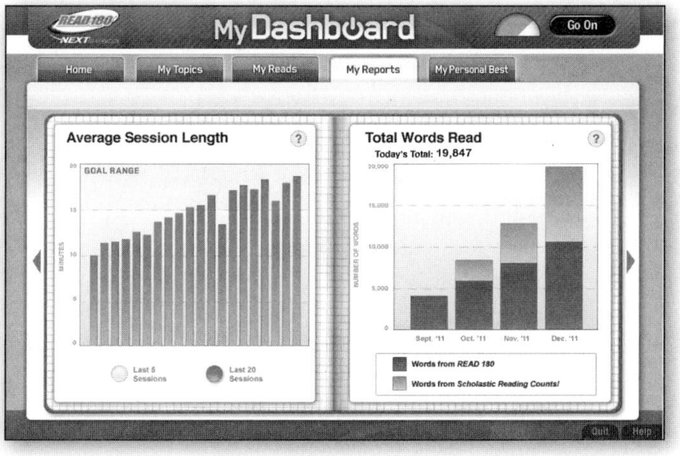

- Displays actionable, student-friendly reports with personalized performance data.
- Encourages students to identify successes and set goals for continued reading growth.

My Personal Best

- Records best scores on Topic Software activities (only the first response to each question counts).
- Awards trophies for reaching milestones such as a set number of words read or *SRC!* quizzes passed.

Previewing the Topic Software

Prepare students for successful independent work during Instructional Software by previewing the Software Topics and Learning Zones that they will complete.

Teacher Tip

Level 1 students work sequentially through the Topic Software, beginning with the first Topic. Students at other levels can choose their own order for completing Topics.

High-Interest Content Areas

Students select from 15 age-appropriate, nonfiction Topics to work on in the daily Instructional Software rotation. Each Topic consists of four segments—different issues related to the same big idea. Each segment takes about five to fifteen sessions to complete, depending on the student's level, performance on activities, and whether the Writing Zone is enabled (see page 159).

Every Topic comes from one of five strands that build student knowledge in key content areas: People & Cultures, Science & Math, History & Geography, Literature & the Arts, and Your World & Beyond. Display the Topic Software Poster in the Instructional Software rotational area to increase interest and support students with selecting Topics.

Make connections between the Topics and current events or content areas that students are studying in other classes.

Explain how the Topics (1–15) and segments (1–4) are numbered.

Introduce the "big idea" of each Topic to build interest when you preview the Software for students.

Read aloud a few segment summaries so students see the full range of engaging Topics to choose from.

Topic Software Poster, Stage B

Topic Software Zone Menu

After exploring the Student Dashboard, students are prompted to move on to the Topic Software Zone Menu. Here they see buttons for five Learning Zones with customized instruction and practice activities. Students also meet Ty, a supportive mentor who provides patient encouragement and specific corrective feedback as students engage in each of the five Zones.

Tech Tip

When starting a new segment, students only see buttons for the Reading, Word, and Spelling Zones on the Zone Menu. They unlock access to the Success and Writing Zones as they complete segment activities.

Five Learning Zones

Students work through five Learning Zones for every segment on the *READ 180* Topic Software. Each Zone offers individualized, adaptive activities to target students' specific instructional needs. See *Getting Started: Your First Three Weeks With READ 180,* available in your Teacher Bookshelf or on the Interactive Teaching System, for suggested classroom activities to introduce each of the five Learning Zones to students.

Reading Zone Students view an Anchor Video and read a leveled passage to build phonics, fluency, vocabulary, and comprehension skills.

Word Zone Students practice decoding and rapid word recognition to build fluency and automaticity with words from the reading passage.

Spelling Zone Students practice their encoding—or spelling—skills with a customized word list from the reading passage.

Success Zone Students demonstrate mastery of comprehension and vocabulary skills and make a final oral recording of the reading passage.

Writing Zone Students write, revise, and publish a scaffolded argument paragraph in response to an engaging prompt related to the Software Topic.

Teacher Tip

Remind students that they may or may not see the Writing Zone for a segment, depending on how you have adjusted *READ 180* Program Settings in SAM (see page 159). Consider writing goals and time on task when deciding whether to change the default setting (enabled for every other segment).

Exploring the Software: Reading Zone

In the Reading Zone on the *READ 180* Topic Software, students develop reading skills and strategies with adaptive instruction, individualized practice, and immediate feedback.

Reading Zone

Students begin each new Topic Software segment in the **Reading Zone.** They view an Anchor Video, read a leveled passage with scaffolds, and answer daily questions to build comprehension and vocabulary skills.

Video

Students will:

- Watch an engaging video (90–180 seconds) to build background knowledge about the Topic.
- Have the option to read along with text captioning of the video narration.
- Have the option to hear a summary in one of five languages before viewing.

How It Helps:

- Develops a mental model to help students make meaning from the reading passage.
- Motivates and engages students with age-appropriate and high-interest content.
- Provides support for students who are hearing-impaired or learning English as a second language.

Video, Stage B

Passage

Students will:

- Read a content-area passage at one of four levels.
- Practice reading with audio support and highlighted text at adjustable speeds.
- Make and hear an initial oral recording of the passage.
- See definitions for targeted vocabulary words.
- Revisit the passage at least four more times to answer a total of 15 Quick Check questions per Software segment.

How It Helps:

- Scaffolds student reading practice with text at their level.
- Allows students to monitor their own reading fluency with audio recordings.
- Builds comprehension, content-area vocabulary, fluency, and reading confidence.

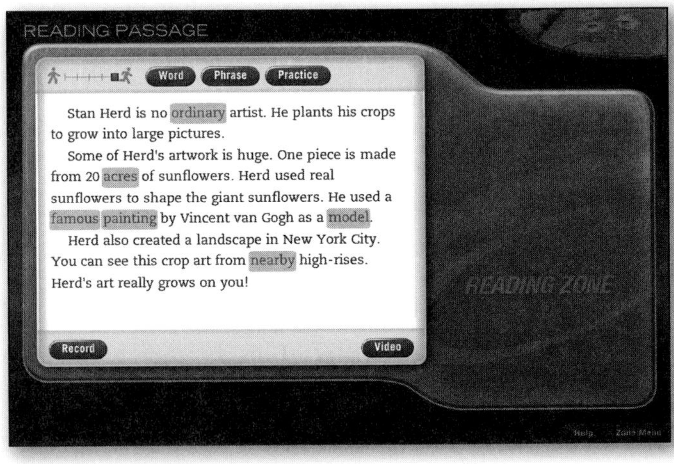

Level 2 Passage, Stage B

Quick Check

Students will:

- Answer three multiple-choice comprehension and vocabulary questions per visit to the Reading Zone.
- Reread the passage to find text evidence for their answers.
- Receive immediate feedback on their answers.

How It Helps:

- Assesses passage comprehension and vocabulary.
- Provides data to inform the Reading CheckPoint groups suggested by the Teacher Dashboard Groupinator.
- Familiarizes students with the format of questions commonly found on standardized tests.

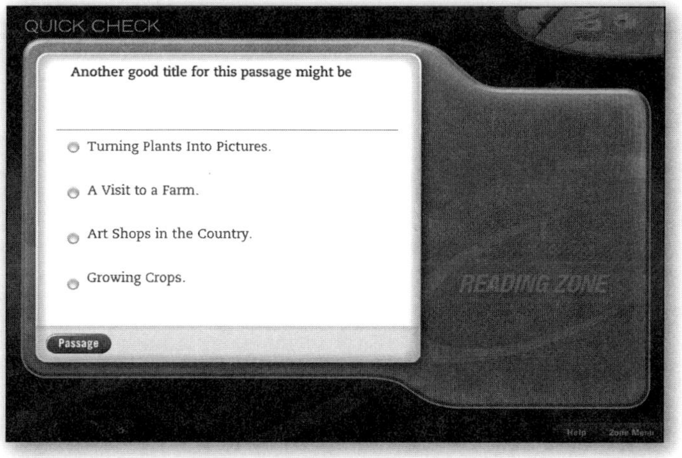

Quick Check Question, Stage B

Supporting Students With the Reading Zone

Encourage your students to start in the Reading Zone each time they log in to the Topic Software. If a student avoids the Reading Zone for two consecutive Software sessions, he or she will automatically begin in the Reading Zone during the next session. This ensures multiple readings of the passage for comprehension and fluency growth. Consider these suggestions for supporting your students' daily independent work in the Reading Zone.

Try This Support Strategy	Here's How
Explain Zone Purpose	*I'll tell students the Reading Zone helps them grow as readers by...*
Share Mastery Requirements	Explain that to complete the Reading Zone for each segment, students must answer all 15 Quick Check questions. Students' *first* attempt on each question is the only score that counts on the SAM data reports, Teacher Dashboard Groupinator (Reading CheckPoint), and Student Dashboard Personal Best Tab.
Check In Regularly	Stop by the Instructional Software rotation and ask students to read aloud their Reading Zone passages. Listen carefully to informally assess their accuracy and fluency. Check that they are reading directly into the microphone to ensure a clear recording.
Monitor Zone Performance	Run the *READ 180* Student Segment Status Report in SAM for an overview of student performance on a Software Topic, including the percentage of correct Quick Check questions and the number of passage readings.

Exploring the Software: Word Zone

In the Word Zone on the *READ 180* Topic Software, students build vocabulary and word-study skills with adaptive instructional activities and immediate corrective feedback.

Word Zone

After visiting the Reading Zone at least once, students unlock the **Word Zone**, where they receive systematic instruction in decoding and word recognition to build automaticity with vocabulary words from the reading passage.

Word Assessment

Students will:

- Listen to vocabulary words read aloud and identify them from a list.
- Differentiate among multiple distractors to identify the right words.
- Find out which words they did not identify quickly enough or accurately. These become their Study Words.

How It Helps:

- Allows assessment to inform instruction by determining which words the student already knows and which need further study.
- Provides feedback on word mastery in a private environment.

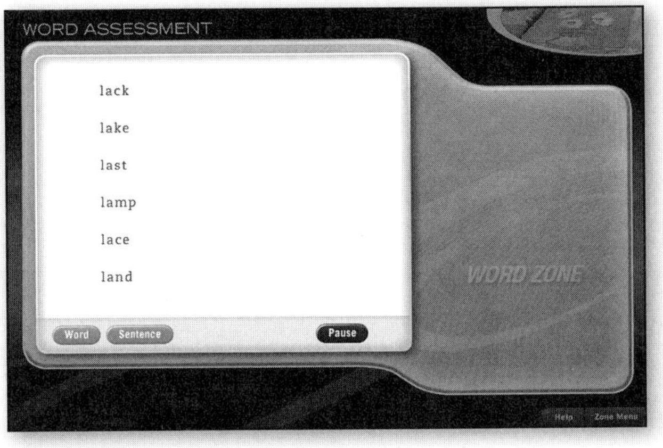

Word Assessment, Stage B

Word Clinic

Students will:

- Listen to the correct pronunciation of their Study Words.
- See and hear concrete tips on how to decode their Study Words.
- Make an audio recording of their Study Words.

How It Helps:

- Begins building automaticity with a customized list of Study Words.
- Minimizes overload of students' working memory with small instructional sets of no more than five Study Words at a time.

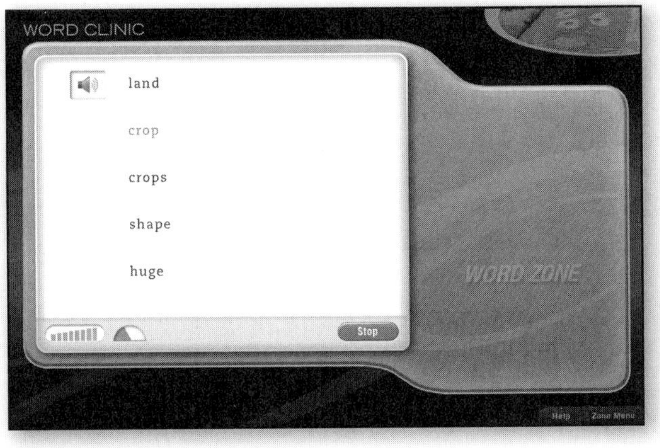

Word Clinic, Stage B

Word Match

Students will:

- Hear their personal recordings of their Study Words.
- Match their recordings to written words in a list.

How It Helps:

- Continues building word recognition and automaticity.
- Develops the connection between the spoken and written forms of each word.

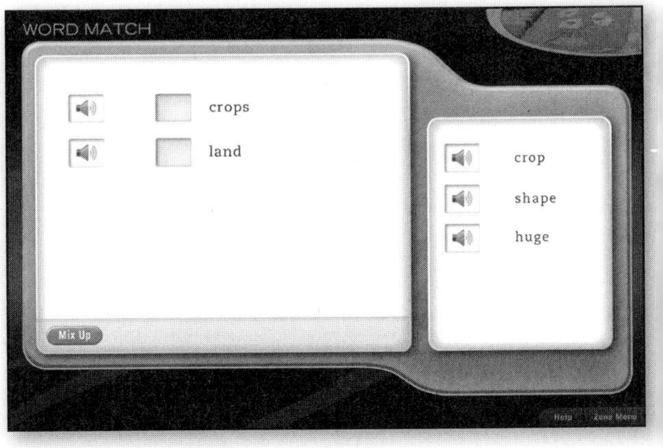

Word Match, Stage B

Self Check

Students will:

- Re-record their Study Words.
- Compare their personal recordings with model versions.
- Click Thumbs-Up or Down to rate their recordings.

How It Helps:

- Shortens available recording time to build automaticity.
- Sharpens listening skills by requiring students to compare and evaluate pronunciation.
- Encourages self-monitoring and ownership for learning.

Self Check, Stage B

Speed Challenge

Students will:

- See a list of six words that includes a Study Word or a Review Word (from a previous Software segment).
- Hear the Study or Review Word spoken aloud.
- Select the spoken word from the list quickly. Words correctly identified are considered "mastered."

How It Helps:

- Allows students to practice rapid word identification.
- Differentiates instruction by focusing on the words that the student struggles with most.

Speed Challenge, Stage B

Supporting Students With the Word Zone

Encourage students to visit the Word Zone every day during the Instructional Software rotation. Consider these suggestions for supporting their independent practice on the computer.

Try This Support Strategy	Here's How
Explain Zone Purpose	*I'll point out that Word Zone activities build vocabulary skills by...*
Share Mastery Requirements	Explain that to complete the Word Zone for each segment, students must master all of the Study Words from the reading passage.
Check In Regularly	When students in Small-Group Instruction are working independently, check in with those at Instructional Software. Listen to students record their Study Words, assess their accuracy, and provide any feedback.
Monitor Zone Performance	Run the *READ 180* Student Diagnostic Report for an overview of student performance on a Software Topic, including the student's most common word-recognition errors in the Word Zone Speed Challenge activity.

Exploring the Software: Spelling Zone

In the Spelling Zone on the *READ 180* Topic Software, students practice their encoding—or spelling—skills with a customized word list, adaptive practice, and corrective feedback.

Spelling Zone

After visiting the Reading Zone at least once, students can access the **Spelling Zone**, where they practice spelling a personalized list of vocabulary words and receive immediate corrective feedback based on their specific errors.

Spelling Assessment

Students will:

- Hear words from the reading passage pronounced aloud, first alone then as part of a sentence.
- Spell the words they hear.
- Find out which words they did not spell correctly. These words become their spelling Study Words.

How It Helps:

- Differentiates instruction by identifying which words students still need to practice for mastery.
- Assesses fluency and automaticity by counting words not spelled within 30 seconds as incorrect.

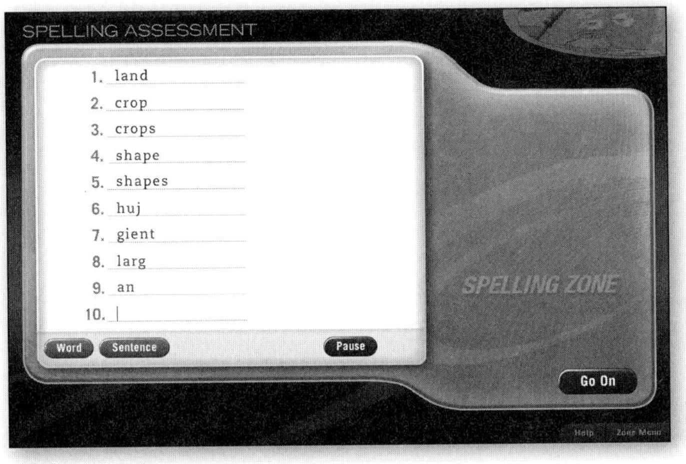

Spelling Assessment, Stage B

Spelling Clinic

Students will:

- Hear Study Words and see a spelling tip for each word.
- Spell each Study Word when prompted.
- Hear and see additional spelling tips that address the specific errors they made.

How It Helps:

- Helps students identify their errors by comparing their spelling to the correct spelling.
- Models how to identify the important parts of the word, segment the word, and blend the word accurately.
- Maintains students' attention and focus with instructional sets of no more than three words at a time.

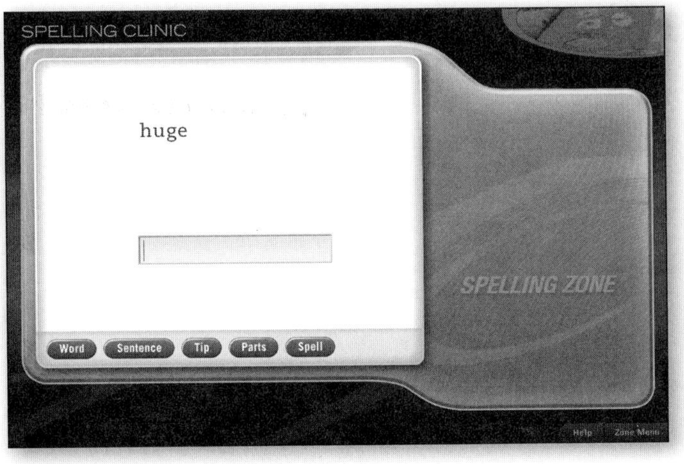

Spelling Clinic, Stage B

Spelling Challenge

Students will:

- Hear and spell their Study and Review Words (from previous Software segments). Words spelled correctly are considered "mastered."
- Receive specific corrective feedback for any misspellings.

How It Helps:

- Repeats Study and Review Words at increasing speed intervals to build fluency and automaticity.
- Motivates students with immediate feedback given in a private, supportive manner.
- Provides systematic review of previously mastered words, or Review Words, to maintain mastery.

Spelling Challenge, Stage B

Proofreading

Students will:

- Read passages that include misspelled words.
- Identify the misspelled words and select correct spellings from a list.

How It Helps:

- Transfers spelling skills to writing activities.
- Emphasizes spelling accuracy by including common misspellings as distractors.
- Builds the good habit of carefully rereading written work.

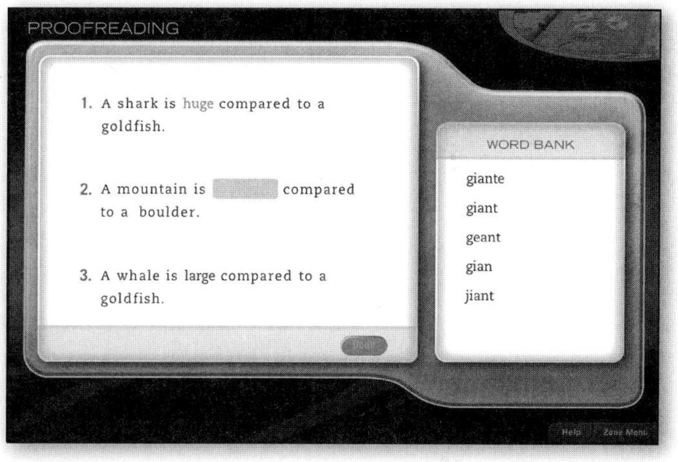

Proofreading, Stage B

Supporting Students With the Spelling Zone

Encourage students to visit the Spelling Zone every day during the Instructional Software rotation. Consider these suggestions for supporting their independent practice on the computer.

Try This Support Strategy	Here's How
Explain Zone Purpose	*I'll tell my students that the Spelling Zone builds literacy skills such as...*
Share Mastery Requirements	Explain that to complete the Spelling Zone for each segment, students must master a set number of Study Words, depending on their level: 6 words for Level 1, 12 for Level 2, 18 for Level 3, and 24 for Level 4.
Check In Regularly	Visit Instructional Software and ask students to read aloud their Spelling Words. Listen carefully to informally assess and support their accuracy.
Monitor Zone Performance	Run the *READ 180* Spelling Skills Grouping Report to see which students are struggling with similar skills—such as letter additions, omissions, and reversals—in the Spelling Clinic and Spelling Challenge.

Exploring the Software: Success Zone

In the Success Zone on the *READ 180* Topic Software, students demonstrate mastery of passage comprehension, vocabulary, and fluency skills.

Success Zone

Students unlock the **Success Zone** after they have met all of the requirements for the Reading, Word, and Spelling Zones and demonstrated mastery of all words in the reading passage.

Discrepancy Passages

Students will:

- Read two to three modified versions of the Reading Zone passage.
- Select the version that accurately summarizes the content of the original passage.
- See the misinformation highlighted if they choose an incorrect version.

How It Helps:

- Activates higher-order thinking skills for evaluating text based on knowledge of the original passage.
- Requires students to read carefully for meaning to see how similar passages contain different information.
- Provides an additional opportunity for repeated reading of the passage to build fluency with connected text.

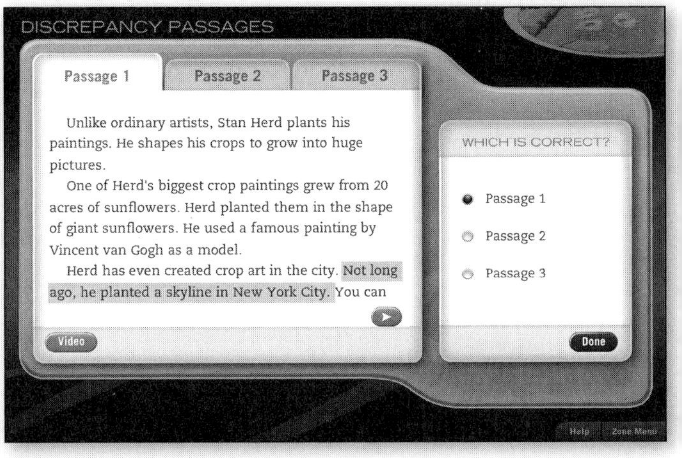

Discrepancy Passage, Stage B

Context Passages

Students will:

- Read three passages that include missing words.
- Choose a word from a list to correctly fill each blank.
- Receive immediate feedback about their answers.

How It Helps:

- Uses a modified cloze procedure to develop comprehension and reinforce vocabulary in context.
- Builds on background because the first two passages are based on the Reading Zone and Discrepancy Passages.
- Challenges students to apply skills to new text with the third passage, which includes some new information.

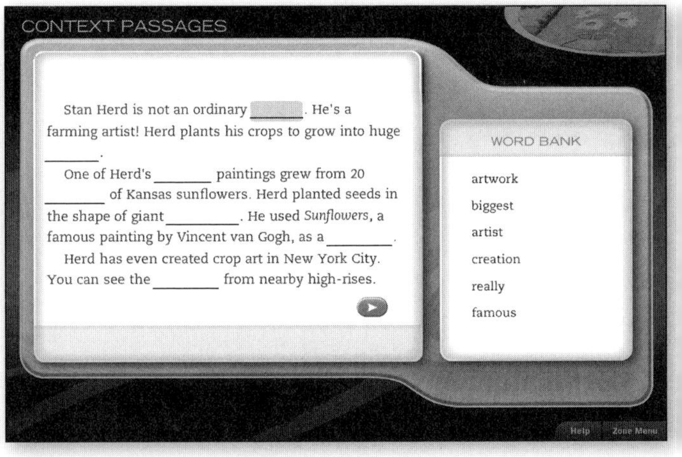

Context Passage, Stage B

Final Recording

Students will:

- Make an audio recording of the original reading passage to demonstrate mastery.
- Listen to their recording to assess their own fluency.
- Re-record the passage until satisfied with the recording.

How It Helps:

- Allows students to hear how much their fluency has improved since their first visit to the Reading Zone.
- Saves the recording in the SAM Student Digital Portfolio so you can listen to it to assess fluency.
- Encourages students to feel a sense of accomplishment and success, which builds motivation and self-esteem.

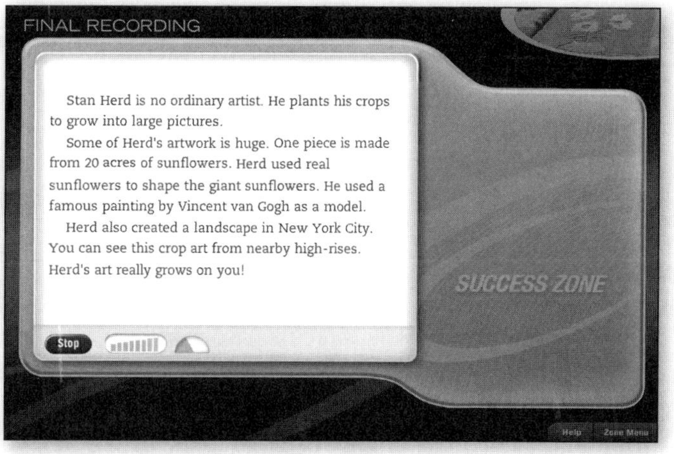

Final Recording, Stage B

Supporting Students With the Success Zone

Remind students that they will only be able to access the Success Zone after they have completed all requirements for the Reading, Word, and Spelling Zones. Consider these tips for supporting them with demonstrating mastery.

Try This Support Strategy	Here's How
Explain Zone Purpose	*I'll encourage students to try their best in the Success Zone because...*
Share Mastery Requirements	Explain that to complete the Success Zone for each Topic Software segment, students make a final oral recording of the reading passage, which you can hear and grade in the SAM Student Digital Portfolio.
Check In Regularly	Encourage your students to read all possible answer choices for the Discrepancy and Context Passages before choosing one. Stress that only their *first* response to each question counts on their SAM reports and Student Dashboard.
Monitor Zone Performance	Click the Portfolio tab in SAM to access the Student Digital Portfolio. Check the My Inbox tab for new Final Recordings ready for grading. Use the copy of the reading passage and the on-screen rubric provided in the SAM Student Digital Portfolio to evaluate each recording. Share results with students during one-to-one conferences to help them improve their fluency.

Exploring the Software: Writing Zone

In the Writing Zone on the *READ 180* Topic Software, students write, revise, and publish an argument paragraph using scaffolds for support.

Writing Zone

The **Writing Zone** allows students the opportunity to write a scaffolded, argument paragraph in response to a Topic-related prompt. Students practice supporting their argument with strong reasons to back up their viewpoint.

Students unlock the Writing Zone on the Topic Software Zone Menu after they have completed all other Zones. Use the *READ 180* Program Settings in SAM (see page 159) to choose how often each student works in the Writing Zone. The default setting is twice per Topic, after every other segment.

Respond & Write: Respond

Students will:

- Hear a survey question based on the content area they explored in the Topic Software segment.
- Select one of two possible answers to respond to the question.
- See how other students on the same school or district server responded to the question.

How It Helps:

- Requires students to think critically and establish a point of view before writing.
- Motivates students by showing them how their opinions compare to those of their peers.

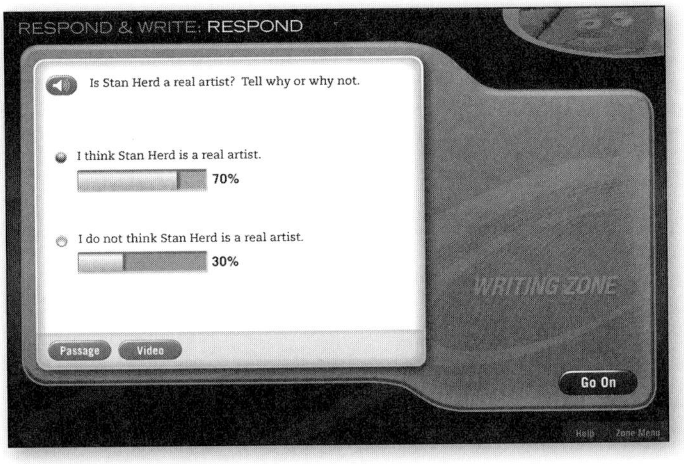

Respond, Stage B

Respond & Write: Write

Students will:

- See how their survey answer has become the topic sentence of a paragraph.
- Receive sentence response frames in one of two versions that matches their *READ 180* Level (1–2 or 3–4).
- Type in responses to complete two support sentences and one conclusion sentence.

How It Helps:

- Models how to organize and structure a written response and use transition words effectively.
- Scaffolds student writing by providing leveled response frames that start each sentence.
- Guides students to cite reasons to develop an argument and support their opinion.

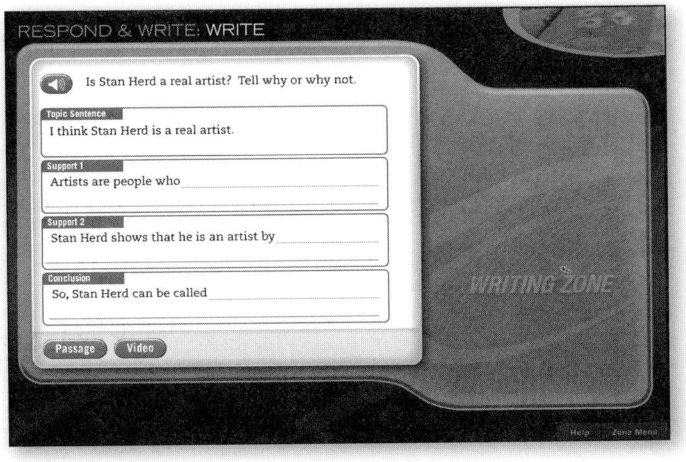

Write, Stage B

Respond & Write: Revise

Students will:

- Reread their draft to check their work.
- Use a rubric, similar to those in *rBook* writing lessons, to evaluate word choice, sentence structure, and spelling.
- Revise their writing based on suggestions provided.

How It Helps:

- Identifies revision as an important step in the writing process.
- Draws attention to the importance of strong word choice.
- Supports students to use more precise vocabulary by providing a list of synonyms to replace "tired" words.

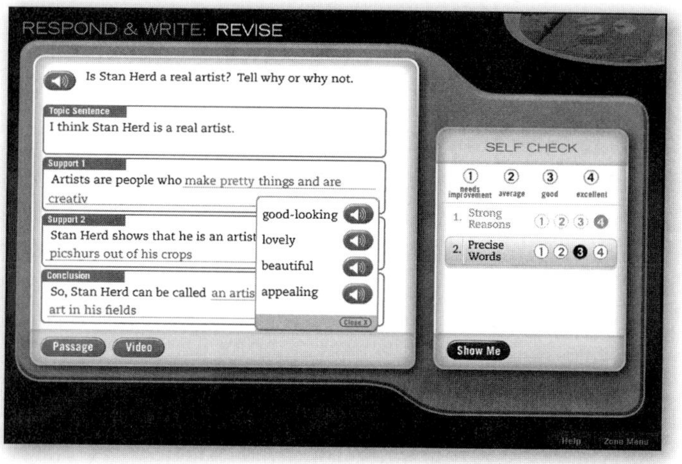

Revise, Stage B

Respond & Write: Publish

Students will:

- Review and edit their writing one last time.
- Make a recording of their paragraph and play it back.
- Submit the final version for grading.

How It Helps:

- Provides students with a sense of closure and success.
- Encourages students to listen for any changes to make.
- Sends the first and final drafts to the SAM Student Digital Portfolio for grading.

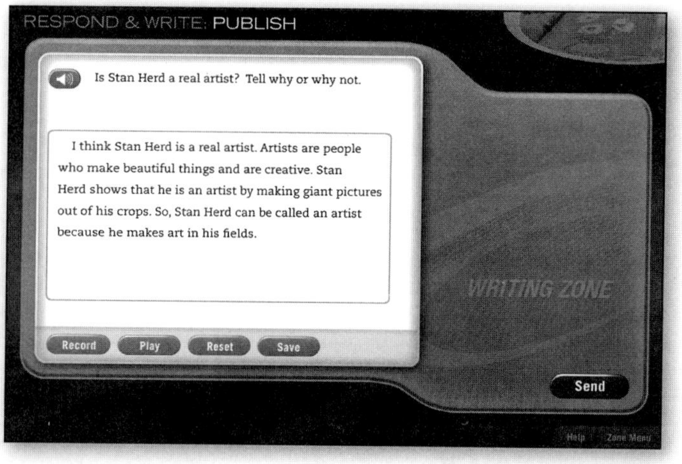

Publish, Stage B

Supporting Students With the Writing Zone

Remind students that they will earn access to the Writing Zone for every other Topic segment after they have completed all other Learning Zones for that segment. Consider these strategies for supporting them with independent writing.

Try This Support Strategy	Here's How
Explain Zone Purpose	*I'll tell students that the Writing Zone teaches key skills such as...*
Share Mastery Requirements	Explain that to complete the Writing Zone, students must send their published paragraph to the SAM Student Digital Portfolio for your review.
Check In Regularly	Check in at the Instructional Software rotation when students in Small-Group Instruction are working independently. Ask students to read aloud their paragraph drafts and offer any suggestions for improvement.
Monitor Zone Performance	Check the My Inbox tab in the SAM Student Digital Portfolio for any new Writing Zone paragraphs to grade. Use the rubric provided to evaluate each paragraph, and share results with students to help them grow as writers.

Using *Teaching Resources* for Software Support

Teaching Resources for Topic Software **is your comprehensive guide for supporting students with success during the independent Instructional Software rotation.**

What's Inside

Use this book throughout the year to monitor students as they work independently on the *READ 180* Topic Software. Look for three key types of support:

- **Professional Development** articles provide research-based background, assessment information, and practical classroom management tips for monitoring Instructional Software.
- **Teaching Support** plans offer insight into the content of each Topic Software segment to help you check in regularly with students and assess their understanding and reading progress.
- **Skills Practice and Assessment** resources help you reinforce fluency and writing skills, increase student engagement with the Software, and hold students accountable for independent work.

***Teaching Resources for Topic Software*, Stage B**

Using the Resources

Teaching Resources for Topic Software also includes classroom and reproducible resources to guide students' daily skills practice during Instructional Software:

- **Teaching Resources:** Use the Software Overview for each Topic to preview the nonfiction content areas, comprehension strategies, and specific word-study and spelling skills your students are learning on the Software.
- **Student Resources:** Make copies of the reproducible QuickWrites and leveled reading passages for students to practice essential writing and fluency skills in the classroom or at home.
- **Additional Resources:** Use the Classroom Management Support reproducibles at the back of the book to evaluate and guide students to improve their fluency and respond to QuickWrite prompts.

Teacher Tip

See the *Software Overview,* available in your Teacher Bookshelf, for a screen-by-screen walkthrough of the Student Dashboard and Topic Software experience.

Software Overviews

Use the Overviews in *Teaching Resources for Topic Software* to find out which words and skills students learn in each Software segment, depending on their level. Determine areas for practice and reinforcement during Whole- and Small-Group Instruction.

Notice the Software segments are numbered first by Topic (1–15) and then by segment (1–4).

Review the vocabulary words your students are learning based on their *READ 180* Level.

Read the "big idea" that connects all four segments in the Topic.

***READ 180* Topic Software 1**

OVERVIEW: Art Attack

TOPIC CONCEPT
The art world is made up of diverse people with unique visions and talents.

Skills covered on the Software are listed here for your reference.

VIDEO SEGMENT	PASSAGE VOCABULARY WORDS				COMPREHENSION	WORD STUDY/SPELLING SKILLS			
1.1 Crop Art 	LEVEL 1 art artist city crops farm grows pictures shops	LEVEL 2 acres famous model nearby ordinary painting	LEVEL 3 fertile grandest imagination imaginative model pattern	LEVEL 4 boundaries fertile grand innovative landscape modeled neighboring	• Main Idea • Summarize • Understand Vocabulary • Make Inferences • Cause and Effect • Compare and Contrast	LEVEL 1 **Phonogram *-op*** crops shops tops	LEVEL 2 **Ending *-ed* With Base Change** created used **Compound Words** artwork sunflowers	LEVEL 3 **Suffixes *-ative, -ive*** creative imaginative innovative **Suffix *-ly*** lovely naturally	LEVEL 4 **Long Vowel /ē/*ei*** deceived
1.2 Halls of Fame 	LEVEL 1 dance drama fans music plan sing special	LEVEL 2 auditions example movie rehearsals students study	LEVEL 3 audition express performing pursue remarks	LEVEL 4 accepted audition devoted established featured plays talented	• Summarize • Understand Vocabulary • Sequence of Events • Read for Detail • Draw Conclusions • Make Inferences • Cause and Effect • Compare and Contrast • Problem and Solution	LEVEL 1 **Phonogram *-an*** fans plan	LEVEL 2 **Long Vowel /ē/*y*** busy study **Ending *-ing*** acting performing	LEVEL 3 **Suffix *-al*** rehearsal **Suffix *-ment*** commitment fulfillment	LEVEL 4 **Ending *-ing* With Base Change** aspiring pursuing
1.3 Young at Art 	LEVEL 1 loves millions money paintings professional sticks	LEVEL 2 famous ordinary painting rare talent teenager	LEVEL 3 abstract average millionaire popularity professional purposely style	LEVEL 4 celebrities customers popularity represented resembles	• Main Idea • Summarize • Understand Vocabulary • Draw Conclusions • Cause and Effect • Compare and Contrast • Problem and Solution	LEVEL 1 **Consonant /k/*ck*** shock sticks	LEVEL 2 ***r*-Controlled Vowel /är/*are*** rare spare **Prefix *un-*** unlikely unrewarded unusual	LEVEL 3 **Prefix *un-*** unrealistic **Compound Words** rollerblade something	LEVEL 4 **Suffix *-al*** exceptional professional
1.4 STOMP 	LEVEL 1 beat claps drum group music song stomp	LEVEL 2 objects sounds stage theater unusual	LEVEL 3 audience cast echo performances rhythms	LEVEL 4 audience cast constructed envision mundane participate rhythm witness	• Understand Vocabulary • Sequence of Events • Read for Detail • Draw Conclusions • Make Inferences • Cause and Effect • Compare and Contrast • Problem and Solution	LEVEL 1 **Phonogram *-ap*** clap rap tap	LEVEL 2 **Blend *nk*** clanking sinks **Suffix *-er*** performer	LEVEL 3 **Suffix *-est*** noisiest strangest	LEVEL 4 **Root *vis*** envision visionary

20 ***READ 180* Topic Software 1**

***READ 180* Overview** 21

Teaching Resources for Topic Software, Stage B

Identify comprehension skills and strategies to reinforce for students during Small-Group Instruction.

Locate words from the leveled passages for word-study and spelling reinforcement activities.

Using *Teaching Resources:* Teaching Plans and QuickWrites

Use the Teaching Plans and QuickWrites in *Teaching Resources for Topic Software* to support student success during the Instructional Software rotation.

Teaching Plans

These plans provide you with tools to monitor and support students with every *READ 180* Topic Software segment. Each plan includes a video summary, discussion questions, fluency practice benchmarks, and links to resources.

***READ 180* Topic Software 1.1**

1.1 Crop Art

An unusual artist doesn't paint pictures, he plants them.

Resources	SAM Keywords
• Passages, pp. 111–114	Crop Art
• QuickWrites, pp. 351–352	Crop Art
• Reading Rate Chart, p. 471	Rate Chart

Video Summary

Stan Herd is an unusual kind of artist. His canvas is the earth and his paintbrush is a tractor. This video captures Herd's artistic process from a sketch on paper, to clearing land with a tractor, to planting crops. One of Herd's finest pictures is a pattern of sunflowers reminiscent of a famous painting by Vincent van Gogh. This 20-acre picture, however, is created from a huge crop of sunflowers!

Discussion Questions

- In what way is Stan Herd both a farmer and an artist? *(He plants crops and uses them to create pictures.)* COMPARE AND CONTRAST
- What kind of guy is Stan Herd? How would you describe him to others? *(He is hardworking, creative, and disciplined.)* ANALYZE CHARACTER
- How has Herd met his challenge of "doing something grand and something innovative that stretches the boundaries"? *(His large-scale artwork allows him to express himself in an unconventional way. He uses materials and techniques not commonly used by artists.)* DRAW CONCLUSIONS

Fluency Practice

Use the leveled passages for fluency practice. Have students read the passage repeatedly and record their timings on the Reading Rate Chart.

	Below Benchmark	Approaching Benchmark	On Benchmark
Level 1 40 words	**34** sec (70 wpm)	**29** sec (82 wpm)	**23** sec (106 wpm)
Level 2 76 words	**56** sec (82 wpm)	**43** sec (107 wpm)	**37** sec (123 wpm)
Level 3 159 words	**89** sec (107 wpm)	**76** sec (126 wpm)	**67** sec (143 wpm)
Level 4 226 words	**108** sec (126 wpm)	**84** sec (161 wpm)	**79** sec (172 wpm)

Reading rate measures are adjusted according to the ability range of each *READ 180* level. See page 11 for further fluency information.

Check Progress

- Reports for monitoring Topic Software progress are available on SAM.

22 ***READ 180*** Topic Software 1.1

Read the Video Summary for an overview of the content area that the segment addresses.

Ask questions during group discussions or individual conferences to reinforce comprehension skills and understanding.

Use the Reading Rate Chart (SAM Keyword: Rate Chart) to track students' fluency growth.

Time students' reading of the Software passage to determine if they meet the benchmark for their *READ 180* Level.

I can run SAM reports to monitor:

____

____

____

***Teaching Resources for Topic Software,* Stage B**

QuickWrites

The QuickWrites are short writing prompts related to the Topic Software segments. They are designed to motivate reluctant writers, build writing fluency and confidence, and hold students accountable for independent work.

Name ______________________

READ 180 **Topic Software**
QuickWrites 1.1
LEVELS 1–2

Crop Art

Here are some writing assignments for this segment. Do the first two as you work on the segment. Do the third one after you finish the segment. Write your answers on the back of this sheet or on a separate piece of paper.

Seen and Herd

DATE

1. Stan Herd's pictures are too big to put in museums. List two ways you can see his pictures.

Grow an Idea

DATE

2. You have a great idea for a picture. You want Stan Herd to grow it on his farm. Describe what you want him to "paint" with plants in his field. Write two or three sentences.

WRITING ZONE

Respond & Write

DATE

Now that you've finished the segment, answer the question below. If you already answered it in the Writing Zone, argue the opposite opinion or support the same opinion with different reasons from the passage.

3. Is Stan Herd a real artist? Tell why or why not.

Use with page 22.

Resource Links
Teaching Resources: p. 351
SAM Keyword: Crop Art

READ 180 Topic Software 1.1 | 351

***Teaching Resources for Topic Software,* Stage B**

Provide students with QuickWrites prompts matched to their *READ 180* Level (1–2 or 3–4).

Make copies of the QuickWrite Response Sheet (SAM Keyword: QuickWrite) for students to use to neatly write out their answers.

Consider having your students complete one QuickWrite prompt each night for homework.

Engaging prompts help reluctant writers because:

____

____

____

Have students use this space or the back of the sheet to write their Study Words from the Word and Spelling Zones for practice at home.

Using *Teaching Resources:* Leveled Passages

Make student copies of the leveled reading passages in *Teaching Resources for Topic Software* for additional fluency practice in the classroom or at home.

Fluency Benchmark Passages

The passages in *Teaching Resources for Topic Software* are reproducible versions of the leveled passages students read in the Reading Zone. Provide students with a copy of their current passage at the right level so they can continue their fluency practice even when they are not on the computer. Below are examples of four leveled passages for a Topic Software segment (Stage B).

Level 1
Lexile Range 200–450L

***READ 180* Topic Software**
Passage 1.1
LEVEL 1

Crop Art

Stan Herd is an artist. His art is not in shops. Herd grows art on [15]
his farm! Herd shapes crops into big pictures. Sometimes Herd even [26]
grows art in the city. Herd is tops in the field of crop art! [40]

TM ® & © Scholastic Inc. All Rights Reserved.

Use for fluency practice.

Resource Links
Teaching Resources: p. 111
SAM Keyword: Crop Art

***READ 180* Topic Software 1.1** 111

Level 2
Lexile Range 400–700L

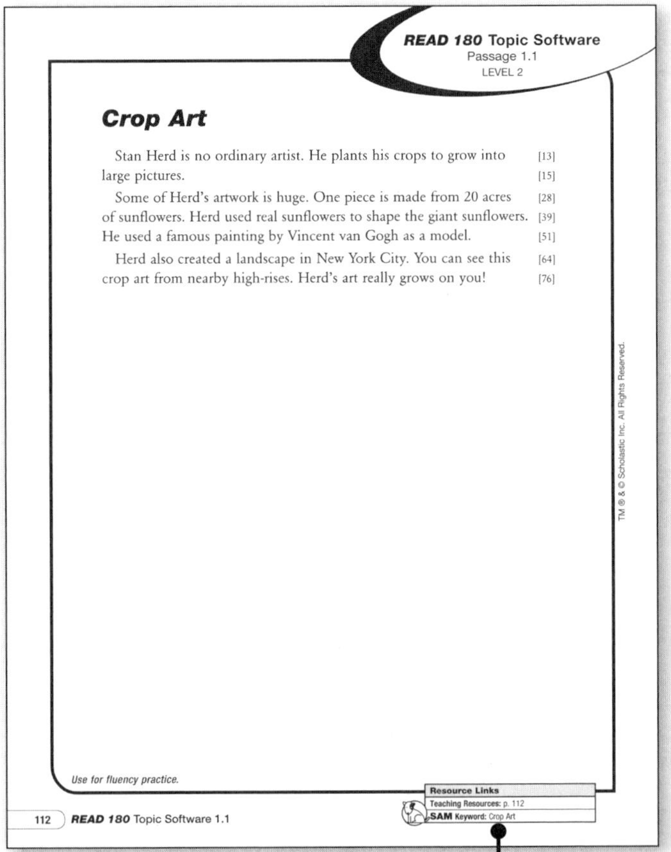
***READ 180* Topic Software**
Passage 1.1
LEVEL 2

Crop Art

Stan Herd is no ordinary artist. He plants his crops to grow into [13]
large pictures. [15]
Some of Herd's artwork is huge. One piece is made from 20 acres [28]
of sunflowers. Herd used real sunflowers to shape the giant sunflowers. [39]
He used a famous painting by Vincent van Gogh as a model. [51]
Herd also created a landscape in New York City. You can see this [64]
crop art from nearby high-rises. Herd's art really grows on you! [76]

TM ® & © Scholastic Inc. All Rights Reserved.

Use for fluency practice.

112 ***READ 180* Topic Software 1.1**

Resource Links
Teaching Resources: p. 112
SAM Keyword: Crop Art

Give students a copy of the Software passage at their *READ 180* Level (1–4).

Reproduce passages or print them from SAM for students' fluency practice with partners or at home.

Teacher Tip

Administer the *Scholastic Reading Inventory (SRI)* to automatically place each student at the right level in the Topic Software: Levels 1–3 for Stage A or Levels 1–4 for Stages B and C. Re-administer the *SRI* three more times during the school year and adjust students' Software levels as needed (see page 159).

Level 3

Lexile Range 600–900L

READ 180 **Topic Software**
Passage 1.1
LEVEL 3

Crop Art

Stan Herd looks like an ordinary farmer. His farm is no ordinary [12]
farm, though. Herd's crops aren't planted on a grid, like the crops on [25]
most farms. Herd's a little more imaginative than that! As a crop [37]
artist, he plants and shapes his crops into huge pictures. In fact, [49]
Herd's creative efforts are so large that you need to view them from [62]
an airplane. [64]

One of Herd's grandest pictures grew from 20 acres of Kansas crops. [76]
Herd planted them in the pattern of sunflowers. He used a famous [88]
painting by Vincent van Gogh as a model. What kind of crops did [101]
Herd use? Naturally, he planted sunflowers! [107]

Of course, you don't have to visit the country to check out Herd's [120]
work. He went to New York City. There, Herd planted a lovely [132]
landscape that can be seen from nearby high-rises. [141]

Stan Herd's a pretty cool guy. From his fertile imagination comes [152]
innovative art that really grows on you. [159]

Use for fluency practice.

Resource Links
Teaching Resources: p. 113
SAM Keyword: Crop Art

READ 180 Topic Software 1.1 | 113

Use these word counts and the benchmarks in the corresponding Topic Software Teaching Plan to assess fluency.

Level 4

Lexile Range 800–1200L

READ 180 **Topic Software**
Passage 1.1
LEVEL 4

Crop Art

Don't be deceived by Stan Herd's appearance. He may look like [11]
any other farmer, but the truth is, he's an artist, too. [22]

Herd uses his farmland as a canvas and his crops are his media. [35]
Instead of planting the crops in a grid, Herd gets on his tractor and [49]
shapes the crops into pictures. [54]

Herd creates his art on a very large scale. To really appreciate it, [67]
you've got to view it from an airplane window. As Herd explains it, [80]
"My inspiration was to do something grand and innovative that [90]
stretches the boundaries." [93]

One of Herd's grandest pictures grew from 20 acres of Kansas [104]
crops planted in the pattern of sunflowers. The crops were–you [115]
guessed it–sunflowers. The work was modeled after a painting by [126]
the famous Dutch artist, Vincent van Gogh. You could call Herd a [138]
"Van Gogh on a tractor." [143]

You can't keep this artist down on the farm, though. Herd visited [155]
a big city in search of a new canvas for his work. Crop art in the city? [172]
You bet! With the help of a couple of first-time city farmers, Herd [186]
planted a beautiful landscape. No need for an airplane here–you can [198]
see the landscape from neighboring high-rises. [205]

Stan Herd's a cool guy with a passion for art. From his fertile [218]
imagination comes pictures that really grow on you! [226]

Use for fluency practice.

114 | ***READ 180*** Topic Software 1.1

Resource Links
Teaching Resources: p. 114
SAM Keyword: Crop Art

I notice that as the Software levels get higher, the passages become:

____

____

Monitoring Software Progress

Launch the Teacher Dashboard for a quick glance at student Software usage and performance. Log in to the Scholastic Achievement Manager (SAM) for in-depth evaluation of reading progress.

Teacher Dashboard Data Snapshots: *READ 180*

Check the *READ 180* Data Snapshot on your Teacher Dashboard Home Page for an at-a-glance look at the class average for time spent on the Topic Software each day. Use the data to ensure that your class schedule allows for the recommended 15–20 minutes per day and monitor whether students are maximizing their time on task in the Instructional Software rotation.

Notice that the target Software usage is 15–20 minutes per day for maximum reading growth.

Click here to see which students are using the Software for less than the target amount of time.

Compare recent usage data to previous data to look for trends over time and adjust your class schedule as needed.

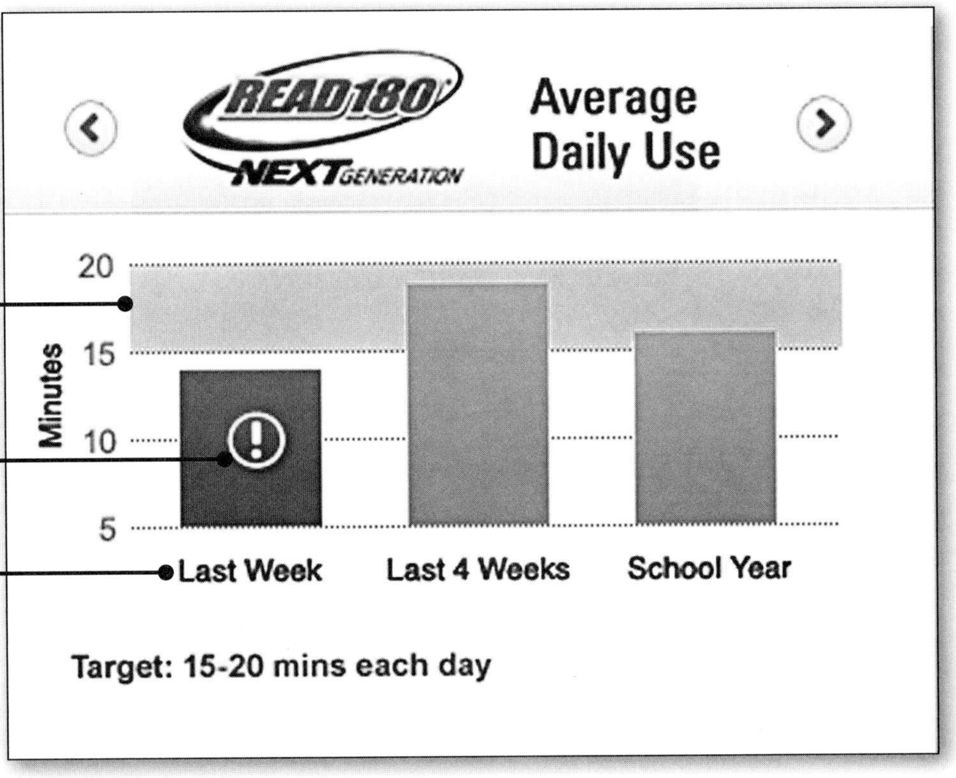

***READ 180* Data Snapshot, Teacher Dashboard**

Tech Tip

You can opt to receive email notifications about key changes in student Software performance, such as low usage or segment completion. Click Notifications on the Teacher Dashboard Home Page to select which notifications you would like to receive.

Additional *READ 180* Data

For more detailed information, go to the Teacher Dashboard Class Page to view the Data Snapshot in List View (see pages 173–174). In addition to time on-task data, List View also includes performance data for comprehension and vocabulary.

For further follow-up, run the following reports in SAM:

- ***READ 180* Reading Progress Report** Run this report for a comprehensive look at student participation and progress in the Software.
- ***READ 180* Comprehension Skills Grouping Report** Refer to this report at Reading CheckPoints for a closer look at the data that powers the Groupinator.
- ***READ 180* Comprehension Skills Report** Use this data to make data-driven adjustments to Groupinator recommendations and inform instructional planning.

SAM Reports

The Scholastic Achievement Manager (SAM) manages student data for all *READ 180* technology components, including the Topic Software. SAM provides you with comprehensive reports to evaluate performance at the class or student level. Run SAM reports every four to six weeks to monitor your students' progress over time.

SAM includes 16 *READ 180* reports to support you with monitoring student performance on the Topic Software. The following table summarizes when and why to run the *READ 180* class and student reports. Look for additional information on each report in the *Placement, Assessment, and Reporting Guide* pages 136–171.

Tech Tip

Use the Report Scheduler on the Teacher Dashboard to have your favorite SAM reports automatically emailed to you at a time of your choosing. Click Schedule a Report on the Dashboard Home Page. Use the pull-down menus to designate which report you want to receive and when.

If You Want to...	Run This Report
Class Reports	
Track the amount of time spent in each Topic Software Learning Zone	*READ 180* Comparative Time on Task Report
Monitor Topic Software progress and Lexile growth	*READ 180* Completion Success Report
Review performance on specific comprehension skills	*READ 180* Comprehension Skills Report
Regroup students at Reading CheckPoints	*READ 180* Comprehension Skills Grouping Report
Assign grades based on Topic Software scores	*READ 180* Grading Report
Track how a class is spending time in the Instructional Software rotation	*READ 180* Participation Report
Group students for decoding or fluency practice	*READ 180* Phonics and Word Study Grouping Report
Monitor overall Topic Software usage and progress	*READ 180* Reading Progress Report
Group students for spelling practice	*READ 180* Spelling Skills Grouping Report
Student Reports	
View progress in each Learning Zone and target instruction	*READ 180* Student Diagnostic Report
Track participation in the Topic Software and *Scholastic Reading Counts!*	*READ 180* Student Reading Report
Check current Topic Software segment scores and track progress over time	*READ 180* Student Segment Status Report
Monitor spelling progress on the Topic Software	*READ 180* Student Spelling Zone Report
Monitor word mastery on the Topic Software	*READ 180* Student Word Zone Report
Introduce families to *READ 180* and update them on their child's Topic Software performance	*READ 180* Parent Reports I and II

Assessing Fluency and Writing

Use the Portfolio tab in the Scholastic Achievement Manager (SAM) to evaluate student work from the Success and Writing Zones on the Topic Software.

SAM Student Digital Portfolio

The SAM Student Digital Portfolio collects and stores students' Final Recordings from the Success Zone and Respond & Write paragraphs from the Writing Zone. Click the purple Portfolio tab in SAM about once per week to see if any of your students have recently completed assignments ready for grading. Use the provided rubrics to evaluate the assignments, and share results with students to help them grow as readers and writers. Revisit stored student assignments throughout the year to monitor reading fluency and writing development over time (see pages 165–166).

Check the SAM Student Digital Portfolio Inbox for new assignments at least once per week.

Click an assignment to open it for grading.

Play Final Recordings during parent conferences so caregivers can hear their child's fluency growth over time.

Compare students' first drafts with their final paragraphs to evaluate their revision process during Respond & Write.

Share assignment grades and feedback with students during one-to-one conferences.

SAM Student Digital Portfolio

Holding Software Conferences

Check in with students during one-to-one conferences to informally assess their engagement, comprehension, and accountability with the *READ 180* Topic Software.

Why Conference?

Conferencing with students about their *READ 180* performance and progress fosters buy-in and increases motivation. One-to-one conferences allow you to discuss each student's Topic Software performance and hold him or her accountable for independent work. This is a good time to check that students understand how to select a Software Topic, engage in the activities, and demonstrate mastery in the Success and Writing Zones.

When to Conference

Consider holding student Software conferences during Small-Group Instruction. Toward the middle or end of *rBook* Workshops—when students are practicing skills with greater independence—have students work independently on an assignment during Small-Group Instruction. Then call one group member at a time to meet with you for a brief one-to-one conference.

Time each discussion so all students in the group have an opportunity to meet with you. Conferences typically last from one to four minutes per student. Aim to hold a conference with each student about once per month.

How to Conference

Follow these steps to facilitate a Topic Software conference with one student at a time.

1. Ask the student for general reactions to his or her current Software Topic and examples of Study Words from the Word and Spelling Zones. Prompt the student to share what he or she likes about the Software and answer any technical questions.
2. Locate the Teaching Plan for the student's current segment in *Teaching Resources for Topic Software.* Use the Discussion Questions to check understanding. Then discuss the prompts on the corresponding QuickWrite.
3. Share individual *READ 180* reports—such as the Reading Progress, Student Reading, or Student Segment Status Reports—with the student to discuss his or her Software usage and performance. Use the report to highlight successes and areas for growth. Guide students to set new learning goals for improvement (see page 247).
4. Find the segment reading passage at the student's level in *Teaching Resources for Topic Software*. Time the student reading the passage aloud, and compare results to the Fluency Benchmark Chart on the Teaching Plan. Have the student record his or her results on the Reading Rate Chart. Provide any follow-up strategies for continued fluency growth.

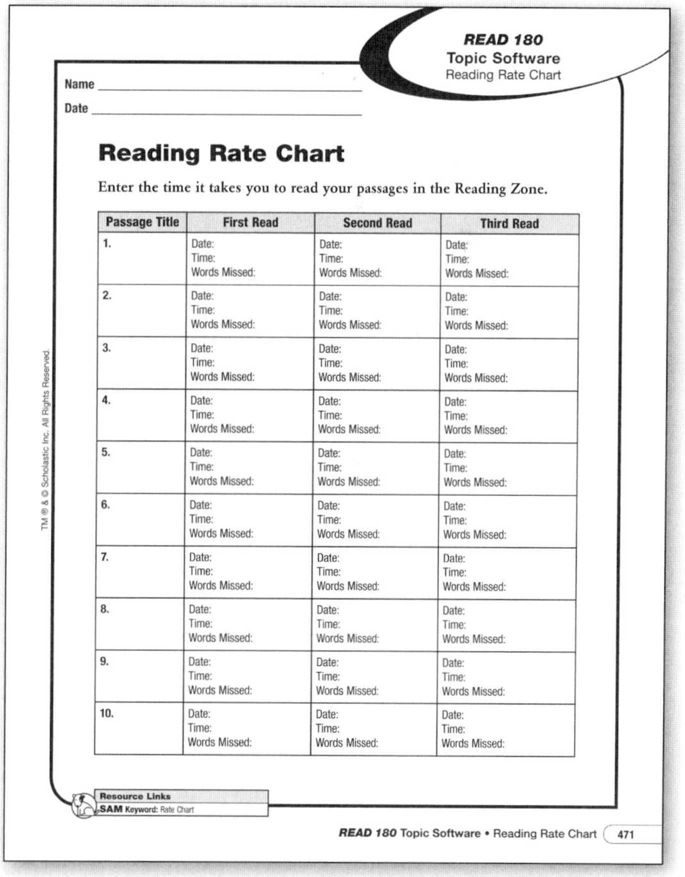

READ 180
Topic Software
Reading Rate Chart

Name ____________
Date ____________

Reading Rate Chart

Enter the time it takes you to read your passages in the Reading Zone.

Passage Title	First Read	Second Read	Third Read
1.	Date: Time: Words Missed:	Date: Time: Words Missed:	Date: Time: Words Missed:
2.	Date: Time: Words Missed:	Date: Time: Words Missed:	Date: Time: Words Missed:
3.	Date: Time: Words Missed:	Date: Time: Words Missed:	Date: Time: Words Missed:
4.	Date: Time: Words Missed:	Date: Time: Words Missed:	Date: Time: Words Missed:
5.	Date: Time: Words Missed:	Date: Time: Words Missed:	Date: Time: Words Missed:
6.	Date: Time: Words Missed:	Date: Time: Words Missed:	Date: Time: Words Missed:
7.	Date: Time: Words Missed:	Date: Time: Words Missed:	Date: Time: Words Missed:
8.	Date: Time: Words Missed:	Date: Time: Words Missed:	Date: Time: Words Missed:
9.	Date: Time: Words Missed:	Date: Time: Words Missed:	Date: Time: Words Missed:
10.	Date: Time: Words Missed:	Date: Time: Words Missed:	Date: Time: Words Missed:

Resource Links
SAM Keyword: Rate Chart

READ 180 Topic Software • Reading Rate Chart 471

Reading Rate Chart, *Teaching Resources for Topic Software*

Managing Instructional Software

Use these classroom management strategies to ensure that students engage in productive independent work during the daily Instructional Software rotation.

Reflection

Picture your classroom. How will you set up an inviting and motivating Software area?

Setting Up the Rotation Area

Ensure success in Instructional Software by setting up a clean, organized, comfortable area in which students can work. Remember that you will need enough computers for at least one-third of the students in each of your classes. Place a long table or several desks along one wall with many electrical outlets. On top, set up individual workstations with enough space between the computers and chairs that students will not get distracted by their peers.

Consider these additional tips for setting up and organizing the Software area:

- Ensure that all computer screens are facing out toward the classroom, instead of facing a wall. This allows you to keep an eye on all screens from your position in Small-Group Instruction and make sure students are staying on task.
- Display the Topic Software Poster to increase interest and help students select engaging Topics.
- Number each computer, to make it easy to identify and assign to students.
- Tape a list of students assigned to each workstation on the side of the computer monitor for your reference.
- Stick adhesive hooks to the side of each computer monitor for students to hang their headsets.
- Keep a file of the leveled passages and QuickWrites from *Teaching Resources for Topic Software*. Encourage students to take copies for additional fluency and writing practice at home.

Teacher Tip

Refer to page 40 of *Getting Started: Your First Three Weeks With READ 180* for a model lesson on teaching Instructional Software procedures to your students.

Establishing Software Procedures

Establish procedures for students to follow during Instructional Software to maximize their daily time on task. Think about what you want your students to accomplish each day and how you want them to handle the *READ 180* materials. Explicitly teach each procedure at the beginning of the year so students understand your expectations for behavior and independent work (see page 93). Create either a large poster to display the Software procedures or small checklists to tape to each computer.

Add any procedures specific to your classroom to the suggested list below:

- Selecting a Topic.
- Logging in and out of the Software.
- Using the Topic Software Daily Log (page 242) to track ongoing progress.
- Recording passages using the microphone.
- Using the leveled reading passages and QuickWrites for additional practice.
- Reporting any technical problems.
- ______________________________________
- ______________________________________

Checking In With Students

Monitor student engagement by briefly visiting the Instructional Software area whenever students in Small-Group Instruction are working independently. Stop by each computer workstation to check in with students and answer any questions. Ask students to summarize the segment video, read aloud their leveled passage or writing paragraph, or share a few of their Study Words.

Remind students that you are using SAM reports to keep track of everything they do on the Topic Software. Routinely check each student's Topic Software Daily Log (page 242) to increase accountability for independent work.

Preparing for Technical Issues

All computers may experience technical difficulties from time to time. A bit of proactive planning will go a long way toward preserving the Instructional Model and keeping students on task even if the computers go down. Consider these tips for handling technical problems that arise during a *READ 180* class:

- Provide each workstation with a red plastic cup or flag. If students experience technical difficulties, they can place the flag on top of their computer monitor or by their chair to let you know that they need help. While they are waiting for assistance, students can begin working on a QuickWrite or reading their independent book so they do not miss out on any learning time.
- Keep a notebook or log in the Instructional Software area to track technical needs that arise. Ask students to use it to record the exact error messages they see on the Software to best assist the technology support team.
- Visit the Scholastic Product Support website at **www.scholastic.com/education/productsupport** to download Software updates and manuals.

Teacher Tip

If your school or district has a Product Maintenance and Support Plan, call Scholastic Tech Support for help with *READ 180* technology issues. Contact them at 1-800-283-5974 or TechSupport@scholastic.com.

"Plan B" Assignments

Have at least one paper-based backup assignment ready to use in case one or more of your *READ 180* computers is down for an entire class period or longer. Try these "Plan B" assignments for students to complete independently during the Instructional Software rotation:

eReads If the problem is with the Topic Software on the server only, not the computer or Internet, then have students read an eReads Collection during this time. Remind them to answer the Think Tank questions and explore the Like This? Read More links to learn all about the selected content area.

QuickWrites Have students catch up on any Topic Software, Paperback, Audiobook, or eReads QuickWrites they have not yet completed. Keep copies of these reproducibles in the Instructional Software and Modeled and Independent Reading areas so students can easily access them on their own.

Library Book Projects *Teaching Resources for Modeled and Independent Reading* includes six engaging Final Book Projects that students can do after finishing a book. For example, students can write a book review, create a new front cover, or make a plot timeline. Reproduce copies of the Final Book Projects to keep in the Instructional Software area. Provide time for students to present their projects to the class when they are done.

Reflecting on Instructional Software

During training, practice Numbered Heads Routine to reflect on how you plan to implement Instructional Software in your classroom.

Research Says

Students learn more from collaborative discussions when they are held accountable for participating and listening actively.
Feldman & Denti, 2004.

Group

The first step of the Numbered Heads Routine is forming small groups for discussion. Get together with three people who are sitting near you in training. Take turns numbering off from one to four so that each person in your group has a number. Write down your number below for reference.

My number is: ______________________________.

Respond

Prepare for your small-group discussion by thinking about how Instructional Software will look in your classroom. Jot down your ideas below.

Consider these questions to guide your reflection: *How will you support students with using the Topic Software effectively? How will you monitor students' Software progress and hold them accountable for productive independent work? What ideas do you have for setting up the rotation area?*

____

____

____

____

Discuss

Take about three minutes to discuss your reflections with the other members of your small group. Use these sentence starters to structure your conversation:

- *I like the way you* ______________________________.
- *I agree with* ______________ *because* ______________.
- *My idea is different. I think* ______________________________.
- *I hear your views, but I disagree because* ______________________.

Share

Listen for your number during the final whole-group discussion. Be prepared to share a summary of what your small group discussed if your number is called.

When sharing, use the sentence starters below to acknowledge similarities and build upon other groups' ideas:

- *We agree, but would also add that* ______________________________.
- *We could combine these ideas by* ______________________________.

Teacher Tip

When using Numbered Heads, prepare an objective method for choosing which group number to share. For example, you could create a spinner or keep a jar with numbered slips of paper. See *rBook Teacher's Edition* pages T120–T121 for additional tips on using this routine.

TEACHER IMPLEMENTATION GUIDE

Modeled and Independent Reading

Overview: Modeled and Independent Reading

The Modeled and Independent Reading rotation supports students with the sustained practice they need to make reading growth.

Understanding the Model for Blended Learning

Modeled and Independent Reading is one of the three small-group rotations that occur after Whole-Group Instruction in the *READ 180* Next Generation Instructional Model. One small group of students works independently in Modeled and Independent Reading while two other groups engage in Small-Group Instruction and Instructional Software. Groups rotate depending on your model to ensure all students experience all three rotations.

READ 180 Instructional Model

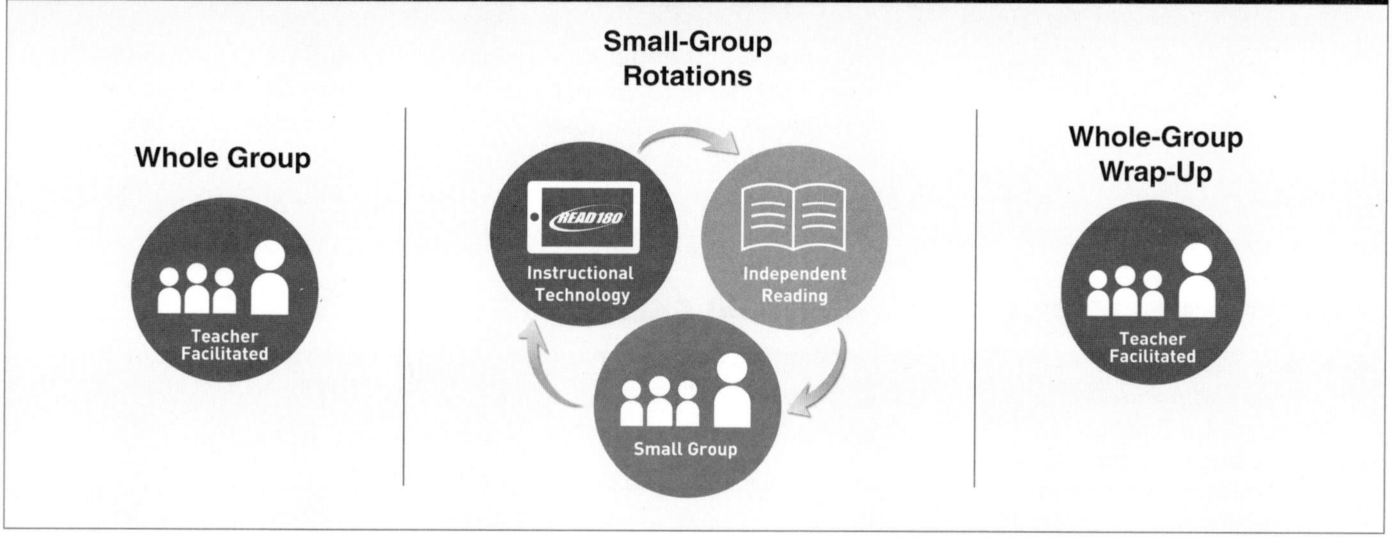

Building Your Knowledge

Track your learning about **Modeled and Independent Reading** using the K-W-L chart below. Use the first column to reflect on what you already know about this rotation from the Student Experience in training. Jot down any questions in the middle column. In the last column, record notes as you learn more about Modeled and Independent Reading.

K	W	L
I already know . . .	*I want to know . . .*	*I have learned . . .*

Understanding Modeled and Independent Reading

Support your students with daily Modeled and Independent Reading to help them build comprehension, fluency, and vocabulary skills for reading success.

Research Says

Different academic disciplines are characterized by different sets of literacy practices. Students need frequent opportunities to apply comprehension strategies in different types of texts.

Biancarosa & Snow, 2006

Purpose

Students experience **Modeled** reading with the *READ 180* Audiobooks and eReads to learn best practices for critical reading. The Audiobooks enable students to access grade-level text with audio support provided by a Narrator and Reading Coach. The Web-based eReads are short nonfiction articles for students to learn more about the content areas they explore on the *READ 180* Topic Software. Students can choose to hear each eRead read aloud by a model reader with accurate fluency, phrasing, and expression.

Students engage in **Independent** reading using the *READ 180* Paperbacks and eReads to get the practice, practice, practice they need for reading growth. The high-interest, age-appropriate Paperbacks allow students to read text at their level to build comprehension, vocabulary, and fluency over time. The eReads are also leveled and include embedded scaffolds to support student independence with complex informational text.

Teacher Tip

See *Getting Started: Your First Three Weeks With READ 180*, available in your Teacher Bookshelf or on ITS, for model lessons on introducing the Instructional Model and teaching students how to engage in Modeled and Independent Reading.

Instructional Focus

Help students become better readers during Modeled and Independent Reading by guiding them to:

- Select Paperbacks at their level for targeted reading practice.
- Use the Audiobooks and CD or mp3 players to access grade-level texts.
- Listen carefully to Audiobook think-alouds that model good reading habits and self-monitoring for understanding.
- Follow along in the Audiobook text as they listen to modeled fluent reading.
- Use eReads to build reading endurance with informational texts.
- Click embedded eReads scaffolds to build vocabulary and critical thinking.
- Keep track of their daily reading progress by completing a Reading Log (SAM Keyword: Reading Log).
- Respond to texts with quick writing assignments and graphic organizers.
- Take *Scholastic Reading Counts! (SRC!)* quizzes to demonstrate understanding of the texts they have read.
- Check the My Reads tab on the Student Dashboard to track and rate their completed books and eReads.

Teacher Materials

Use *Teaching Resources for Modeled and Independent Reading* to support students with Teaching Plans, Book Overviews, Comprehension Graphic Organizers, and QuickWrites. Display the Paperbacks and Audiobooks Poster and the eReads Poster in your classroom to help students with selecting high-interest texts.

Teaching Resources for Modeled and Independent Reading

Library Posters

Student Materials

Monitor students as they independently read the Audiobooks, Paperbacks, and eReads for daily practice with comprehension, fluency, vocabulary, and self-monitoring.

Audiobooks

Paperbacks

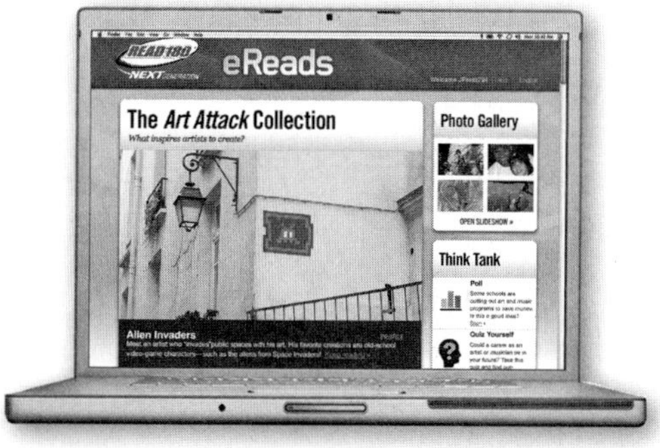

eReads

Assessment Materials

Administer the *Scholastic Reading Inventory (SRI)* College & Career to identify student reading levels. Use *Scholastic Reading Counts! (SRC!)* quizzes to assess students' understanding of Paperbacks, Audiobooks, and eReads. Log in to SAM, the Scholastic Achievement Manager, to monitor performance on *SRI* and *SRC!* Use the *Placement, Assessment, and Reporting Guide* for comprehensive support with assessing progress in Modeled and Independent Reading.

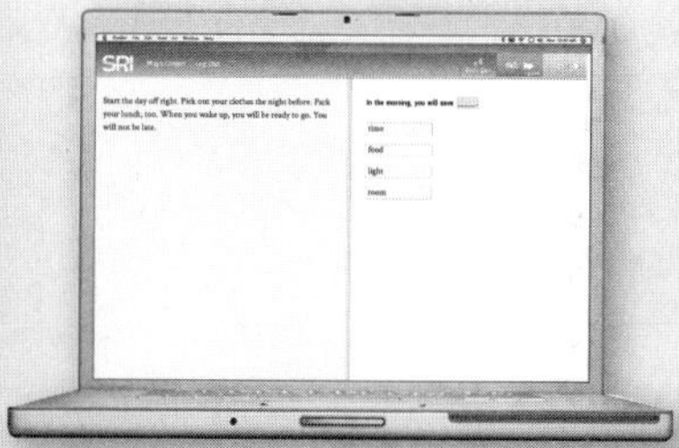

Scholastic Reading Inventory (SRI) **College & Career**

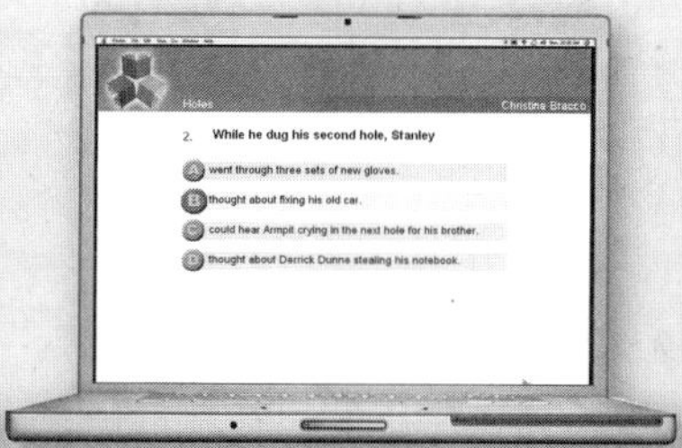

Scholastic Reading Counts! (SRC!)

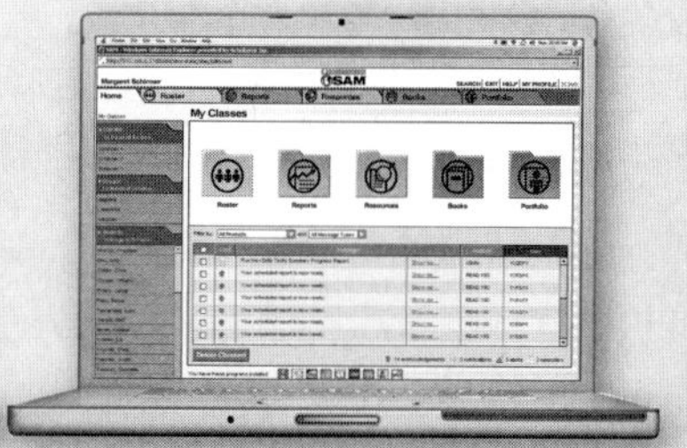

Scholastic Achievement Manager (SAM)

Placement, Assessment, and Reporting Guide

Targeting Reading Practice: Paperbacks

The *READ 180* Paperbacks provide students with opportunities to read age-appropriate books at their level and experience reading confidence and success.

Selection of Titles

Your *READ 180* Library offers a comprehensive selection of engaging Paperbacks at a range of levels to motivate your students with independent reading. Stage A includes 51 different Paperbacks, with 17 titles at each Level (1–3). Stages B and C each include 60 different Paperbacks, with 15 titles at each Level (1–4). All Stages have five copies of each title. The Paperbacks come in a range of genres, such as historical fiction, graphic classics, and debates. About half of the titles are nonfiction to build proficiency with informational text.

Key Features for Reading Growth

The Paperbacks incorporate research-based features to promote students' independent reading success and growth.

Research-Based Feature	Why It Helps
Leveled text	Reading success results from practice with texts that have the right level of challenge—not too easy, not too hard (National Reading Panel, 2000). The Paperbacks come in a range of levels—3 in Stage A, 4 in Stages B and C—so all of your students have the opportunity to read independently with confidence.
High-interest, relevant, age-appropriate topics	Motivation is a strong predictor of reading comprehension, especially for students with disabilities (Heo, 2007). Every Paperback has a relevant, high-interest topic so students feel motivated and *want* to read each day.
Wide variety of genres and text types	Students benefit from reading a diverse array of texts in a range of subjects to build knowledge and broaden their perspectives (Common Core State Standards, 2010). The Paperbacks provide practice with a variety of genres—such as historical fiction, biography, and graphic classics—and text types, such as news articles, short stories, and plays.

Explore a *READ 180* Paperback

Many of your older struggling readers may have never read an entire book before. Embedded scaffolds in the Paperbacks—such as illustrations, critical reading questions, chapter previews, and word definitions—help students feel comfort and control while reading. Their increased confidence will make them *want* to keep reading until the end!

Encourage students to read the chapter previews to build a mental model for what is to come next.

The bomb squad's job is not a blast. One false move can mean it's all over!

Bomb-Squad Techs: *Life or Death*

The clock is ticking. A powerful bomb has been left on a train! In seconds, it will blow up. The bomb will rip through the train. It will send scraps of metal flying. If that happens, you are dead!

You are on the Bomb Squad. It is your job to **defuse** the bomb.

A bomb squad is a team of specialists. They protect people from explosive devices. These devices vary in size and power. Some are small pipe bombs. Others are high-tech car bombs.

Luckily, bomb-squad technicians don't defuse huge bombs every day. In fact, most "techs" face mega-threats like this only during training.

12

Stage B Paperback

anyone in the area.

"Bomb techs are the best of the best," Carter says. They have to be. If they are wrong, things can blow up in their faces!

Why would a bomb-squad tech have to be patient?

Today, techs use robots to check out possible bombs.

17

Refer students to the glossary in the back of many Paperbacks to see definitions for words they may not know.

Guide students to monitor their understanding with end-of-chapter questions in many of the Paperbacks.

Teacher Tip

Hold students accountable for careful reading by having them write out answers to end-of-chapter questions in a notebook. Review their responses during one-to-one conferences to discuss books and assess understanding.

Accessing Grade-Level Text: Audiobooks

The *READ 180* Audiobooks allow struggling readers to develop good reading skills and strategies while enjoying authentic grade-level literature.

Selection of Titles

Every *READ 180* Audiobook consists of a book on CD with a corresponding paperback copy. Students listen to the CD while following along in the hard-copy version. Each *READ 180* Stage includes 12 different Audiobooks, with five copies of each title. All of the Audiobooks are authentic, unabridged, grade-level texts, so your struggling students can access the same complex literature that their peers in other classes are reading.

Key Features for Reading Growth

Research-based features in the Audiobooks build good reading habits and comprehension strategies for success.

Research-Based Feature	Why It Helps
Complex text	The ability to read complex text is essential for achievement in college, career, and life (Adams, 2009). The Audiobooks scaffold authentic grade-level literature for your struggling readers to help them access and develop proficiency with complex text.
Literary narratives	Students build literary and cultural knowledge through wide and deep reading of literary texts (Common Core State Standards, 2010). The Audiobooks allow students to enjoy the same classic and contemporary works as their grade-level peers and learn about different cultures, times, and perspectives.
Embedded think-alouds	Internal questioning is automatic for good readers, but must be modeled repeatedly for struggling readers to help them internalize good reading habits (Moats, 2001). The Reading Coach on each Audiobook thinks aloud to model reading skills and strategies, which helps students understand how to question and self-monitor as they read.

Explore a ***READ 180*** Audiobook

The Audiobooks offer struggling readers the opportunity to develop good reading skills and habits while enjoying grade-level literature. Each Audiobook is narrated by one voice, while a second voice occasionally interjects to think aloud and model best practices for reading comprehension and self-monitoring. Therefore, when reading an Audiobook, students will always hear two distinct voices that support them with building reading independence:

- **The Audiobook Narrator,** who reads aloud, modeling fluent phrasing and reading expression as the student tracks the hard-copy text.
- **The Reading Coach,** who models the comprehension, vocabulary, and self-monitoring strategies that successful readers employ while reading.

Prepare your students for success with the Audiobooks by explaining that they will hear two voices. Share the purpose of each voice and encourage students to practice the good habits and self-monitoring strategies they learn from the Reading Coach whenever they are reading.

Audiobooks Excerpt

From *The Star Fisher*,
by Laurence Yep (Scholastic, 1991)

Stage B Audiobook

Narrator: Mama put her arms around us and ushered us down the hall. “Make sure you bring two cups of water to Papa,” she instructed me. “One cup for drinking and one cup for his ink. I have a feeling he’ll have a lot of poetry tonight.”

Reading Coach: “Write a lot of poetry”? Huh? Oh, I get it. Remember a few pages back, when Mama said Papa always feels better after he’s written a poem? Well, tonight he’s got a lot to be upset about. Dinner got burned. He didn’t exactly hit it off with the landlady. And then those creeps came to vandalize the house. Papa’s going to have to write a lot of poems to recover from all of that.

Tech Tip

Some Audiobooks are also accessible as mp3 files. Download a list of available titles, with instructions for downloading the files, from SAM Resources using the Keyword: MP3A, MP3B, or MP3C, depending on your *READ 180* Stage.

Diving Into Content Areas: eReads

The nonfiction eReads enable students to dive deep into the engaging content areas that they explore on the *READ 180* Topic Software and build proficiency with rigorous informational text.

Collections of Articles

The Web-based eReads library consists of 15 nonfiction Collections that correspond to the 15 Software Topics in your *READ 180* Stage. Each Collection contains four engaging, informational texts of different types, such as news articles, interviews, editorials, and science articles. Every eRead is available in two different levels—one for students in *READ 180* Levels 1 and 2, and one for students in Levels 3 and 4—to promote independent reading success. The software automatically provides the appropriate version based on each student's Software level.

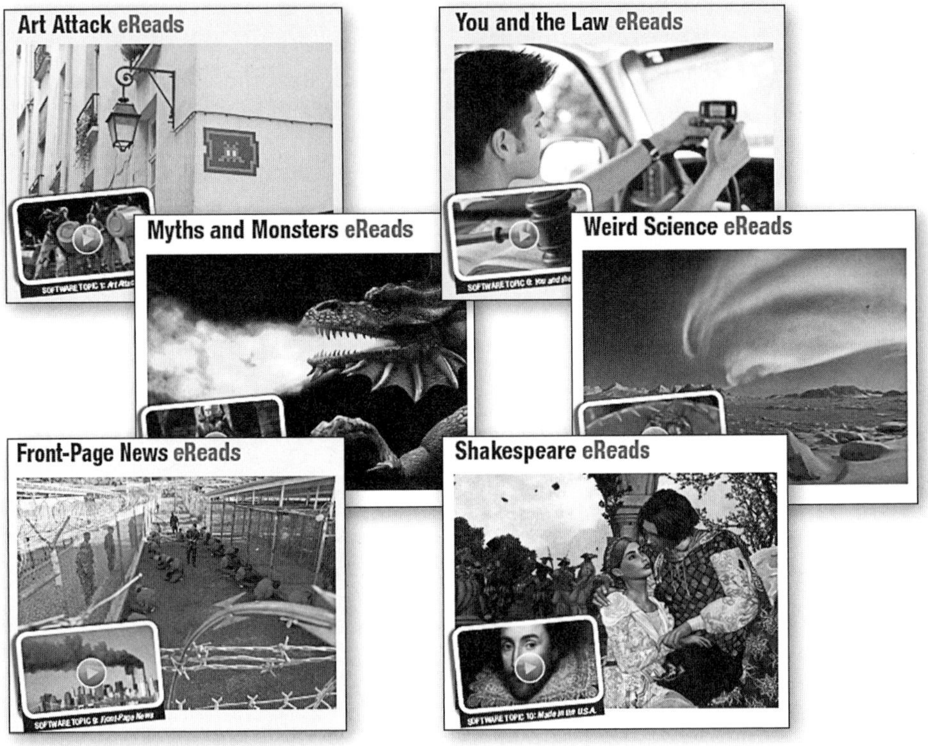

Key Features for Reading Growth

The research-based eReads help students build reading independence for future college and career success.

Research-Based Feature	Why It Helps
Informational text	Informational literacy is central to success, and even survival, in schooling, the workplace and the community (Duke, 2010). The scaffolded eReads support students with developing reading independence and confidence with rigorous informational text.
Critical reading questions	"The ability to find, analyze, and synthesize written information provides access to lifelong learning in a rapidly changing world" (Daggett & Hasselbring, 2007). eReads support students with building critical reading skills with embedded higher-order thinking prompts.
Content-area connections	Knowledge acquired through learning about content is fundamental for successful reading comprehension (Hirsch, 2003). The nonfiction eReads help students build a foundation of content and vocabulary knowledge for successful comprehension across content areas.

Explore an eRead

Guide your students to access the online eReads to learn more about their Software Topics. Every eRead incorporates comprehension, vocabulary, and read-aloud support, so students can experience independent reading success in the classroom or at home. The default setting for eReads is "off," so use the *READ 180* Program Settings menu in SAM to allow your students access to the eReads website (see page 159).

eReads Art Attack Collection, Stage B

Explain that students can "unlock" a Collection once they have started work in the corresponding Topic on the Software.

Tell struggling students to listen to the eRead read aloud by a model reader to hear fluent phrasing and expression.

Remind students to click highlighted academic and content words to see and hear their definitions.

Encourage students to reflect on embedded critical thinking prompts to self-monitor their reading comprehension.

Tech Tip

Access all eReads Collections for your *READ 180* Stage by clicking [eReads icon] in the Web Gateway on the Teacher Dashboard Home Page. Click Print at the top of any eRead for a hard-copy version that students can read in the classroom or at home.

Participating in the eReads Student Experience

During training, use the *READ 180* Next Generation Software Simulator to explore the engaging, Web-based eReads from a student's perspective.

Choose a Collection

Select an unlocked eReads Collection to learn more about a Software Topic.

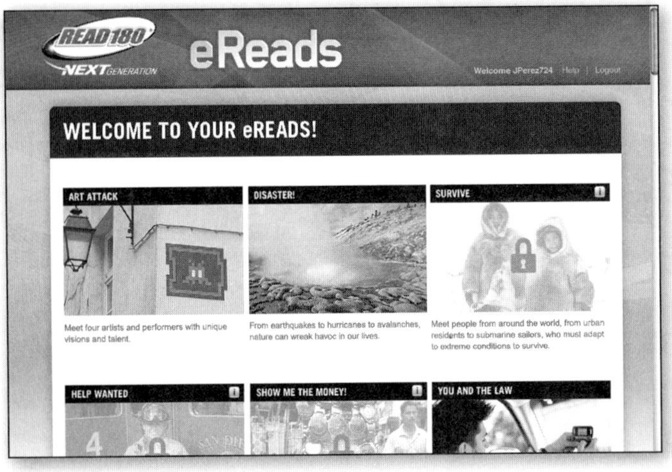

Directions

1. Log in by clicking **eReads** on the **Student Access** screen. Enter your username and password. Your eReads Home Page will appear.
2. See which eReads Collections you have unlocked by working in the corresponding Software Topic. Locked Collections are grayed out with a lock icon.

> **Tech Tip**
> **Once a Collection unlocks, it stays unlocked. The student can revisit it as many times as he or she wants throughout the year, as long as you have set eReads to "on" for that student (see page 159).**

3. Read each unlocked Collection title and essential question. Hover your mouse over a Collection to see a summary of the four eReads it contains.
4. Click an image to open the Collection.

> **Tech Tip**
> **You can access all eReads Collections by clicking in the Web Gateway on the Teacher Dashboard Home Page.**

Read an Article

Read an eRead article with scaffolded support to learn more about a content area.

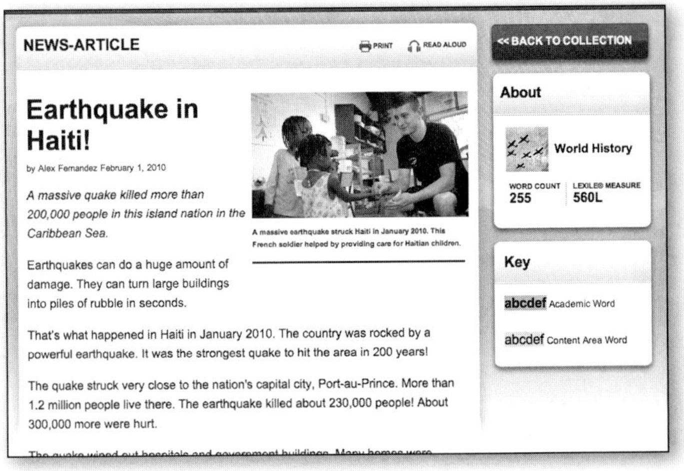

Directions

1. Log in to eReads using your username and password. Click a Collection to open it.
2. Select one of the four articles that appear under the Collection name by clicking either the title or the accompanying photo.

> **Tech Tip**
> **The article in the largest space below the Collection title rotates, so all four articles are featured in turn.**

3. Click the **Read Aloud** icon at the top right of the article to hear the text read aloud fluently.
4. Click each highlighted academic and content-area vocabulary word to see and hear the definition.
5. Click the + icon at the end of each section or paragraph to reveal a higher-order thinking prompt to reflect on mentally as you read.
6. Scroll down to read the complete article and see a glossary for all highlighted vocabulary words.
7. Click **Print** at the top of the screen to print a hard-copy of the eRead.

Complete Think Tank Activities

Complete the engaging Think Tank activities after exploring all four eReads in a Collection.

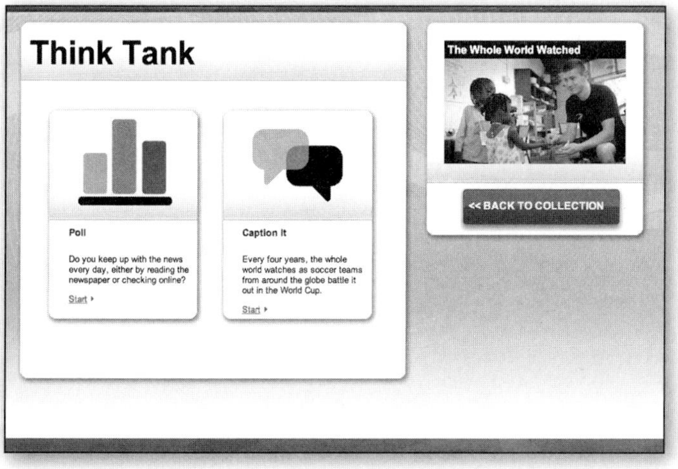

Directions

1. Log in to eReads using your username and password. Click a Collection to open it.
2. Click **Open Think Tank** on the right of the Collection Home Page to access two related activities.

> **Tech Tip**
>
> **For each Think Tank, students receive two out of four possible activities: Poll, Rank It, Quiz Yourself, and Say What? Student responses are not reported.**

3. Click **Start** at the bottom of each Think Tank box to reveal a pop-up with the activity and directions.
4. Follow the activity directions to answer all questions. Then click **OK** to review your responses.
5. Click **OK** again to exit the activity.
6. Click **Back to Collection** on the right side of the screen to return to the Collection Home Page.

> **Tech Tip**
>
> **Encourage students to explore the Photo Gallery on the eReads Collection Home Page. The Photo Gallery has 10 Topic-related images and captions.**

Extend Your Learning

Use the Read More links to learn more about an eReads content area.

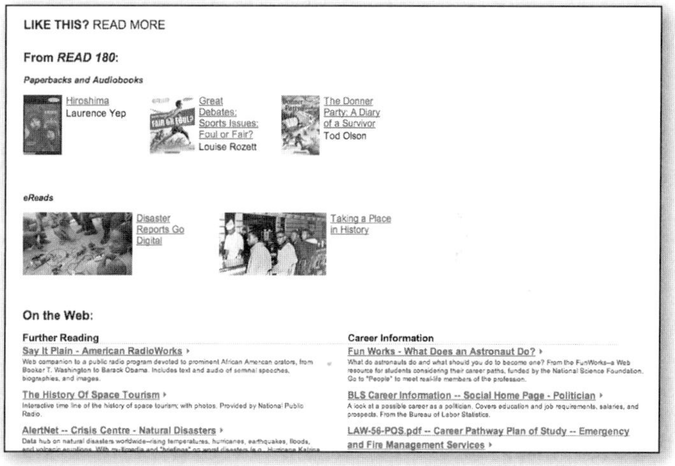

Directions

1. Log in to eReads using your username and password. Click a Collection to open it.
2. Scroll down to view the **Like This? Read More** section at the bottom of the Collection Home Page.
3. See recommended titles of *READ 180* Library books and eReads that relate to the Collection.

> **Tech Tip**
>
> **Hover your computer mouse over the cover of each recommended text to see a pop-up with a brief description, including the Lexile measure.**

4. Click the **On the Web: Further Reading** links to visit age-appropriate, student-friendly websites for more information about the Collection content area.
5. Click the **On the Web: Career Information** links to visit websites with more information on real-world careers related to the Collection.

Matching Students to Texts

Set your students up for independent reading success by matching them to engaging texts that they *can* read and *want* to read.

Targeting Reading Levels

Help your students grow as readers by matching them to texts at the right level. Research shows that "just-right books"—texts that are not too hard or too easy—allow students to feel confident and engaged with reading while also providing just enough of a challenge to encourage reading growth.

Administering *SRI* to Identify Student Lexile Measures

The *Scholastic Reading Inventory (SRI)* is a computer-based assessment that makes it easy to identify your students' independent reading levels, as represented by the Lexile Framework for Reading. Administer *SRI* College & Career at the beginning of the year to identify a baseline Lexile for each student. The *READ 180* Topic Software uses these Lexile measures to place students at the appropriate level for reading on the Software.

You can also use the Lexile measures to match students to independent books they can read using the chart below. The *READ 180* Paperbacks are leveled based on Lexile measures to make it easy to match your students to just-right books. Re-administer *SRI* College & Career three more times during the year to track reading growth. As your students' Lexile measures grow, continue to match them to Paperbacks at the right *READ 180* Level to encourage ongoing reading enjoyment and success.

***READ 180* Level**	**Grade-Level Equivalent**	**Lexile Range**
Level 1	Grades 1.5–2.5	200L–450L
Level 2	Grades 2.5–4.0	400L–700L
Level 3	Grades 4.0–6.9	600L–900L
Level 4	Grades 6.0–8.9 (Stage B) or 12.0 (Stage C)	800L–1200L

Using Lexile Measures to Select Books

The Lexile Framework is different from other reading measurements because it places both readers and texts on a common scale. When the Lexile measures for a student and a text match, students are able to read with 75% comprehension, which promotes reading growth without frustration. See pages 20–25 in the *Placement, Assessment, and Reporting Guide,* or visit **www.Lexile.com** to learn more about the Lexile Framework for Reading.

Match students to books at or below their Lexile measures for independent reading. It is important for students to experience success and enjoyment so they want to keep reading on their own. A good rule of thumb is to **guide students to choose independent reading books that fall within a range of 100L below to 50L above their Lexile measure**. For example, a student with a Lexile of 500L could select independent reading books with Lexile measures of 400L to 550L. You may want to guide your reluctant readers to choose texts with even lower Lexile measures to build confidence at the beginning of the school year.

Run the *SRI* Text Complexity Report for support with identifying easy, on level, and challenging texts for your students. The **On Level** range is 100L below to 50L above each student's Lexile measure.

Other Factors to Consider

In addition to reading levels, consider these other factors when matching students to texts for independent reading.

- **Text Complexity** The complexity of a text depends on quantitative difficulty (Lexile), qualitative aspects, and the specific reader and task. Qualitative aspects of a text include its levels of meaning, structure, language, concepts, and knowledge demands. Check the summary for each Paperback, Audiobook, or eRead in *Teaching Resources for Modeled and Independent Reading* to see the text's complexity. Carefully consider maturity, background knowledge, and attitude about reading before matching students to more complex texts. For example, a book with a low Lexile and a high qualitative measure can be deceptively challenging for reluctant readers.
- **Areas of Interest** Research shows that students are more motivated to read books that match their personal interests. Guide students to identify their interests using the Reader's Survey (SAM Keyword: Survey). Display the *READ 180* Library Posters for students to peruse for texts that match their interests.
- **Content Knowledge** Familiarity with a topic and its content-specific vocabulary enables students to read texts at a more challenging level than usual. Encourage students to choose more challenging texts—such as eReads—to learn more about topics they already know a lot about. Conversely, guide them to select less challenging texts on topics that are new to them.

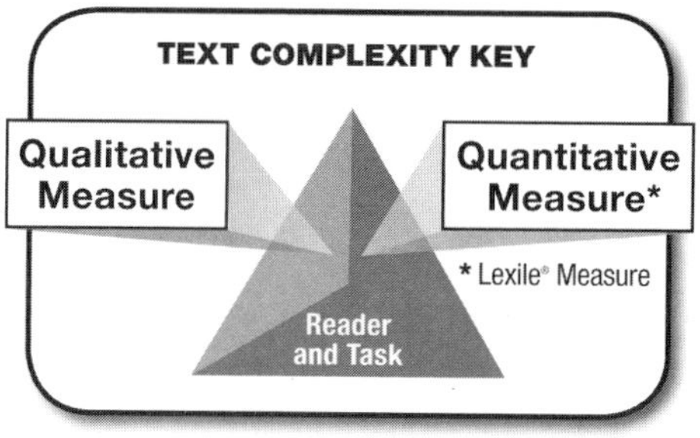

Procedure for Choosing a Book

After directing students to a selection of texts at the right level, allow them to make their own choices about which ones to read. This increases motivation and ownership. Support students with making good choices by explicitly teaching how to select a book. Here is a suggested teaching plan:

1. Explain how the *READ 180* Library books are organized in their crates. Point out the different types of texts: Paperbacks, Audiobooks, and eReads.
2. Model how to use the Paperbacks and Audiobooks Poster by scanning the available book covers and reading a few of the summaries.
3. Point out how the Paperbacks are categorized by level to help narrow down the selection to books within students' Lexile ranges.
4. Select two or three Paperbacks or Audiobooks that appeal to you from the poster. Demonstrate how to locate them in the crates. (For eReads, project the website onto your board and demonstrate how to log in. Then model previewing and choosing an unlocked Collection that seems interesting to you. Explain that Collections become unlocked for reading once students have started work in the corresponding Software Topic.)
5. Model previewing each book by thinking aloud and asking questions like:
   - *What does the cover tell me about what this book might be like?*
   - *Let me read the back. Does the topic or story seem interesting?*
   - *Do the text features or illustrations grab my attention?*
6. Select the book that most appeals to you and explain why.

Teacher Tip

See page 39 of *Getting Started: Your First Three Weeks With READ 180*, available in your Teacher Bookshelf or on ITS, for a model lesson on teaching students how to select books they will enjoy.

Using *Teaching Resources* for Reading Support

Teaching Resources for Modeled and Independent Reading **is your comprehensive guide for supporting students with success during the Modeled and Independent Reading rotation.**

What's Inside

Use this book throughout the year to monitor students as they independently read the Paperbacks, Audiobooks, and eReads. Look for three key types of support:

- **Professional Development** articles provide research-based background, assessment information, and practical classroom management tips for Modeled and Independent Reading.
- **Teaching Support** plans offer insight into the content of the independent reading texts to help you recommend and discuss books with your students and monitor their understanding.
- **Skills Practice and Assessment** resources help you reinforce comprehension and writing skills, increase reading engagement, and hold students accountable for independent work.

***Teaching Resources for Modeled and Independent Reading*, Stage B**

Using the Resources

Teaching Resources for Modeled and Independent Reading also includes classroom and reproducible resources to guide students' daily independent skills practice:

- **Teaching Resources:** Use the Overviews and Teaching Plans to learn about your students' independent books and support them during reading.
- **Student Resources:** Make copies of the reproducible Comprehension Graphic Organizers, QuickWrites, and Higher-Order Thinking (H.O.T.) Pages for students to apply key comprehension skills and strategies for reading success.
- **Additional Resources:** Use the Final Projects, Classroom Management pages, and Answer Keys to motivate, manage, and assess your students' daily independent reading.

Tech Tip

Access digital versions of the book's resources on SAM. Refer to the Resource Links at the bottom of pages to find the SAM Keywords. Enter the exact Keyword in the SAM Resource Quick Search to download and print a resource for use in your classroom.

Teaching Plans

The Teaching Plans provide you with tools to monitor and support students with the Paperbacks, Audiobooks, and eReads. Each plan includes a summary, discussion questions, comprehension skill practice, and links to resources.

Resources for Modeled and Independent Reading

Moderate 1 | HL530L

Text Complexity | Genre: Nonfiction | Pages: 40

Danger Is My Business

The World's Deadliest Jobs

by John DiConsiglio

SAM Keywords

Resources	SAM Keywords
• **Comprehension:** Problem and Solution, p. 115	Deadliest Jobs
• QuickWrites, p. 116	Deadliest Jobs
• Final Projects, pp. 257–262	Final Projects
• Reading Log, p. 263	Reading Log

Comprehension:
✓Problem and Solution

SCAFFOLDING TRACKER

✓ **Skill:** Problem and Solution

Teach Practice Apply Review Reteach

Introduced in Teacher's Edition, p. 121

Apply Have students complete the graphic organizer as they read to identify the problems and solutions for each job.

p. 115

Paperback Summary

Danger Is My Business will introduce kids to six extremely dangerous jobs: Motocross driver, bomb-squad technician, Alaskan crab fisher, miner, tornado chaser, and yes, believe it or not, competitive ballroom dancer. Each chapter tells exactly what makes the job so dangerous, and why people feel compelled to do the job. In some cases the thrill of the risk makes it worthwhile, and in others the financial reward for taking the risk is the payoff. Kids will learn about the injuries that people sustain doing these jobs, and in some cases, the fatalities.

Create Interest *Not every job involves going to an office or sitting at a desk. Some people chase killer storms or perform death-defying stunts for a crowd! Read about people who perform the world's most dangerous jobs—and discover why they picked these careers.*

Discussion Questions

After Chapter 2 Both Motocross drivers and bomb-squad technicians get a thrill from their work. How might the thrill be different for each job? *(The drivers might get a thrill from doing stunts that impress the crowd. The technicians might get a thrill from knowing that their work might save lives, or end their own!)* **MAKE INFERENCES**

After Chapter 3 How do fishers catch Alaskan king crabs? What is dangerous about this part of the job? *(They fill giant pots with fish, then lower the pots into the waves. This attracts the crabs. Then they pull the pots back up. The heavy pots can knock the fishers off the boats. Also, the pots hang from gears that can crush the fishers.)* **SUMMARIZE**

After Chapter 5 What causes cave-ins in a mine? *(Large columns hold up rock that separates the mine from the surface. When miners dig for coal, these columns can shift, and collapse. This can cause the rock to come crashing down.)* **CAUSE AND EFFECT**

After Chapter 6 Why do you think competitive dancing is getting faster and faster? *(The faster dancers move, the more exciting and impressive the dancing looks.)* **DRAW CONCLUSIONS**

Check Progress

Scholastic Reading Counts! computer book quiz

• Assessment Guide, p. 271

34 ***READ 180*** Paperbacks • LEVEL 2

Enter Keywords in SAM to download and print related resources.

Read the plot summary to engage students in discussing the book.

Hook students' interest to motivate them to read books on new topics.

One benefit of discussing books is:

____

____

____

Teaching Resources for Modeled and Independent Reading, Stage B

Using *Teaching Resources:* Graphic Organizers and QuickWrites

Make copies of the reproducibles in *Teaching Resources for Modeled and Independent Reading* to reinforce students' comprehension during and after reading.

Comprehension Graphic Organizers

The *Teaching Resources* book has one Comprehension Graphic Organizer for each Paperback and Audiobook. Have students use it after finishing the text to increase accountability and provide practice with applying a specific skill.

Name ____________________

***READ 180* Paperbacks**
Comprehension Graphic Organizer
LEVEL 2

Danger Is My Business

Problem and Solution

As you read, use this chart to record the problems and solutions that are listed for each job. The first one is done for you.

1. Bomb Squad Tech's Problem A bomb squad tech doesn't want to reveal any information that may be useful to bomb makers.	→	**The Solution** Everyone on the squad keeps quiet about the methods and technology they use.
2. Crab Fisher's Problem A fisher has to get the crabs into the giant steel pots.	→	**The Solution**
3. Tornado Chaser's Problem A tornado chaser has to get information about wind speed, temperature, and direction from the tornados.	→	**The Solution**
4. Miner's Problem	→	**The Solution** Miners pick and drill through the rock in a coal mine.

Use with page 34.

Resource Links
Teaching Resources: p. 115
SAM Keyword: Deadliest Jobs

***READ 180* Paperbacks • Danger Is My Business** 115

Graphic organizers build comprehension skills by:

____

____

____

Suggest that students carefully examine the model response so they better understand how to complete the organizer.

Guide students to complete the organizer using details from the text.

Enter the Keyword in SAM to download the resource for student use.

***Teaching Resources for Modeled and Independent Reading,* Stage B**

QuickWrites

Every Paperback, Audiobook, and eReads Collection has one QuickWrites page in *Teaching Resources for Modeled and Independent Reading*. The QuickWrites are short prompts that guide students to reflect on their reading and respond in writing.

Name ______________________

READ 180 **Paperbacks**
QuickWrites
LEVEL 2

Danger Is My Business

Here are some ideas to write about while you're reading the book. Write your answers on the back of this sheet or on a separate piece of paper.

Super Stunt *(After Chapter 1)*

DATE

1. Imagine you are a Motocross driver. You have come up with a new stunt that you will perform for hundreds of excited fans. Describe the stunt you will perform. Then give the stunt a name.

How Much Would It Take? *(After Chapter 3)*

DATE

2. Alaskan crab fishers can make a lot of money, but their job may be the most dangerous job in America! Would you risk your life at a job in order to make a lot of money? Why or why not? List at least two reasons.

Wanted: Storm Chaser *(After Chapter 5)*

DATE

3. You are a scientist who studies weather, and you need an assistant. Write a help-wanted ad for a storm chaser. Describe the job and make it sound as exciting as possible. Remember, you want adventurous people to apply!

Play by Play *(After Chapter 6)*

DATE

4. You are a reporter backstage at a reality TV show about dancing. One of the dancers has just been injured. Interview the injured dancer about what happened. Write two questions and two responses.

Use with page 34.

Resource Links
Teaching Resources: p. 116
SAM Keyword: Deadliest Jobs

116 ***READ 180*** Paperbacks • Danger Is My Business

***Teaching Resources for Modeled and Independent Reading,* Stage B**

Notice that the complexity of QuickWrite prompts corresponds to the Level (1–4) of the text.

Have students use the QuickWrite Response Sheet (SAM Keyword: QuickWrite) to neatly write their answers.

Stopping to reflect during reading helps students:

____

____

____

Promote accountability by having students fill in the date that they answer each question or prompt.

Teacher Tip

Instead of a Comprehension Graphic Organizer, students can complete a Higher-Order Thinking (H.O.T.) Page for each eReads Collection. The H.O.T. Pages, available in *Teaching Resources for Modeled and Independent Reading,* structure practice of critical reading skills, such as synthesizing, evaluating, and analyzing.

Assessing Comprehension With *Scholastic Reading Counts!*

Guide students to take *Scholastic Reading Counts!* quizzes to assess their understanding of Modeled and Independent Reading texts.

What Is *SRC!*?

Scholastic Reading Counts! (SRC!) is a computer-based assessment program that helps you monitor and support your students' independent reading success. It consists of short, multiple-choice quizzes for students to take after finishing each *READ 180* Paperback, Audiobook, or eRead that they read independently.

If your students are reading appropriately leveled books, they should be able to pass the quizzes. Their success will motivate them to read more and more. Launch the Teacher Dashboard or Scholastic Achievement Manager (SAM) to monitor your students' *SRC!* quiz results and reading progress.

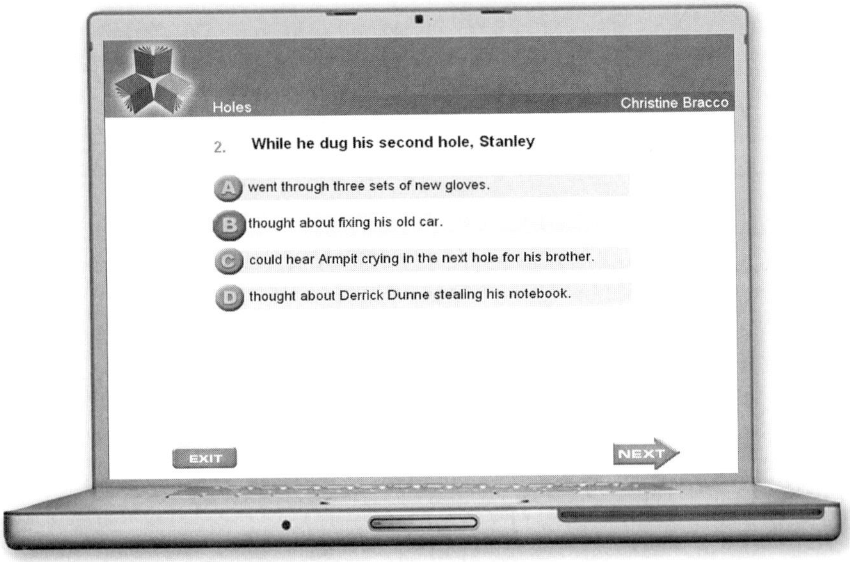

***SRC!* Quiz Question, Stage B**

Understanding Quiz Basics

Familiarize your students with the *SRC!* format before they take their first quiz. When taking an *SRC!* quiz, students:

- Enter the text title to search for the appropriate quiz.
- Receive randomly selected questions from a database of 30 possible questions (10 for eReads). For Paperbacks and Audiobooks, the default is 10 questions per quiz. For eReads, the default is 5 questions. Use the *SRC!* Program Settings menu in SAM to adjust the number of quiz items for your entire class or for individual students (see page 159).
- Answer modified cloze (fill-in-the-blank), embedded cloze, and direct questions.
- View a personalized congratulations screen upon passing the quiz.
- Rate the book using the Read-O-Meter scale after they pass.
- Have the option to view wrong answers. The correct answers are not displayed, to encourage students to go back to the book to review what they missed.
- Retake a different version of the quiz if they do not pass.

Congratulations Screen

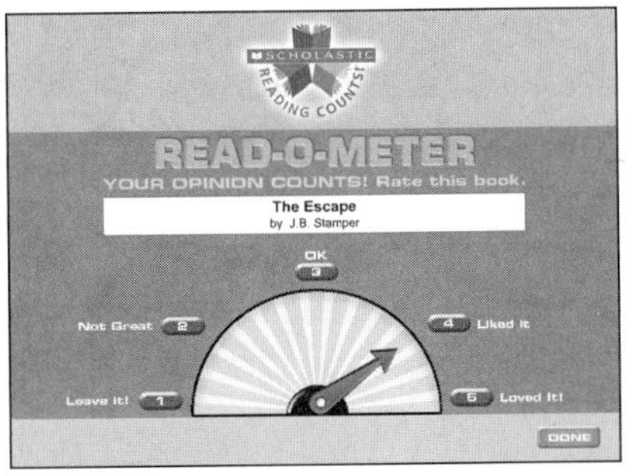

Read-O-Meter

Teacher Tip

The eReads *SRC!* quizzes specifically assess six higher-order thinking skills—identify, analyze, synthesize, evaluate, summarize, and vocabulary—to help you monitor your students' college and career readiness.

How It Helps

SRC! helps you assess and monitor your students' self-directed work in Modeled and Independent Reading, while motivating students and holding them accountable for what they read.

Assessment and Progress Monitoring

Launch the Teacher Dashboard to see Data Snapshots of *SRC!* performance for your classes or log in to SAM for more detailed class and student reports. The *SRC!* data will help you:

- Assess student comprehension of independent reading texts.
- Check that students are reading carefully for understanding.
- Track student progress from book to book.
- Compare how much each student is reading relative to his or her peers.
- Share results and progress with students, parents, and administrators.

Student Accountability and Motivation

SRC! includes several features to hold students accountable for reading carefully and motivate them to read more and more. Each time they take a quiz, students can:

- Receive immediate feedback on their quiz results including number of correct answers.
- See a personalized, grade-appropriate congratulations screen if they pass.
- Review which questions they got wrong.
- Share their opinion using the Read-O-Meter feature, which allows them to rate the book on a scale of 1 (Leave It!) to 5 (Loved It!).
- View their Student Reading Report to monitor their own *SRC!* results and reading progress.
- Earn a predetermined number of points for each *SRC!* quiz they pass, depending on the complexity and length of the book. Consider displaying each student's accumulated *SRC!* points on a bulletin board throughout the year to motivate continued success.
- Check their reading progress by viewing the *SRC!* Progress Report in the My Reports tab on the Student Dashboard.

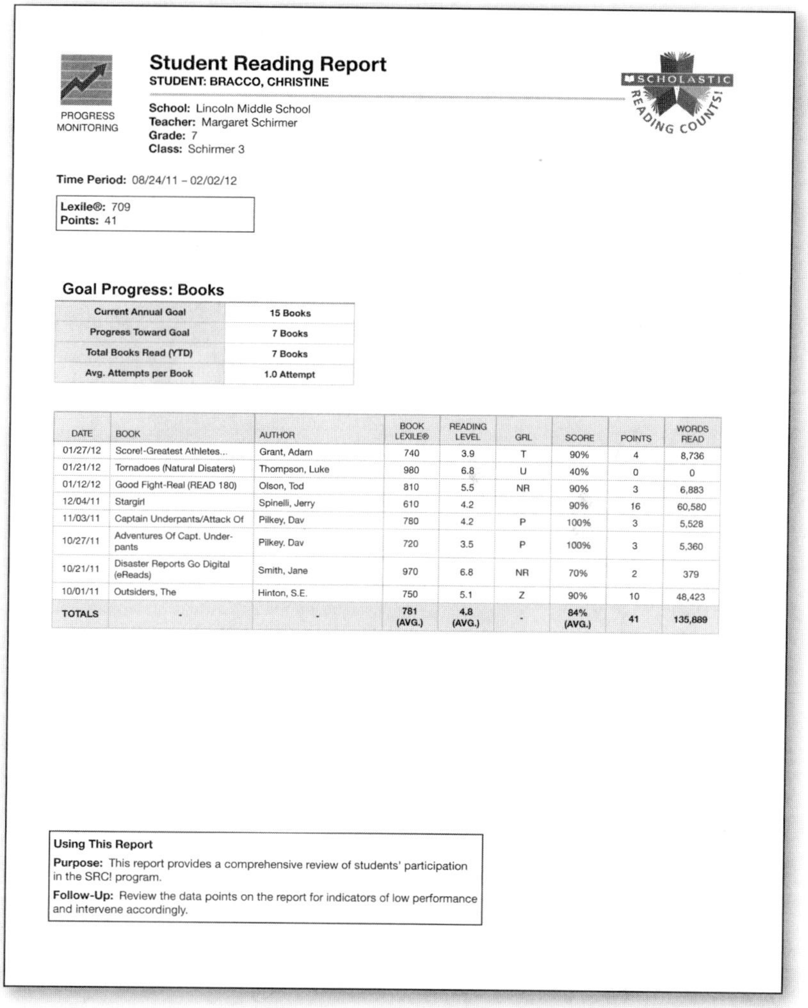

PROGRESS MONITORING

Student Reading Report
STUDENT: BRACCO, CHRISTINE

School: Lincoln Middle School
Teacher: Margaret Schirmer
Grade: 7
Class: Schirmer 3

SCHOLASTIC READING COUNTS!

Time Period: 08/24/11 – 02/02/12

Lexile®: 709
Points: 41

Goal Progress: Books

Current Annual Goal	15 Books
Progress Toward Goal	7 Books
Total Books Read (YTD)	7 Books
Avg. Attempts per Book	1.0 Attempt

DATE	BOOK	AUTHOR	BOOK LEXILE®	READING LEVEL	GRL	SCORE	POINTS	WORDS READ
01/27/12	Score!-Greatest Athletes...	Grant, Adam	740	3.9	T	90%	4	8,736
01/21/12	Tornadoes (Natural Disaters)	Thompson, Luke	980	6.8	U	40%	0	0
01/12/12	Good Fight-Real (READ 180)	Olson, Tod	810	5.5	NR	90%	3	6,883
12/04/11	Stargirl	Spinelli, Jerry	610	4.2		90%	16	60,580
11/03/11	Captain Underpants/Attack Of	Pilkey, Dav	780	4.2	P	100%	3	5,528
10/27/11	Adventures Of Capt. Under-pants	Pilkey, Dav	720	3.5	P	100%	3	5,360
10/21/11	Disaster Reports Go Digital (eReads)	Smith, Jane	970	6.8	NR	70%	2	379
10/01/11	Outsiders, The	Hinton, S.E.	750	5.1	Z	90%	10	48,423
TOTALS	-	-	**781 (AVG.)**	**4.8 (AVG.)**	-	**84% (AVG.)**	**41**	**135,889**

Using This Report
Purpose: This report provides a comprehensive review of students' participation in the SRC! program.
Follow-Up: Review the data points on the report for indicators of low performance and intervene accordingly.

***SRC!* Student Reading Report**

Monitoring Reading Progress

Sign in to the Teacher Dashboard for a quick glance at your classes' *SRC!* usage and performance. Use the Scholastic Achievement Manager (SAM) for in-depth evaluation of reading progress.

Teacher Dashboard Data Snapshots: *SRC!*

Check the *SRC!* Data Snapshot on the Teacher Dashboard for a quick view of how your students are performing on their *Scholastic Reading Counts!* quizzes. Use the data to determine if students are reading enough and comprehending the texts that they choose during Modeled and Independent Reading.

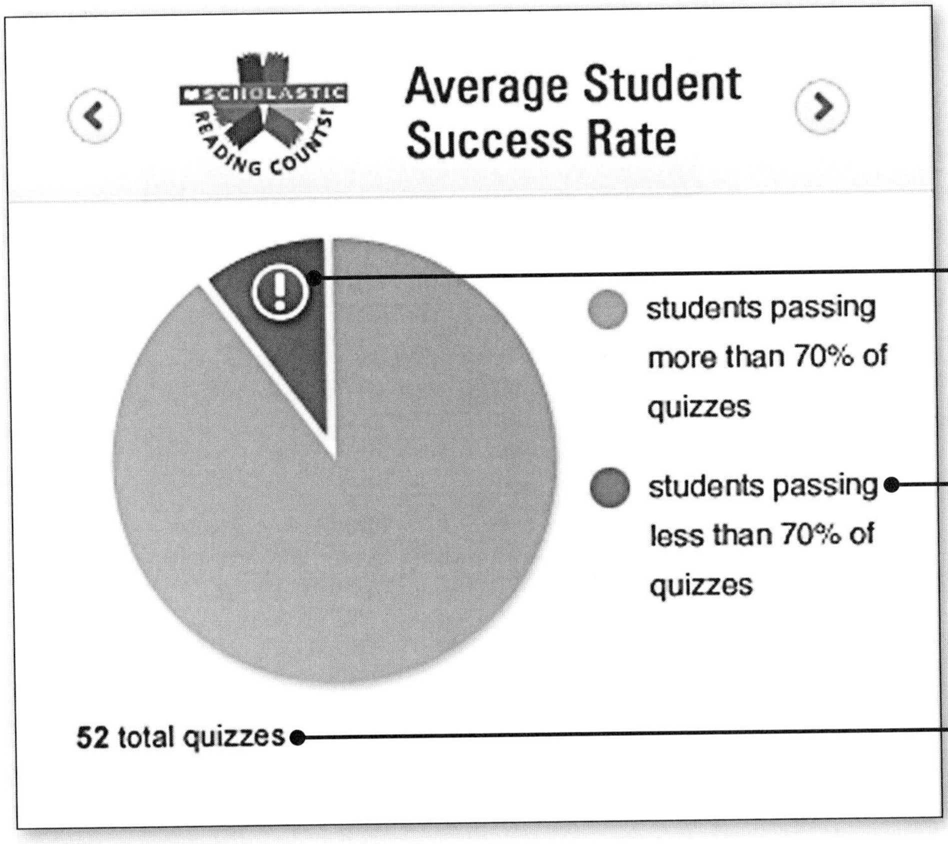

***SRC!* Data Snapshot, Teacher Dashboard**

Click here to see which students are struggling to pass their *SRC!* quizzes.

Check in with struggling students to identify and address their challenges (see page 148).

Monitor whether your classes are using *SRC!* as often as you expect.

Tech Tip

From the Teacher Dashboard Class Page, you can see Data Snapshots in graph view ( ) or list view ( ).

SAM Reports

The Scholastic Achievement Manager (SAM) manages student data for all *READ 180* technology-based components, including *Scholastic Reading Counts! (SRC!)*. SAM provides comprehensive reports for evaluating performance at the class and student level. Run SAM reports every four to six weeks to monitor reading progress over time.

SAM includes 14 *SRC!* reports to support you with monitoring student performance in Modeled and Independent Reading. The following table summarizes when and why to run the *SRC!* class and student reports. See *Placement, Assessment, and Reporting Guide* pages 218–241 for more information on these reports.

Teacher Tip

Use the Teacher Dashboard Data Snapshots to identify which student reports to run. Click the red exclamation mark (if applicable) on the *SRC!* Data Snapshot to see who is struggling with the quizzes. Run reports for these students to pinpoint challenges and identify steps for follow-up support.

If You Want to...	Run This Report
Class Reports	
Acknowledge students' reading achievements	*SRC!* Award Report
Track how many quizzes students have passed	*SRC!* Books Read Report
Find out which books are most popular in a class	*SRC!* Book Frequency and Rating Report
See which quizzes students have taken most often	*SRC!* Most Frequent Quizzes Report
Track the total points earned for passed quizzes	*SRC!* Points Report
Identify students who may be struggling with quizzes	*SRC!* Quiz Alert
Acknowledge students who are successfully reading books above their Lexile	*SRC!* Reading Growth Acknowledgment
Monitor overall *SRC!* participation and progress	*SRC!* Reading Progress Report
Student Reports	
Help a student select appropriate books	*SRC!* Recommended Reading Report
Review results for quizzes a student has passed	*SRC!* Student Quiz Success Report
Monitor a student's quiz progress	*SRC!* Student Reading Report
Introduce families to *Scholastic Reading Counts!*	*SRC!* Parent Report I
Provide families updates about their child's progress in independent reading	*SRC!* Parent Reports II and III

Monitoring Reading Progress

Monitor, celebrate, and support your students' *SRC!* performance throughout the school year to keep them on track for reading mastery.

Celebrating Successes

Recognize your students' reading successes to motivate them to keep up the good work. Try these strategies for celebrating *SRC!* progress in your classroom:

- **Create personalized certificates** using the Certificates link in the *SRC!* Program Settings menu in SAM. Print them for students when they pass a set number of *SRC!* quizzes or whenever they need an extra boost of encouragement.
- **Use the optional *SRC!* points system** to motivate students. Every Paperback, Audiobook, and eRead has an assigned point value based on complexity and length. When students pass an *SRC!* quiz, they earn a certain number of points depending on the book. Check *SRC!* reports in SAM to track students' earned points. Guide students to work towards class or individual *SRC!* points goals.

***SRC!* Certificate from SAM**

- **Chart reading growth** on a class bulletin board. Display an *SRC!* goal and path for growth on the board and assign each student a colorful place marker. Allow students to move their marker forward along the path toward the goal whenever they pass an *SRC!* quiz.
- **Plan special events** to acknowledge students who have passed a certain number of *SRC!* quizzes. Celebrations can include a "Read Aloud Day" where community members visit and share from their favorite books or a "Book Banquet" where students share their favorite books while enjoying a treat.
- ____________________
- ____________________

Reflection

Reflect on how you plan to monitor student performance in Modeled and Independent Reading. Place a star or check mark next to strategies on this page that you want to try. Add any additional ideas to the blank lines.

Addressing Challenges

Check in with students who are struggling to pass *SRC!* quizzes to identify their challenges. Consider these ideas for providing follow-up support when a student does not pass an *SRC!* quiz:

- Make sure that the student has read the entire text.
- Review the QuickWrites and Graphic Organizer to check understanding.
- Ask the student to read an excerpt from the text to assess fluency.
- Remind the student to review wrong answers after taking an *SRC!* quiz.
- Have the student reread and clarify key ideas before retaking the quiz.
- Sit with the student during the quiz retake. Ask him or her to think aloud while answering.
- For a third quiz attempt, review all 30 quiz questions (not answers) with the student.
- ____________________
- ____________________

Holding Reading Conferences

Check in with students during one-to-one conferences to informally assess their engagement, comprehension, and accountability with independent reading.

Why Conference?

One-to-one reading conferences allow you to check in with students about their independent reading progress and make sure they are choosing and finishing Paperbacks at their level. During conferences, students have the chance to share ideas in a safe environment and build reading enjoyment through engaging discussions.

When to Conference

Consider holding brief conferences about the Paperbacks, Audiobooks, and eReads during small-group rotations. Get students in Small-Group Instruction started on an independent assignment they can complete with little supervision. Then call on one or more group members at a time to meet with you for a one- to four-minute reading conference. Aim to conference with each student at least once per month.

How to Conference

Follow these steps to facilitate a reading conference with individuals or small groups of students who are reading the same Paperback, Audiobook, or eReads Collection.

1. Ask students for general reactions to their book. Prompt them to give reasons for their reactions and examples from the text to support their ideas.
2. Encourage students to relate book characters, events, topics, and ideas to their lives, to other texts they have read, and to their background knowledge. Ask follow-up questions to build on their responses:
   - *Are you glad you chose this book? Why or why not?*
   - *Does the character remind you of anyone you know?*
   - *What did you learn from reading this book?*
3. Locate the Teaching Plan for the Paperback, Audiobook, or eReads Collection in *Teaching Resources for Modeled and Independent Reading*. Use the Discussion Questions to facilitate conversation. Then discuss responses to the corresponding QuickWrite prompts.
4. Have students complete an entry in the Independent Reading Log at the back of their *rBook*. The log provides space for students to keep track of which books they have read and record their reactions.

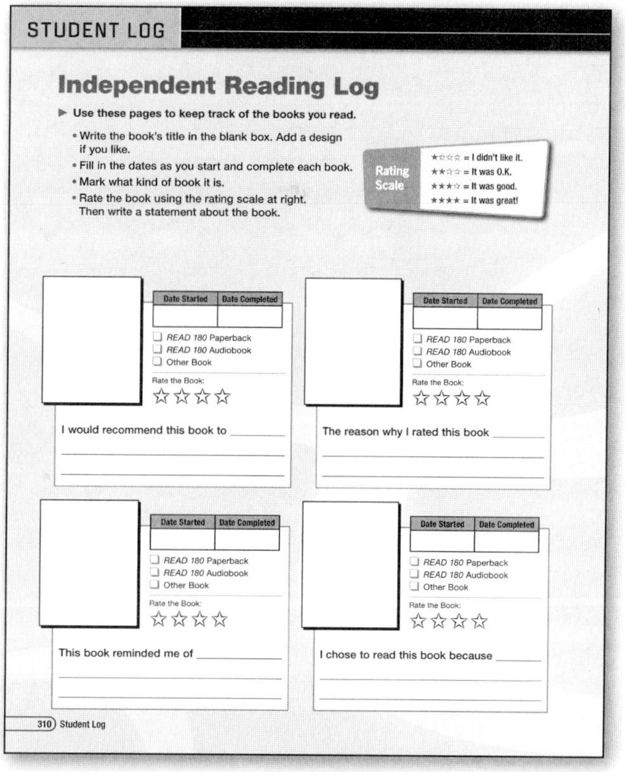

STUDENT LOG

Independent Reading Log

► Use these pages to keep track of the books you read.

- Write the book's title in the blank box. Add a design if you like.
- Fill in the dates as you start and complete each book.
- Mark what kind of book it is.
- Rate the book using the rating scale at right. Then write a statement about the book.

Rating Scale: ★☆☆☆ = I didn't like it. ★★☆☆ = It was O.K. ★★★☆ = It was good. ★★★★ = It was great!

Date Started | Date Completed — ❑ *READ 180* Paperback ❑ *READ 180* Audiobook ❑ Other Book — Rate the Book: ☆☆☆☆

I would recommend this book to ______

The reason why I rated this book ______

This book reminded me of ______

I chose to read this book because ______

310 Student Log

Independent Reading Log, *rBook*

Managing Modeled and Independent Reading

Set students up for success by creating a comfortable Modeled and Independent Reading area, establishing procedures, and checking in frequently to maintain accountability.

Setting Up the Rotation Area

Create an organized and inviting Modeled and Independent Reading area so your struggling readers will be excited to read each day. Situate the rotation area far enough away from Small-Group Instruction that independent readers do not get distracted. Use comfortable furniture, rugs, lamps, and live plants to arrange the space. Consider these additional tips for setting up and organizing Modeled and Independent Reading:

- Use the Paperback and Audiobook crates as a room divider, to create a feeling of a separate space.
- If possible, set up a computer workstation in the area with Internet access, so students can use eReads and take *SRC!* quizzes during this rotation.
- Display the Paperbacks and Audiobooks and eReads Posters to help students choose texts that interest them.
- Set up storage for CD players and headphones.
- Organize student-accessible copies of the Reading Logs, QuickWrites, Comprehension Graphic Organizers, and H.O.T. Pages from *Teaching Resources for Modeled and Independent Reading*.
- Provide clipboards for students to use when completing written work.
- Use a three-tier storage bin—with one tier for each of the three small groups—to store a binder or folder for every student and resealable plastic bags for checked-out books.

Reflection

Picture a place you go to read for pleasure. What makes it welcoming? Jot down details you think of below, and consider them when setting up a cozy reading area.

Establishing Procedures

Establish and display a list of procedures that you want students to follow during Modeled and Independent Reading to maximize their daily time on task. Think about what you want your students to accomplish each day during this rotation and how you want them to handle the *READ 180* materials. Explicitly teach each procedure at the beginning of the year so students understand your expectations for behavior and independent work (see page 93). Add any procedures that are specific to your classroom to the suggested list below:

- Selecting a book.
- Handling CDs and CD players.
- Using the eReads website.
- Marking your place in a book.
- Completing Reading Logs, QuickWrites, and Comprehension Graphic Organizers.
- Turning in completed work.
- Taking an *SRC!* quiz.
- ______
- ______
- ______

Promoting Student Accountability

Check in frequently with students in Modeled and Independent Reading to ensure that they are selecting books they enjoy, engaging with the text, and completing related resources for accountability.

Check Reading Logs

Make copies of the Modeled and Independent Reading Log, available on page 243 or SAM (Keyword: Reading Log). Have students complete one entry per day at the end of Modeled and Independent Reading. Collect and check the logs once per week to ensure that students are completing them correctly and reading their books at an expected pace. Consider briefly checking logs at the start of Small-Group Instruction each day to provide immediate accountability, check for understanding, and address any questions.

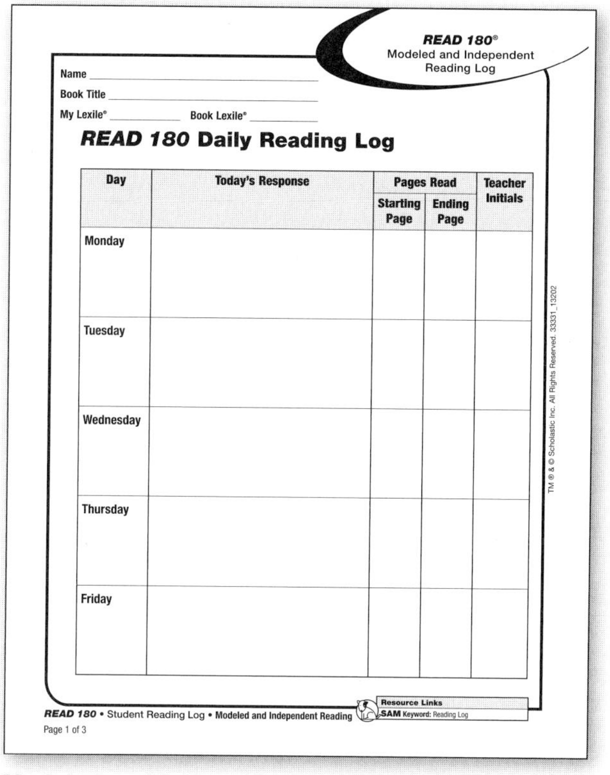
READ 180® Modeled and Independent Reading Log

Name

Book Title

My Lexile® Book Lexile®

***READ 180* Daily Reading Log**

Day	Today's Response	Pages Read		Teacher Initials
		Starting Page	Ending Page	
Monday				
Tuesday				
Wednesday				
Thursday				
Friday				

READ 180 • Student Reading Log • Modeled and Independent Reading

Page 1 of 3

Resource Links SAM Keyword: Reading Log

TM ® & © Scholastic Inc. All Rights Reserved. 33331_13202

Modeled and Independent Reading Log

Make Reading Count

Consider making Modeled and Independent Reading a part of student grades. This helps students understand the importance of independent reading and celebrates their progress. Use the following resources for accountability, assessment, and grading in this rotation. See also pages 216–217 for additional support with determining *READ 180* grades.

- **QuickWrites and Comprehension Graphic Organizers** These resources allow students to engage with and think about the text they are reading. Make copies from *Teaching Resources for Modeled and Independent Reading* and keep them accessible to students in the rotation area. Have students turn in completed pages so you can check and grade their responses using the Assessment Guides and Answer Keys in the back of the *Teaching Resources* book.
- ***SRC!* Quizzes** These assessments test student understanding of each independent reading text. Have students take the quiz after finishing all other work for a book. Run *SRC!* reports in SAM to see student quiz results and inform your grading.

Checking In With Students

Visit the Modeled and Independent Reading area whenever students in Small-Group Instruction are working on their own. Check in with each reader to ensure that they are working productively and engaging with their books. When checking in, ask students to read aloud a few paragraphs so you can evaluate their fluency. Then ask follow-up questions such as: *Are you enjoying your book? Why or why not? How did you choose that book to read? What have you learned so far? About how many pages are you reading per day?*

> **Teacher Tip**
>
> **Increase engagement by guiding students to select books that match their personal interests. Use the Reader's Survey (SAM Keyword: Survey) and the model lesson on *Getting Started: Your First Three Weeks With READ 180* page 16 to survey your students' reading interests.**

Making It Work in Your Classroom

During training, practice the Think (Write)-Pair-Share Routine to reflect on how you plan to implement Modeled and Independent Reading in your classroom.

Research Says

Incorporating extended talk time and structured peer discussions into literacy instruction provides students with multiple opportunities to practice and hear academic language.

Dutro & Kinsella, 2010

Think and Write

How will Modeled and Independent Reading look in *your* classroom, with *your* students? Take a moment to reflect on the questions below and jot down your implementation ideas.

1. **What are your three next steps for organizing the reading area and materials in your classroom?**

   ____

   ____

2. **How will you support your students with selecting independent books that they *can* and *want* to read?**

   ____

   ____

3. **What strategies will you use to hold students accountable for working productively during this rotation?**

   ____

   ____

Teacher Tip

When using Think (Write)-Pair-Share, guide students to use the 4L's for partnering:

- **Look** at your partner.
- **Lean** toward each other.
- Use **low voices** to share.
- **Listen** to your partner.

Pair

Partner with someone sitting next to you. Take turns exchanging ideas using the following sentence starters:

- *One next step I'll take is* ______________ *because* ______________.
- *I can support my students with selecting books by* ______________.
- *A strategy I'll use to manage this small-group rotation is* ______________.

Share

Be prepared to share an idea with the whole group, using the following sentence starters to structure your response.

- *One idea my partner and I discussed is* ______________.
- *We plan to support our students by* ______________.
- *A strategy we both want to try is* ______________.

TEACHER IMPLEMENTATION GUIDE

Navigating the System Technology

Teaching With Technology

***READ 180* Next Generation includes easy-to-use technology tools to support you with planning, teaching, and monitoring student progress.**

Next Generation Teaching Tools

Use these 21st Century teaching tools to plan lessons, differentiate instruction, manage student data, and monitor ongoing progress:

Scholastic Achievement Manager (SAM) Sign in to SAM from the Educator Access screen to adjust program settings, run data-rich reports, access downloadable resources, and evaluate student writing and fluency recordings.

Teacher Dashboard Launch the Teacher Dashboard from the Educator Access screen for step-by-step support with daily lesson planning, student grouping, performance monitoring, and point-of-use professional development.

Interactive Teaching System (ITS) Connect to ITS from the Teacher Dashboard to access digital versions of the *rBook Teacher's Edition* and other instructional materials as well as project *rBook* pages to increase engagement.

Research Says

Technology is an important tool for teachers. It minimizes the loss of instructional time by providing an efficient method of collecting, organizing, and analyzing student data.

Bransford, Brown, & Cocking, 2003

Accessing Your Technology Toolbox

Talk to your school's technical coordinator to discuss how the Educator Access screen is bookmarked and find out your SAM username and password. Then follow these steps to log in to SAM and the Teacher Dashboard from school:

1. Open an Internet browser, such as Internet Explorer or Firefox, by double-clicking the icon on your computer desktop or selecting it from the Start menu.
2. Click **Bookmarks** at the top of the browser window. Select the bookmark for the **Educator Access** screen. (If you do not see this bookmark, ask your school's technical coordinator about the server-specific URL that he or she received as part of the SAM installation process. Enter the URL into the browser address bar to access the Educator Access screen.)
3. To access SAM, click **SAM** on the **Educator Access** screen. Enter your SAM username and password on the SAM login screen. Then click **Sign In.**
4. To access the Teacher Dashboard, click **Dashboard** on the **Educator Access** screen. Enter your SAM username and password on the Teacher Dashboard login screen. Then click **Sign In.**
5. After logging in to the Teacher Dashboard, access ITS from the Teacher Dashboard Home Page by clicking ITS in the **Web Gateway** or by clicking the lesson links in **Today's Summary**.

Tech Tip

From home, access the Teacher Dashboard and ITS by going to www.read180.com/teacherdashboard. Enter your school's zip code and select your school district from the pull-down menu. Then click Go.

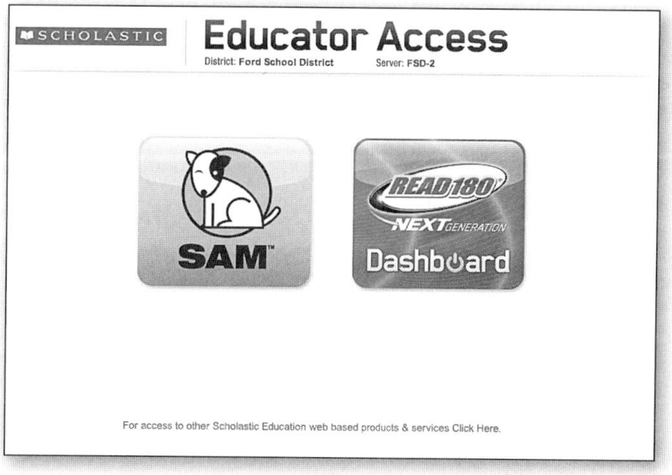

Educator Access Screen

Using the Scholastic Achievement Manager

Manage enrollment, adjust program settings, and monitor student performance data with the Scholastic Achievement Manager (SAM).

Tech Tip

Ask your school or district technical coordinator for the personalized username and password you can use to log in to SAM.

Teacher Tip

Learn more about SAM by downloading program-specific SAM manuals from the Product Support website at www.scholastic.com/read180ng/productsupport.

Getting to Know SAM

The Scholastic Achievement Manager, or SAM, is a computer-based management and reporting system that gathers usage and performance data for all *READ 180* technology-based components:

- *READ 180* Next Generation Topic Software
- *rSkills* College & Career
- *Scholastic Reading Inventory (SRI)* College & Career
- *Scholastic Reading Counts! (SRC!)*

READ 180 is grounded in data-driven instruction. The four technology-based program components generate data on student performance each time a student logs in. SAM collects and organizes this data to enable you to monitor student progress and target instruction throughout the school year.

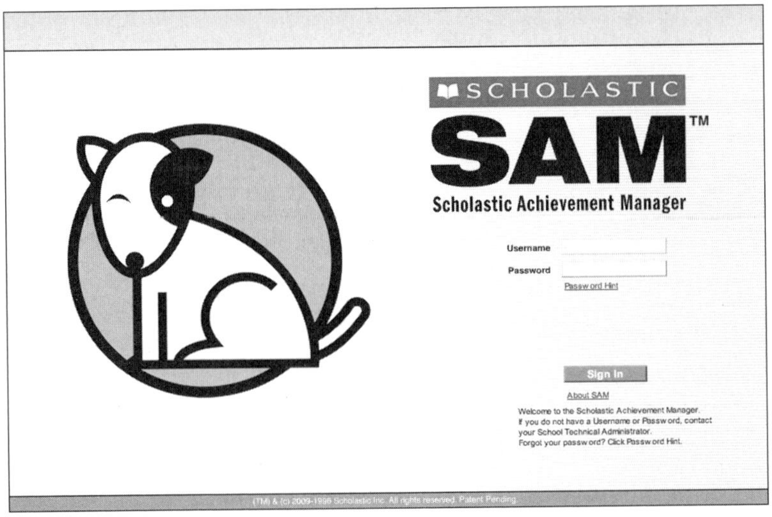

SAM Login

Purpose

SAM allows teachers and administrators to monitor their *READ 180* implementation, manage performance data, and provide data-driven instruction with easy-to-use tools for:

- Managing class rosters and program settings.
- Generating reports on student performance at the individual, group, class, school, and district levels.
- Locating helpful resources for classroom instruction.
- Searching for books to match students' reading levels.
- Evaluating and storing open-ended student responses from the Topic Software and *rSkills Tests*.

Navigating SAM

The Home Page is the first screen you will see after signing in to SAM with your username and password. The gray SmartBar on the left displays the names of all students enrolled in *READ 180.* The five color-coded tabs across the top allow you to access each SAM feature to complete key tasks for effective program implementation.

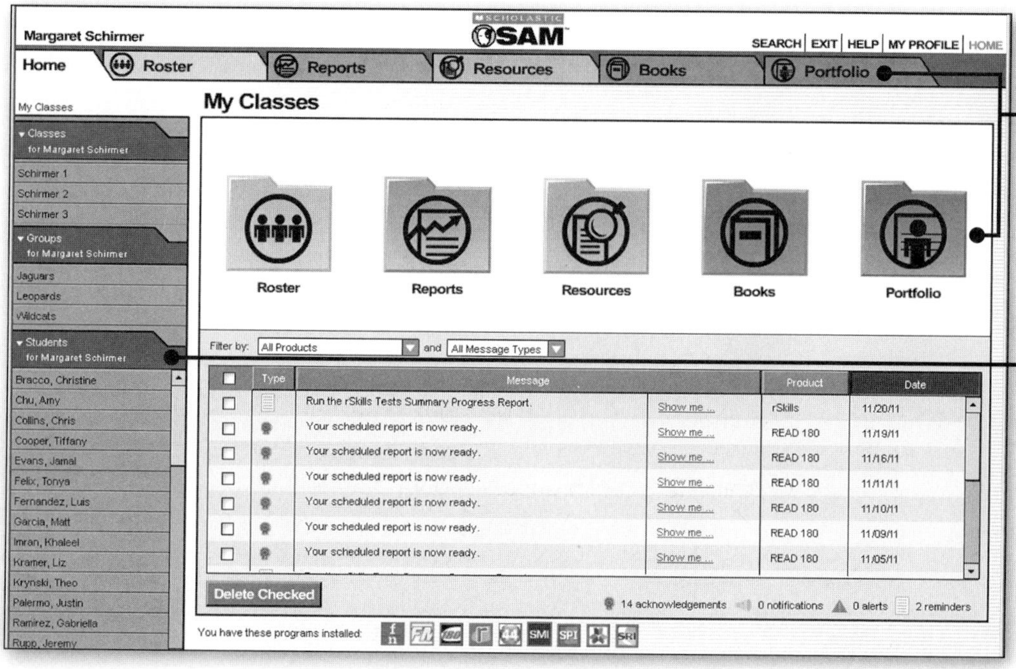

Click one of the five main tabs to get started with key *READ 180* management tasks.

Navigate the SmartBar to manage data at a class, group, or student level.

SAM Home Page

The SmartBar

The SmartBar is the core of SAM navigation. It appears as a gray column along the left side of every SAM screen. It is the quickest route to displaying information about classes and students who are using *READ 180* Next Generation. Whatever you select on the SmartBar will appear in the main display in the center of the screen.

Five Color-Coded Tabs

SAM is divided into five main sections, identified by tabs along the top of every screen. The tabs are color-coded, so you can always see which section you are using with a quick glance.

- **Roster** Use the yellow tab to enroll students in the software and manage program settings.
- **Reports** Explore the blue tab to generate data-driven reports for progress monitoring.
- **Resources** Click the green tab to locate downloadable resources such as lesson plans, rubrics, and student practice pages.
- **Books** Select the red tab to search for instructional and independent texts for your students to read.
- **Portfolio** Use the purple tab to evaluate student writing and fluency recordings from the Topic Software and *rSkills Tests.*

For Administrators

Add a School

Set up your school in SAM.

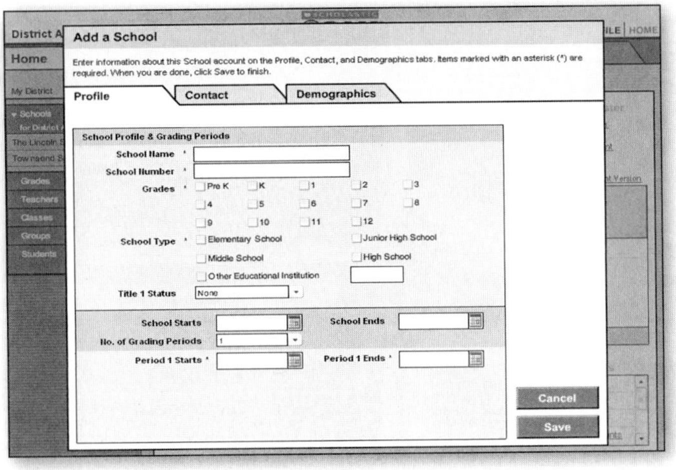

Directions

1. Log in to SAM with the default username (**dadmin**) and password (**SAM@dm1n**). Click **Roster.**
2. Click **Add a School** under **Manage Roster** on the district **Profile** screen to open the **Add a School** window.
3. Use the **Profile** tab to enter basic information about the school, including school ID number and grades using *READ 180* Next Generation. Items marked with an asterisk (*) are required.
4. Click **Save** to save your entries and return to the district **Profile** screen, or click **Cancel** to exit without saving your changes.
5. Add additional schools by repeating steps 2–4.

Tech Tip

SAM needs to be initially set up by someone with administrator rights to your computer network.

For Administrators

Add a Class

Set up the *READ 180* Next Generation classes.

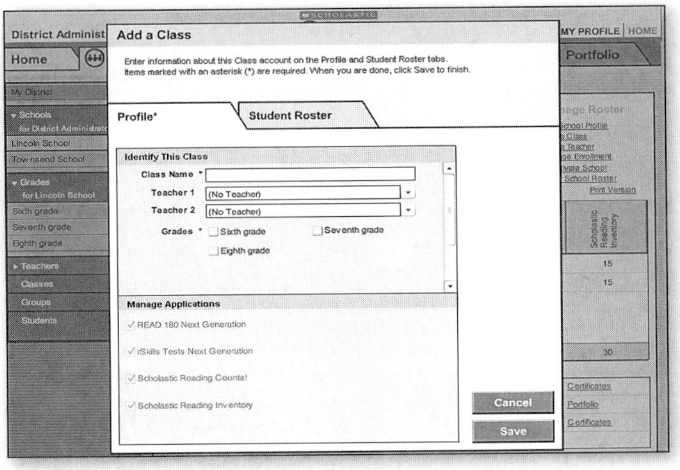

Directions

1. Log in to SAM with the default username (**dadmin**) and password (**SAM@dm1n**). Double-click a school name in the **SmartBar.**
2. Click **Add a Class** under **Manage Roster** on the school **Profile** screen.
3. Enter the class information in the **Profile** tab of the **Add a Class** window. Follow these recommended naming conventions when entering a **Class Name**: Teacher name, Class period, Program Name. For example: "Schirmer, P1, R180."

Tech Tip

The name you enter next to Class Name on the Add a Class screen will identify the class on the Teacher Dashboard Home Page.

4. Use the check boxes under **Manage Applications** to associate these programs with the class: *READ 180* Next Generation, *rSkills Tests* Next Generation, *Scholastic Reading Counts!,* and *Scholastic Reading Inventory.*
5. Click **Save** to return to the school **Profile** screen. The class name will now appear in the **SmartBar.**

For Administrators

Add a Teacher

Add all *READ 180* Next Generation teachers to SAM.

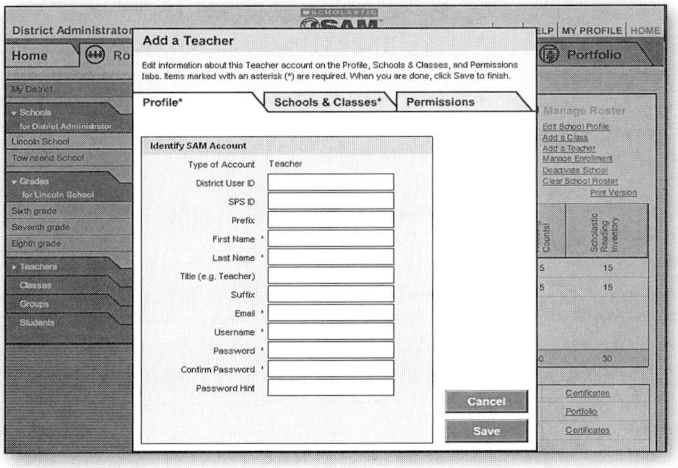

Directions

1. Log in to SAM with the default username (**dadmin**) and password (**SAM@dm1n**). Double-click a school name in the **SmartBar.**
2. Click **Add a Teacher** under **Manage Roster** on the school **Profile** screen.
3. Enter the teacher's information in the **Profile** tab of the **Add a Teacher** window.

Tech Tip

For teachers using more than one version of SAM, be sure to assign the same SAM username and password to avoid confusion.

4. Click the **Schools & Classes** tab and use the check boxes to assign the teacher to classes.
5. If you want to allow the teacher to remove students from SAM when they exit out of *READ 180* or leave the school, click the **Permissions** tab and the **Deactivate Student** check box.
6. Click **Save** to return to the school **Profile** screen. The teacher's name will appear in the **SmartBar.** The teacher can also now add additional classes to SAM, using steps 2–5 on page 156.

Add a Student

Add students to SAM and assign them to a *READ 180* Next Generation class.

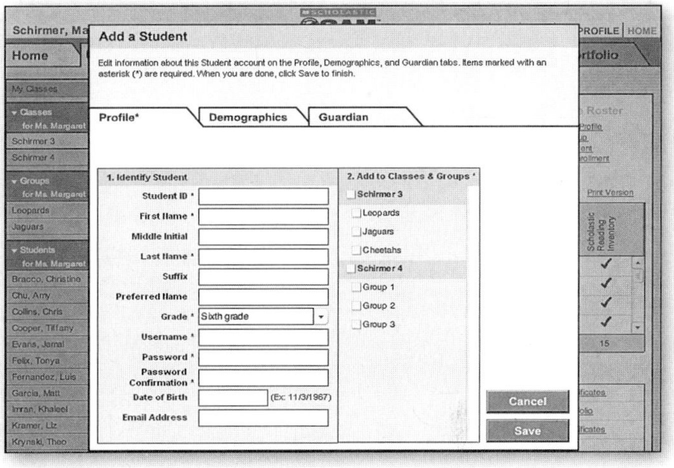

Directions

1. Log in to SAM with your teacher username and password. Double-click a class name in the **SmartBar.**
2. Click **Add a Student** under **Manage Roster** on the class **Profile** screen.
3. Enter the student's information in the **Profile** tab of the **Add a Student** window.
4. Use the check boxes under **Add to Classes & Groups** to assign the student to a particular class and group.
5. Click the **Demographics** tab and use the check boxes to enter any demographic information about the student.
6. Click **Save** to return to the class **Profile** screen. The student's name will now appear in the **SmartBar.**

Tech Tip

When a student leaves *READ 180*, first unenroll him or her from programs (see page 158). Then remove the student from SAM by clicking his or her name in the SmartBar. Click Deactivate Student under Manage Roster on the student Profile screen.

Enroll Students in Programs

Enroll students in *SRI, READ 180* Next Generation, *rSkills Tests* Next Generation, and *SRC!*

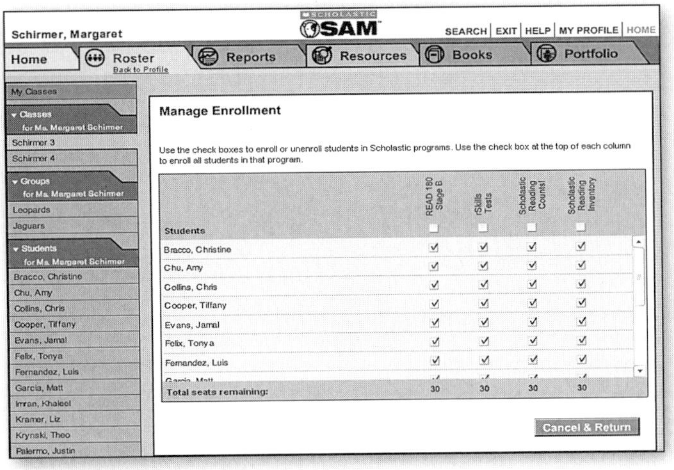

Directions

1. Log in to SAM with your username and password. Double-click a class name in the **SmartBar** to see the class **Profile** screen.
2. Click **Manage Enrollment** under **Manage Roster.**
3. Use the check boxes next to students' names to enroll them in *SRI*, *READ 180* Next Generation, *rSkills Tests* Next Generation, and *SRC!* This allows students to use all four technology-based program components and includes their performance data in the Teacher Dashboard Data Snapshots.

Tech Tip

Enroll all students in a program at once by checking the box at the top of the column. To unenroll students from programs, uncheck the check boxes.

4. Click **Save & Return** to return to the class **Profile** screen, or click **Save** to save your changes and stay on the **Manage Enrollment** screen.

Target *SRI* Reading Levels

Target estimated reading levels before students take the first *Scholastic Reading Inventory (SRI)* test.

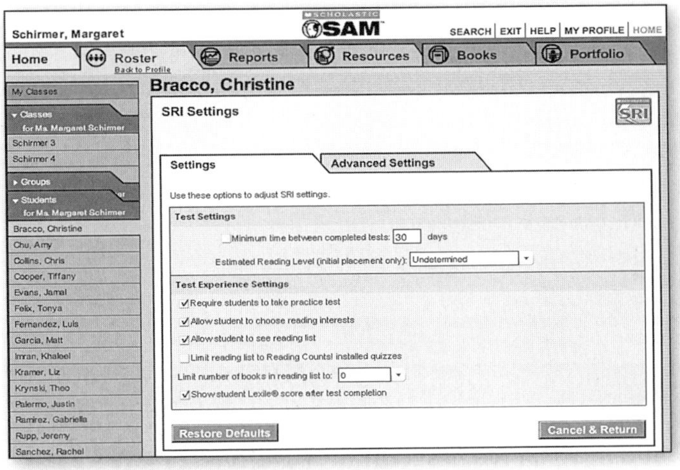

Directions

1. Log in to SAM with your username and password. Double-click a student name in the **SmartBar** to access the student **Profile** screen.
2. Click **Settings** next to ***Scholastic Reading Inventory*** in the **Programs** menu at the bottom of the screen to access ***SRI* Settings**.
3. Use the pull-down menu next to **Estimated Reading Level** under **Test Settings.** Choose **Far below grade level, Below grade level, On grade level, Above grade level,** or **Far above grade level** to estimate the student's reading level.

Tech Tip

If all students in a class are reading Below or Far below grade level, select the class name from the SmartBar instead of a student name. Then follow steps 2 and 3 to target them all at once.

4. Click **Okay** on the confirmation window to confirm the estimated reading level.
5. Click **Save & Return** to return to the student **Profile** screen, or click **Save** to save your changes and stay on the ***SRI* Settings** screen.

Modify *READ 180* Settings

Individualize the *READ 180* Software experience for each student.

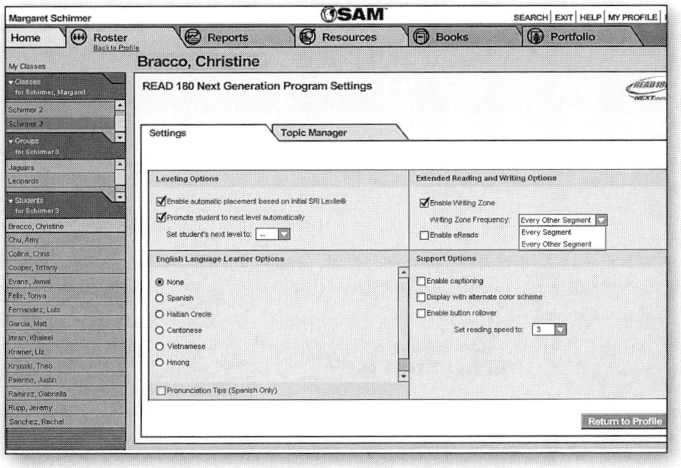

Directions

1. Log in to SAM with your username and password. Double-click a student name in the **SmartBar** to access the student **Profile** screen.
2. Click **Settings** next to ***READ 180* Next Generation** in the **Programs** menu to access ***READ 180* Next Generation Program Settings.**
3. To change access to the Topic Software Writing Zone in *READ 180* Next Generation, click the check box for **Enable Writing Zone.** Use the pull-down menu to adjust **Writing Zone Frequency.** The default is **Every Other Segment.**
4. To allow access to eReads in *READ 180* Next Generation, click the check box for **Enable eReads**. The default is unchecked.
5. Use the check boxes and buttons under **English Language Learner Options** and **Support Options** to address any individual learning needs.

Tech Tip

After administering each *SRI*, check test results to decide whether to adjust a student's Topic Software level. Use the check boxes and pull-down menu under Leveling Options to make any adjustments.

6. Click **Save & Return** to return to the student **Profile** screen, or click **Save** to save your changes and stay on the ***READ 180* Program Settings** screen.

Modify *SRC!* Settings

Customize the *Scholastic Reading Counts! (SRC!)* quiz experience for students.

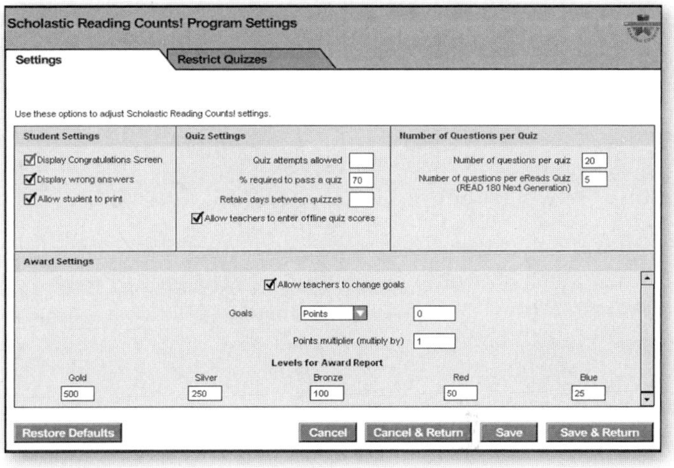

Directions

1. Log in to SAM with your username and password. Double-click a student or class name in the **SmartBar** to see the **Profile** screen.
2. Click **Settings** next to ***Scholastic Reading Counts!*** in the **Programs** menu at the bottom of the screen to access ***Scholastic Reading Counts!* Program Settings.**
3. Use the check boxes to activate or deactivate **Student Settings.** Type any changes to the boxes under **Quiz Settings** and **Number of Questions per Quiz.**

Tech Tip

Quizzes for Paperbacks and Audiobooks have a bank of 30 possible questions. Quizzes for eReads have a bank of 10 possible questions.

4. Click **Save & Return** to return to the **Profile** screen, or click **Save** to save your changes and stay on the ***Scholastic Reading Counts!* Program Settings** screen.

Modify *rSkills* Settings

Individualize the *rSkills Tests* Next Generation settings to include modifications.

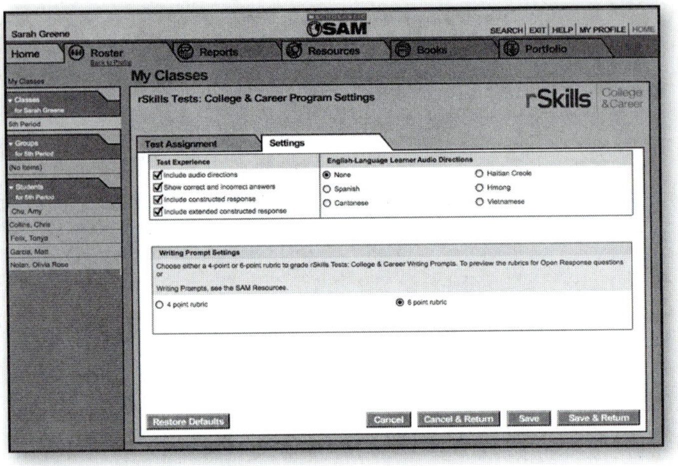

Directions

1. Log in to SAM with your username and password. Double-click a student or class name in the **SmartBar** to access the **Profile** screen.
2. Click **Settings** next to ***rSkills Tests:* College & Career** in the **Programs** menu at the bottom of the screen to access ***rSkills Tests:* College & Career Program Settings.**
3. Click the **Settings** tab. Use the check boxes under **Test Experience** to adjust test settings. Based on your classroom needs, click **Include constructed response** and **Include extended constructed response** to provide additional writing practice.

Tech Tip

Click Restore Defaults on the Settings tab to return to the recommended *rSkills Tests* settings.

4. Select a language under **English-Language Learner Audio Directions** to enable language support for students who speak a second language.
5. Click **Save & Return** to return to the **Profile** screen, or click **Save** to save your changes and stay on the ***rSkills Tests:* College & Career Program Settings** screen.

this test is to assess how students are doing. Students cannot skip questions or it can't be graded.

Assign *rSkills* Tests

Assign *rSkills Tests* to each student at the end of every *rBook* Workshop.

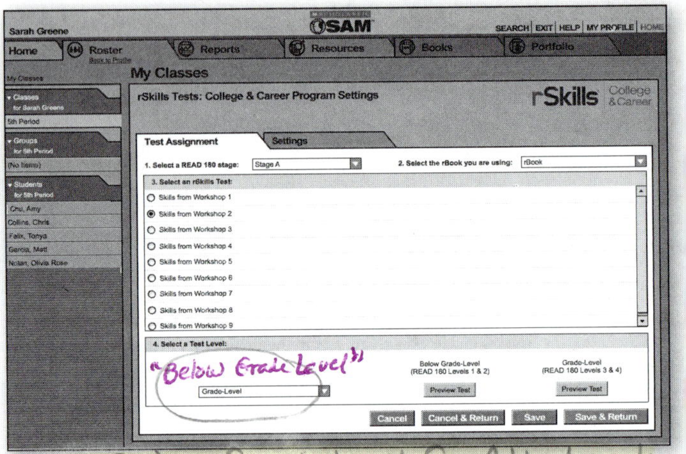

Assign Below Grade Level for ALL LEVELS, not just I & II, because it is challenging enough for all 4 levels

Directions

1. Log in to SAM with your username and password. Double-click a student name in the **SmartBar** to see the student **Profile** screen.

Tech Tip

Assign the same *rSkills Test* to all students in a class at once by double-clicking a class name instead of a student name in the SmartBar.

2. Click **Settings** next to ***rSkills Tests:* College & Career** in the **Programs** menu to access ***rSkills Tests:* College & Career Program Settings.**
3. Choose your *rBook* from the pull-down menu. Then click a button under **Select an rSkills Test** to assign the *rSkills Test* for the Workshop.
4. Use the pull-down menu to choose the below or on grade-level version. Click **Automatic Leveling** if you want the software to choose based on the student's *READ 180* Topic Software Level.
5. Click **Preview Test** to see each version and answer key in an Adobe Acrobat window. Click **Print** in the Adobe Acrobat **File** menu to print a copy.
6. Click **Save & Return** to return to the student **Profile** screen, or click **Save** to save your changes and stay on the ***rSkills Tests:* College & Career Program Settings** screen.

Use the Reports Index

Run data-rich reports for students, groups, and classes to inform instruction and monitor progress.

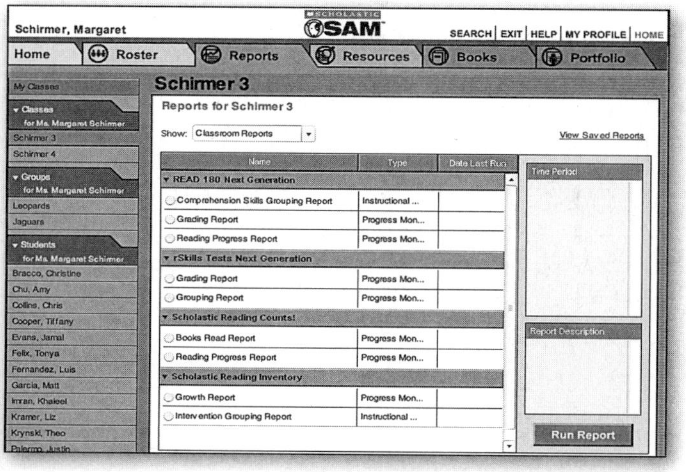

Directions

1. Log in to SAM with your username and password. Click the **Reports** tab.
2. Double-click a class name in the **SmartBar** to access the Reports Index for that class.

> **Tech Tip**
>
> **Double-click a student name in the SmartBar to see the Report Index for that student.**

3. Choose from the pull-down menu next to **Show** to sort the reports by **Multi-Classroom, Classroom,** or **Student.**
4. Click the button next to the report you want to run. Read the **Report Description** to the right of the Reports Index to review the report purpose.
5. Click **Run Report** to view an on-screen version of the selected report.

Save and Print a Report

Save and print reports to track student progress throughout the school year.

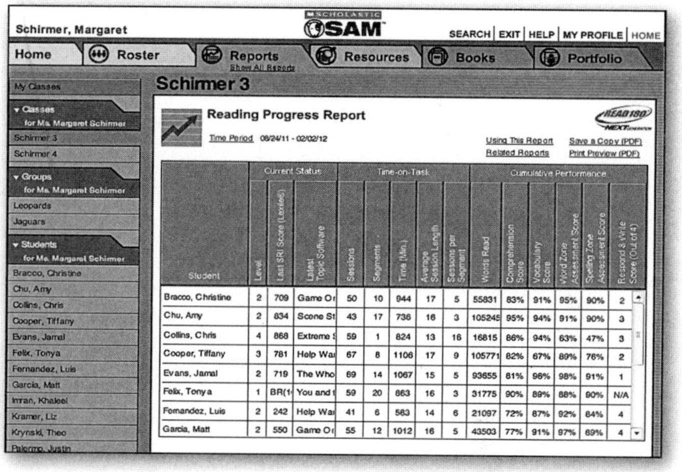

Directions

1. Log in to SAM with your username and password. Click the **Reports** tab.
2. Double-click a class or student name in the **SmartBar** to access the Reports Index for that class or student.
3. Click the button next to the report you want to run. Then click **Run Report** to view an on-screen version of the selected report.
4. To save the report to your computer, click **Print Preview (PDF)** at the top of the screen to open the report in Adobe Acrobat. Click **File** in the Adobe Acrobat toolbar and then select **Save** from the pull-down menu.

> **Tech Tip**
>
> **To save a copy of the report to the SAM server, click Save a Report (PDF) at the top of the screen, then click Save. To view all saved reports on SAM, click the View Saved Reports link.**

5. To print the report, click **File** in the Adobe Acrobat toolbar. Then select **Print** from the pull-down menu.

Use Advanced Reporting

Customize time period settings to narrow the data on a report.

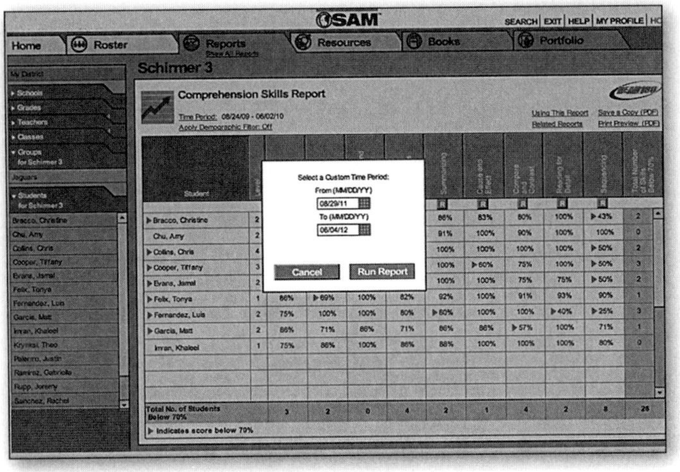

Directions

1. Log in to SAM with your username and password. Click the **Reports** tab.
2. Double-click a class or student name in the **SmartBar** to access the Reports Index for that class or student.
3. Click the button next to a report name to select it. Then click **Run Report** to see an on-screen version of the selected report.
4. Click the **Time Period** link below the report title at the top of the screen.
5. Use the calendar tool in the pop-up window to select new dates for the report.
6. Click **Run Report** to view the on-screen report for the dates specified.

Tech Tip

You can also customize the time period for a report before you run it by choosing an option in the Time Period menu to the right of the Reports Index.

Access Resources From a Report

Access printable resources for targeted skills instruction directly from a report.

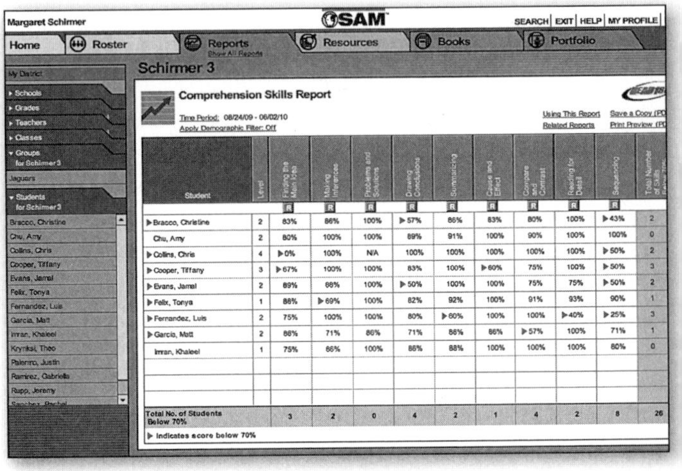

Directions

1. Log in to SAM with your username and password. Click the **Reports** tab.
2. Double-click a class or student name in the **SmartBar** to access the Reports Index for that class or student.
3. Click the button next to a report name to select it. Then click **Run Report** to see an on-screen version of the selected report.

Tech Tip

Nine reports link directly to related SAM Resources. See *Placement, Assessment, and Reporting Guide* page 125 for a list of the reports with resource links.

4. On the on-screen version of the report, click the green R's to see related **Resources** in the **Search Results** screen.
5. Click the column headings to sort resource results by **Name, Type, Program,** or **Grade/Level.**
6. Click a **Resource Name** to open that resource in Adobe Acrobat.
7. To print the resource, click **File** in Adobe Acrobat. Then select **Print** from the pull-down menu.

Search for Resources

Find downloadable resources to support and differentiate instruction.

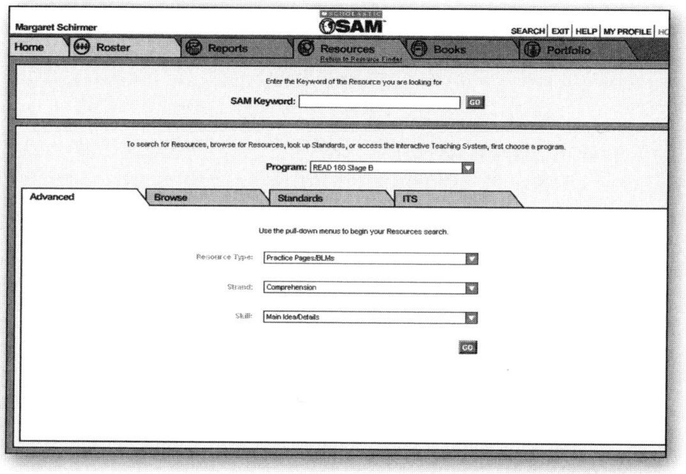

Directions

1. Log in to SAM with your username and password. Click the **Resources** tab.
2. If you know the Keyword for a resource, enter it in the **SAM Keyword** field. Then click **Go.**

> **Tech Tip**
>
> **Type Keyword Index in the SAM Keyword field to download a list of all SAM resources and their Keywords for your *READ 180* Stage.**

3. If you do not know the Keyword for a resource, select the program name from the **Program** pull-down menu.
4. Click the **Browse** tab to search for a resource based on your needs.
5. Click **Go** to access the resource.

Advanced Resource Search

Refine search criteria to find targeted resources that meet your classroom needs.

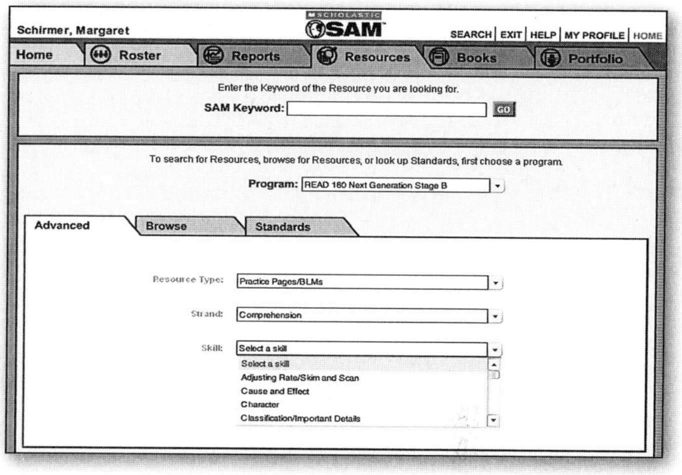

Directions

1. Log in to SAM with your username and password. Click the **Resources** tab.
2. Select the program name from the **Program** pull-down menu.
3. Use the pull-down menus on the **Advanced** tab to select the type of resource, strand, and/or skill. Then click **Go.**
4. Click the column headings in the **Search Results** screen to sort results by **Name, Type, Program,** or **Grade-level.**
5. Click a **Resource Name** to open that resource in Adobe Acrobat.
6. To save the resource, select **Save** from the Adobe Acrobat **File** menu. To print, select **Print** from the **File** menu.

Search *SRC!* Book Expert

Search thousands of *Scholastic Reading Counts! (SRC!)* book titles to create custom reading lists.

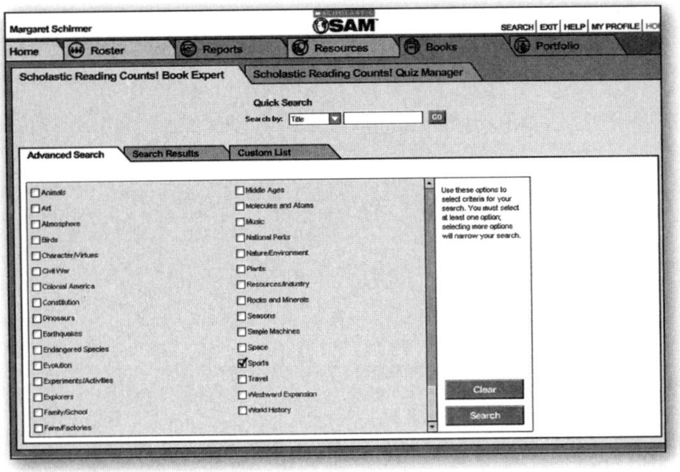

Directions

1. Log in to SAM with your username and password. Click the **Books** tab.
2. To search for a specific book, use the pull-down menu under **Quick Search** and enter a book title or author. To search for a general type of book, click any check boxes in the **Advanced Search** tab.
3. Click **Search** to display your results.

Tech Tip

Click any book title in the Search Results or Custom List tab to open the Book Info window, which lists Lexile, reading level, and word count.

4. Click the check boxes next to titles to add them to a custom book list. A counter on the lower left indicates the number of titles selected.
5. Click **View Custom List** to view your selections.
6. Click **Print List of Titles** to print a list of 30 titles or more.

Use *SRC!* Quiz Manager

Locate, manage, and print *SRC!* quizzes.

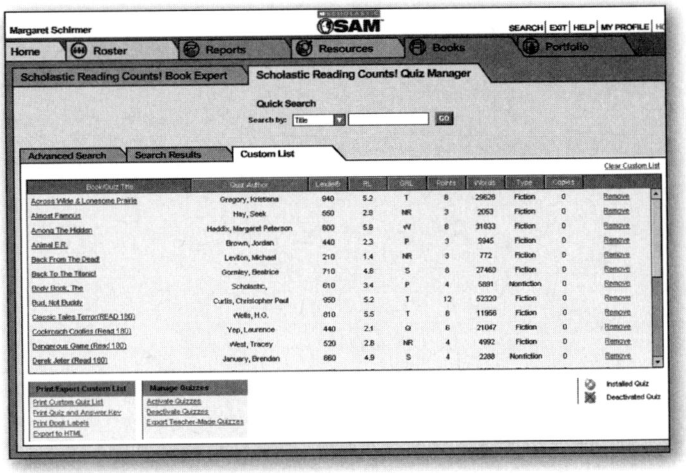

Directions

1. Log in to SAM with your username and password. Click the **Books** tab.
2. Click the ***Scholastic Reading Counts!* Quiz Manager** tab.
3. Use the **Quick Search** or the **Advanced Search** tools to locate *SRC!* quizzes.
4. Click the check boxes next to titles to add them to a custom book list. Then click the **Custom List** tab.
5. Click **Print Quiz** in the **Print/Export Custom List** menu.
6. Enter a value in the **Number of Questions** field to specify how many questions you want on your printed quiz. Click the check box if you also want an answer key.
7. Click **Previous** and **Next** to move to different quizzes on your custom list.
8. Click the **Preview** button to view a PDF file of the quizzes on your list. Click **File** then **Print** in the Adobe Acrobat toolbar to print the quizzes.

Access the Student Digital Portfolio

Select student assignments to grade in the SAM Student Digital Portfolio.

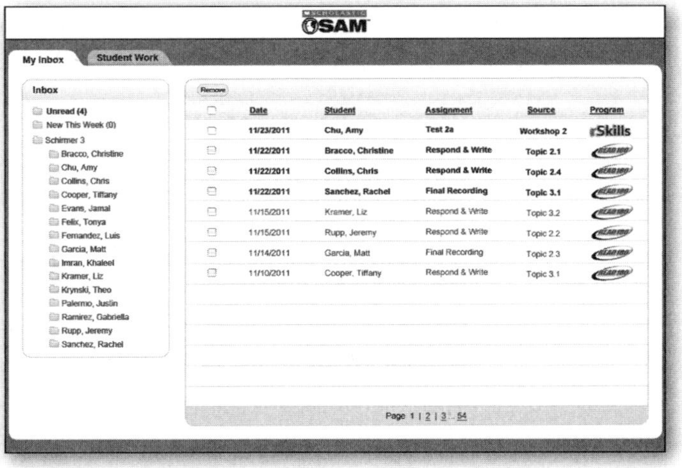

Directions

1. Log in to SAM with your username and password. Click the purple **Portfolio** tab to open the **Student Digital Portfolio** in a new window.
2. Click the **My Inbox** tab to see all ungraded assignments. The total number of ungraded assignments appears in parentheses.

Tech Tip

Only ungraded assignments appear in the My Inbox tab. Once assignments have been graded, they automatically move to the Student Work tab.

3. Click **Unread** under **Inbox** to see all ungraded assignments that you have not read yet.
4. Click **New This Week** under **Inbox** to see only the most recent ungraded assignments.
5. Click the class or student folders under **Inbox** to see ungraded assignments for specific classes or students.
6. Click the **Date, Student, Assignment, Source,** or **Program** columns to sort the assignments by type.
7. Click an assignment name to open it.

Evaluate Final Fluency Recordings

Assess student fluency recordings from the Topic Software Success Zone.

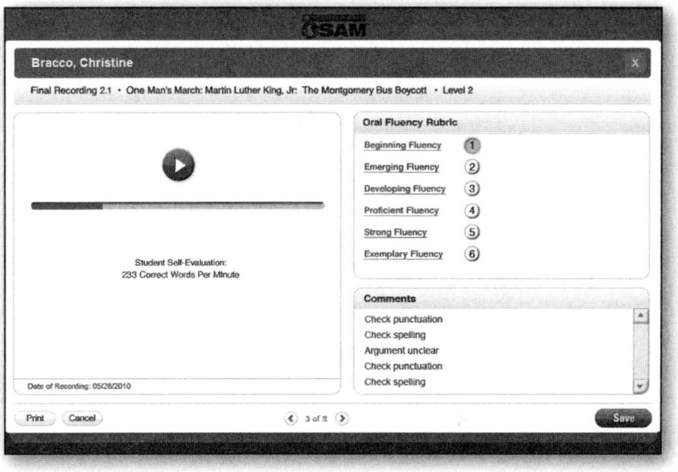

Directions

1. Log in to SAM with your username and password. Click the purple **Portfolio** tab to open the **Student Digital Portfolio** in a new window.
2. Click the **My Inbox** tab to see all ungraded assignments. Click a row that says **Final Recording** in the **Assignment** column to open a student's Success Zone recording.
3. Click **Level** (1–4) at the top of the screen to view the passage text in a pop-up window. Read along as you listen to the student's recording.
4. Click the arrow to play the recording.
5. Click a Fluency Rating under **Oral Fluency Rubric** to see a description. Click a number (1–6) to rate the student's recording.
6. Enter any feedback for the student in the **Comments** section.
7. Click **Save** to save your changes.
8. Click **Print** for a copy of your evaluation and comments.

Tech Tip

Use the arrows at the bottom of the screen to scroll through all ungraded assignments in the My Inbox tab. Be sure to save your work first.

Assess Respond & Write Responses

Evaluate student paragraphs from the Topic Software Writing Zone.

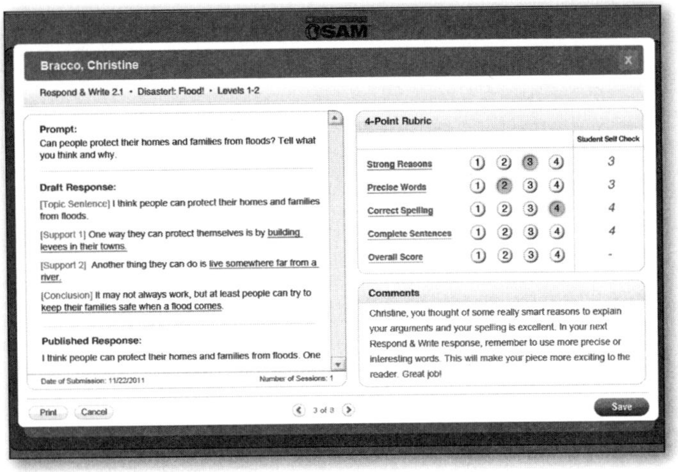

Directions

1. Log in to SAM with your username and password. Click the purple **Portfolio** tab to open the **Student Digital Portfolio** in a new window.
2. Click the **My Inbox** tab to see all ungraded assignments. Click a row that says **Respond and Write** in the **Assignment** column to open a student's Writing Zone paragraph.
3. Use the scroll bar to read the **Prompt, Draft Response,** and **Published Response.**
4. Click the criteria links under **Rubric** to see descriptors for each rubric criterion. Click a number to rate the student on that criterion.

Tech Tip

Examine the Student Self Check column to see how students graded themselves on each criterion.

5. Enter any feedback for the student in the **Comments** section.
6. Click **Save** to save your changes.
7. Click **Print** for a hard copy of the student's drafts, the student's self-check evaluation, your evaluation, and comments.

Evaluate *rSkills* Writing

Grade student answers to open response and writing questions on an *rSkills Test.*

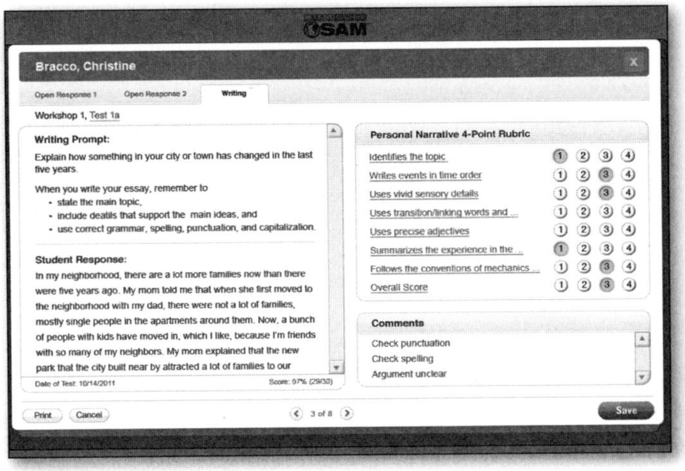

Directions

1. Log in to SAM with your username and password. Click the purple **Portfolio** tab to open the **Student Digital Portfolio** in a new window.
2. Click the **My Inbox** tab to see all ungraded assignments. Click a row that says **Test** (1–9) in the **Assignment** column to open a student's *rSkills Test* written responses (if assigned).
3. Use the scroll bar in the **Open Response 1** tab to read the **Writing Prompt** and **Student Response.**
4. Click the criteria links under **Rubric** to see descriptors for each rubric criterion. Click a number to rate the student on that criterion.
5. Enter any feedback for the student in the **Comments** section.
6. Click the **Open Response 2** and **Writing** tabs to see the student's responses to other *rSkills Test* questions. Repeat steps 3–5 to evaluate them.
7. Click **Save** to save your changes.
8. Click **Print** for a hard copy of the student's writing, your evaluation, and comments.

Review Graded Student Work

Revisit saved work in the SAM Student Digital Portfolio to monitor progress over time.

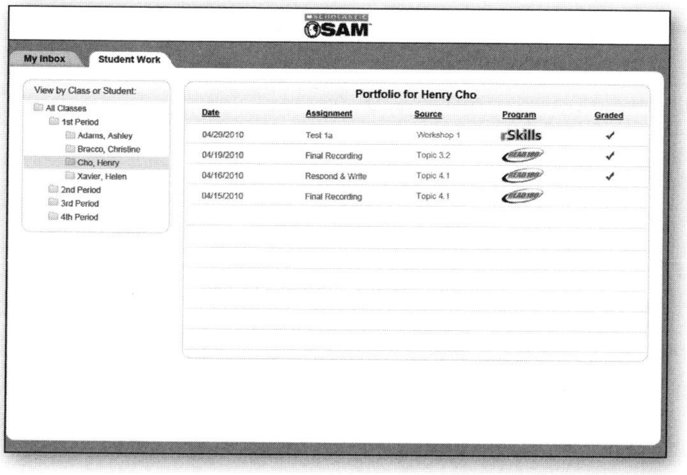

Directions

1. Log in to SAM with your username and password. Click the purple **Portfolio** tab to open the **Student Digital Portfolio** in a new window.
2. Click the **Student Work** tab in the **Student Digital Portfolio**.
3. Click a class, period, or student folder on the left side of the screen to open it.
4. Click the row for an assignment to open it.

Tech Tip

Look for check marks in the Graded column in the Student Work tab to ensure that you have graded all available assignments.

5. When you are done reviewing the assignment, click **Save** to save any changes you made, or **X** to return to the **Student Work** tab without saving changes.

Remove an Assignment

Remove an assignment from your Student Digital Portfolio inbox without grading it.

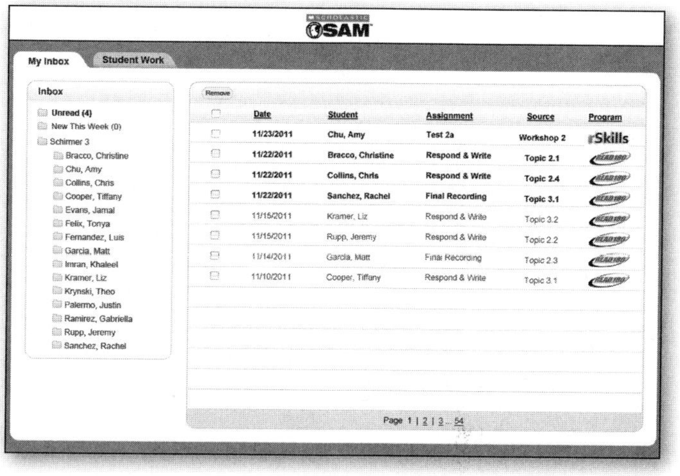

Directions

1. Log in to SAM with your username and password. Click the purple **Portfolio** tab to open the **Student Digital Portfolio** in a new window.
2. Click the **My Inbox** tab to see all ungraded assignments.
3. Use the scroll bar along the right side of **My Inbox** to locate the assignment you want to remove.
4. Click the check box under **Remove** to select the assignment.
5. Click **Remove** to delete the assignment from **My Inbox.**

Tech Tip

If you remove an assignment from your Inbox by mistake, you can find a copy of it in the student's folder in the Student Work tab.

Navigating the Teacher Dashboard

The Teacher Dashboard supports you with planning lessons, differentiating instruction, grouping students, monitoring performance, and engaging in daily professional development.

Teacher Dashboard Home Page

Use your SAM login information to launch the Teacher Dashboard from the Educator Access screen. The Home Page is the first screen you will see each time you log in. Use the Home Page for an at-a-glance overview of student performance and daily instruction for each of your *READ 180* classes.

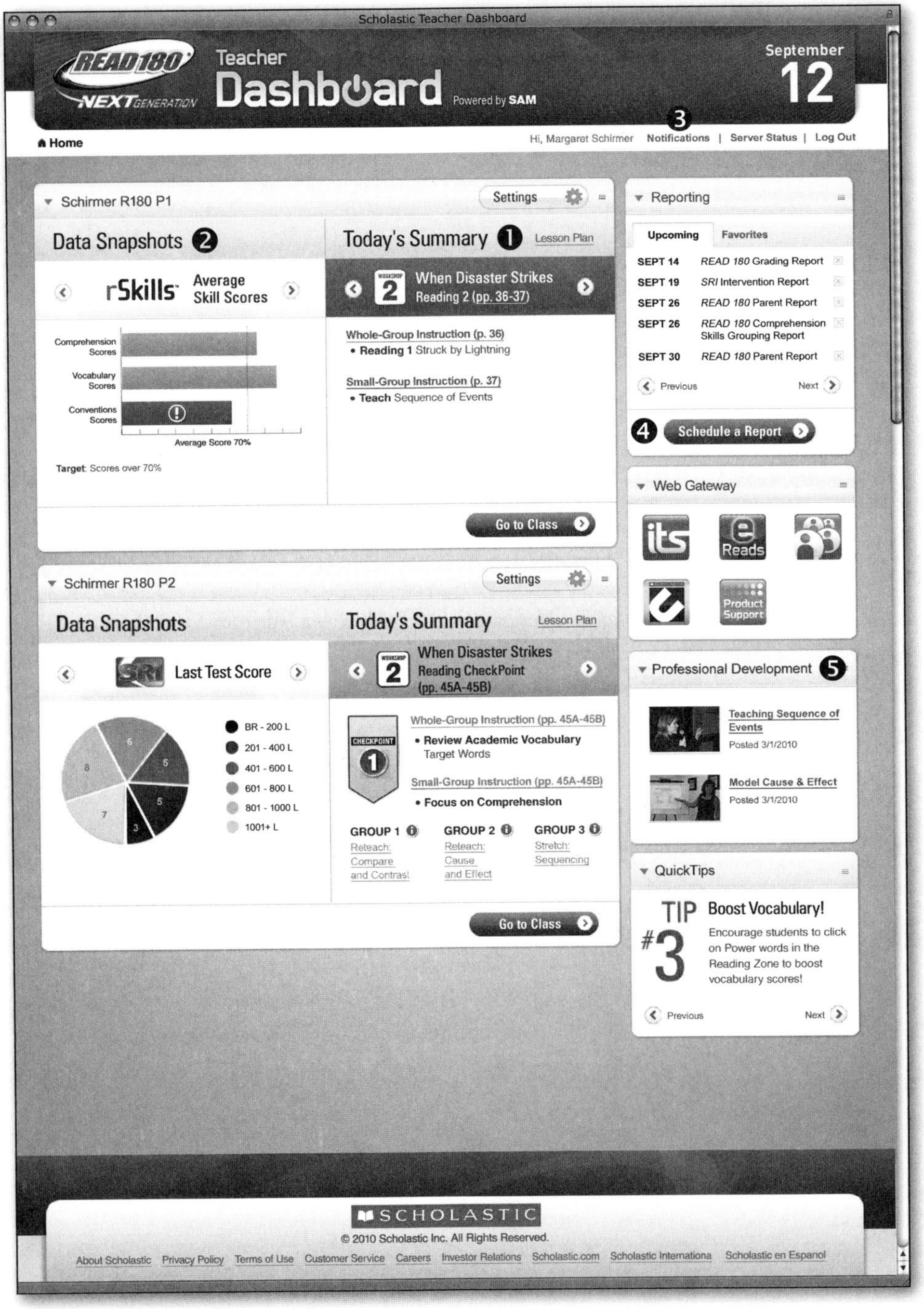

Teacher Dashboard Home Page

❶ Plan Instruction
Click lesson links to plan daily Whole- and Small-Group Instruction using the digital resources in the Interactive Teaching System (ITS). Generate, save, and print standards-aligned lesson plans.

❷ Monitor Performance Data
Review class performance data for each technology-based component—*READ 180* Topic Software, *SRI*, *rSkills Tests*, and *SRC!*—to inform instruction and plan targeted support.

❸ Receive Notifications
Receive weekly email notifications to monitor student reading progress, such as completion of a Topic, and key factors for implementation success, such as average time on task.

❹ Schedule Reports
Arrange for SAM to automatically run a class or student data report and email it to you at a designated time.

❺ Access Professional Development
Engage in ongoing learning with videos, presentations, and articles connected to daily instruction.

Teacher Dashboard Class Page

Detailed information for each of your *READ 180* classes is available on the Teacher Dashboard Class Page. Click the **Go to Class** button on the Home Page to navigate to the Class Page. Use the Class Page to drill down on class performance data and group students for differentiated instruction.

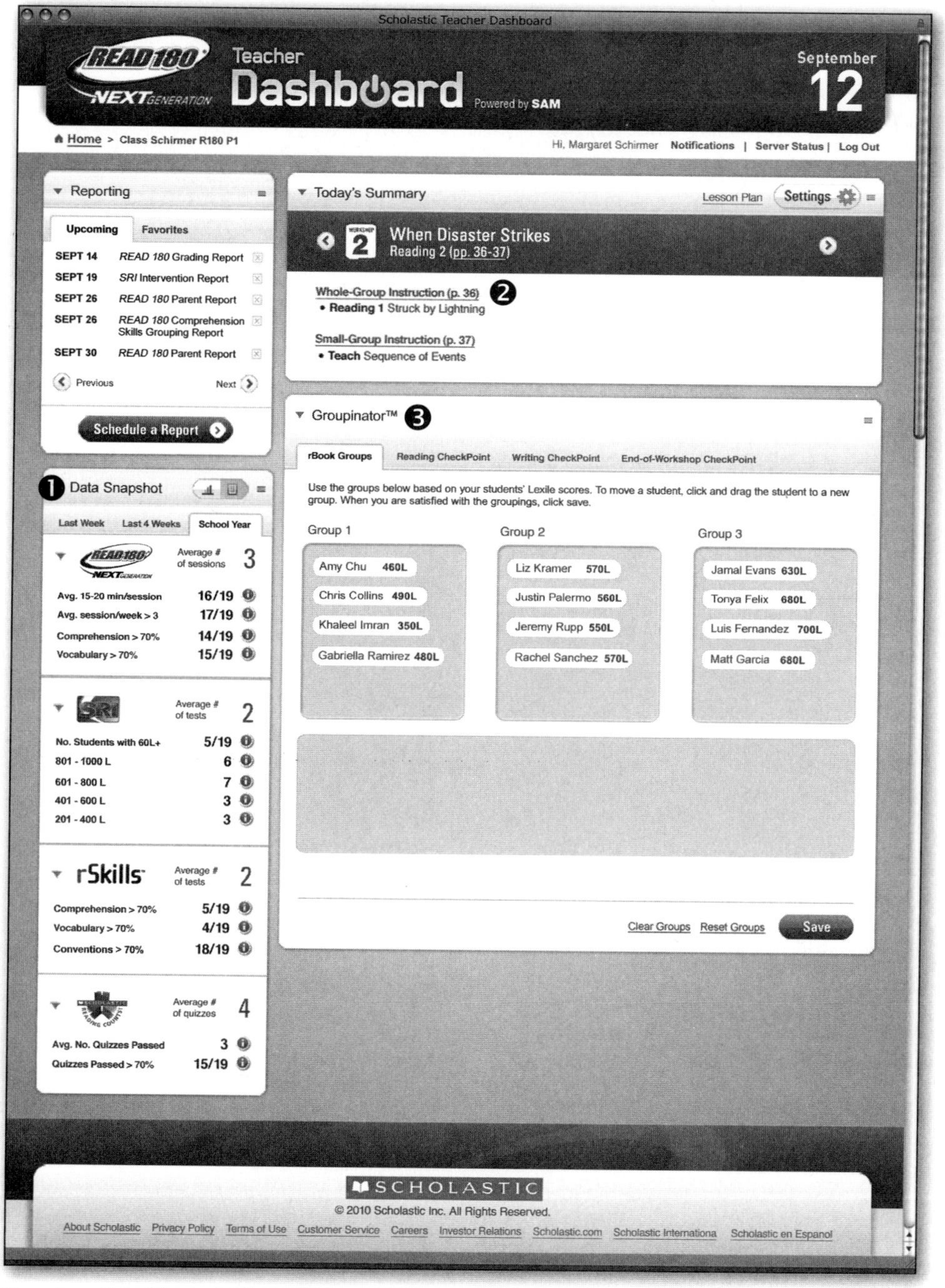

Teacher Dashboard Class Page

❶ View Additional Data
View performance and usage data for each technology-based component from the last week, the last four weeks, or the entire year to monitor program implementation and student progress over time.

❷ Plan Instruction
Click the Whole- and Small-Group Instruction links to plan daily lessons using the *rBook Teacher's Edition* on the Interactive Teaching System (ITS).

❸ Review and Adjust Groups
Check the Groupinator for dynamic and flexible student grouping throughout an *rBook* Workshop, including daily *rBook* groups and groups for the Reading, Writing, and End-of-Workshop CheckPoints. Review and adjust the recommended groups based on your classroom needs.

Select a Lesson

Select an *rBook* Workshop and lesson to teach.

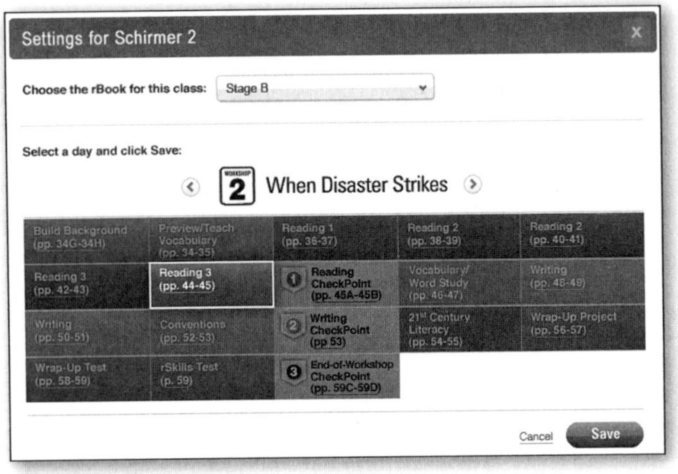

Directions

1. Sign in to the Teacher Dashboard with your SAM username and password.
2. On the Teacher Dashboard Home Page, click **Settings** to adjust the *rBook* settings for a class.
3. Use the pull-down menu next to **Choose the rBook for this class** to select your *rBook* Stage.
4. Use the left and right arrows under **Select a day and click Save** to select a Workshop 1–9.
5. Click a box to select the lesson. The lesson will appear in **Today's Summary** on the Teacher Dashboard Home and Class Pages.

Tech Tip

The highlighted lesson on the Settings page is what is currently featured in Today's Summary for that class.

6. Click **Save** to save your changes and return to the Teacher Dashboard Home Page.
7. Use the left and right arrows in **Today's Summary** on the Home Page to locate previous and future lessons within the selected Workshop.

Preview the Lesson in ITS

Preview the selected lesson on the Interactive Teaching System (ITS).

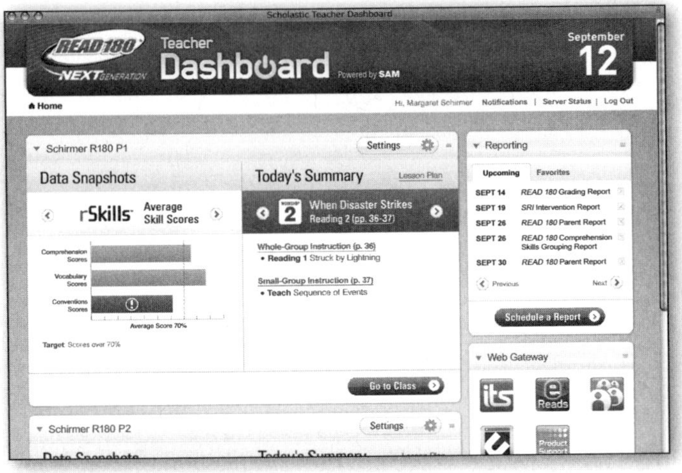

Directions

1. Sign in to the Teacher Dashboard with your SAM username and password.
2. On the Teacher Dashboard Home Page, click **Whole-Group Instruction** in **Today's Summary** to view the day's Whole Group lesson in the digital *rBook Teacher's Edition* on ITS.
3. Click **Small-Group Instruction** in **Today's Summary** to view the day's Small Group lesson in the digital *rBook Teacher's Edition* on ITS.
4. When viewing the *rBook* lesson in ITS, click its Do Now and its Wrap-Up to view brief activities to begin and end the day's class. Click its Scaffolded Support to view strategies for differentiating the day's instruction.
5. To preview lessons on CheckPoint days, click **Group 1, Group 2,** and **Group 3** in **Today's Summary** on the Teacher Dashboard Home Page. This links you to recommended lessons in *Resources for Differentiated Instruction 1–3* on ITS.

Tech Tip

On CheckPoint days, click the blue i icons next to Group 1, 2, and 3 in Today's Summary to see a list of students in each small group.

View and Customize a Lesson Plan

View a printable lesson plan for Whole- and Small-Group Instruction.

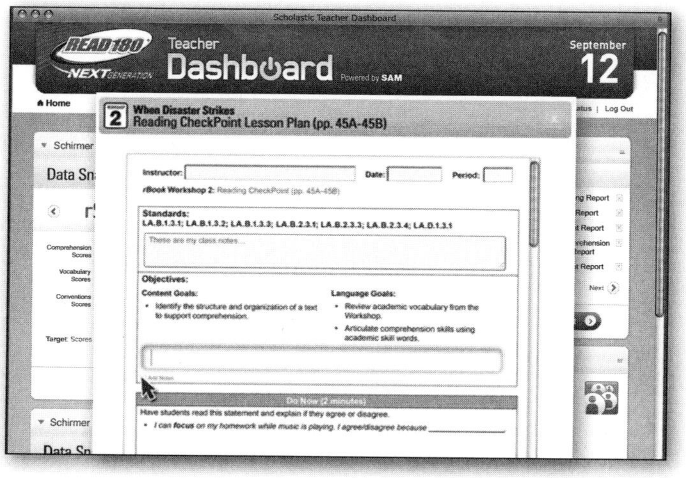

Directions

1. Sign in to the Teacher Dashboard with your SAM username and password.
2. On the Teacher Dashboard Home Page, click **Lesson Plan** to the right of **Today's Summary** to view the day's lesson plan for that class.

> **Tech Tip**
>
> **Before viewing a lesson plan, remember to first click Settings or use the navigation arrows in Today's Summary to select a Workshop lesson.**

3. Enter your class information in the fields next to **Instructor, Date,** and **Period** at the top of the lesson plan pop-up window.
4. Click the **+Add Notes** buttons throughout the lesson plan to enter your own comments.
5. Scroll down to the bottom of the lesson plan and click **Save** to save a copy of the lesson plan to your computer.

Print or Email a Lesson Plan

Print or email a lesson plan for Whole- and Small-Group Instruction.

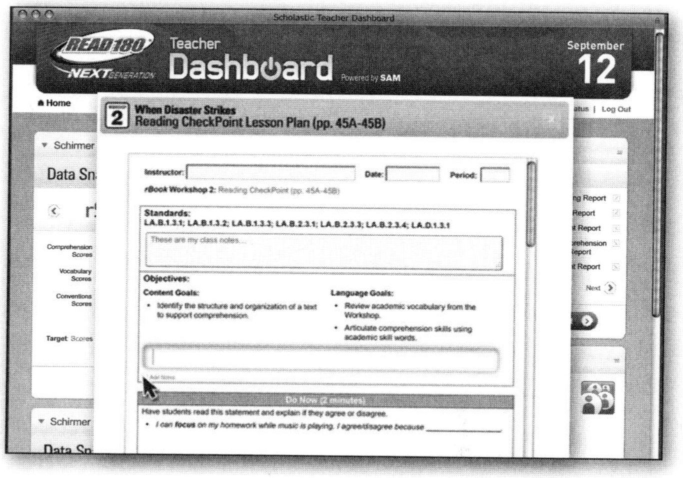

Directions

1. Sign in to the Teacher Dashboard with your SAM username and password.
2. On the Teacher Dashboard Home Page, click **Lesson Plan** to the right of **Today's Summary** to view the day's lesson plan for that class.
3. Click **+Add Notes** to enter any comments on the lesson plan pop-up window.
4. Click **Preview (PDF)** to see a PDF version of the lesson plan in Adobe Acrobat.
5. To print the lesson plan, click **File** on the Adobe Acrobat toolbar. Then click **Print**.
6. To email the lesson plan, click **File** on the Adobe Acrobat toolbar. Then click **Save** to save a copy of the lesson plan to your computer. Add the saved file as an email attachment.

> **Tech Tip**
>
> **Student names and groups from the Groupinator automatically appear under Small-Group Rotations on the printable lesson plan.**

View and Adjust Small Groups

See recommended small groups for daily rotations and make adjustments based on your classroom needs.

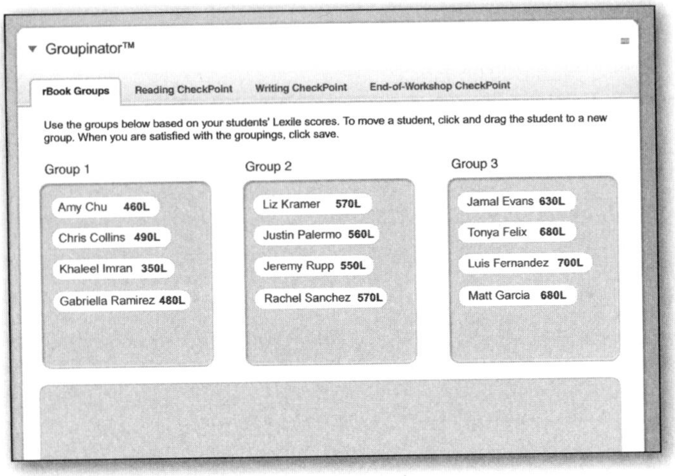

Directions

1. Sign in to the Teacher Dashboard with your SAM username and password.
2. On the Teacher Dashboard Home Page, click **Go to Class** to open the Class Page, which includes the **Groupinator**.
3. Click the ***rBook* Groups, Reading CheckPoint, Writing CheckPoint,** or **End-of-Workshop CheckPoint** tab and request groups.
4. To make adjustments, click student names and drag them from one group to another. You can also drag student names to the blank space at the bottom of the **Groupinator** as you decide how to group them.
5. To create new groups, click **Clear Groups.** Click and drag student names into the spaces under **Group 1, Group 2,** and **Group 3.**

Tech Tip

Click Get Groups to undo your changes and return to the Groupinator recommendations. Then click Save to save the refreshed groups.

6. Click **Save** to save your changes. Click **X** to close the confirmation pop-up.

Change CheckPoint Lessons

Make adjustments to the recommended skills to target for each small group on CheckPoint days.

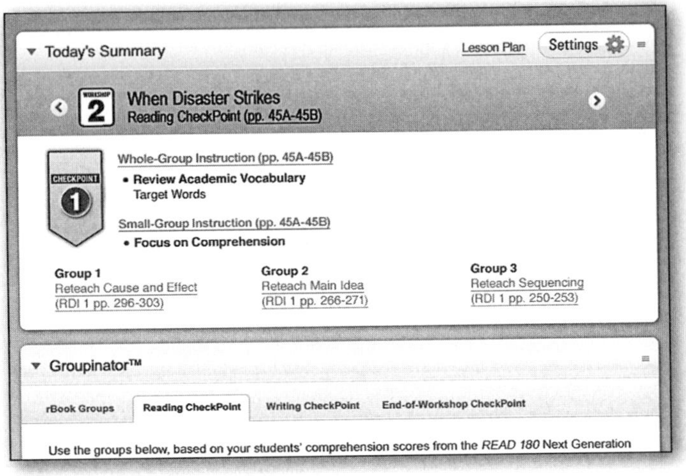

Directions

1. Sign in to the Teacher Dashboard with your SAM username and password.
2. On the Teacher Dashboard Home Page, ensure that a yellow CheckPoint lesson appears in **Today's Summary**. If not, use the left and right arrows in **Today's Summary** to scroll to the CheckPoint lesson that you want.
3. Click **Go to Class** to open the Teacher Dashboard Class Page.
4. Click the **Reading CheckPoint, Writing CheckPoint,** or **End-of-Workshop CheckPoint** tab in the **Groupinator.**
5. Use the pull-down menus under **Group 1, Group 2,** and **Group 3** in the **Groupinator** to select a skill to target for each small group.
6. Click **Save** to save your changes when you are satisfied with the selected skills.

Tech Tip

Make any necessary adjustments to the students in the groups first. Then select which skills to target depending on the specific needs of each group.

View Data Snapshots

See all four Data Snapshots for each of your *READ 180* classes to monitor their progress.

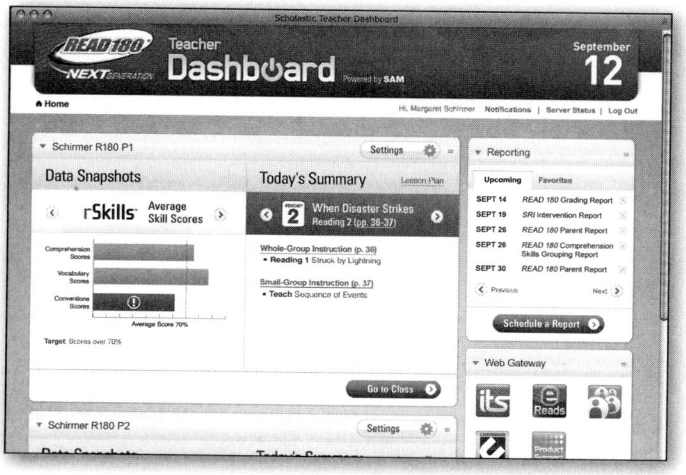

Directions

1. Sign in to the Teacher Dashboard with your SAM username and password.
2. On the Teacher Dashboard Home Page, click the left and right arrows below **Data Snapshots** to scroll through the four Data Snapshots for a class.
3. Click **Go to Class** to open the Teacher Dashboard Class Page, which displays all four Data Snapshots along the left side of the screen.

Tech Tip

The Data Snapshots include class performance data for all students enrolled in *READ 180* Next Generation. Keep enrollment up-to-date in SAM (see page 158) to ensure accurate class data.

See Additional Data

See the Data Snapshots in List or Graph View to analyze student data.

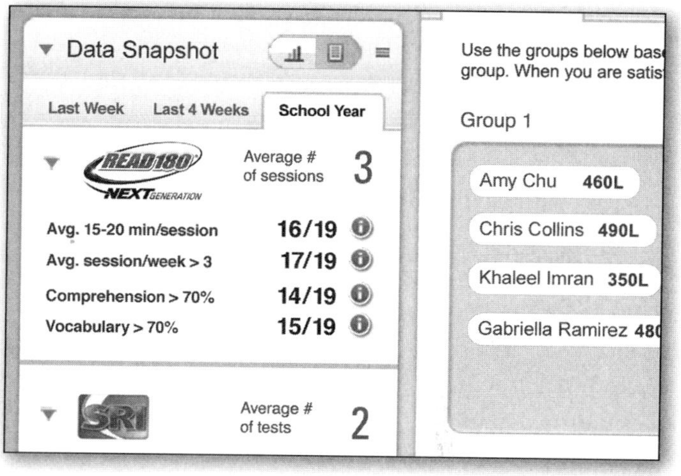

Directions

1. Sign in to the Teacher Dashboard with your SAM username and password.
2. On the Teacher Dashboard Home Page, click **Go to Class** to open the Class Page.
3. Click to the right of **Data Snapshot** to see the four snapshots in Graph View, which shows the data visually displayed in graphs.
4. Click to the right of **Data Snapshot** to see the four snapshots in List View, which shows detailed data written out with text and numbers.

Tech Tip

The List View of the *READ 180* Data Snapshot shows students' comprehension and vocabulary scores, in addition to the Software usage data from the Graph View.

5. Click the **Last Week, Last 4 Weeks,** and **School Year** tabs in List View to view data by time period.

Explore the *READ 180* Snapshot

Explore the *READ 180* Data Snapshot for an overview of Topic Software performance.

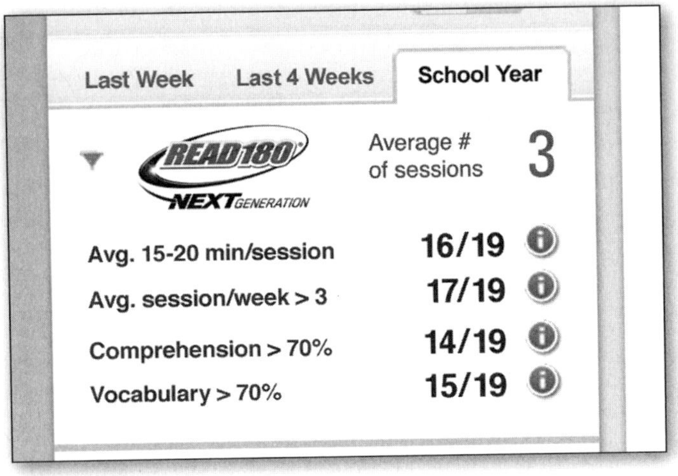

Directions

1. Sign in to the Teacher Dashboard with your SAM username and password.
2. On the Teacher Dashboard Home Page, click **Go to Class** to open the Class Page.
3. Click next to **Data Snapshot** to see the Data Snapshots in Graph View.
4. In the *READ 180* Data Snapshot, click the red exclamation mark (if available) to see students with low average daily Software use. Click **X** to close the pop-up window.

Tech Tip

Red exclamation marks appear on the *READ 180, rSkills,* and *SRC!* Data Snapshots if students are not meeting performance benchmarks. Otherwise, the entire graph will be green.

5. Click next to **Data Snapshot** to see the Data Snapshots in List View.
6. Click the **Last Week, Last 4 Weeks,** and **School Year** tabs to look for data trends over time.
7. Click the blue **i** icons to view a **Students to Watch** list to guide follow-up. Click **X** to close each pop-up window.

Explore the *SRI* Snapshot

Use the *SRI* College & Career Data Snapshot to review your students' Lexile measures.

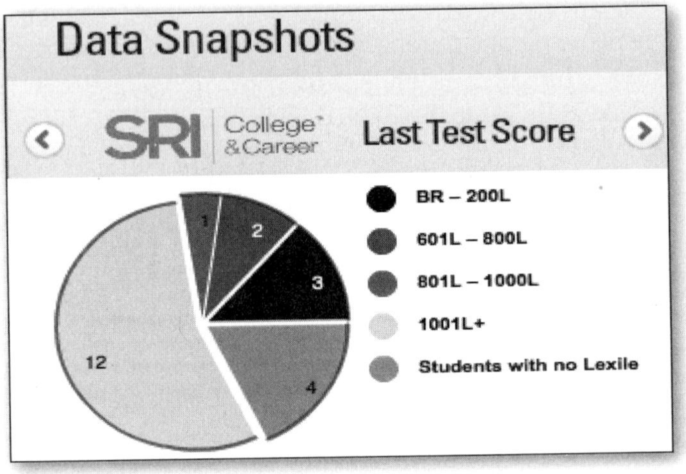

Directions

1. Sign in to the Teacher Dashboard with your SAM username and password.
2. On the Teacher Dashboard Home Page, click **Go to Class** to open the Class Page.
3. Click next to **Data Snapshot** to see the Data Snapshots in Graph View.
4. In the *SRI* Data Snapshot, click a section of the pie graph to see a list of students who scored within that Lexile range. Click **X** to close the pop-up window.
5. Click next to **Data Snapshot** to see the Data Snapshots in List View.
6. Click the blue **i** icons to see a list of students and their Lexile measures for each Lexile range. Click **X** to close each pop-up window.

Tech Tip

The *SRI* Data Snapshot updates only after students take an *SRI* test. Check the snapshot the Monday after administering each *SRI* test to see new data.

Explore the *rSkills* Snapshot

Check the *rSkills* Data Snapshot to monitor student performance on *rSkills* College & Career.

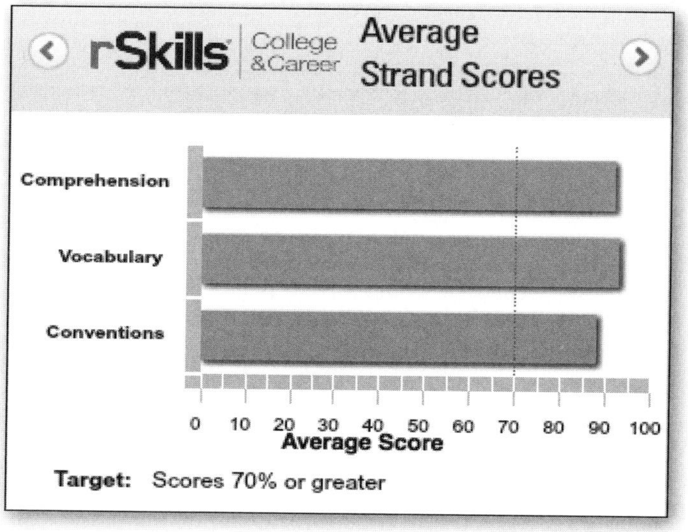

Directions

1. Sign in to the Teacher Dashboard with your SAM username and password.
2. On the Teacher Dashboard Home Page, click **Go to Class** to open the Class Page.
3. Click next to **Data Snapshot** to see the Data Snapshots in Graph View.
4. In the *rSkills* Data Snapshot, click the red exclamation mark (if available) to see a list of students with below 70% mastery. Click **X** to close the pop-up window.
5. Click next to **Data Snapshot** to see the Data Snapshots in List View.
6. Click the **Last Week, Last 4 Weeks,** and **School Year** tabs to look for data trends over time.

Tech Tip

To see updated data, check the Last Week tab of the *rSkills* Data Snapshot on the Monday after administering an *rSkills Test*.

7. Click the blue **i** icons to view a **Students to Watch** list to guide follow-up. Click **X** to close each pop-up window.

Explore the *SRC!* Snapshot

Explore the *SRC!* Data Snapshot to monitor independent reading progress.

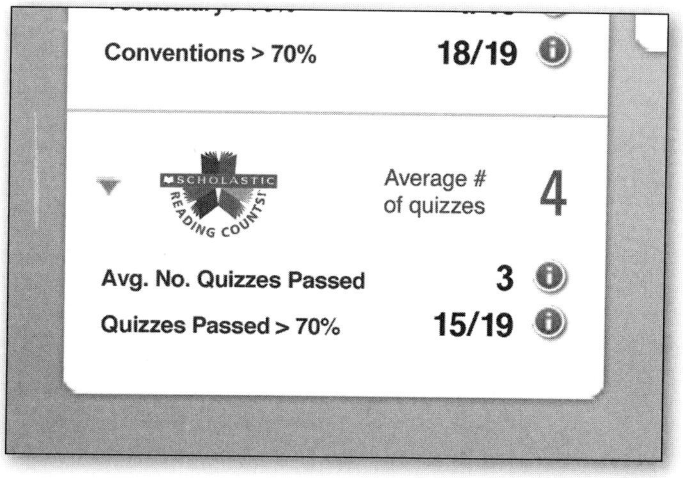

Directions

1. Sign in to the Teacher Dashboard with your SAM username and password.
2. On the Teacher Dashboard Home Page, click **Go to Class** to open the Class Page.
3. Click next to **Data Snapshot** to see the Data Snapshots in Graph View.
4. In the *SRC!* Data Snapshot, click the red exclamation mark (if available) to see students who are passing less than 70% of their quizzes. Click **X** to close the pop-up window.
5. Click next to **Data Snapshot** to see the Data Snapshots in List View.
6. Click the **Last Week, Last 4 Weeks,** and **School Year** tabs to look for data trends over time.
7. Click the blue **i** icons to view a **Students to Watch** list to guide follow-up. Click **X** to close each pop-up window.

Tech Tip

The *SRC!* and *READ 180* Data Snapshots are updated weekly, so check them each Monday morning to see new student data.

Select Notifications

Select the notifications you want emailed weekly to stay alert to changes in program usage and progress.

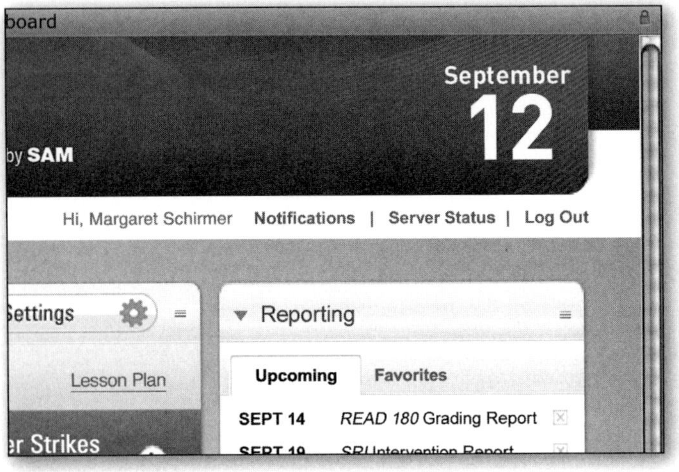

Directions

1. Sign in to the Teacher Dashboard with your SAM username and password.
2. On the Teacher Dashboard Home Page, click **Notifications** in the upper right corner to open the **Notifications Opt-in** pop-up.
3. Use the check boxes to indicate which notifications you want to receive in a weekly email. Notice that the notifications are organized by program component: *READ 180* Topic Software, *Scholastic Reading Inventory (SRI)*, *rSkills Tests*, and *Scholastic Reading Counts! (SRC!)*.

Tech Tip

Notifications are automatically sent to the email address that you have registered with SAM.

4. Click **Save** to save your selections and return to the Teacher Dashboard Home Page.

Opt-Out of Notifications

Cancel weekly email notifications.

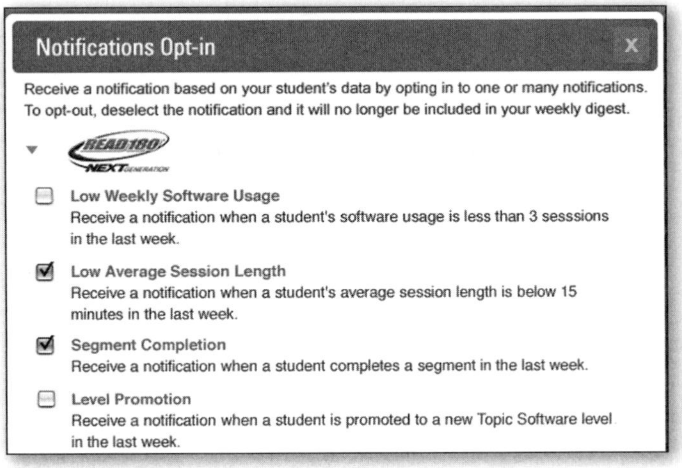

Directions

1. Sign in to the Teacher Dashboard with your SAM username and password.
2. On the Teacher Dashboard Home Page, click **Notifications** in the upper right corner to open the **Notifications Opt-in** pop-up.
3. Click any checked boxes to uncheck them. These notifications will no longer be sent to your designated email address.
4. Click **Save** to save your changes and return to the Teacher Dashboard Home Page.

Tech Tip

Click the gray arrow to the left of each program logo (e.g., *READ 180*) to reveal or hide the available notifications for that program component.

Schedule a Report

Schedule SAM to run a report and email it to you at a designated time.

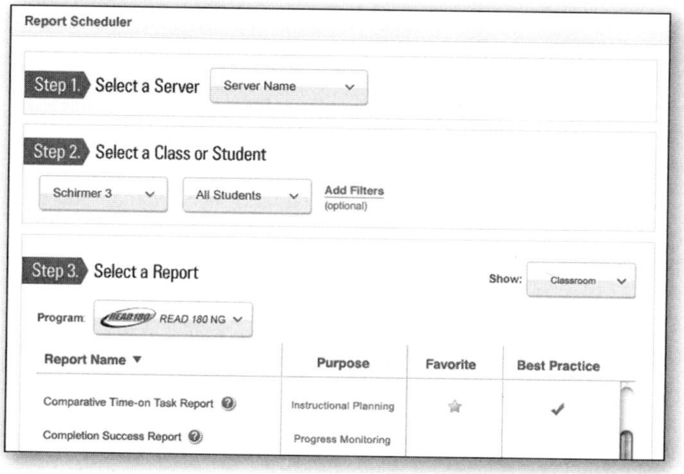

Directions

1. Sign in to the Teacher Dashboard with your SAM username and password.
2. On the Teacher Dashboard Home Page, click **Schedule a Report.**
3. In **Step 1** of the **Report Scheduler Wizard,** use the pull-down menu to select the server that stores your *READ 180* data. (If you do not know your server, ask your school's technical coordinator.) Then click the **Next** arrow.
4. In **Step 2,** use the first pull-down menu to select a class. Use the second pull-down menu to select **All Students** to run a class report or a student name to run a student report. Then click the **Next** arrow.
5. In **Step 3,** use the pull-down menu next to **Program** to choose what kind of report you want. Click a report name to select it. Then click the **Next** arrow.
6. In **Step 4,** use the pull-down menu to select the time period for the report data. If you choose **Custom,** specify dates in the **From** and **To** fields. Then click the **Next** arrow.
7. In **Step 5,** enter the date you want SAM to run and email the report to you. Then click the **Next** arrow.
8. Review your selections for the scheduled report. Click the **Previous** arrow to make any changes. Click **Schedule** to schedule the report.

Review Scheduled Reports

Review upcoming scheduled reports.

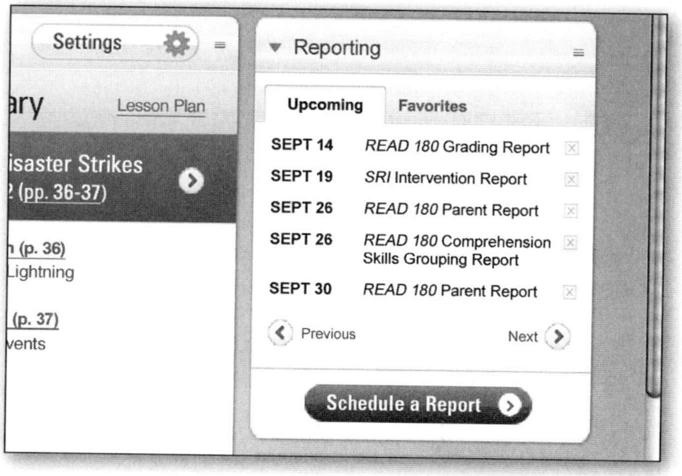

Directions

1. Sign in to the Teacher Dashboard with your SAM username and password.
2. On the Teacher Dashboard Home Page, click the **Upcoming** tab under **Reporting.**
3. Use the **Previous** and **Next** arrows to scroll through a list of all reports you have scheduled.
4. To delete a scheduled report, click the **X** to the right of the report name.

Tech Tip

Scheduled reports are automatically sent to the email address that you have registered with SAM.

Mark a Report as Favorite

Designate your "go-to" reports as Favorites for quick reference when scheduling them.

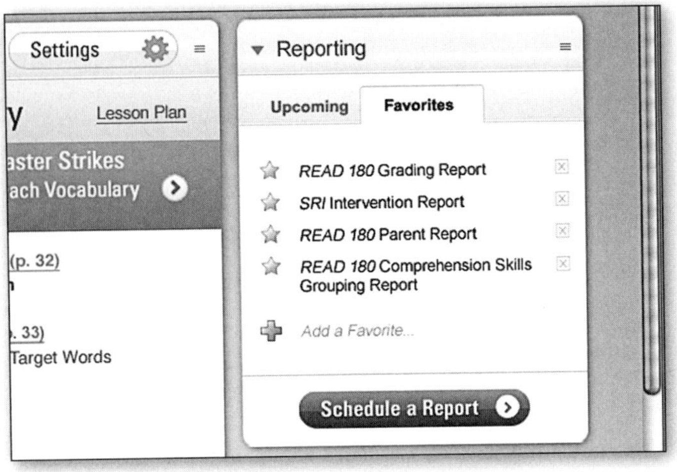

Directions

1. Sign in to the Teacher Dashboard with your SAM username and password.
2. On the Teacher Dashboard Home Page, click the **Favorites** tab under **Reporting.**
3. Click + **Add a Favorite**.
4. Click a report name from the pull-down menu to select it.
5. Click **Save** to save the selected report as a Favorite. The report will now appear in the **Favorites** tab.
6. To delete a report from the **Favorites** tab, click the **X** to the right of the report name.

Tech Tip

The Favorites tab will automatically display recommended Best Practice Reports unless you add other SAM reports as your Favorites.

Access Professional Development

Access videos, presentations, and articles for effective teaching and *READ 180* best practices.

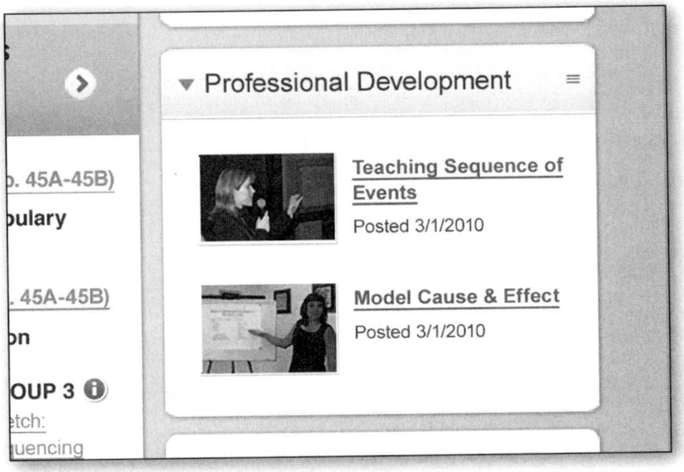

Directions

1. Sign in to the Teacher Dashboard with your SAM username and password.
2. Check the **Professional Development** section on the right side of the Teacher Dashboard Home Page to see resources related to daily instruction.

Tech Tip

The Professional Development resources relate to whichever Workshop lessons are displayed in the Today's Summary sections of the Teacher Dashboard Home Page.

3. To view a video resource, click the arrow icon to play it in a pop-up window.
4. To view a PDF resource, click the resource link to open it in Adobe Acrobat. Click **File** in Adobe Acrobat to **Print** or **Save** the PDF resource.
5. To view a Community resource, click the resource link to access it on the *READ 180* Community website, which will open in a new window. Enter your Community username and password if you are not already logged in.

View Daily QuickTips

Read brief tips to enhance your daily instruction and program implementation.

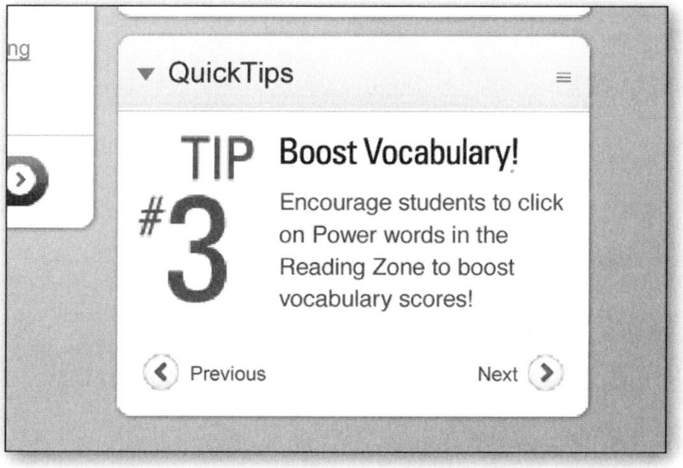

Directions

1. Sign in to the Teacher Dashboard with your SAM username and password.
2. Check the **QuickTips** section on the right side of the Teacher Dashboard Home Page to see a recommendation for effective *READ 180* implementation.
3. Click the **Previous** and **Next** arrows to scroll through all available QuickTips.

Tech Tip

The QuickTips automatically update so a new recommendation will appear every weekday throughout the school year.

Use the Web Gateway

Use the Web Gateway to connect to additional Scholastic resources and build *READ 180* expertise.

Directions

1. Sign in to the Teacher Dashboard with your SAM username and password.
2. On the Teacher Dashboard Home Page, click in the **Web Gateway** to access the Interactive Teaching System (ITS).
3. To explore the eReads Collections your students are reading, click in the **Web Gateway.**
4. To connect to the *READ 180* Community, click in the **Web Gateway.** Log in with your Community username and password.
5. To link to professional development resources, click in the **Web Gateway.**

Tech Tip

Click to access the *READ 180* online course (see pages 226–227), Training Zone, or Scholastic U, depending on the professional development resources your school has purchased.

6. To connect to the Product Support website, click in the **Web Gateway.** Log in with your Product Support username and password.

Exploring the Interactive Teaching System

The Interactive Teaching System (ITS) consists of digital versions of *READ 180* instructional materials for convenient lesson preparation and increased student engagement.

Anytime, Anywhere Lesson Planning

The Interactive Teaching System (ITS) makes it easy to plan and prepare lessons for daily Whole- and Small-Group Instruction. Connect to ITS from the Web Gateway on the Teacher Dashboard Home Page, or access ITS directly at **www.read180.com/its**. ITS allows you to:

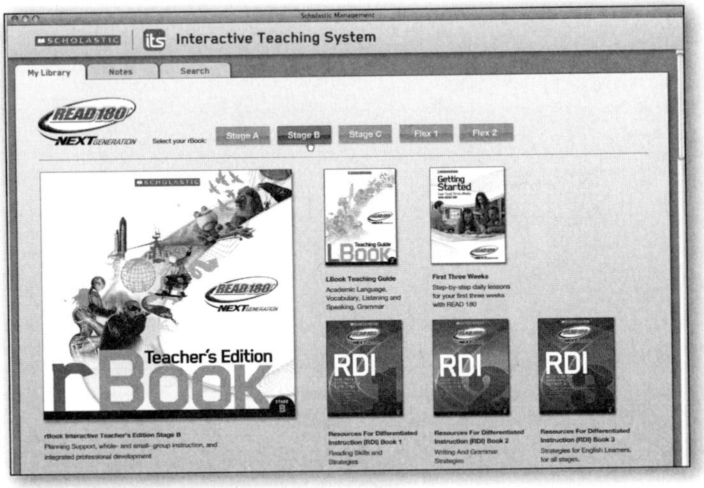

Interactive Teaching System (ITS)

- Explore digital versions of the *rBook Teacher's Edition, Resources for Differentiated Instruction,* and *Getting Started: Your First Three Weeks With READ 180.*
- Access additional instructional content, including a Do Now, Wrap-Up, and Scaffolded Support for every Whole and Small Group lesson.
- Download SAM Resources by clicking hyperlinks in every lesson.
- View embedded Anchor Videos for *rBook* Workshops at point of use.
- Review RED Routine steps and see routines in action with professional development videos.
- Create virtual sticky notes on the digital lesson plans for later reference.

Increasing Student Engagement

Use ITS to project *rBook* lessons and practice pages during class to provide visual support and scaffolding for your students. If you have an interactive whiteboard, increase engagement and motivation by allowing students to use the whiteboard-compatible ITS tools to annotate pages.

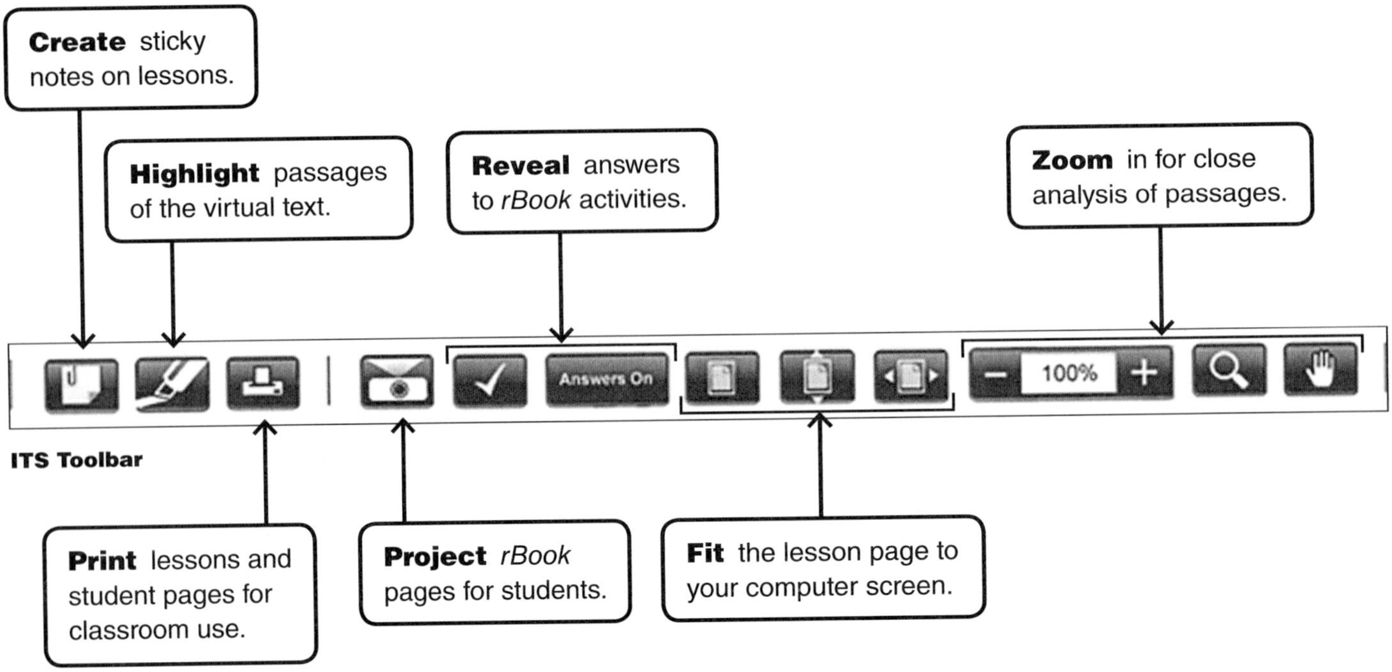

ITS Toolbar

Accessing Additional Instruction

ITS offers additional instructional content to begin and wrap up each class period as well as differentiate lessons based on student readiness. Click the red **ITS** icons embedded in each lesson in the interactive *rBook Teacher's Edition* to access:

- **Do Now** questions or prompts for students to respond to orally or in writing at the beginning of the class period.
- **Wrap-Up** activities for students to reflect on the day's learning during Whole-Group Wrap-Up in the last ten minutes of class.
- **Scaffolded Support** strategies that help you differentiate Small-Group Instruction to meet student needs. Use the "Boost" strategies with your most struggling students to support them for lesson success. Use the "Stretch" strategies to extend the lesson for students who are ready for a challenge.

Do Now (2 Minutes)

Have students write at least two things they already know about hurricanes.

1. I already know that hurricanes _______.
2. Also, I know that they _______.

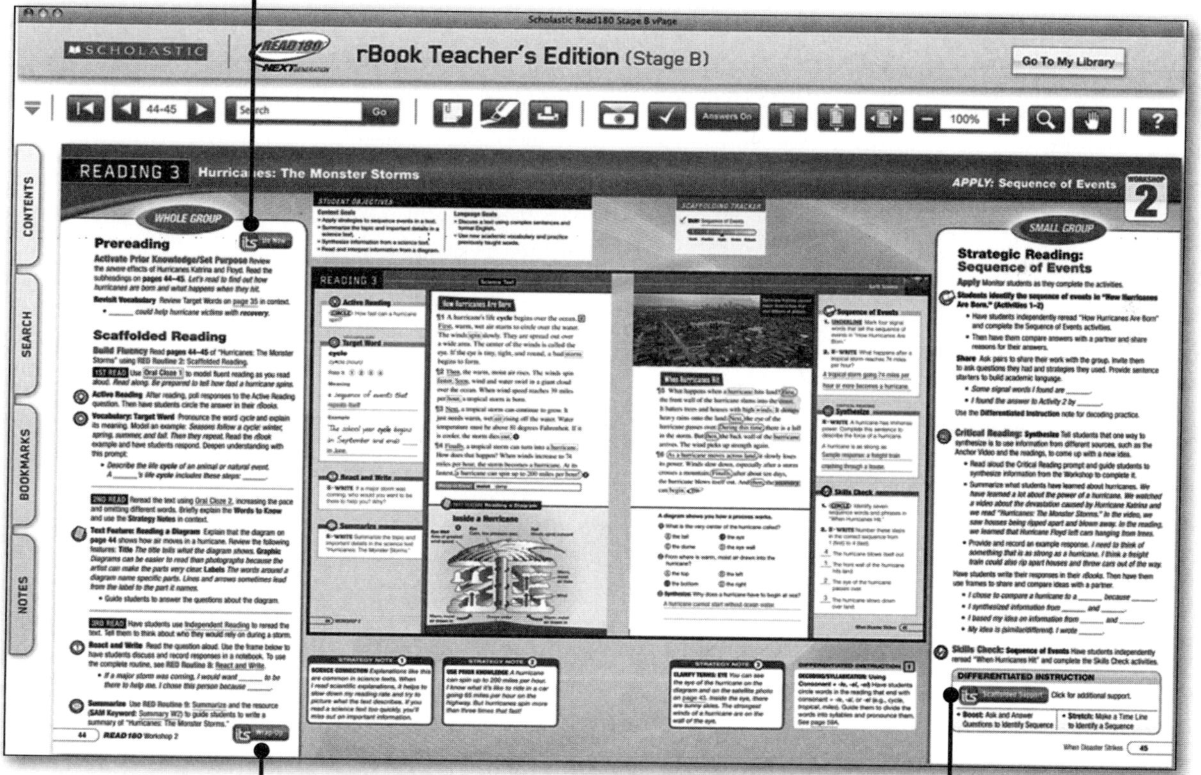

Wrap-Up (8-10 Minutes)

Write two new things that you learned about hurricanes.

1. I learned that hurricanes _______.
2. Also, I learned that one effect of Hurricane _______ was that _______.

Scaffolded Support

BOOST

When to Differentiate: After students complete Activity 3 (p. 43)

Self-Monitoring With a Text Marking

Read aloud paragraphs 3–4 of "Hurricanes: The Monster Storms" and guide students to number the events in order from 1–4. Then have them check the order they wrote for Activity 3 to make sure it matches the numbers they marked in the text.

STRETCH

When to Differentiate: After students complete Activity 3 (p. 43)

Self-Monitoring With a Partner

Have partners check the order of events for paragraphs 3–4 of "Hurricanes: The Monster Storms." Direct one partner to read the events in the order they marked while the other partner listens to see if it makes sense. Then switch roles and have students make any corrections.

Select a Resource on ITS

Choose a digital teaching resource from your Interactive Teaching System (ITS) library.

Directions

1. Sign in to the Teacher Dashboard with your SAM username and password.
2. On the Teacher Dashboard Home Page, click in the **Web Gateway** to launch the **Interactive Teaching System** in a new window.

Tech Tip

You can also access the Interactive Teaching System by visiting www.read180.com/its. Log in with your SAM username and password.

3. Use the pull-down menu in the upper right corner of the screen to select ***READ 180* Next Generation.**
4. Click the button for your *READ 180* Stage next to **Select your rBook** in the **My Library** tab.
5. Click a book cover or title to select and open it.

Navigate a Resource on ITS

Use the ITS navigation tools to explore your selected digital resource.

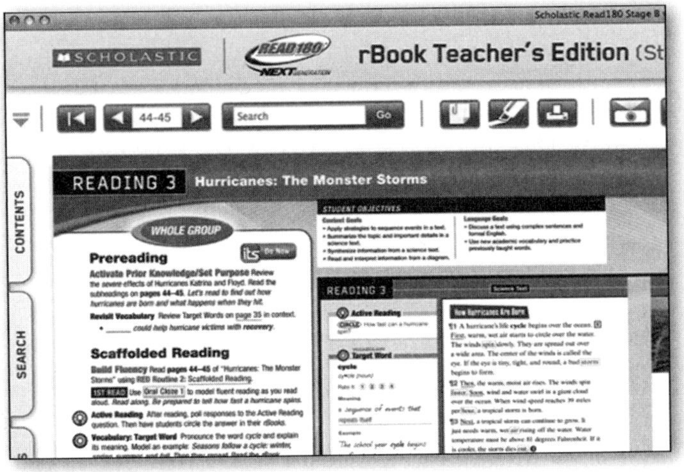

Directions

1. Sign in to the Teacher Dashboard with your SAM username and password.
2. On the Teacher Dashboard Home Page, click in the **Web Gateway.** Select a resource from your **ITS** library to open it.
3. Click the **Contents** tab on the left side of the screen to see a list of sections in the resource. Click a section heading to go to the first page of that section, or click + to view a list of pages in that section. Click a page heading to go to that page.

Tech Tip

View a list of sections at any time by clicking Contents on the left side of every ITS screen.

4. Click on the far left in the ITS toolbar to revisit the last page you viewed in the resource.
5. Enter a number in the blank entry field on the left side of the ITS toolbar to jump to a specific page.
6. Click the **Previous** and **Next** buttons in the ITS toolbar to scroll through pages in the resource.

Preview the Do Now and Wrap-Up

Preview brief activities in ITS to begin and end the day's class period.

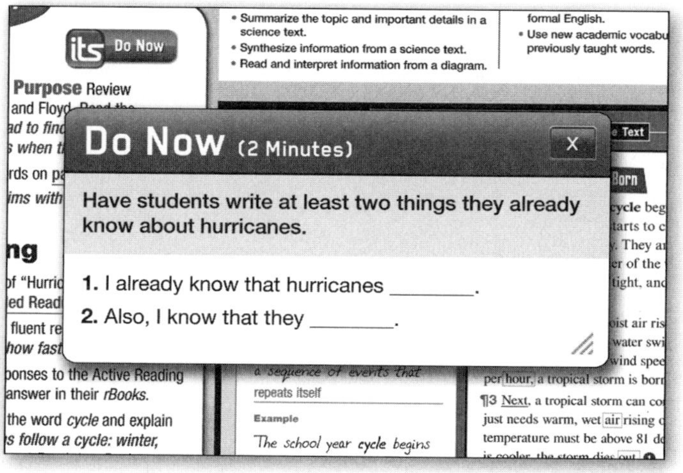

Directions

1. Sign in to the Teacher Dashboard with your SAM username and password.
2. On the Teacher Dashboard Home Page, click **Whole-Group Instruction** in **Today's Summary** to view the day's Whole Group lesson in the digital *rBook Teacher's Edition* on ITS.
3. Click its Do Now near the top of the Whole Group lesson to see a Do Now activity to begin the class period. Click **X** to close the **Do Now** window.
4. Click its Wrap-Up near the bottom of the Whole Group lesson to see a Wrap-Up activity to end the class period. Click **X** to close the **Wrap-Up** window.

Tech Tip

Display the activities by clicking in the ITS toolbar. Click near the top of the projected *rBook* page and select Do Now or Wrap-Up from the pull-down menu.

Plan Scaffolded Support

Integrate Boost and Stretch strategies during the lesson to differentiate instruction for your students.

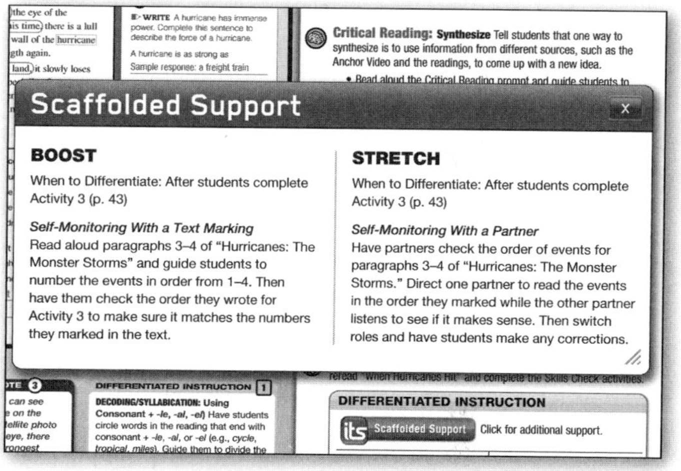

Directions

1. Sign in to the Teacher Dashboard with your SAM username and password.
2. On the Teacher Dashboard Home Page, click **Small-Group Instruction** in **Today's Summary** to view the day's Small Group lesson in the digital *rBook Teacher's Edition* on ITS.
3. Click its Scaffolded Support near the bottom of the Small Group lesson to see Boost and Stretch strategies. Use **Boost** strategies to provide extra support for struggling students. Use **Stretch** strategies to extend learning for advanced students.
4. Click **X** to close the **Scaffolded Support** window.

Tech Tip

Click in the ITS toolbar, then select Scaffolded Support to print the strategies, which also appear on printed lesson plans (see page 171).

Access Teaching Support Tools

Access instructional and support resources on ITS for comprehensive lesson planning.

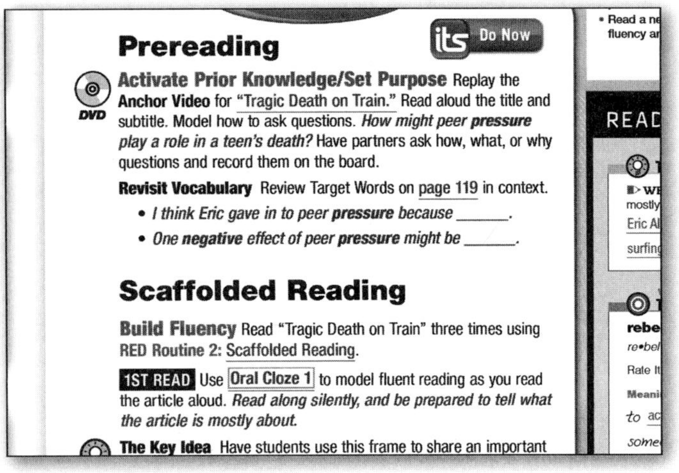

Directions

1. Sign in to the Teacher Dashboard with your SAM username and password.
2. On the Teacher Dashboard Home Page, click the page links in **Today's Summary** to access that lesson in the digital *rBook Teacher's Edition* on ITS.
3. Click [its Do Now], [its Wrap-Up], and [its Scaffolded Support] for additional content for Whole- and Small-Group Instruction. In Reading lessons, click **DVD** under **Prereading** to play the Anchor Video for the passage.
4. Click underlined **RED Routines** to review the routine steps in ITS. Some routines also offer videos of program experts modeling them.
5. Click any page links in the digital lesson to jump to those pages in ITS.

Tech Tip

Click [icon] in the ITS toolbar to return to your original lesson page after jumping to a different page in ITS.

6. Click any underlined SAM Keywords to view a PDF of that SAM resource in Adobe Acrobat.

Annotate Lessons in ITS

Highlight and leave notes in ITS for later reference when planning or teaching lessons.

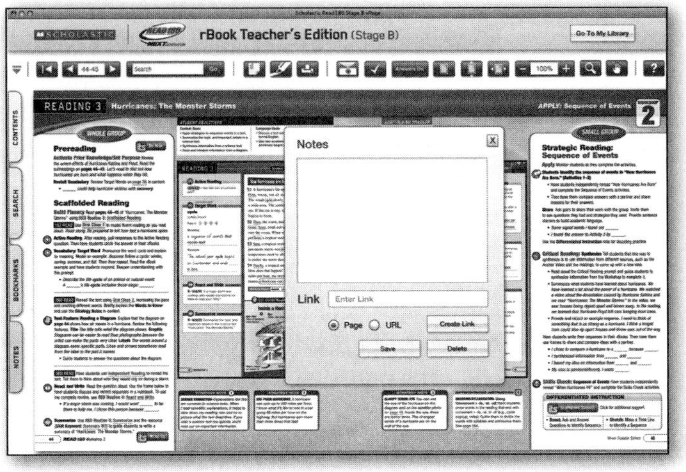

Directions

1. Sign in to the Teacher Dashboard with your SAM username and password.
2. On the Teacher Dashboard Home Page, click the page links in **Today's Summary** to access that lesson in the digital *rBook Teacher's Edition* on ITS.
3. Click [icon] in the ITS toolbar to activate the highlighting tool. Drag the highlighter icon over passages on the lesson pages to highlight them. Click [icon] again to stop highlighting.
4. Click [icon] in the ITS toolbar to create a virtual sticky note. Click anywhere on the lesson page to "stick" a virtual note to that spot.
5. Type your notes in the **Notes pop-up.**
6. Create a link to another page in the *rBook Teacher's Edition* by typing a number in the blank field next to **Link.** Click **Page**, then click **Create Link.**
7. Create a link to a website by entering a Web address in the blank field next to **Link.** Check the button next to **URL,** then click **Create Link.**
8. Click **Save** to save your note. View the note later by clicking [icon] within the lesson to open saved notes.

Project Pages for Students

Project *rBook* pages during class to increase student engagement and scaffold learning.

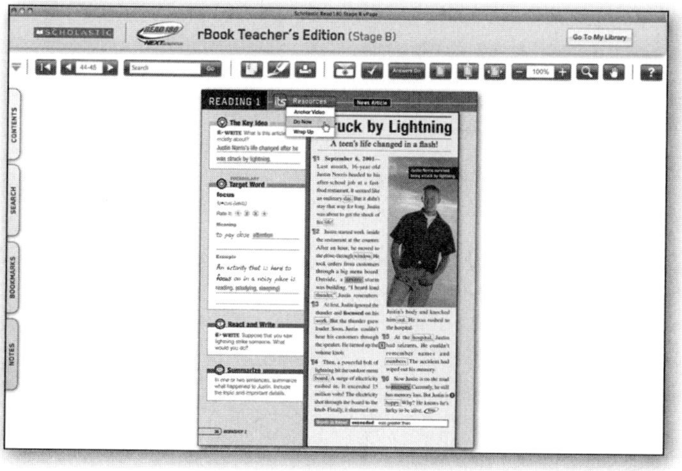

Directions

1. Sign in to the Teacher Dashboard with your SAM username and password.
2. On the Teacher Dashboard Home Page, click the page links in **Today's Summary** to access that lesson in the digital *rBook Teacher's Edition* on ITS.
3. Click in the ITS toolbar to project the corresponding student *rBook* pages.
4. Click at the top of the *rBook* page to display the **Anchor Video, Do Now,** or **Wrap-Up.** Click **X** to close each pop-up window.
5. Click **Answers On** in the ITS toolbar to reveal all answers for lesson activities. Click the button again to hide the answers.
6. Click **Select Answers** in the ITS toolbar to reveal answers to lesson activities one at a time. Drag the check mark icon across the lesson page until it turns green. Then click to reveal the answer.

Tech Tip

Connect your computer to an LCD projector to project ITS pages onto your board or interactive whiteboard during class.

Adjust ITS Sizing

Zoom in to focus on pages and passages in ITS.

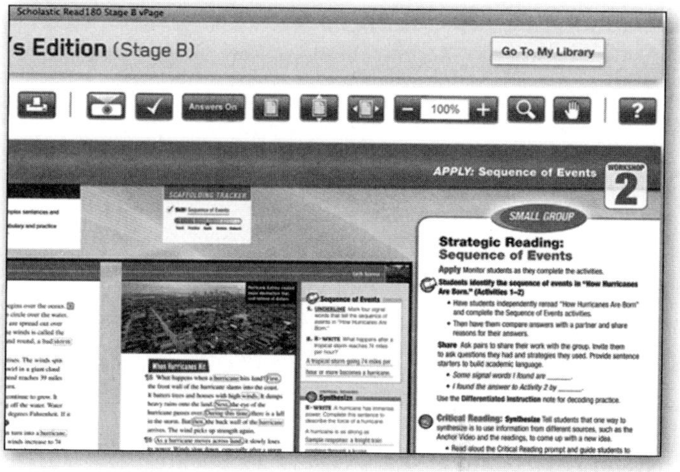

Directions

1. Sign in to the Teacher Dashboard with your SAM username and password.
2. On the Teacher Dashboard Home Page, click the page links in **Today's Summary** to access that lesson in the digital *rBook Teacher's Edition* on ITS.
3. Click or in the ITS toolbar to view one or two pages at once.
4. Click or in the ITS toolbar to fill the screen with the page vertically or horizontally.
5. Click **Zoom In** or **Zoom Out** in the ITS toolbar to increase or decrease the size of the lesson page.
6. Click in the ITS toolbar, then click and drag your mouse over a section of the page for a close-up of that section. Click **Zoom to 100%** to return to viewing the entire lesson page.

Tech Tip

After zooming in, click in the ITS toolbar. Click the lesson and move your mouse around to see different areas of the page.

Reflecting on Next Generation Technology

Complete the chart below to review and reflect on teaching with technology in *READ 180*.

Teaching Tool	Review and Reflect
Scholastic Achievement Manager (SAM)	*A key task I'll do in SAM to get my students started with* READ 180 *is…*
SAM Student Digital Portfolio	*I look forward to using the SAM Student Digital Portfolio to…*
Teacher Dashboard Today's Summary	*Today's Summary will help me plan and prepare for lessons by…*
Teacher Dashboard Groupinator	*The Groupinator supports me with differentiating because…*
Teacher Dashboard Data Snapshots	*I can check the Data Snapshots to…*
Interactive Teaching System (ITS)	*One ITS resource or tool I plan to use for my instruction is…*

Teacher Tip

Find additional support for *READ 180* technology on the Product Support website at www.scholastic.com/read180ng/productsupport.

TEACHER IMPLEMENTATION GUIDE

Assessment and Data-Driven Instruction

What Is Data-Driven Instruction?

Analyzing *READ 180* Next Generation assessment data regularly can help you monitor progress and identify your students' individual needs to differentiate instruction.

Differentiation Within the Instructional Model

Explicit teacher-directed instruction for a whole class is essential for accelerating reading performance. However, it alone cannot meet the various needs of a diverse group of learners. Struggling students benefit from intensive individualized instruction that is targeted to address their specific reading challenges. The *READ 180* Instructional Model promotes a balance of direct and differentiated instruction every day.

Whole-Group Instruction incorporates structured Instructional Routines, such as Scaffolded Reading and Think (Write)-Pair-Share, to ensure that all students are actively participating during reading, writing, and discussion.

Small-Group Instruction provides an opportunity to flexibly group students and target instruction to meet their specific reading and writing needs.

Instructional Software allows students to engage with "intelligent software" that collects ongoing data based on their responses and adapts content and pacing to meet their individual needs.

Modeled and Independent Reading offers high-interest, leveled texts to help students build fluency, vocabulary, comprehension, and confidence at their individual reading levels.

> **Research Says**
>
> **Teachers who rely mostly on whole-group instruction do not adequately meet the individual needs of their students who require extra literacy support.**
>
> Avalos, 2006

Dynamic Grouping

The Teacher Dashboard streamlines the process of differentiating instruction. The Groupinator on the Teacher Dashboard Class Page gathers student performance data from the Scholastic Achievement Manager (SAM). The Groupinator uses this data to group students for small-group rotations and recommend targeted lessons to meet their needs.

The groups recommended by the Groupinator are dynamic. They change four times per Workshop—for daily *rBook* instruction and for each of the three differentiation CheckPoints.

Check the Groupinator at the start of a Workshop to see recommended *rBook* Groups, which are based on student Lexile measures. Check the Groupinator again before each Workshop CheckPoint for support with grouping students based on their Topic Software, *rBook* writing, and *rSkills Test* performance (see page 172 for directions). Use SAM report data and observations about student class performance to inform any adjustments to the three small groups.

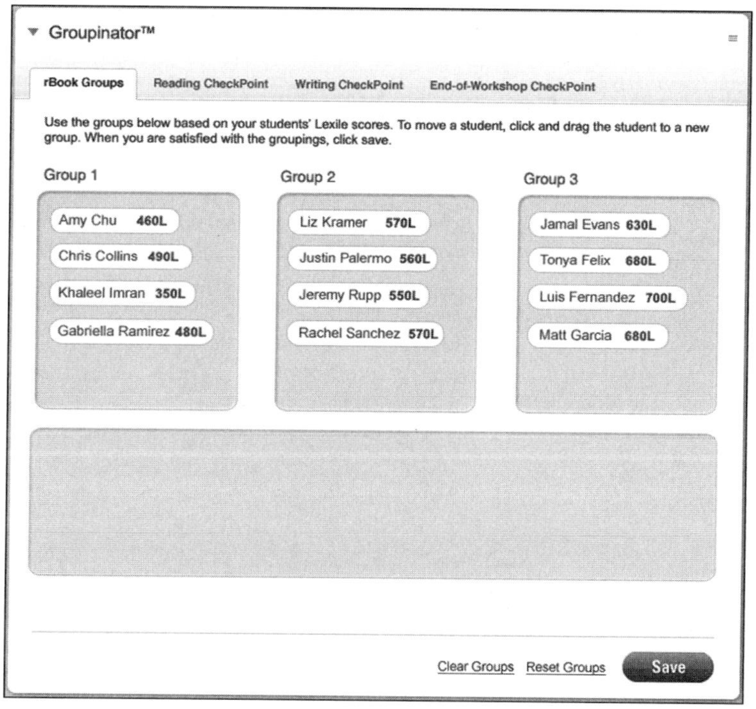

Groupinator, Teacher Dashboard Class Page

Understanding *READ 180* Assessments

***READ 180* includes a range of assessments to help you plan data-driven instruction, group students, monitor progress, and diagnose individual needs.**

	Assessment Tool	Purpose	What It Assesses	Frequency
SCREENING & PLACEMENT	***Scholastic Reading Inventory (SRI)***	• Screen students for appropriate intervention • Place students appropriately	• Baseline reading level • Placement within *READ 180*	**Once a year**
PROGRESS MONITORING	***Scholastic Reading Inventory (SRI)***	• Monitor student reading progress • Place students appropriately	• Current reading level • Reading gains	**2 times a year** (in addition to initial screening)
	rSkills Tests	• Measure acquisition of *rBook* Workshop skills • Group students for additional support	• Comprehension • Vocabulary/ Word Study • Conventions • Critical reading • Writing	**9 times a year** At the end of each *rBook* Workshop
	Oral Fluency Assessment	Monitor decoding and oral fluency progress	• Word recognition • Decoding speed and accuracy • Oral expressiveness	**3 times a year**
CURRICULUM-EMBEDDED	***READ 180* Topic Software**	• Monitor student progress • Diagnose reading strengths and challenges • Group students for targeted instruction	• Comprehension • Vocabulary • Fluency • Phonics • Spelling/ Encoding • Writing	**Daily** During Instructional Software Rotation
	Scholastic Reading Counts!	• Assess reading comprehension • Track independent reading progress	• Reading comprehension	When students complete books and eReads in Modeled and Independent Reading
	rBook	• Track mastery of *rBook* Workshop skills • Provide targeted instruction and instructional support	• Comprehension • Vocabulary/ Word Study • Conventions • Critical Reading • Writing	**Daily** Throughout each *rBook* Workshop
SUMMATIVE	***Scholastic Reading Inventory (SRI)***	• Monitor student reading progress • Place students appropriately	• Current reading level • Reading gains	**Once a year** (In addition to screening and progress monitoring)
	rSkills Summative Tests	Measure curriculum mastery	• Comprehension • Vocabulary • Conventions • Critical reading • Listening • Writing	**Midyear** **End-of-year**

Placement, Assessment, and Reporting Guide

Results	Diagnostic and Intervention Planning
Normative Data NCE, Stanine, Percentile **Performance Standards** Below Basic, Basic, Proficient, Advanced	**IF students are reading at grade level...** ...use grade-level curriculum. **IF students are reading below grade level...** ...begin *READ 180* at the designated level.
Normative Data NCE, Stanine, Percentile **Performance Standards** Below Basic, Basic, Proficient, Advanced	**Use results to...** ...group students with similar Lexile levels for Small-Group rotations. ...assign appropriate instructional and independent reading materials.
Test Results Comprehension, Vocabulary, Word Study, Conventions, Open Response: Critical Thinking, Writing Prompt	**IF students need further support/challenge...** ... review *READ 180* Reports to cross-reference results. ...regroup students and provide targeted support during Small-Group rotations.
Oral Fluency Results Percentile based on WCPM (Words Correct Per Minute)	**IF students need further support...** ...provide phonics or fluency support from *Resources for Differentiated Instruction* at *rBook* CheckPoints
Comprehension Results Reading for Detail, Sequencing, Finding the Main Idea, Summarizing, Cause and Effect, Compare and Contrast, Problem and Solution, Making Inferences, Drawing Conclusions **Other Results** Phonics, Spelling, Fluency, Writing, Time On-Task	**IF students need further support...** ...regroup students to provide targeted support during Small-Group rotations. ...monitor software usage. **IF students need challenge...** ...provide opportunities to apply skills with less scaffolding. ...ensure appropriate software level.
Quizzes passed Number of quizzes attempted Percentage of goal achieved	**IF students are not meeting individual goals...** ...provide additional support in daily independent reading
Writing Rubric Results Results align to writing type assessed **Wrap-Up Project Rubric Results** Results align to project type assessed **Workshop Rubric Results** Progress and performance on *rBook* tasks	**USE writing rubric results to...** ...provide support in revision during each Writing CheckPoint **USE Wrap-Up Project rubric results to...** ...provide feedback on project performance and track progress **USE Workshop rubric results to...** ...monitor overall performance and share results with students
Normative Data NCE, Stanine, Percentile **Performance Standards** Below Basic, Basic, Proficient, Advanced	**IF students are reading at grade level...** ...use grade-level curriculum. **IF students are reading below grade level...** ...begin *READ 180* at the designated level.
Test Results Comprehension, Vocabulary, Word Study, Conventions, Open Response: Critical Thinking, Writing Prompt	**IF students need further support/challenge...** ... review *READ 180* Reports to cross-reference results. ...provide targeted support during Small-Group rotations.

Managing Assessment Data

Run reports on the Scholastic Achievement Manager (SAM) and launch the Teacher Dashboard to access student performance data and make follow-up instructional decisions.

Scholastic Achievement Manager

The Scholastic Achievement Manager, or SAM, captures performance data each time students use one of the four technology-based program components: *READ 180* Topic Software, *rSkills Tests*, *Scholastic Reading Inventory (SRI)*, and *Scholastic Reading Counts! (SRC!)*. You can access this student performance data by logging in to SAM.

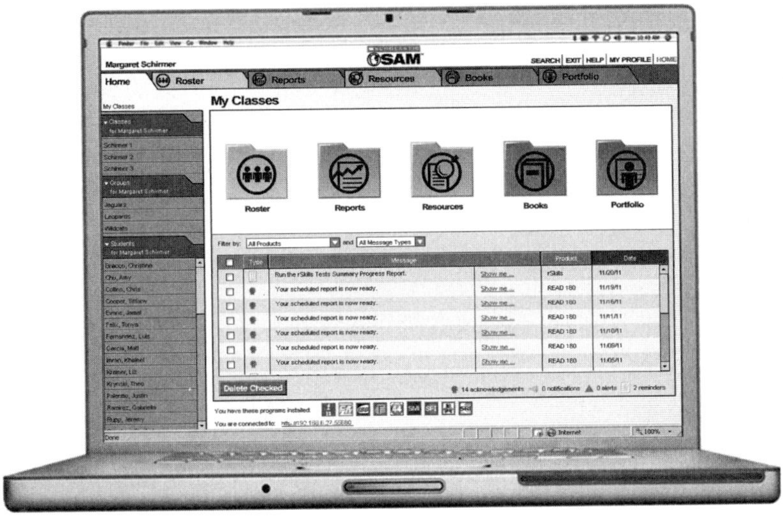

SAM Home Page

Reports SAM aggregates the performance data into data-rich reports. You can run the reports to see data for individual students, groups, or an entire class. The clearly organized reports enable you to monitor your students' progress, target instruction, and share results with administrators or families.

SAM Student Digital Portfolio SAM stores student responses for grading the following activities: Success Zone Final Fluency Recording, Writing Zone Respond & Write Published Response, and *rSkills Tests* Open Response and Writing Questions. You can access and evaluate student work on these assignments using the SAM Student Digital Portfolio. Use the rubrics provided to grade your students' work, then share constructive feedback to help them grow as readers and writers.

Teacher Dashboard

Your Teacher Dashboard is powered by SAM. The Dashboard pulls key data from SAM to run the following features that make it easy to keep track of student assessment results:

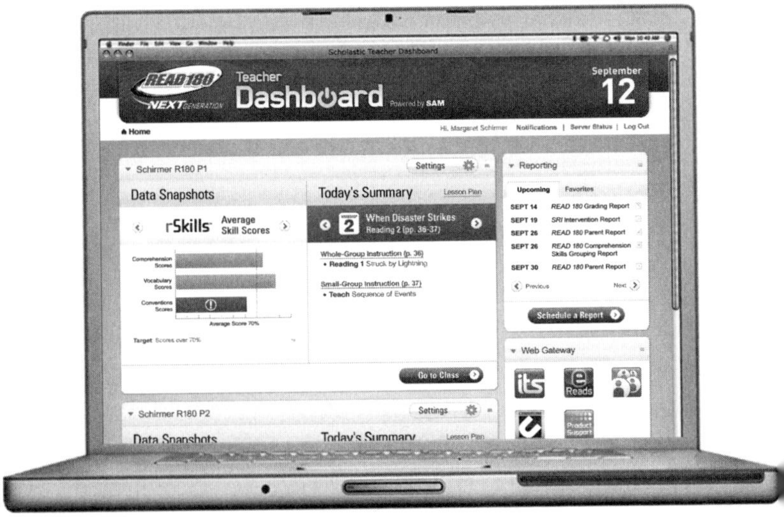

Teacher Dashboard Home Page

- **Data Snapshots** show the most crucial student data metrics for effective *READ 180* implementation, updated weekly.
- **Groupinator** uses student performance data to recommend small groups for differentiated instruction during daily *rBook* lessons and Workshop CheckPoints.
- **Notifications** help you monitor program usage, such as average Software session time, and let you know when your students achieve *READ 180* milestones, such as making Lexile growth or completing a Software Topic.
- **Report Scheduler** allows the Dashboard to automatically run your favorite SAM reports for you and send them to a designated email account.

Focusing on Best Practice Reports

Manage assessment data in SAM by regularly running the Best Practice Reports to monitor student progress and make instructional decisions.

Understanding the Reports

As students progress through the software, SAM captures and organizes the results of their work in easy-to-access reports. The Best Practice Reports represent the 16 most foundational reports to use regularly for progress monitoring and instructional decision-making across the technology components. Focus on the Best Practice Reports during your first year with *READ 180.* As you become more comfortable with the program, continue to use the Best Practice Reports as a foundation while you also run additional reports to drill down even further on student data.

Best Practice Class/Group Reports

Run these eight Best Practice Reports to monitor progress and target instruction for an entire class or group.

Best Practice Report	Frequency	Use to Determine
Instructional Planning Reports		
SRI Instructional Planning Report	4 times a year (after each *SRI* test)	*rBook* Groups and reading levels
READ 180 Comprehension Skills Grouping Report	Once per *rBook* Workshop (before Reading CheckPoints)	*rBook* Reading CheckPoint groups
rSkills College & Career Grouping Report	Once per *rBook* Workshop (after *rSkills Tests*)	*rBook* End-of-Workshop CheckPoint groups
SRC! Books Read Report	Monthly	Support needed for Modeled and Independent Reading
Progress Monitoring Reports		
SRI Growth Report	4 times a year (after each *SRI* test)	Student reading gains
READ 180 Reading Progress Report	Monthly	Student participation and progress in the Topic Software
rSkills College & Career Grading Report	Once per *rBook* Workshop (after *rSkills Tests*)	Student results on *rSkills Tests*
SRC! Reading Progress Report	Monthly	Student participation and success on *SRC!* quizzes

Best Practice Student Reports

To follow up on class reports, run and analyze the following eight Best Practice Reports for individual students:

- *SRI* Student Action Report
- *SRI* Student Progress College & Career Report
- *READ 180* Student Diagnostic Report
- *READ 180* Student Reading Report
- *rSkills* College & Career Student Skills Report
- *rSkills* College & Career Student Progress Report
- *SRC!* Recommended Reading Report
- *SRC!* Student Reading Report

Assessing Reading With *SRI*

Administer the *Scholastic Reading Inventory (SRI)* College & Career to place students in *READ 180* and monitor their reading progress throughout the school year.

Overview

The *Scholastic Reading Inventory (SRI)* College & Career is a research-based, computer-adaptive assessment that measures students' reading comprehension and reports their current reading levels.

As each student takes the test, the program "adapts" to his or her performance, adjusting the level and number of questions until it arrives at an accurate score. If the student misses a question, the next question will be slightly easier. If the student answers correctly, the next question will be slightly more difficult. The final *SRI* score is reported as a Lexile—a measure from BR ("Beginning Reader") to above 1500L—that represents the student's reading level.

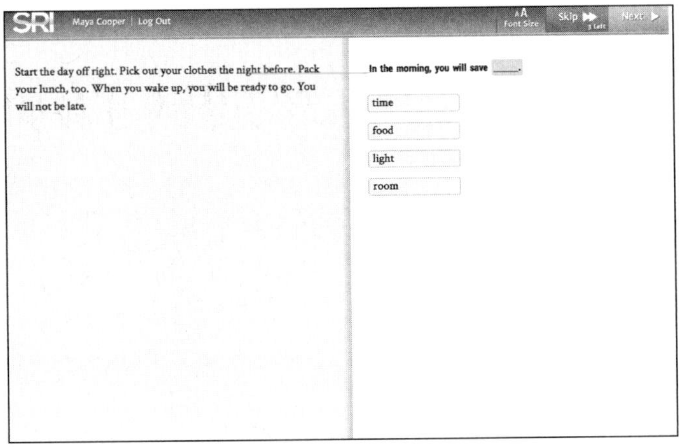

***SRI* Test Question**

Test Items

SRI has a bank of over 5,000 test items, which come from authentic fiction and nonfiction texts. When taking the *SRI,* students answer fill-in-the-blank, or cloze, questions, similar to those found on many standardized tests. *SRI* tests typically have 20 to 25 questions that should take students about 20 minutes to complete.

Administer *SRI* College & Career for Placement

Administer the *SRI* to determine student placement in *READ 180* and report students' test scores, or Lexile measures, to SAM. SAM uses the Lexile measures to automatically place each student in the appropriate *READ 180* Level on the Topic Software. The Groupinator on the Teacher Dashboard also uses students' Lexile measures to form small groups for daily *rBook* instruction.

Targeting Student Levels Before administering the first *SRI* test at the start of the school year, be sure to estimate—or target—your students' reading levels in SAM. Targeting helps *SRI* select an appropriate reading level for the first test question for each student. This reduces testing time and promotes more accurate results. See page 158 for directions on targeting in SAM.

Checking *SRI* Results After administering the *SRI,* run the *SRI* Instructional Planning Report in SAM to see student Lexile measures. The Topic Software uses the Lexile measures to automatically place students at the right level. You can also use Lexile measures to guide student selection of Paperbacks for independent reading.

Level	Stage A	Stage B	Stage C
1	200L–450L	200L–450L	200L–450L
2	400L–700L	400L–700L	400L–700L
3	600L–900L	600L–900L	600L–900L
4	N/A	800L–1200L	800L–1200L

***READ 180* Topic Software and Paperback Levels**

Administer *SRI* for Progress Monitoring

After using *SRI* results to place students in *READ 180*, administer the *SRI* test three more times during the year to monitor their reading growth. As the year progresses, revisit *SRI* data to regroup students and adjust instruction as needed.

Establishing a Testing Cycle It is recommended that students take the *SRI* four times each year, with at least 30 days between tests. Spacing out the assessments allows time for students to make meaningful gains through instruction and practice. The most effective *READ 180* classrooms "frontload" the *SRI* by administering two tests in the Fall, followed by one test in the Winter and a final summative test in the Spring. This ensures a reliable baseline score in the Fall for determining accurate placement and making instructional plans.

Test	Time of Year	Purpose
1	First three weeks of instruction	Determine initial placement
2	Fall	Establish goals
3	Winter	Forecast annual growth
4	Spring	Evaluate overall growth

***SRI* Testing Cycle**

Setting Growth Expectations Expected Lexile growth on the *SRI* tests varies for each student, depending on the student's grade level and how close he or she is reading to grade-level proficiency. Depending on their grade level, students reading at the 25th percentile can expect to grow an average of 140L (elementary), 70L (middle school), or 50L (high school) per year. In general, you can expect more growth from students with lower Lexile measures.

For additional information on growth expectations and support with setting individual growth targets, see pages 62–63 in the *Placement, Assessment, and Reporting Guide.*

Preparing Students to Take the *SRI*

Support your students to do their best on the *SRI* by sharing the following test-taking strategies with them. You may want to practice reading example test questions with the class and modeling how to apply each strategy.

- **Read Directions Carefully** Make sure you understand the directions before beginning the test or answering a question.
- **Identify Important Ideas** While reading each passage, look for ideas you think might be important, especially in the first and last sentences.
- **Complete the Sentence** Fill in the blank with your selected answer. Then read the whole sentence and ask yourself: *Does this sentence make sense? Does it match the passage?*
- **Eliminate Incorrect Answers** If you know an answer is incorrect, eliminate it. Consider the remaining answers before making your choice.
- **Use Your Skips** You can skip up to three questions without penalty. Use a skip if you do not understand the subject matter of a passage.

Participating in the *SRI* Student Experience

Use the steps below during training to experience taking the *Scholastic Reading Inventory (SRI)* from a student's perspective.

Choose Book Interests

Log in as a student and indicate your reading interests.

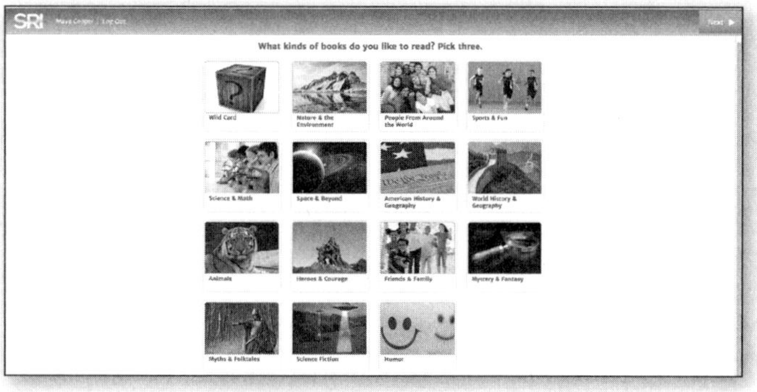

Directions

1. Navigate to the SRI Demo on the Literacy Simulator.
2. Enter your username and password and click **Go On**.
3. After logging in, select **Reading Comprehension**.
4. Select three reading categories or interests.
5. Click **Next** to move on.

Tech Tip

The chosen reading interests inform the *SRI* College & Career Recommended Reading Report that students receive at the end of the test. They do not influence the selection of *SRI* test questions.

Take a Practice Test

Listen to the instructions and take a practice test.

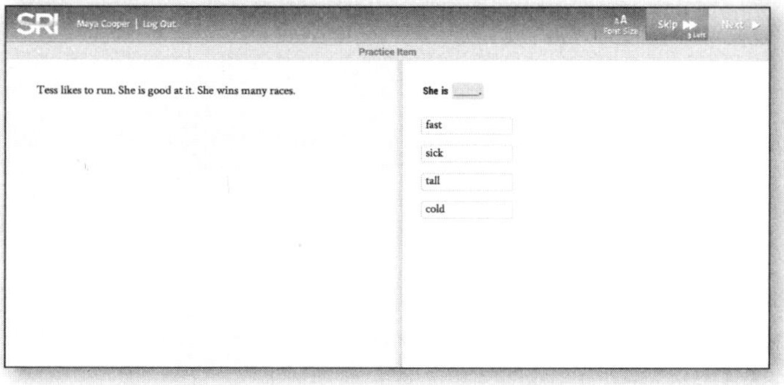

Directions

1. Use your headphones to listen to the directions as they are read aloud. Then click **Next** to move on.
2. Answer three practice questions, one at a time. For each question, click your answer choice. Then click **Next.**

Tech Tip

The Practice Test checks that the student knows how to use the computer to answer test questions. It offers passages that are lower than the student's estimated reading level in SAM.

3. You may skip up to three questions by clicking **Skip.**

Tech Tip

If a student receives a pop-up to ask you for help, review the *SRI* directions and purpose with him or her. Then monitor as he or she retakes the Practice Test and provide follow-up support as needed.

Take an *SRI* Test

Take an *SRI* test that has three questions. In a real *SRI* test, students answer 20 to 25 questions.

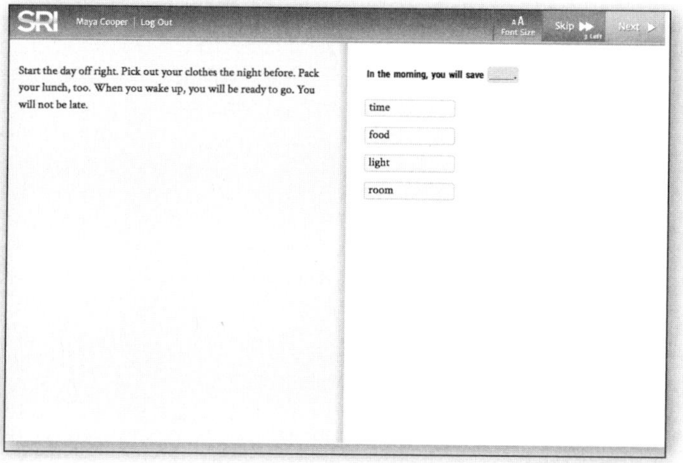

Directions

1. After selecting reading interests, click **Next** to move on to the practice test.
2. Read each passage and corresponding question. Choose an answer by clicking its box.
3. Click **Next** to move on to the next question. Notice that the questions increase in difficulty as you answer them correctly.

Tech Tip

Tell students to press Esc on their keyboard if they need to exit before finishing the test. Their progress will be saved so they can pick up exactly where they left off next time they log in to *SRI*.

View and Print a Reading Report

View and print a personalized reading list based on your Lexile and selected reading interests.

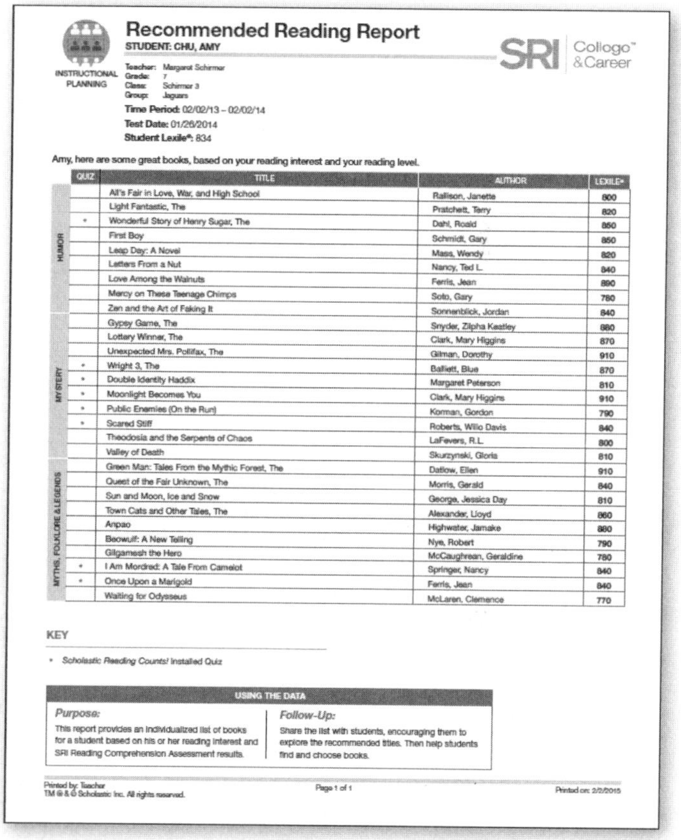

Recommended Reading Report
STUDENT: CHU, AMY

SRI College & Career

INSTRUCTIONAL PLANNING

Teacher: Margaret Schirmer
Grade: 7
Class: Schirmer 3
Group: Jaguars
Time Period: 02/02/13 – 02/02/14
Test Date: 01/26/2014
Student Lexile®: 834

Amy, here are some great books, based on your reading interest and your reading level.

	QUIZ	TITLE	AUTHOR	LEXILE®
HUMOR		All's Fair in Love, War, and High School	Rallison, Janette	800
		Light Fantastic, The	Pratchett, Terry	820
	•	Wonderful Story of Henry Sugar, The	Dahl, Roald	850
		First Boy	Schmidt, Gary	850
		Leap Day: A Novel	Mass, Wendy	820
		Letters From a Nut	Nancy, Ted L.	840
		Love Among the Walnuts	Ferris, Jean	890
		Mercy on These Teenage Chimps	Soto, Gary	780
		Zen and the Art of Faking It	Sonnenblick, Jordan	840
MYSTERY		Gypsy Game, The	Snyder, Zilpha Keatley	880
		Lottery Winner, The	Clark, Mary Higgins	870
		Unexpected Mrs. Pollifax, The	Gilman, Dorothy	910
	•	Wright 3, The	Balliett, Blue	870
	•	Double Identity Haddix	Margaret Peterson	810
	•	Moonlight Becomes You	Clark, Mary Higgins	910
	•	Public Enemies (On the Run)	Korman, Gordon	790
	•	Scared Stiff	Roberts, Willo Davis	840
		Theodosia and the Serpents of Chaos	LaFevers, R.L.	800
		Valley of Death	Skurzynski, Gloria	810
MYTHS, FOLKLORE & LEGENDS		Green Man: Tales From the Mythic Forest, The	Datlow, Ellen	910
		Quest of the Fair Unknown, The	Morris, Gerald	840
		Sun and Moon, Ice and Snow	George, Jessica Day	810
		Town Cats and Other Tales, The	Alexander, Lloyd	860
		Anpao	Highwater, Jamake	880
		Beowulf: A New Telling	Nye, Robert	790
		Gilgamesh the Hero	McCaughrean, Geraldine	780
	•	I Am Mordred: A Tale From Camelot	Springer, Nancy	840
	•	Once Upon a Marigold	Ferris, Jean	840
		Waiting for Odysseus	McLaren, Clemence	770

KEY

• *Scholastic Reading Counts!* Installed Quiz

USING THE DATA

Purpose:
This report provides an individualized list of books for a student based on his or her reading interest and SRI Reading Comprehension Assessment results.

Follow-Up:
Share the list with students, encouraging them to explore the recommended titles. Then help students find and choose books.

Printed by: Teacher
TM ® & © Scholastic Inc. All rights reserved.
Page 1 of 1
Printed on: 2/2/2015

Directions

1. Upon test completion, you will receive a Recommended Reading List.
2. You can take a screen grab of the list, or you can print a Recommended Reading Report (pictured above) from SAM.
3. Click **Log Out** to log out of SRI.

Tech Tip

The computer workstation must be connected to a printer for students to print their *SRI* Recommended Reading Report.

Identifying Students for *READ 180*

Work with your school leaders and colleagues to determine how you will select students who will benefit most from *READ 180* intervention.

Teacher Tip

Ask colleagues who teach the grade level below yours which students struggled to keep up during the previous school year. Use these observations to identify candidates for *SRI* screening and possible placement in *READ 180*.

Screening Students Using *SRI*

Screen all students who are possible candidates for reading intervention using the *Scholastic Reading Inventory (SRI)*. *SRI* assesses reading comprehension using the Lexile Framework for Reading to determine if students are reading above, on, or below grade level.

After administering SRI, check test results by logging into SAM and running the *SRI* Intervention Grouping Report (see page 197). Students who fall in the Below Basic and Basic Performance Standards—which are colored red and yellow—make good candidates for *READ 180.* They likely need extra intervention and support to achieve grade-level reading proficiency.

Reviewing State Test Results

State test scores may reveal a need for reading intervention. Work with your administrators to look at recent standardized test results and identify student achievement gaps. Consider selecting students in the bottom two quartiles who are reading below grade level for further screening with *SRI*.

Other Selection Criteria

Additional signs that a student might benefit from participation in *READ 180* include:

- Formal proficiency exams show that a student is reading below grade level.
- Teacher observations and informal assessments indicate that a student is reading below grade level and needs intervention.
- Student displays frustration and does not participate during class or complete classwork.
- Student is an English language learner reading below grade level.
- Student is in a special education program and needs intervention to address reading challenges.

Reflection

I'll consider these criteria when recommending students for my* READ 180 *class(es)…

SRI Instructional Planning Report

This Best Practice Report groups students based on *SRI* performance standards. Use it to check *SRI* test results and select students for *READ 180* intervention.

Select "This School Year" as the report time period to see the most current *SRI* test results.

Compare your students' Lexiles to national norms to set goals.

Use *SRI* settings in SAM to align the proficiency bands with your district standards.

Notice that students fall into four color-coded groups based on *SRI* performance.

Instructional Planning Report

INSTRUCTIONAL PLANNING

CLASS: Schirmer 3

SRI College™ & Career

School: Lincoln Middle School
Teacher: Margaret Schirmer
Grade: 7

Time Period: 08/24/13 – 02/02/14

PERFORMANCE LEVEL	STUDENT	GRADE	LEXILE®	DATE	NORMATIVE DATA		
					PERCENTILE RANK	NCE	STANINE
	Krynski, Theo	7	1130	01/25/14	80	68	7
	Collins, Chris	7	968	01/26/14	52	53	5
	Ramirez, Gabriella	7	1042	01/28/14	65	60	6
	Rupp, Jeremy	7	1027	01/27/14	63	59	6
	Chu, Amy	7	834	01/26/14	32	41	4
	Kramer, Liz	7	909	01/26/14	43	48	5
	Sanchez, Rachel	7	792	01/25/14	26	36	4
	Cooper, Tiffany	7	841	01/25/14	32	41	4
	Imran, Khaleel	7	792	01/25/14	26	36	4
	Evans, Jamal	7	781	01/25/14	25	35	4
	Bracco, Christine	7	778	01/27/14	25	35	4
	Garcia, Matt	7	770	09/01/13	23	34	4
	Palermo, Justin	7	538	01/25/14	5	13	2
	Fernandez, Luis	7	342	01/25/14	1	1	1
	Felix, Tonya	7	BR	01/25/14	1	1	1

KEY

BR = Beginning Reader
ADVANCED
PROFICIENT
BASIC
BELOW BASIC
▸ Test taken in less than 15 minutes

YEAR-END PROFICIENCY RANGES					
GRADE 1	190–530L	GRADE 5	830–1010L	GRADE 9	1050–1260L
GRADE 2	420–650L	GRADE 6	925–1070L	GRADE 10	1080–1335L
GRADE 3	520–820L	GRADE 7	970–1120L	GRADE 11	1185–1385L
GRADE 4	740–940L	GRADE 8	1010–1185L	GRADE 12	1185–1385L

USING THE DATA

Purpose:	*Follow-Up:*
This report groups students by performance level on the SRI Reading Comprehension Assessment.	Plan appropriate instruction for students at each performance level. Provide additional support or intervention for students at the Basic or Below Basic level.

Printed by: Teacher

Page 1 of 1
Printed on: 2/2/2015

***SRI* Instructional Planning Report**

For additional information on this report, see pages 194–197 in the *Placement, Assessment, and Reporting Guide*.

SRI Growth Report

This Best Practice Report measures student Lexile growth between two *SRI* tests within a selected time period.

Growth Report

TEACHER: Margaret Schirmer

PROGRESS MONITORING

School: Lincoln Middle School
Grade: 7

Time Period: 08/31/11 – 02/02/12

STUDENT	GRADE	FIRST TEST IN SELECTED TIME PERIOD LEXILE®	FIRST TEST IN SELECTED TIME PERIOD DATE	LAST TEST IN SELECTED TIME PERIOD LEXILE®	LAST TEST IN SELECTED TIME PERIOD DATE	GROWTH IN LEXILE®*
Chu, Amy	7	443	09/01/11	834	01/26/12	391
Krynski, Theo	7	984	09/04/11	1120	01/25/12	136
Collins, Chris	7	784	09/04/11	868	01/26/12	84
Ramirez, Gabriella	7	661	09/02/11	743	01/28/12	82
Bracco, Christine	7	643	08/31/11	709	01/27/12	66
Evans, Jamal	7	665	08/31/11	719	01/25/12	54
Fernandez, Luis	7	200	08/31/11	242	01/25/12	42
Palermo, Justin	7	400	09/12/11	438	01/27/12	38
Rupp, Jeremy	7	691	09/02/11	727	01/27/12	36
Kramer, Liz	7	775	09/02/11	809	01/26/12	34
Sanchez, Rachel	7	783	09/02/11	792	01/25/12	9
Imran, Khaleel	7	710	08/31/11	719	01/25/12	9
Garcia, Matt	7	550	09/01/11	N/A	N/A	N/A
Felix, Tonya	7	BR (20)	09/01/11	BR (10)	01/25/12	(-10)
Cooper, Tiffany	7	880	09/02/11	781	01/25/12	(-99)

* Scale for bar chart is based on highest Lexile® growth within selected time period.

Using This Report

Purpose: To identify the growth each student is making, check the dates of the two tests for an individual student. On average, students are expected to grow approximately 75-100 Lexiles per year.

Follow-Up: Provide opportunities to challenge students who show significant progress. Provide appropriate levels of intervention and support to students who are showing little growth. If zero or negative Lexile growth is recorded, check to see if students' test experience is problematic in some way and retest accordingly.

***SRI* Growth Report**

Analyzing This Report

Use the steps below to closely analyze the data in this report.

1. Check that all students took both *SRI* tests during the selected time period.

   I see that ________________ did not take the second SRI test in the selected time period.

2. Identify students who are making strong reading gains of at least 50L.

   ________ out of 15 students in Ms. Schirmer's class have increased their score by at least 50 Lexile measures. The student who made the biggest gains is ________________.

3. Look for students who experienced decreases in their Lexile measures.

   ________________ and ________________ experienced drops in their Lexile measures during the selected time period.

Using This Report

Write down strategies you would use to address the strengths and challenges you identified above.

1. *To ensure that I have complete SRI data for all students, I would:*

   ____

   ____

   ____

   ____

2. *I would celebrate the success of students who are making strong gains by:*

   ____

   ____

   ____

   ____

3. *To support students who had decreases in their Lexile measures, I would:*

   ____

   ____

   ____

   ____

For additional information on this report, see pages 190–193 in the *Placement, Assessment, and Reporting Guide.*

READ 180 Comprehension Skills Grouping Report

This Best Practice Report places students into three groups based on comprehension results from the *READ 180* Topic Software.

INSTRUCTIONAL PLANNING

Comprehension Skills Grouping Report

CLASS: SCHIRMER 3

SCHOLASTIC *READ 180* NEXT GENERATION

School: Lincoln Middle School
Teacher: Margaret Schirmer

Time Period: 08/24/11 – 02/02/12

Group 1

COMPREHENSION SKILL	STUDENT	LEVEL	COMPREHENSION SCORE
Stretch: Current rBook Workshop Skill*	Collins, Chris	4	86%
	Cooper, Tiffany	3	82%
	Krynski, Theo	4	97%
	Ramirez, Gabriella	3	81%
	Sanchez, Rachel	3	81%

Group 2

COMPREHENSION SKILL	STUDENT	LEVEL	SEQUENCING SCORE
Reteach: Sequencing	Bracco, Christine	2	43%
	Evans, Jamal	2	57%
	Fernandez, Luis	2	0%
	Kramer, Liz	4	0%
	Palermo, Justin	1	75%

Group 3

COMPREHENSION SKILL	STUDENT	LEVEL	FINDING THE MAIN IDEA SCORE
Reteach: Finding the Main Idea	**Chu, Amy**	2	78%
	Felix, Tonya	1	92%
	Garcia, Matt	2	83%
	Imran, Khaleel	2	71%
	Rupp, Jeremy	3	75%

STUDENTS WITH NO DATA
No Data to Report

* For rBook Literature Workshops, the Stretch skill is Making Inferences

Using This Report

Purpose: This report places students into Stretch or Reteach groups based on comprehension results in the software. Launch the Groupinator on the Teacher Dashboard for assistance in grouping and finding appropriate instructional resources.

Follow-Up: Use these results to group students for rBook Reading Check Points. Address specific Comprehension needs during Small-Group Instruction.

***READ 180* Comprehension Skills Grouping Report**

Analyzing This Report

Use the steps below to closely analyze the data in this report.

1. Identify which comprehension skills to reinforce for each "Reteach" group during the Reading CheckPoint.

   Ms. Schirmer can reteach __________ *to Group 2 and* __________ *to Group 3.*

2. Look for students who may need extra support or scaffolding to master the targeted comprehension skill.

   In Group 2, __________ *and* __________ *will likely need the most support with sequencing because they both scored* ______ *%.*

3. Check if any students placed into a "Stretch" group for extended practice with the Workshop skill during the Reading CheckPoint.

   Ms. Schirmer can use the Workshop Stretch text to challenge these five students: __________, __________, __________, __________*, and* __________.

Using This Report

Write down strategies you would use to address the strengths and challenges you identified above.

1. *To prepare for reteaching comprehension skills during the Reading CheckPoint, I would:*

   ____

   ____

   ____

   ____

2. *The strategies I would use to provide additional support for the most struggling students are:*

   ____

   ____

   ____

   ____

3. *I would extend learning and increase engagement for students who are ready for a challenge by:*

   ____

   ____

   ____

   ____

For additional information on this report, see pages 142–143 in the *Placement, Assessment, and Reporting Guide.*

READ 180 Student Diagnostic Report

This Best Practice Report details a student's skills performance in each of the five Learning Zones on the *READ 180* Topic Software.

DIAGNOSTICS

SCHOLASTIC READ 180 NEXT GENERATION

Student Diagnostic Report

STUDENT: IMRAN, KHALEEL

School: Lincoln Middle School
Teacher: Margaret Schirmer
Grade: 7
Class: Schirmer 3

Time Period: 08/24/11 – 02/02/12

READ 180 Level: 2
Last SRI Score (Lexile®): 719

Reading Zone: Comprehension and Vocabulary

SKILL	CORRECT	% CORRECT*	SKILL	CORRECT	% CORRECT*
Finding the Main Idea	12 of 17	71%	Understanding Vocabulary	68 of 69	99%
Sequencing	9 of 12	75%	Cause and Effect	15 of 15	100%
Drawing Conclusions	12 of 15	80%	Compare and Contrast	14 of 14	100%
Making Inferences	12 of 14	85%	Problems and Solutions	14 of 14	100%
Summarizing	11 of 13	86%	Reading for Detail	16 of 16	100%

Word Zone: Most Common Word Recognition Error Types

WORDS WITH PHONOGRAMS	HIGH FREQUENCY WORDS	COMPOUND WORDS	NON-DECODABLE WORDS	OTHER CONSONANTS
(18 errors)	(18 errors)	(16 errors)	(15 errors)	(12 errors)
Recent Examples:	**Recent Examples:**	**Recent Examples:**	**Recent Examples:**	**Recent Examples:**
shops	will	sometimes	want	brings
mop	way	someday	your	spends
crops	be	everywhere	who	sing
wing	get	earthquakes	they	trip
soon	go	earthquake	would	trick

*Benchmark=70%

Using This Report

Purpose: This report shows a student's skills progress, recent word and spelling errors, and fluency scores to help you identify successes and prioritize the student's needs.

Follow-Up: Check individual skill scores. Look for error patterns on the student's word lists. Use Resources for Differentiated Instruction to provide individual support as needed.

***READ 180* Student Diagnostic Report**

Analyzing This Report

Use the steps below to closely analyze the data in this report.

1. Identify which comprehension and vocabulary skills the student still needs to master in the Reading Zone.
   Two skills that Khaleel still needs to master are ________________ and ________________.

2. Look for patterns in the student's word recognition errors from activities in the Word Zone.
   ________ *out of five errors in the Other Consonants column have the "tr" spelling pattern.*

3. Check which word patterns the student has the most difficulty spelling (on page 2 of the report).

4. Track ongoing progress with reading comprehension and fluency in the Success Zone (on page 2 of the report).

5. See median scores on the Respond & Write paragraphs from the Writing Zone (on page 2 of the report).

Using This Report

Write down strategies you would use to address the strengths and challenges you identified above.

1. *I would reinforce Khaleel's mastery of key comprehension and vocabulary skills by:*

2. *To help Khaleel master the "tr" spelling pattern, I would:*

3. *During a one-to-one Software conference with Khaleel, I would use the report data to:*

For additional information on this report, see pages 156–157 in the *Placement, Assessment, and Reporting Guide.*

READ 180 Reading Progress Report

This Best Practice Report provides an overview of student participation and performance in the *READ 180* Topic Software.

PROGRESS MONITORING

Reading Progress Report

CLASS: SCHIRMER 3

School: Lincoln Middle School
Teacher: Margaret Schirmer
Grade: 7

SCHOLASTIC READ 180 NEXT GENERATION

Time Period: 08/24/11 – 02/02/12

	CURRENT STATUS			TIME-ON-TASK					CUMULATIVE PERFORMANCE					
STUDENT	LEVEL	LAST SRI SCORE (LEXILE®)	LATEST TOPIC SOFTWARE	SESSIONS	SEGMENTS	TIME (MIN.)	AVG. SESSION LENGTH	SESSIONS PER SEGMENT	WORDS READ	COMPREHENSION SCORE	VOCABULARY SCORE	WORD ZONE ASSESSMENT SCORE	SPELLING ZONE ASSESSMENT SCORE	RESPOND & WRITE SCORE (OUT OF 4)
Bracco, Christine	2	709	Beating the Odds	50	10	944	17	5	55,831	83%	91%	95%	90%	2
Chu, Amy	2	834	Scene Stealers	43	17	736	16	3	105,245	95%	94%	91%	90%	3
Collins, Chris	4	868	Extreme Sports	59	1	824	14	16	16,815	86%	94%	63%	47%	3
Cooper, Tiffany	3	781	Help Wanted	67	8	1106	17	9	105,771	82%	67%	89%	76%	2
Evans, Jamal	2	719	The Whole World Watched	69	14	1067	15	5	93,655	81%	96%	98%	91%	1
Felix, Tonya	1	BR (10)	You and the Law	59	20	863	16	3	31,775	90%	89%	88%	90%	N/A
Fernandez, Luis	2	242	Help Wanted	41	6	583	14	6	21,097	72%	87%	92%	84%	4
Garcia, Matt	2	550	Game On!	55	12	1012	16	5	43,503	77%	91%	97%	89%	4
Imran, Khaleel	2	719	Help Wanted	44	12	545	13	3	289,267	88%	98%	81%	86%	3
Kramer, Liz	4	809	The Big Giveback	52	1	588	12	21	15,792	67%	82%	82%	67%	3
Krynski, Theo	4	1120	Show Me the Money!	54	5	814	14	9	30,096	97%	93%	91%	88%	4
Palermo, Justin	1	438	Survive	22	10	379	16	3	24,537	87%	76%	88%	92%	N/A
Ramirez, Gabriella	3	743	Extreme Sports	49	4	585	12	14	15,715	81%	63%	92%	80%	1
Rupp, Jeremy	3	727	Show Me the Money!	54	3	815	14	13	17,793	79%	39%	86%	54%	2
Sanchez, Rachel	3	792	First Person	59	15	1007	16	4	251,855	81%	81%	99%	94%	3
AVERAGE	-	**718**	-	**52**	**9**	**803**	**15**	**8**	-	**83%**	**83%**	**89%**	**81%**	

Using This Report

Purpose: This is an overview of students' overall progress in the READ 180 Software during the selected time period.

Follow-Up: Check regularly for Software usage patterns and correlations between time and performance data. Use other reports to "drill down" on individual student performance.

***READ 180* Reading Progress Report**

Analyzing This Report

Use the steps below to closely analyze the data in this report.

1. Look for students who are spending less than the recommended 15 minutes per day on the Software.

   _________ out of 15 students in Ms. Schirmer's class have an Average Session Length of less than 15 minutes.

2. Identify who is completing Software segments too quickly or too slowly. Students should average 4–15 sessions per segment, depending on their *READ 180* Level and whether the Writing Zone is enabled.

   I notice that Amy Chu takes an average of _________ sessions to complete a segment, and Liz Kramer takes an average of _________ sessions to complete a segment.

3. Look for low cumulative performance scores of less than 70% to plan targeted skills instruction.

   Gabriella Ramirez may need extra support with ________________ because she scored _________%.

Using This Report

Write down strategies you would use to address the strengths and challenges you identified above.

1. I would follow up with students who are using the Software for less than 15 minutes per day by:

   ____

   ____

   ____

   ____

2. For students who appear to be completing Software segments too quickly, I would:

   ____

   ____

   ____

   ____

3. I would support students who appear to be completing Software segments too slowly by:

   ____

   ____

   ____

   ____

For additional information on this report, see pages 150–153 in the *Placement, Assessment, and Reporting Guide*.

READ 180 Student Reading Report

This Best Practice Report tracks a student's annual progress in the *READ 180* Topic Software and on *Scholastic Reading Counts!* quizzes.

SCHOLASTIC READ 180 NEXT GENERATION

PROGRESS MONITORING

Student Reading Report

STUDENT: IMRAN, KHALEEL

School: Lincoln Middle School
Teacher: Margaret Schirmer
Grade: 7
Class: Schirmer 3

Time Period: 08/24/11 – 02/02/12

READ 180 Level: 2
Current Topic Software: Help Wanted
Last SRI Score (Lexile®): 719

READ 180 Software Progress

TOPIC SOFTWARE AND SEGMENT	LEVEL	DATE STARTED	DATE COMPLETED	NO. OF SESSIONS PER SEGMENT	COMPREHENSION AND VOCABULARY			WORDS MASTERED	
					COMP. SCORE	VOCAB. SCORE	CONTEXT PASSAGE SCORE	FLUENT	SPELLING
Help Wanted									
In the Funnies	2	02/05/12	In Progress	4	75%	87%	N/A	22	39
Jump Shot	2	01/26/12	02/05/12	8	75%	83%	100%	17	33
Show Me the Money									
Making Money	1	01/15/12	01/21/12	2	100%	100%	100%	26	44
Bogus Bill	1	01/11/12	01/12/12	2	100%	100%	100%	22	32
Fighting Forgery	1	01/04/12	01/08/12	2	100%	100%	100%	24	43
Mangled Money	1	12/03/11	12/16/11	4	75%	100%	88%	18	15
Disaster!									
Volcano!	1	11/23/11	12/02/11	3	80%	100%	100%	17	31
Avalanche!	1	11/12/11	11/23/11	5	75%	100%	100%	28	35
Earthquake!	1	11/05/11	11/12/11	5	80%	100%	100%	27	31
Flood!	1	10/29/11	11/05/11	3	100%	100%	100%	29	39
The Big Giveback									
Room to Read	1	10/20/11	10/27/11	5	100%	100%	100%	34	33
Hometown Hero	1	10/16/11	10/19/11	2	100%	100%	100%	38	39
Get Pumped!	1	09/22/11	10/15/11	8	100%	100%	100%	36	36
Tunes 4 the Troops	1	09/15/11	09/22/11	5	75%	100%	100%	35	33
TOTAL SEGMENTS COMPLETED: 13				**N/A**	**88%**	**98%**	**99%**	**373**	**483**

Using This Report

Purpose: This report shows an individual student's progress on READ 180 Topic Software CDs and segments, as well as independent reading progress using Scholastic Reading Counts!

Follow-Up: Share this report with the student to discuss results and set goals. Investigate areas of concern using the appropriate Student Diagnostic Report.

***READ 180* Student Reading Report**

Analyzing This Report

Use the steps below to closely analyze the data in this report.

1. Look for segments that took the student longer than usual to complete.

   It took Khaleel ________ sessions to complete Jump Shot and Get Pumped!

2. Compare Comprehension, Vocabulary, and Context Passage Scores to see in which area the student needs the most support.

   For the 13 segments Khaleel has completed, he has the lowest average scores in ______________.

3. Check if the student has moved up to a higher *READ 180* Level. (**Note:** Level 1 students do not move to Level 2 automatically. You must increase their level manually using *READ 180* Program Settings in SAM.)

   Ms. Schirmer moved Khaleel from Level 1 to Level 2 after he completed ______________.

4. Monitor the student's performance on *SRC!* quizzes in the selected time period (on page 2 of the report).

Using This Report

Write down strategies you would use to address the strengths and challenges you identified above.

1. *I would follow up with Khaleel about segments that took longer to complete by:*

2. *To help Khaleel improve his comprehension scores, I would:*

3. *After increasing Khaleel's Software Level from 1 to 2, I would monitor his progress by:*

For additional information on this report, see pages 158–161 in the *Placement, Assessment, and Reporting Guide.*

rSkills Grading Report

This Best Practice Report shows *rSkills Test* results for all students in a class or group, summarized by assessment strand.

Grading Report

CLASS: SCHIRMER 3

PROGRESS MONITORING

rSkills College & Career

School: Lincoln Middle School
Teacher: Margaret Schirmer
Grade: 7

Test 3b (Stage Flex II)
Average Test Score: 76%
Number of Students Tested: 7

Time Period: 1/15/14 – 1/30/14

Reading

Claim: Students can read closely and analytically to comprehend a range of increasingly complex texts.

		COMPREHENSION						VOCABULARY		
Student	Test Date	CRAFT AND STRUCTURE: FIGURATIVE LANGUAGE	STORY ELEMENTS: PLOT	CRAFT AND STRUCTURE: MOOD	STORY ELEMENTS: POINT OF VIEW	STORY ELEMENTS: THEME	* TEXT EVIDENCE	SUFFIXES	PREFIXES	READING SUBTOTAL
Bracco, Christine	1/25/14	1 of 2 (50%)	2 of 2 (100%)	1 of 3 (33%)	1 of 1 (100%)	1 of 1 (100%)	1 of 2	3 of 4 (75%)	3 of 3 (100%)	75%
Evans, Jamal	1/25/14	1 of 2 (50%)	2 of 2 (100%)	2 of 3 (67%)	1 of 1 (100%)	1 of 1 (100%)	1 of 2	3 of 4 (75%)	3 of 3 (100%)	81%
Felix, Tonya	1/25/14	1 of 2 (50%)	2 of 2 (100%)	1 of 3 (33%)	1 of 1 (100%)	1 of 1 (100%)	1 of 2	2 of 4 (50%)	3 of 3 (100%)	69%
Fernandez, Luis	1/25/14	1 of 2 (50%)	2 of 2 (100%)	1 of 3 (33%)	1 of 1 (100%)	1 of 1 (100%)	1 of 2	3 of 4 (75%)	3 of 3 (100%)	75%
Garcia, Matt	1/26/14	2 of 2 (100%)	2 of 2 (100%)	3 of 3 (100%)	1 of 1 (100%)	1 of 1 (100%)	1 of 2	2 of 4 (50%)	3 of 3 (100%)	88%
Imran, Khaleel	1/25/14	2 of 2 (100%)	2 of 2 (100%)	2 of 3 (67%)	1 of 1 (100%)	1 of 1 (100%)	1 of 2	2 of 4 (50%)	3 of 3 (100%)	81%
Palermo, Justin	1/26/14	2 of 2 (100%)	1 of 2 (50%)	1 of 3 (33%)	1 of 1 (100%)	1 of 1 (100%)	1 of 2	2 of 4 (50%)	3 of 3 (100%)	69%
Average Skill Score		71%	93%	52%	100%	100%	NA	61%	100%	77%

Writing

Claim: Students can produce effective and well-grounded writing for a range of purposes and audiences.

	CONVENTIONS			SHORT AND EXTENDED CONSTRUCTED RESPONSE			
				Constructed Response 1 (2-Point Rubric)	Constructed Response 2 (2-Point Rubric)	Extended Constructed Response	
Student	RUN-ON SENTENCES	WORD ORDER	WRITING SUBTOTAL			Score	Rubric Value
Bracco, Christine	2 of 2 (100%)	2 of 2 (100%)	100%	ungraded	ungraded	ungraded	6
Evans, Jamal	1 of 2 (50%)	2 of 2 (100%)	75%	ungraded	ungraded	ungraded	6
Felix, Tonya	0 of 2 (0%)	1 of 2 (50%)	25%	ungraded	ungraded	ungraded	6
Average Skill Score	50%	83%	67%	ungraded	ungraded	ungraded	6

STUDENT(S) NOT TESTED
Brad, Grady

Key
* These items are additional data points to assess students' ability to demonstrate their thinking.

Using This Report
Purpose: This report shows student results on one rSkills Test. Constructed Response items will appear as "ungraded" until they are scored in the Student Digital Portfolio.

Follow-Up: Include student progress from all parts of the *Read 180* Instructional Model in your grading assessment.

Printed by: District Administrator

Page 1 of 1

***rSkills* Grading Report**

Analyzing This Report

Use the steps below to closely analyze the data in this report.

1. Check whether all students in the class took the assigned *rSkills Test.*

   I notice that ______________________ did not take this rSkills Test.

2. Scan overall test scores to evaluate student mastery of assessed skills.

   The class average on this test was ______%. ______________________ scored the highest with ______%. ______________________ scored the lowest with ______%.

3. Look for skills that multiple students struggled with, scoring less than 70% (indicated by a red flag).

   Two skills that many students struggled with were ______________________ and ______________________.

Using This Report

Write down strategies you would use to address the strengths and challenges you identified above.

1. To ensure that I have complete rSkills Test data for the class, I would:

   ____

   ____

   ____

   ____

2. I would follow up with students who have overall test scores of less than 70% by:

   ____

   ____

   ____

   ____

3. The strategies and resources I would use to reinforce Summarizing and Using Commas in a Series are:

   ____

   ____

   ____

   ____

For additional information on this report, see pages 174–177 in the *Placement, Assessment, and Reporting Guide.*

SRC! Reading Progress Report

This Best Practice Report provides an overview of students' *Scholastic Reading Counts!* quiz participation and progress.

PROGRESS MONITORING

Reading Progress Report

CLASS: SCHIRMER 3

SCHOLASTIC READING COUNTS!

School: Lincoln Middle School
Teacher: Margaret Schirmer
Grade: 7

Time Period: 08/24/11 – 02/02/12

Year to Date Totals

Quizzes Taken	128
Quizzes Passed	86
Quiz Success Rate	64.3%
Points Earned	655
Words Read	869,301

STUDENT	GRADE	LEXILE®	QUIZZES PASSED/ TAKEN	QUIZ SUCCESS RATE	AVG. QUIZ SCORE	BOOKS READ	POINTS EARNED	ANNUAL GOAL	% OF GOAL ACHIEVED
Bracco, Christine	7	709	7/8	88%	84%	7	43	20(B)	47%
Chu, Amy	7	834	6/7	86%	86%	6	32	15(B)	40%
Collins, Chris	7	868	6/8	75%	▸ 62%	6	32	15(B)	40%
Cooper, Tiffany	7	781	10/12	83%	▸ 65%	10	26	17(B)	58%
Evans, Jamal	7	719	15/17	88%	▸ 49%	15	23	18(B)	83%
Felix, Tonya	7	BR (10)	6/13	46%	83%	6	24	30(B)	20%
Fernandez, Luis	7	242	2/3	67%	▸ 67%	2	7	30(B)	7%
Garcia, Matt	7	550	2/13	15%	▸ 35%	2	9	22(B)	9%
Imran, Khaleel	7	719	9/10	90%	89%	9	85	20(B)	45%
Kramer, Liz	7	809	2/5	40%	▸ 54%	2	6	18(B)	11%
Krynski, Theo	7	1120	4/4	100%	83%	4	15	13(B)	31%
Palermo, Justin	7	438	7/8	88%	76%	7	32	23(B)	30%
Ramirez, Gabriella	7	743	1/5	20%	▸ 62%	1	3	18(B)	6%
Rupp, Jeremy	7	727	0/0	N/A	N/A	0	0	18(B)	0%
Sanchez, Rachel	7	792	9/15	60%	73%	9	55	17(B)	53%
TOTALS	-	**700 (AVG.)**	**86/128**	**64% (AVG.)**	▸ **64% (AVG.)**	**86**	**352**	-	**31% (AVG.)**

(B)=Books ▸ Indicates Score Below 70%

Using This Report

Purpose: This report provides an overview of students' progress in the program. In addition to tracking group quiz success rates, the report shows individual quiz performance and achievement.

Follow-Up: Use the information in the report to plan incentives and to help students monitor their progress. You may also use the report to guide instruction and create reading groups.

***SRC!* Reading Progress Report**

Analyzing This Report

Use the steps below to closely analyze the data in this report.

1. Check the overall class performance on *SRC!* quizzes in the selected time period.
   Ms. Schirmer's students have taken a total of ________ quizzes, of which they have passed ________.
   That's why the class average quiz success rate is ________%.

2. Identify who is making strong progress and who is not making sufficient progress toward the annual goal.
   Jamal's annual goal is to read ________ books, and he has achieved ________% of this goal. Jeremy's annual goal is to read ________ books, and he has read ________ books so far.

3. Look for students with low average quiz scores of less than 70% (indicated by a red flag).
   ________ of the 15 students in Ms. Schirmer's class have average quiz scores of less than 70%.

Using This Report

Write down strategies you would use to address the strengths and challenges you identified above.

1. To increase the overall quiz success rate for the class, I would:

____

____

____

____

2. To motivate students to reach their annual SRC! goal, I would:

____

____

____

____

3. I would support individual students who have low average quiz scores by:

____

____

____

____

For additional information on this report, see pages 230–233 in the *Placement, Assessment, and Reporting Guide.*

Setting Up a Data Notebook

Organize the SAM reports that you run and analyze throughout the year in a data notebook, which you can use to track progress and share data with others.

Research Says

To provide optimal support for adolescent literacy intervention, teachers, principals, and administrators should have easy access to data to inform student-level, school-level, and district-wide decision-making.

Carnegie Council on Advancing Adolescent Literacy, 2010

What Is a Data Notebook?

A "data notebook" is a binder, portfolio, or filing system that you routinely add to throughout the year to track your students' *READ 180* progress. You can use the data notebook to store and organize SAM reports, Conferencing Logs, and standardized test results. Having all of your data archived in one place makes it easy to quickly reference and share with administrators, parents, or students.

Think about how many data notebooks you want to set up for your *READ 180* classes. Then establish a clear system for organizing each notebook so your data is easy to navigate throughout the year. Consider the following options:

- One notebook per class period, with tabs dividing it by grading period or technology-based program component.
- One notebook per grading period, with tabs dividing it by class.
- One notebook per report type (class/group reports and student reports), with tabs dividing it by class or student.

Adding to Your Notebook

Regularly add class and student data to your notebook throughout the year to create a comprehensive and dynamic picture of *READ 180* progress.

Data to Include

Decide what kind of data you want to gather and archive to track student progress and share results with others. Your data notebook may include:

- Progress Monitoring Best Practice Reports for each technology component (*READ 180* Topic Software, *rSkills Tests, SRI,* and *SRC!*).
- Conferencing Logs from one-to-one student conferences.
- State or district standardized test results.
- Sample student work from the *rBook, rSkills Tests,* or *RDI* lessons.

Tech Tip

After establishing a schedule for analyzing data, use the Report Scheduler on the Teacher Dashboard to have SAM reports automatically emailed to you at set times.

Establish a Schedule

Ensure ongoing monitoring of each *READ 180* component by establishing a schedule to run, analyze, and add SAM reports to your data notebook. Use your school calendar, *rBook* Workshop Planning Guides, and *SRI* testing cycle to decide when would be the best times to run class and student reports.

When establishing a schedule for adding to your data notebook, consider questions such as: *Which days of the week are most convenient to analyze results? When will I conference with students? When are my grading periods?*

Plan to run and analyze at least one class or student report each week. Place your completed schedule at the front of your data notebook for reference.

See *Placement, Assessment, and Reporting Guide* pages 126–127 for additional support on establishing a report schedule for the school year.

Holding Report Conferences

Conduct regular one-to-one report conferences with students to share performance data and progress, set goals, and celebrate achievement.

Why Conference?

Research shows that when students are included in monitoring their own progress, they better understand their academic growth, gain motivation, and acquire a sense of ownership over their learning (Andrade, 2007/8; Forster, 2009; Hupert & Heinze, 2006). Making performance data visible increases motivation and engagement by helping students see that their hard work is paying off.

Share report data with students during individual conferences to help them understand their reading progress, identify personal strengths and challenges, and discuss their goals in a private setting. Additionally, use the SAM reports to remind students that you are keeping an eye on everything that they do on the computer, which can increase productivity in the Instructional Software rotation.

When to Conference

Structuring regular time within your class schedule to conference creates a sense of stability and structure. In a *READ 180* classroom, the best opportunity for student conferencing is during rotations on predetermined days. Assign students in Small-Group Instruction an assignment they can complete independently. After they begin work, pull students out of the group one at a time for brief one-to-one report conferences. Communicate your report conferencing plans to students beforehand.

How to Conference

Follow the steps below to hold a one-to-one report conference with a student. See pages 112–113 in the *Placement, Assessment, and Reporting Guide* for additional tips on conferencing with students.

1. Prepare all materials beforehand, including printing a copy of the Student Conferencing Log (SAM Keyword: Conference Log).
2. Time each conference so that all students have the opportunity to meet with you. Conferences typically range from one to four minutes per student.
3. Begin by explaining that the purpose of the conference is to discuss progress based on SAM reports.
4. Share the types of reports you have and the data they contain.
5. Guide the student to reflect on the following questions: *What does this report demonstrate about my work? What changes can I make based on this information? What support do I need in order to make these changes?*
6. Work with the student to complete the Conferencing Log to set new goals for growth.
7. Ensure the student understands outcomes expected for the next conference and end on a positive note.

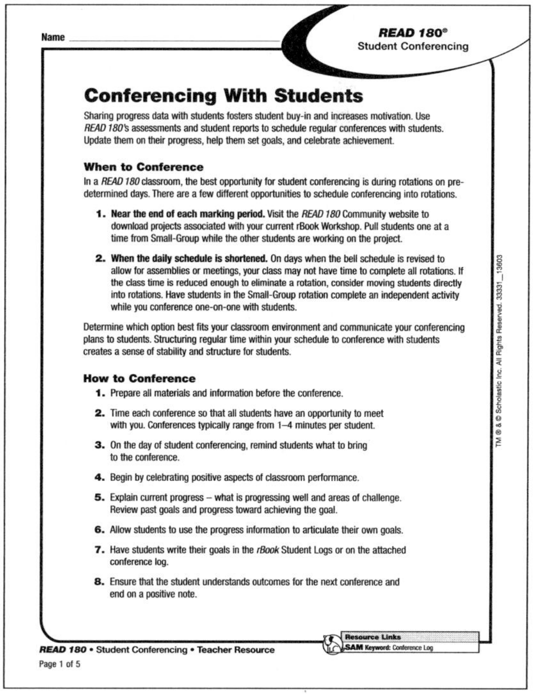
Name ____________

READ 180®
Student Conferencing

Conferencing With Students

Sharing progress data with students fosters student buy-in and increases motivation. Use *READ 180*'s assessments and student reports to schedule regular conferences with students. Update them on their progress, help them set goals, and celebrate achievement.

When to Conference

In a *READ 180* classroom, the best opportunity for student conferencing is during rotations on pre-determined days. There are a few different opportunities to schedule conferencing into rotations.

1. **Near the end of each marking period.** Visit the *READ 180* Community website to download projects associated with your current rBook Workshop. Pull students one at a time from Small-Group while the other students are working on the project.
2. **When the daily schedule is shortened.** On days when the bell schedule is revised to allow for assemblies or meetings, your class may not have time to complete all rotations. If the class time is reduced enough to eliminate a rotation, consider moving students directly into rotations. Have students in the Small-Group rotation complete an independent activity while you conference one-on-one with students.

Determine which option best fits your classroom environment and communicate your conferencing plans to students. Structuring regular time within your schedule to conference with students creates a sense of stability and structure for students.

How to Conference

1. Prepare all materials and information before the conference.
2. Time each conference so that all students have an opportunity to meet with you. Conferences typically range from 1–4 minutes per student.
3. On the day of student conferencing, remind students what to bring to the conference.
4. Begin by celebrating positive aspects of classroom performance.
5. Explain current progress – what is progressing well and areas of challenge. Review past goals and progress toward achieving the goal.
6. Allow students to use the progress information to articulate their own goals.
7. Have students write their goals in the *rBook* Student Logs or on the attached conference log.
8. Ensure that the student understands outcomes for the next conference and end on a positive note.

Resource Links
SAM Keyword: Conference Log

READ 180 • Student Conferencing • Teacher Resource
Page 1 of 5

Student Conferencing Log
SAM Keyword: Conference Log

Assessing Student Fluency

Use these strategies to assess your students' fluency, or the ability to read connected text at a pace that allows for comprehension of grade-level reading materials.

Why Is Fluency Important?

Fluent readers can read aloud with appropriate speed, accuracy, phrasing, and expression. Fluency is critical to reading comprehension because when students read text slowly in a laborious manner, it is difficult for them to remember what they have read and relate it to their background knowledge (NRP, 2000). Being able to read fluently allows students to focus on overall meaning, rather than on decoding each individual word. By regularly assessing your students' fluency, you can quickly identify who may need additional support to achieve reading proficiency.

Monitoring Fluency Practice

Students make final recordings of their Topic Software reading passages in the Success Zone. You can listen to these recordings in the SAM Student Digital Portfolio (see page 165 for directions). Use the on-screen rubric to evaluate your students' reading fluency practice and enter constructive feedback. Revisit stored student recordings throughout the year to monitor fluency growth over time and share during parent conferences.

Administering Oral Fluency Assessments

An Oral Fluency Assessment, or OFA, formally measures the number of words correct per minute (WCPM) that a student can read. You can compare your students' WCPM scores with national averages to see if their reading fluency is above, below, or on grade level.

Administer an OFA to each of your students three times per year during one-to-one conferences to monitor their fluency growth over time. See pages 104–108 in the *Placement, Assessment, and Reporting Guide* to learn how to administer an OFA and determine a WCPM score.

Make copies of grade-level OFA passages from *Resources for Differentiated Instruction 1.* You can also print copies from SAM, which has three passages for each Grade (3 to 12). Check the SAM Resources Index (SAM Keyword: Keyword Index) to locate the SAM Keyword for each OFA passage.

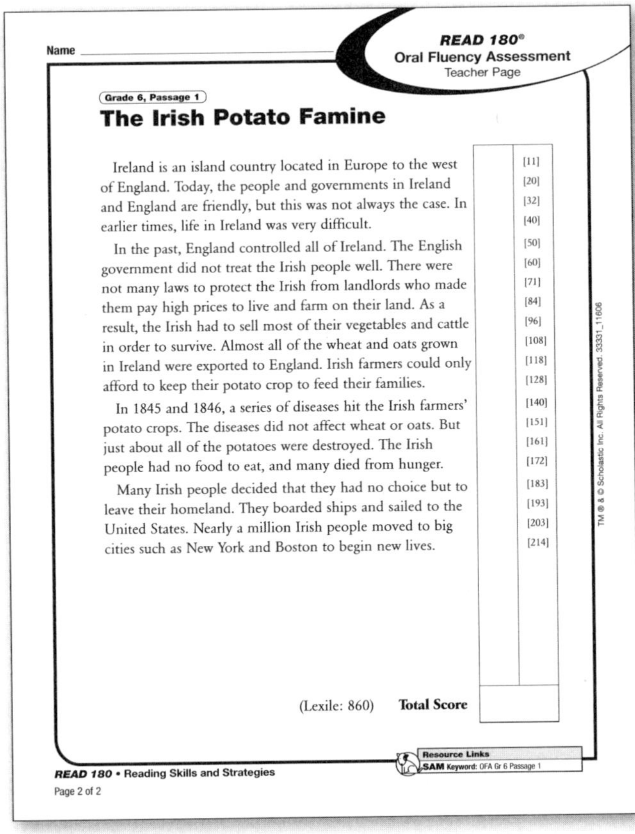

Name ____________

***READ 180*®**
Oral Fluency Assessment
Teacher Page

Grade 6, Passage 1

The Irish Potato Famine

Ireland is an island country located in Europe to the west [11]
of England. Today, the people and governments in Ireland [20]
and England are friendly, but this was not always the case. In [32]
earlier times, life in Ireland was very difficult. [40]

In the past, England controlled all of Ireland. The English [50]
government did not treat the Irish people well. There were [60]
not many laws to protect the Irish from landlords who made [71]
them pay high prices to live and farm on their land. As a [84]
result, the Irish had to sell most of their vegetables and cattle [96]
in order to survive. Almost all of the wheat and oats grown [108]
in Ireland were exported to England. Irish farmers could only [118]
afford to keep their potato crop to feed their families. [128]

In 1845 and 1846, a series of diseases hit the Irish farmers' [140]
potato crops. The diseases did not affect wheat or oats. But [151]
just about all of the potatoes were destroyed. The Irish [161]
people had no food to eat, and many died from hunger. [172]

Many Irish people decided that they had no choice but to [183]
leave their homeland. They boarded ships and sailed to the [193]
United States. Nearly a million Irish people moved to big [203]
cities such as New York and Boston to begin new lives. [214]

(Lexile: 860) **Total Score**

Resource Links
SAM Keyword: OFA Gr 6 Passage 1

READ 180 • Reading Skills and Strategies
Page 2 of 2

Oral Fluency Assessment for Grade 6
SAM Keyword: OFA Gr 6 Passage 1

Using Grading Rubrics

Use *READ 180* rubrics to evaluate student performance on various assignments, and share results with students to help them grow as readers and writers.

Rubrics in *READ 180*

Rubrics support you with objectively evaluating student work and determining meaningful grades. A rubric breaks down an assignment into its key criteria and outlines what different levels of proficiency for each criterion might look like. This makes it easy to identify student strengths and challenges, provide constructive feedback, and set expectations before an assignment.

READ 180 has rubrics to assess each of the following assignment types:

- ***rBook* Workshop** (SAM Keyword: Workshop Rubric)
- ***rBook* Writing** (in *rBook* writing lessons)
- ***rBook* Wrap-Up Project** (SAM Keywords: Debate Rubric, Presentation Rubric, Proposal Rubric)
- ***rSkills Tests* Constructed Response and Extended Constructed Response** (on the SAM Student Digital Portfolio)
- **Topic Software Final Fluency Recording** (on the SAM Student Digital Portfolio)
- **Topic Software Respond & Write Published Responses** (on the SAM Student Digital Portfolio)
- **Software and Reading QuickWrites** (in *Teaching Resources* books)

Research Says

Using scoring guides or rubrics for self-assessment helps students understand the key elements of an assignment and evaluate and improve the quality of their work.

Andrade, 2007/8

How to Assess With a Rubric

Follow these steps for using a rubric to evaluate a completed assignment:

1. Write the student's name and the date at the top of the page.
2. Review the assignment criteria in the first column.
3. For each criterion, read the proficiency level descriptions in the numbered columns.
4. For each criterion, compare the student's work to the proficiency level descriptions. Decide which level the work most closely matches. Write that number in the last column. Repeat for all criteria.
5. Consider all of the scores in the last column to determine an overall assignment score for the student. Write it at the bottom.

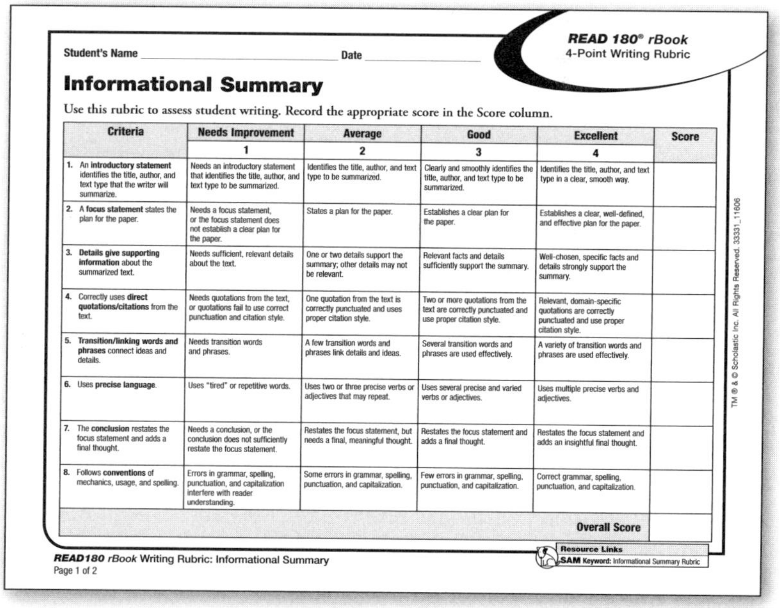

Student's Name ______ Date ______

READ 180® rBook
4-Point Writing Rubric

Informational Summary

Use this rubric to assess student writing. Record the appropriate score in the Score column.

Criteria	Needs Improvement 1	Average 2	Good 3	Excellent 4	Score
1. An **introductory statement** identifies the title, author, and text type that the writer will summarize.	Needs an introductory statement that identifies the title, author, and text type to be summarized.	Identifies the title, author, and text type to be summarized.	Clearly and smoothly identifies the title, author, and text type to be summarized.	Identifies the title, author, and text type in a clear, smooth way.	
2. A **focus statement** states the plan for the paper.	Needs a focus statement, or the focus statement does not establish a clear plan for the paper.	States a plan for the paper.	Establishes a clear plan for the paper.	Establishes a clear, well-defined, and effective plan for the paper.	
3. **Details give supporting information** about the summarized text.	Needs sufficient, relevant details about the text.	One or two details support the summary; other details may not be relevant.	Relevant facts and details sufficiently support the summary.	Well-chosen, specific facts and details strongly support the summary.	
4. Correctly uses **direct quotations/citations** from the text.	Needs quotations from the text, or quotations fail to use correct punctuation and citation style.	One quotation from the text is correctly punctuated and uses proper citation style.	Two or more quotations from the text are correctly punctuated and use proper citation style.	Relevant, domain-specific quotations are correctly punctuated and use proper citation style.	
5. **Transition/linking words and phrases** connect ideas and details.	Needs transition words and phrases.	A few transition words and phrases link details and ideas.	Several transition words and phrases are used effectively.	A variety of transition words and phrases are used effectively.	
6. Uses **precise language**.	Uses "tired" or repetitive words.	Uses two or three precise verbs or adjectives that may repeat.	Uses several precise and varied verbs or adjectives.	Uses multiple precise verbs and adjectives.	
7. The **conclusion** restates the focus statement and adds a final thought.	Needs a conclusion, or the conclusion does not sufficiently restate the focus statement.	Restates the focus statement, but needs a final, meaningful thought.	Restates the focus statement and adds a final thought.	Restates the focus statement and adds an insightful final thought.	
8. Follows **conventions** of mechanics, usage, and spelling.	Errors in grammar, spelling, punctuation, and capitalization interfere with reader understanding.	Some errors in grammar, spelling, punctuation, and capitalization.	Few errors in grammar, spelling, punctuation, and capitalization.	Correct grammar, spelling, punctuation, and capitalization.	
				Overall Score	

READ180* *rBook Writing Rubric: Informational Summary
Page 1 of 2

Resource Links
SAM Keyword: Informational Summary Rubric

Informational Summary Rubric

6. Enter the overall score in your grade book and share constructive feedback with the student. If you completed a computer-based rubric, the results will be included on SAM reports.

Assigning *READ 180* Grades

Consider the complete picture of student progress and performance in your *READ 180* classroom when assigning periodic grades.

Setting Up a Grading System

When setting up your grade book for the year, carefully consider how you want to balance assignments from each part of the *READ 180* Instructional Model. Since students spend an equal amount of time in each rotation, you may wish to balance the grading weights for each rotation:

- Whole-Group Instruction: 25%
- Small-Group Instruction: 25%
- Instructional Software: 25%
- Modeled and Independent Reading: 25%

If you choose to assign homework, you may wish to add that to your grade book and adjust weighting accordingly. If you choose to factor in daily participation, effort, and motivation, consider questions such as: *Is the student engaged and focused in class? Is the student trying his or her best? Does the student answer questions and collaborate productively with peers each day?*

READ 180 Grading Form

To assign periodic grades, download the *READ 180* Grading Form from SAM (Keyword: Grading Form) or make copies from page 217. Use the *READ 180* Grading Report, *rBook,* and any other assignments to complete the form for each student. Store copies of completed forms in your data notebook to share with parents during conferences.

Completing the Grading Form

Follow these steps to complete the *READ 180* Grading Form (page 217) for each of your students:

1. Decide which criteria on the Grading Form you want to factor into student grades. Use the blank rows to add any additional criteria. Cross out rows for any criteria that you do not want to consider.
2. Use SAM reports, especially the *READ 180* Grading Report, to identify a student's performance on each criterion that you are considering. Record the performance score as a percentage in the **Grade** column. Example: 85%.
3. Assign each criterion a weight in order to prioritize bigger assignments. Ask yourself: *Which of these criteria do I consider most important? Least important?* For accurate class assessment, apply the same weight to each criterion for every student. Record this percentage in the **Weight** column. Example: 25%.
4. Multiply each grade by the weight of importance. Convert percentages to decimals when multiplying. Example: 85% = .85. Record the results in the **Subtotal** column.
5. Add all subtotals together and multiply by 100. Record the result in the space for **Final Grade**. Convert this number to a letter grade if required.

READ 180 Grading Form

Complete the table below to determine a *READ 180* class grade for each of your students. See page 216 of the *Teacher Implementation Guide* for additional information and directions.

Criterion	Grade	Weight	Subtotal
Whole- and Small-Group Instruction			
rSkills Tests Overall Score (*READ 180* Grading Report)			
rBook Workshop Rubric			
rBook Writing Rubric			
rBook Wrap-Up Project Rubric			
Daily Participation & Motivation (Teacher Observation)			
Instructional Software			
Comprehension Score (*READ 180* Grading Report)			
Vocabulary Score (*READ 180* Grading Report)			
Word Fluency (*READ 180* Grading Report)			
Spelling Score (*READ 180* Grading Report)			
Context Passage (*READ 180* Grading Report)			
Final Fluency Recording (*READ 180* Grading Report)			
Respond & Write Score (*READ 180* Grading Report)			
QuickWrites			
Daily Participation & Motivation (Teacher Observation)			
Modeled and Independent Reading			
SRC! Quiz Average (*READ 180* Grading Report)			
QuickWrites & Graphic Organizers			
Daily Reading Log			
Daily Participation & Motivation (Teacher Observation)			
Total			_____(100)=_____

FINAL GRADE: ______________________%

FINAL LETTER GRADE: ______________________

Resource G_s
SAM Keyword: Grading Form

Exiting Students From *READ 180*

Work with your administrators to establish criteria for assessing student readiness to transition from the *READ 180* intervention classroom.

Assessing Student Readiness

Your *READ 180* students will likely have a wide range of academic skills and reading levels. As they respond to the program, students make gains at their own rates. Some may accelerate through the Topic Software but take longer to increase their Lexile measures. Others may be successful using the *rBook* during direct instruction but need more practice to transfer strategies to independent reading or other classes. Be mindful of your students' individual strengths, needs, and growth rates when considering whether to exit them from *READ 180*.

Using Multiple Measures of Success

Most schools set their own criteria to determine when students are ready to exit *READ 180*. Some districts promote students when they reach a certain performance level, such as Proficient on *SRI* or *READ 180* Level 4, or when students can successfully read grade-level texts. Students may also leave *READ 180* when they change schools or to make way for students with greater intervention need.

When establishing exit criteria, use multiple formal and informal measures to get an overall picture of student readiness to move beyond the *READ 180* classroom. Formal and informal measures to consider may include:

- Substantial Lexile growth.
- *SRI* proficiency scores and normative data (percentiles, NCEs, or stanines).
- State or district standardized test results.
- Scores on grade-level (Level b) *rSkills Tests*.
- Topic Software data (e.g., high scores in comprehension and vocabulary).
- *rBook* completion and success level.
- Observations of skill proficiency, motivation, attitude, and behavior.
- Number and level of books read (or *SRC!* quizzes passed).
- Demonstrated proficiency with independently reading grade-level texts with comprehension.

Supporting Students Beyond *READ 180*

Ensure that students are placed into supportive classrooms when they leave *READ 180*. Work with your students' new teachers to monitor their progress as they encounter more challenging content and reading materials. To foster continued success after *READ 180*, encourage students to continue choosing books at their Lexile levels, especially for independent reading.

TEACHER IMPLEMENTATION GUIDE

Ongoing Professional Development

Best Practices for Professional Development

***READ 180* Next Generation offers comprehensive professional development resources to build and enhance effective strategies for teaching struggling readers.**

Characteristics of Effective Professional Development

Several federal initiatives, including the American Recovery and Reinvestment Act of 2009, emphasize the importance of developing teachers' professional skills to help raise student achievement. According to federal guidelines, the most effective teacher development programs have five common characteristics. Look for these five characteristics integrated throughout all *READ 180* trainings and professional development resources to support you with continued skill-building:

1. **Sustained**
   Sustained professional development occurs on an ongoing, regular basis to support you with continually acquiring new strategies and enhancing your teaching skills.
2. **Job-Embedded**
   Job-embedded professional development provides just-in-time information to support you with immediate classroom issues and enhance your teaching skills as you engage in your daily work.
3. **Collaborative**
   Collaborative professional development allows you to work together with your colleagues to share best practices, reflect on challenges, and learn new professional skills.
4. **Data-Driven**
   Data-driven professional development uses school and district data to identify and target your specific instructional needs for supporting your students' reading achievement.
5. **Focused on Student Needs**
   Professional development that is focused on your students' learning needs helps you concentrate on developing strategies that are directly targeted to accelerate their academic achievement.

Reflection

How do you learn best: online or in person? In short daily chunks or extended periods of concentration? Reflect on your learning preferences below. Keep them in mind as you explore options for *READ 180* professional development in this section.

Building Expertise With the *rBook Teacher's Edition*

Explore the red tabs in the back of your *rBook Teacher's Edition* for embedded support with incorporating instructional strategies to raise student reading achievement.

Research Foundations

The red Research Foundations tab in your *rBook Teacher's Edition* has 15 professional articles to build knowledge about the big ideas underlying *READ 180* instruction and assessment. The Research Foundations tab supports you with implementing research-based strategies, including:

- Using adaptive technology and ongoing assessment to target instruction.
- Building students' comprehension and critical reading skills.
- Reading complex, informational, literary, and content-area texts.
- Supporting students with developing academic language and vocabulary.
- Teaching multi-paragraph writing for college and career readiness.
- Differentiating instruction for English language learners and students with special needs.

Learn practical tips for incorporating research-based strategies into your daily instruction.

Identify additional research articles to further your learning about the topic.

Preview the basics of what the research says and why it helps students achieve reading success.

Read the article to build knowledge on the research foundation and how it impacts student learning.

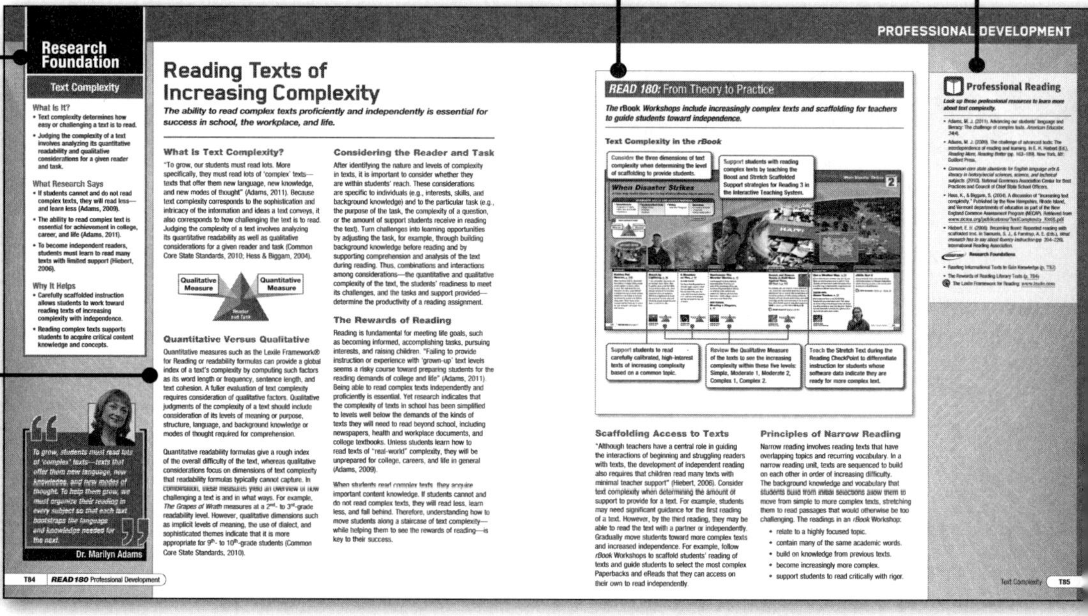

***rBook Teacher's Edition,* Research Foundations Tab**

Instructional Routines

The Instructional Routines tab in your *rBook Teacher's Edition* helps you implement nine RED Routines during daily Whole- and Small-Group Instruction. Explore this tab to learn the research behind each routine, step-by-step directions, and tips for using the routines effectively in your classroom.

Understand why the routine is important and how it supports students.

Preview how the routine looks in action during Whole- and Small-Group Instruction.

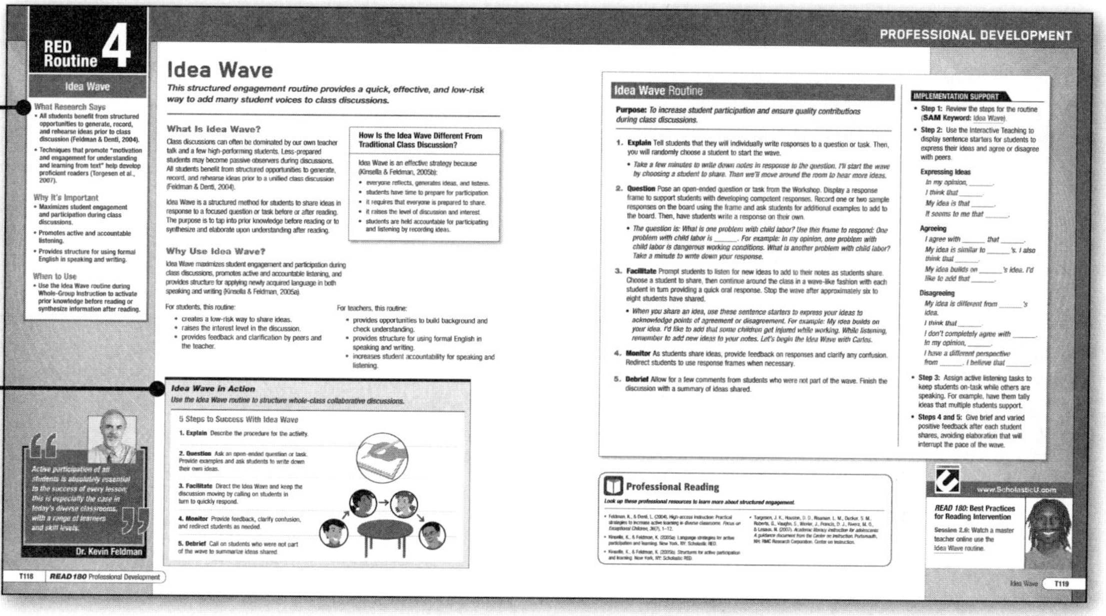

***rBook Teacher's Edition*, Instructional Routines Tab**

Best Practices

Explore the Best Practices tab in your *rBook Teacher's Edition* for professional development on effective instructional strategies for literacy intervention. You will find background research, model lessons, and academic language for teaching students key skills such as synthesizing, evaluating, and analyzing.

Learn about a Best Practices strategy, when to teach it, and how to target individual student needs.

Use the model lesson to teach students how to apply the strategy while reading or writing.

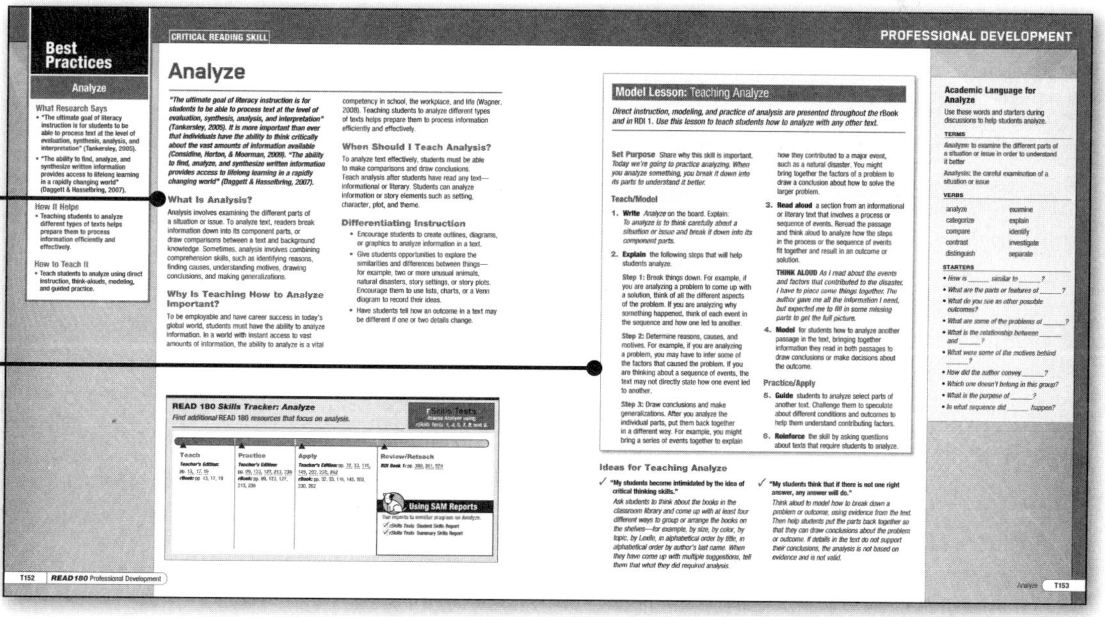

***rBook Teacher's Edition*, Best Practices Tab**

Enhancing Strategies With Your Dashboard

Build new teaching strategies and enhance your professional skills day by day directly from the *READ 180* Teacher Dashboard.

Professional Development

Refer to the Professional Development section on the right side of the Teacher Dashboard Home Page for resources to support you with implementing *READ 180*. Here you will find classroom videos, professional presentations, and downloadable articles related to that day's lesson. Click a resource link to spend a few minutes engaging in on-demand professional development before planning or teaching your lessons.

Learn best practices for teaching Whole- and Small-Group Instruction with training presentations and professional articles from *READ 180* experts.

Watch videos of master teachers and program authors modeling *rBook* lessons and routines.

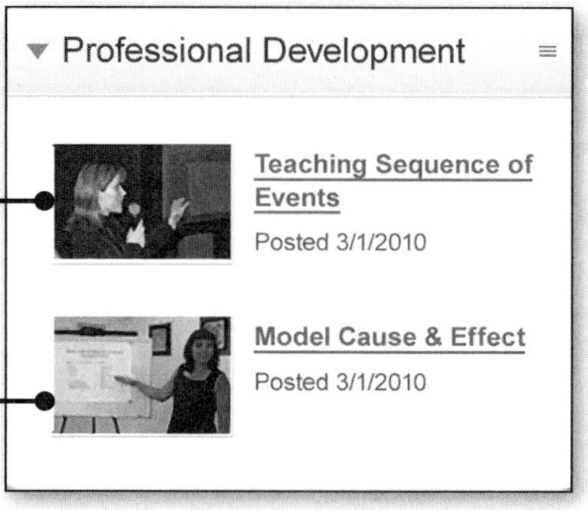

Teacher Dashboard Home Page

QuickTips

Read the daily QuickTips on your Teacher Dashboard Home Page for pointers and reminders about implementing *READ 180* effectively. The QuickTips address key implementation topics such as setting up the learning environment, teaching Whole- and Small-Group Instruction, and using the program technology. Use the arrows at the bottom to scroll through all available QuickTips.

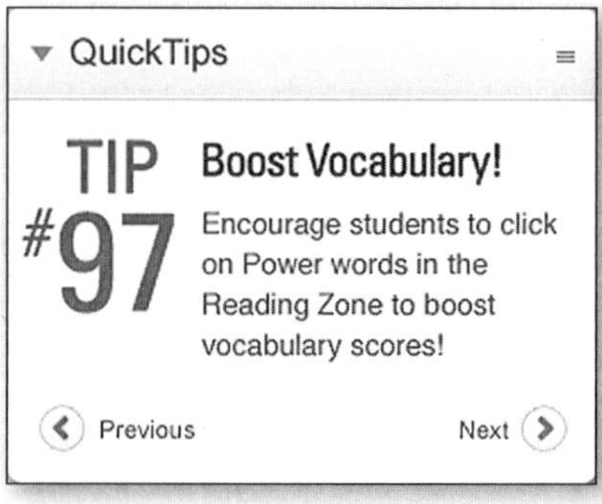

Teacher Dashboard Home Page

Tech Tip

You can also engage in daily professional development directly from *rBook* lessons in the Interactive Teaching System. Click the RED Routines links to review the steps and watch videos of the routines in action.

Getting Started With Implementation Videos

Watch the *READ 180* Implementation Videos for support with beginning the program, including setting up your classroom and implementing the Instructional Model.

Implementing for Success

The Implementation Videos explain the research behind *READ 180* and offer tips for integrating all program components. Watch the videos before getting started with *READ 180* to plan your classroom setup and learn strategies for effectively implementing the Instructional Model. Look for these features to support you:

- Videos of real *READ 180* classrooms and master teachers in action.
- Interviews with experienced *READ 180* teachers and leaders who can offer expert advice on classroom management, assessment, report analysis, and targeted instruction.
- Chapters to show students to introduce them to *READ 180*.

Implementation Videos

Reflect While Watching

As you watch the Implementation Videos, reflect on how you will implement the *READ 180* Instructional Model in your classroom. Pause after watching each chapter to jot down your reflections below.

DVD Chapter	Reflections
Welcome to *READ 180* Next Generation	To what extent do you see your students struggling with the "failure cycle"?
Implementing the Instructional Model	Jot down a tip you learned for implementing each part of the Instructional Model.
Getting to Know the Teacher Technology	How do you think the Teacher Dashboard will help increase success in your classroom?
Teaching an *rBook* Workshop	Jot down ideas on how to introduce Stretch Texts to the class to increase rigor.
Screening and Assessing	How will you prepare students for taking the SRI College & Career assessment at the start of the year?

Connecting With the *READ 180* Community

Join and interact with the *READ 180* Community to access downloadable resources, view and post ideas on message boards, and connect with other teachers from around the country.

Making Professional Connections

As a *READ 180* teacher, you are connected to thousands of other educators across the country. Once you register for the free *READ 180* Community website, you will have a virtual network of teaching colleagues who you can turn to for advice, resources, and support. Use the "Ask Dee" feature to submit questions and receive advice from a master *READ 180* teacher.

Create a personal profile for networking with other *READ 180* educators across the country.

Explore the Resource Library for hundreds of downloadables developed by Scholastic and other Community members.

Collaborate with colleagues nationwide to discuss shared interests, such as teaching students with disabilities or English language learners.

Post a question and get answers from *READ 180* colleagues who have solved similar challenges.

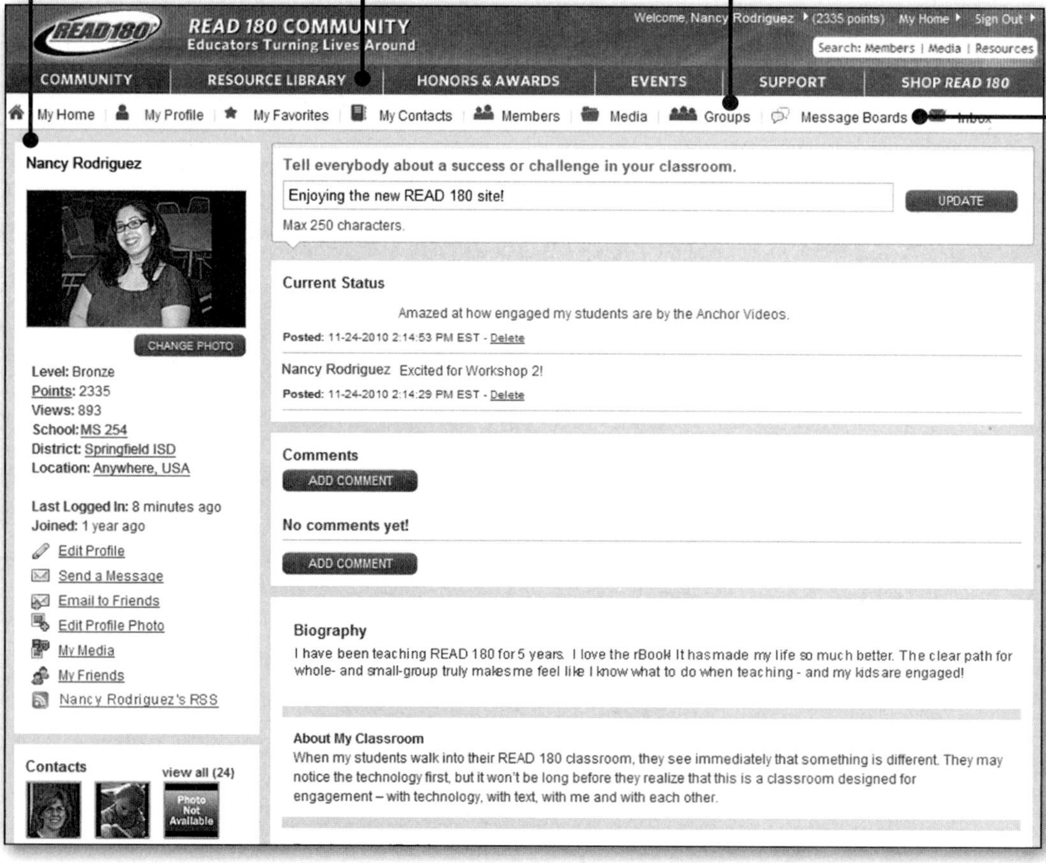

www.read180.com/community

Become a Member

Follow these steps to create your own account on the free *READ 180* Community website:

1. Sign in to the Teacher Dashboard from the **Educator Access** screen. On the Teacher Dashboard Home Page, click in the **Web Gateway.** Alternately, you can use an Internet browser to go to **www.read180.com/community.**
2. Click **Join Now** in the upper right corner of the *READ 180* Community welcome screen. A **Join the Community Now!** page will appear.
3. Enter your first name, last name, and email address in the blank fields near the top of the page. Scholastic highly recommends using the same email address that you have registered with SAM.
4. Create a Community username and password by completing the blank fields in the middle of the page. Scholastic highly recommends that you use your SAM username and password.
5. Enter your school zip code in the appropriate field near the bottom of the page. Then use the pull-down menus to select answers to the remaining questions on the form.
6. Upload an optional photo to appear on your personalized Community profile by clicking the **Choose File** button and selecting a photo that is stored on your computer
7. Copy the letters that are in the box under **Enter the text from the image below.** Check the two boxes below it.
8. Click **Join** to complete your registration.

Getting to Know the Community

After completing your registration, complete the tasks below to get familiar with the resources available to you as a member of the *READ 180* Community.

Community Task	My Findings
Identify a feature that will support you on the "New *READ 180* Teachers" Group Page.	
Find an answer to a question you have on the Message Board for your *READ 180* Stage.	
Search the Resource Library to find a Classroom Management resource that is helpful for new teachers.	

Participating in Your Online Course

Enroll in a graduate-level online course, *READ 180 Next Generation: Building Literacy for College and Career Readiness,* for support with successful program implementation in your classroom.

READ 180 Next Generation: Building Literacy for College and Career Readiness

READ 180 Next Generation: Building Literacy for College and Career Readiness is an interactive, graduate-level professional development course designed to support new *READ 180* teachers. Your *READ 180* program purchase includes access to this course directly from your Teacher Dashboard. The course is self-paced, and you can choose to apply for graduate credit (see page 231).

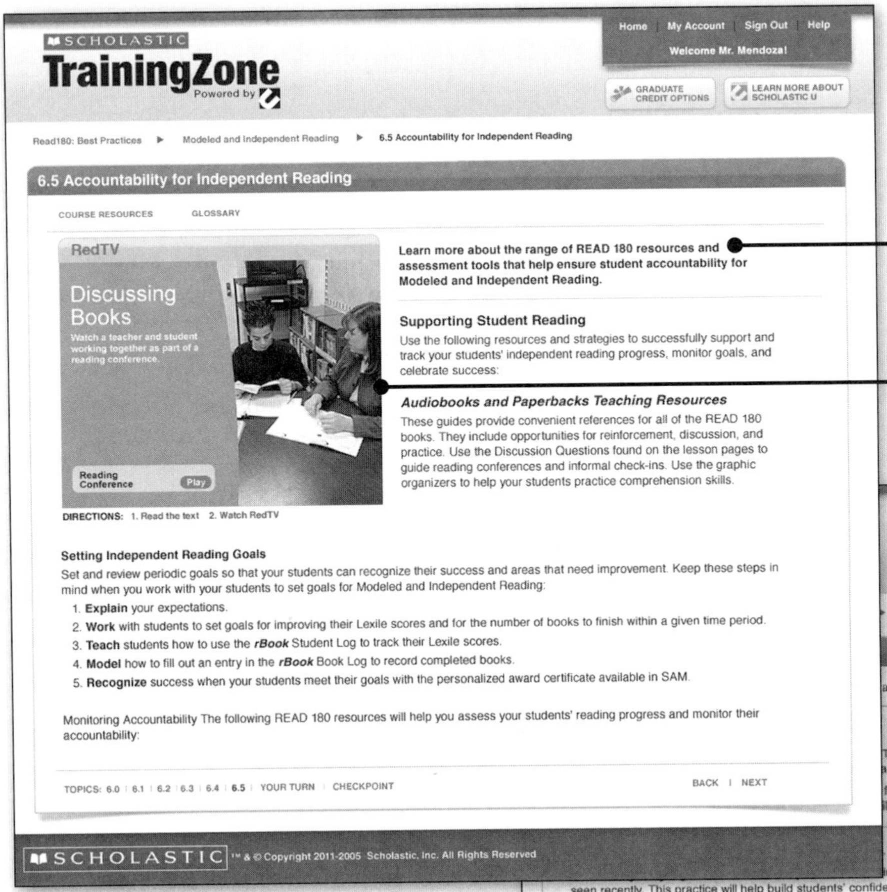

Learn research-based instructional strategies for raising your students' reading achievement.

Watch program authors and master teachers share best practices for implementing *READ 180.*

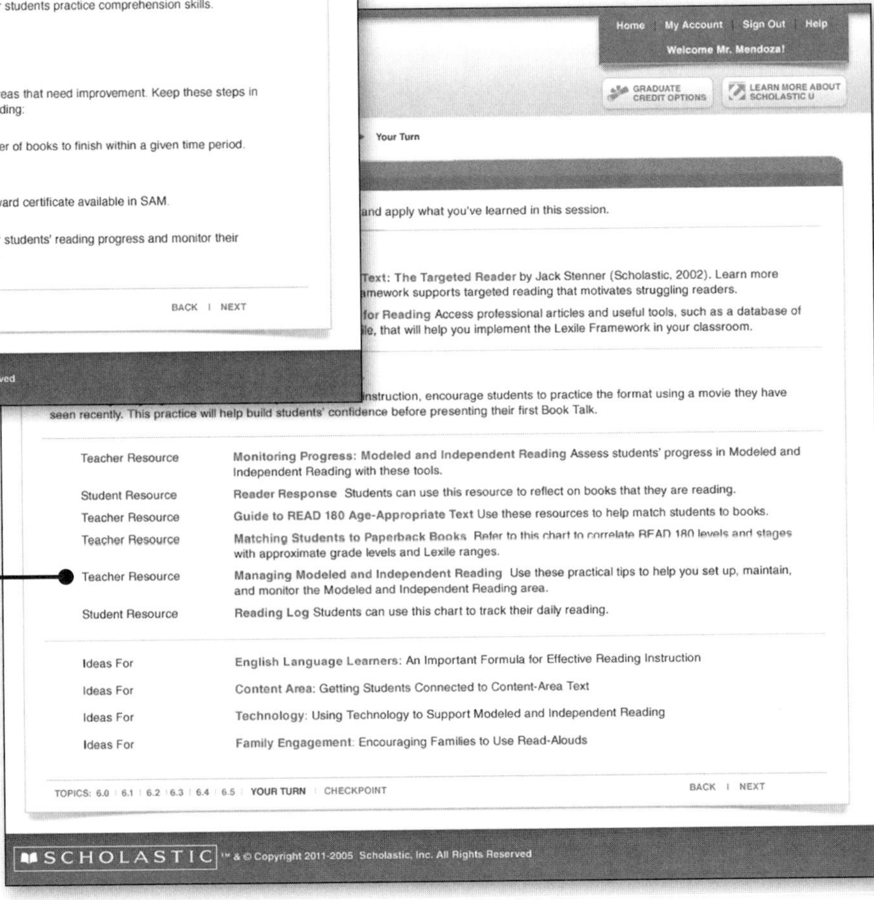

Download professional articles, reproducibles, and Web links to extend your learning about key *READ 180* topics.

Previewing the Online Course

The course includes six sessions to build your knowledge on key components of successful program implementation. The sessions provide background on struggling readers, research-based teaching strategies, and guidelines for effective usage of the Topic Software and *READ 180* assessments.

Session 1: Course Introduction: Getting Started With *READ 180* Next Generation Session 1 provides a course overview and introduces *READ 180.* It explains how to set up the *READ 180* classroom, establish clear procedures, and plan instruction based on the Instructional Model.

Session 2: Whole- and Small-Group Instruction: Close Reading of Text Session 2 defines the elements of reading instruction and explores how you can provide explicit instruction that supports students to read increasingly complex texts.

Session 3: Whole- and Small-Group Instruction: Writing and Research Session 3 explains how to scaffold the writing process to support your struggling readers with single- and multi-paragraph writing.

Session 4: Personalized Learning With *READ 180* Software Session 4 shows you how to maximize the benefits of the *READ 180* Topic Software to accelerate your students' reading achievement.

Session 5: Modeled and Independent Reading: Range and Quality Session 5 explains how to support students to build reading independence and fluency, use Lexile measures to match students to texts, extend reading practice with eReads, and increase student accountability during daily independent reading.

Session 6: Assessing, Reporting, and Data-Driven Instruction Session 6 focuses on how to use the Teacher Dashboard and analyze *READ 180* data to guide instruction, inform student groupings, and determine final grades. It also explores ways to collaborate with leaders and families to ensure student progress.

How to Enroll

Follow these steps to get started with *READ 180 Next Generation: Building Literacy for College and Career Readiness,* available on the Training Zone powered by Scholastic U:

1. Launch the Teacher Dashboard from the **Educator Access** screen. Sign in with your SAM username and password.
2. On the Teacher Dashboard Home Page, click the icon in the **Web Gateway**. This will connect you to the Course Home Page, Training Zone, or Scholastic U, depending on your school or district's level of access. If you connect to the Training Zone or Scholastic U, select ***READ 180 Next Generation: Building Literacy for College and Career Readiness*** from the list of available courses to access the Course Home Page.
3. On the Course Home Page, click the **Session 1** link to access the **Session at a Glance** screen.
4. On the **Session at a Glance** screen, click the links under **Step 1: Learn** to explore key topics for successful program implementation. For each topic, read the text along the right side of the screen. Click the **RedTV** on the left to watch a short video or interact with a multimedia tutorial.
5. On the **Session at a Glance** screen, click **Your Turn** under **Step 2: Extend and Apply** to view research articles, lesson plans, and classroom resources related to the Session topics.
6. On the **Session at a Glance** screen, click **CheckPoint** under **Step 3: Check** to complete an informal assessment of your learning before unlocking the next Session of the course.

Accessing the Training Zone

If your school or district has a Premium Maintenance and Support Plan, access the Training Zone from the Teacher Dashboard for *READ 180* implementation resources.

Premium Maintenance and Support

Scholastic offers a variety of technical support plans to ensure that *READ 180* works efficiently for optimal student achievement results. The Premium Maintenance and Support Plan provides unlimited technical support and in-person service as well as full access to the Training Zone, a comprehensive website with implementation resources for Scholastic programs. Check with your administrators to see if your school or district has purchased the Premium Maintenance and Support Plan.

Supporting Your *READ 180* Implementation

The comprehensive Training Zone website provides resources specific to *READ 180* to support you with successful program implementation. "Get in the Zone" to access downloadable classroom resources, videos of model lessons and trainings, on-demand tutorials, interactive webinars, and graduate-level online courses with best practices to support Scholastic programs.

Access hundreds of program-specific implementation resources.

Sign in to the Training Zone using your SAM username and password.

Watch short How-To tutorials to learn or review key tasks for successful implementation.

Register for interactive training webinars to build expertise with *READ 180.*

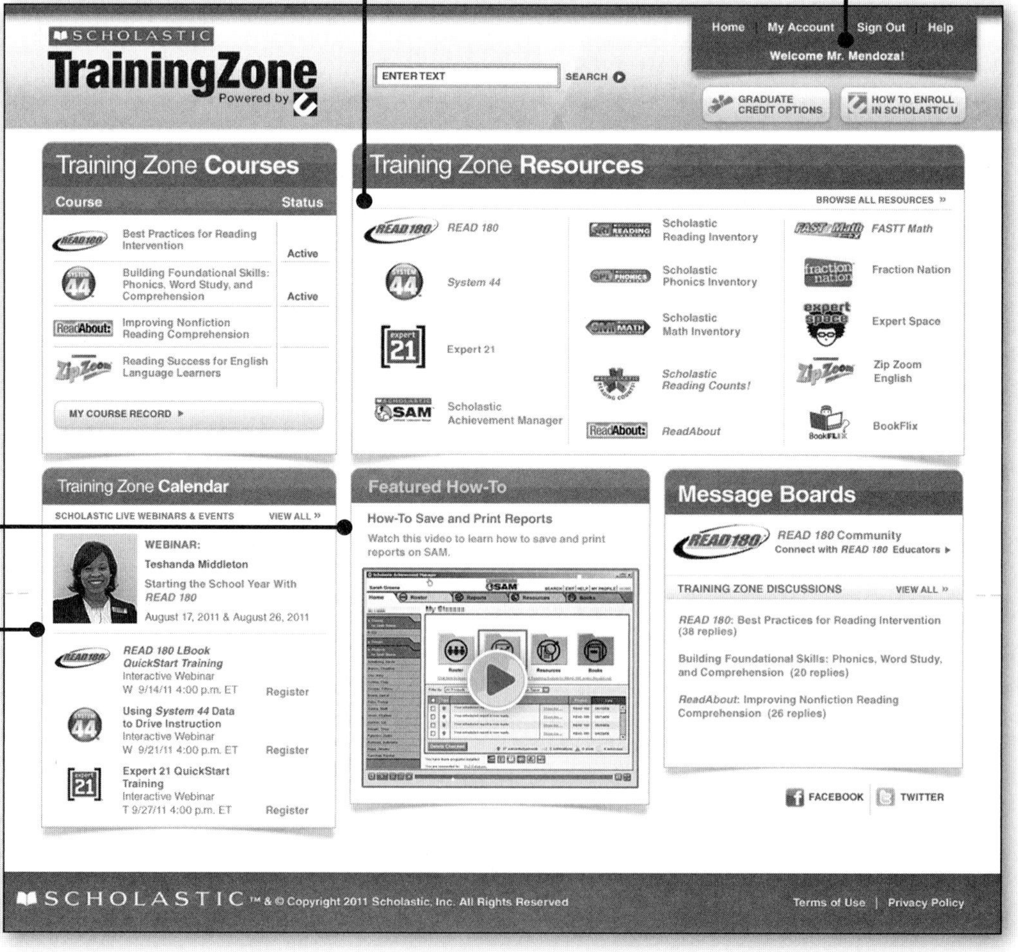

www.scholastic.com/tz

On-Demand Support and Learning

The Training Zone includes the following resources to support you with implementing *READ 180* effectively in your classroom:

- **Downloadables** Browse a library of hundreds of downloadable resources for teachers, students, and parents to support your *READ 180* classroom. Available resources include lesson plans, professional articles, reproducibles for classroom management, and more.
- **How-Tos** Watch short—3 to 5 minutes—video tutorials to learn how to perform key tasks for successful program implementation, such as enrolling students in SAM, supporting independent reading, and targeting instruction for small groups.
- **Digital Overviews** View longer—15 to 20 minutes—video tutorials for an in-depth look at key *READ 180* topics, such as classroom management and using the Interactive Teaching System (ITS).
- **Training Videos** Play videos of actual *READ 180* Implementation Trainings to refresh your knowledge about key topics for effective program implementation.
- **Webinars** Participate in live online training sessions to develop increasing expertise with all *READ 180* components, including the Teacher Dashboard, *SRI*, and *SRC!*
- **Graduate-Level Online Courses** Access your free course, *READ 180 Next Generation: Best Practices for Reading Intervention,* to learn best practices for instruction, management, and assessment.
- **Discussion Boards** Interact with other *READ 180* teachers across the country by posting questions and viewing answers on the Training Zone discussion boards.

How to Access

If your school or district has purchased the Premium Maintenance and Support Plan, access the Training Zone directly from your Teacher Dashboard. On the Teacher Dashboard Home Page, click in the **Web Gateway.** This will connect you to the Training Zone Home Page where you can begin exploring downloadables, video tutorials, webinars, and other resources to support successful program implementation in your classroom.

Access the online course, *READ 180 Next Generation: Best Practices for Reading Intervention,* by selecting it from the list of available courses under **Training Zone Courses** on the Training Zone Home Page.

Deepening Learning With Scholastic U

Explore Scholastic U—available with a purchased subscription—for comprehensive professional development resources for effective teaching across all content areas.

Scholastic U Subscription

Scholastic U is an online destination for educators that provides anytime, anywhere access to professional development resources for raising student achievement in all content areas. Access to Scholastic U is available through a purchased yearly subscription. Check with your administrators to find out if your school or district has purchased a Scholastic U subscription.

Building Your Professional Skills

Scholastic U includes thousands of resources to help you build your teaching skills, including:

- Dozens of graduate-level online courses.
- An extensive library of thousands of Just-in-Time Learning resources—including lesson plans, classroom management tools, classroom videos, interactive tutorials, and assessments.
- Discussion boards for interacting with educators across the country.
- Data reports and a calendar to help you monitor your professional learning and goals.

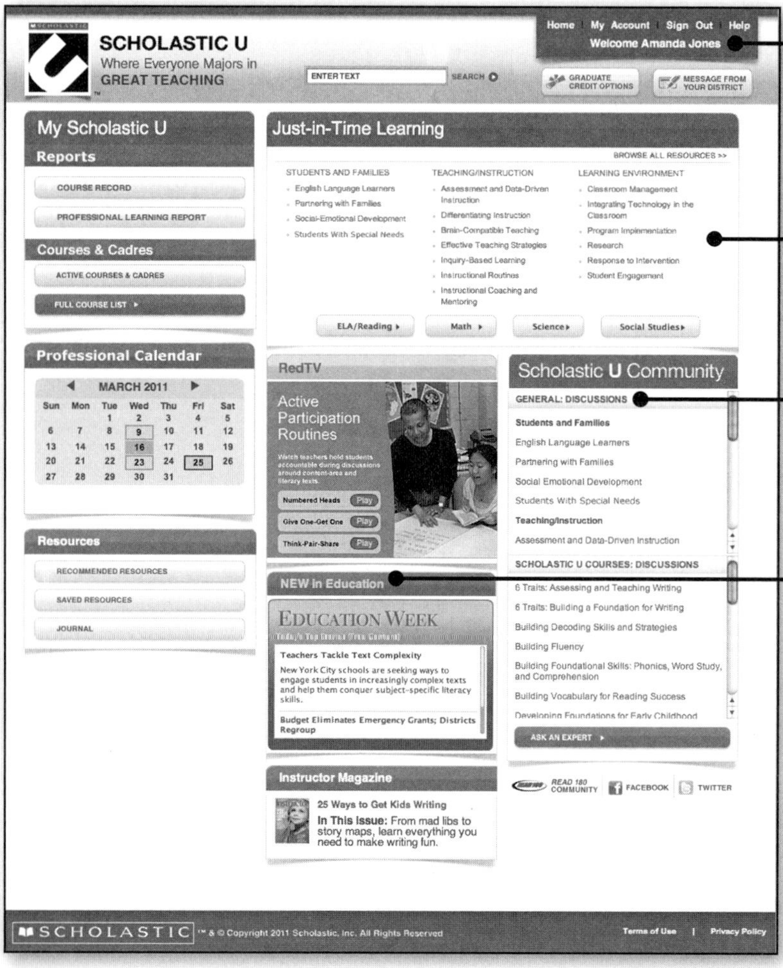

Sign in to Scholastic U using your SAM username and password.

Find hundreds of Just-in-Time resources organized by learning theme or content area.

Discuss resources, courses, and teaching strategies with other learners nationwide.

Stay up-to-date on current research, news, and trends in education.

www.ScholasticU.com

Participating in Online Courses

Scholastic U graduate-level courses offer a balance of online and in-person work, peer discussion, and individual study to provide convenient, targeted professional development. A Scholastic U subscription provides access to all available courses, including the following (visit **www.ScholasticU.com** for a complete listing):

- *6 Traits: Assessing and Teaching Writing*
- *Building Foundational Skills: Phonics, Word Study, and Comprehension*
- *Building Vocabulary for Reading Success*
- *English: A Universal Tool*
- *Exploring the Lexile Framework for Reading*
- *Improving Fluency*
- *Leading a Literacy-Focused School*
- *Middle School Literacy: Improving Text Comprehension*
- *High School Literacy: Comprehension Through Active, Strategic Reading*
- *Reading Success for English Language Learners*

Teacher Tip

Scholastic U offers courses and resources targeted for facilitators and leaders to support school-wide professional development across content areas.

Earning Course Credit

During your Scholastic U enrollment, you can sign up for graduate credit or continuing education units (CEUs) from accredited university partners. Credits may be transferred to a degree program, but it is important to first consult with the degree-granting institution. Credits are usually used for teacher certification and/or salary enhancement purposes. Visit **www.ScholasticU.com** or call toll-free 1-866-888-5392 for more information about Scholastic university partners and graduate credit opportunities.

How to Enroll

If your school or district has a purchased subscription, access Scholastic U directly from the Teacher Dashboard. On the Teacher Dashboard Home Page, click in the **Web Gateway.** This will connect you to the Scholastic U Home Page where you can begin exploring online courses, Just-in-Time Learning resources, and discussion boards to build your teaching skills across content areas.

Access the online course, *READ 180 Next Generation: Best Practices for Reading Intervention,* by clicking **Full Course List** under **Courses & Cadres** on the Scholastic U Home Page. Then click the course name to begin your learning.

Tracking Your Professional Growth

Monitor your own learning by recording the professional development experiences that you engage in throughout the school year.

Scholastic Implementation Trainings	**Date(s)/Notes**
Getting Started Training (Part 1) Explore the basics for beginning to implement *READ 180* effectively.	
Getting Started Training (Part 2) Continue learning strategies for successful program implementation.	
Conversion Training (for existing *READ 180* teachers) Learn about the exciting new enhancements to *READ 180* Next Generation.	
Follow-Up Training Enhance your *READ 180* expertise to further support student achievement.	
Scholastic Online Learning	**Date(s)/Notes**
Teaching With Technology Webinar Participate in an interactive training about using the *READ 180* technology.	
READ 180 Next Generation: Building Literacy for College and Career Readiness Enroll in a graduate-level course to support effective program implementation.	
Program-Embedded Professional Development	**Date(s)/Notes**
rBook Teacher's Edition: Research Foundations Tab Read about the research underlying *READ 180* instruction and assessments.	
rBook Teacher's Edition: Instructional Routines Tab Learn how to incorporate RED Routines into your daily instruction.	
rBook Teacher's Edition: Best Practices Tab Explore strategies for teaching key reading and writing skills.	
Teacher Dashboard: Professional Development Engage in daily learning to take your *READ 180* instruction to the next level.	
Other Professional Learning Experiences	**Date(s)/Notes**

TEACHER IMPLEMENTATION GUIDE

Additional Resources

Overview: Additional Resources

Use the *READ 180* Next Generation parent, teacher, and student resources in this section to take your program implementation to the next level of success.

Previewing Additional Resources

This section includes information and resources to support you with:

- **Getting Started** Start your year off right by completing key tasks for successful implementation during your first three weeks with *READ 180*.
- **Building a Home-to-School Connection** Learn strategies for developing a collaborative relationship with your students' families.
- **Managing Effective Rotations** Support students to work productively during each part of the Instructional Model.
- **Motivating the *READ 180* Student** Keep students engaged in learning and help them monitor their progress throughout the school year.

Tech Tip

Use the SAM Keyword in the Resource Links box at the bottom of each reproducible page in this section to download and print copies from SAM.

Reproducible Pages

Make copies of the reproducible pages in this section to use in your classroom and give to students and their families. The chart below outlines when to use each of the available parent, teacher, and student resources.

Resource	Page	Purpose
Welcome to *READ 180* Next Generation	238	Introduce the program to families at the beginning of the year.
Tips for Supporting Reading at Home	239	Offer strategies for encouraging student reading practice at home.
Rotation Chart	241	Display the groups and rotation order for the Instructional Model.
Daily Software Log	242	Hold students accountable for working productively on the Software.
Daily Reading Log	243	Hold students accountable for daily independent reading.
Exit Slips	244	Facilitate student reflection during Whole-Group Wrap-Up.
Daily Reflection Journal	245	Guide students to reflect on their learning in Whole-Group Wrap-Up.
READ 180 Goal Setting	247	Motivate students by helping them set goals for each rotation.
Analyzing SAM Reports	248	Analyze class and student reports to inform instructional decisions.

Getting Started: Your First Three Weeks

Use this time line as a guide for preparing your classroom, introducing *READ 180* to students, and connecting with families for a successful start to the school year.

Make sure *READ 180* Next Generation is installed on your school or district server.

Sign in to SAM to enroll students in *READ 180, rSkills, SRI,* and *SRC!* using the steps in the Technology Quick Reference.

Label rotation areas, organize materials, and post procedures.

Send home the Welcome to *READ 180* Next Generation letter to introduce the program.

Sign in to the Teacher Dashboard to plan your first three weeks online.

Introduce the Instructional Model, Topic Software, Student Dashboard, and *rBook.*

Set up an organizational system for frequently used handouts, such as the Reading Log.

Introduce the *READ 180* Library and online eReads.

WEEK 1

Participate in community-building activities.

Watch the Special Features: For Students chapter on the ITS Implementation Videos.

Preview *READ 180* Paperback, Audiobook, and eRead titles.

Get acquainted with the Student Dashboard.

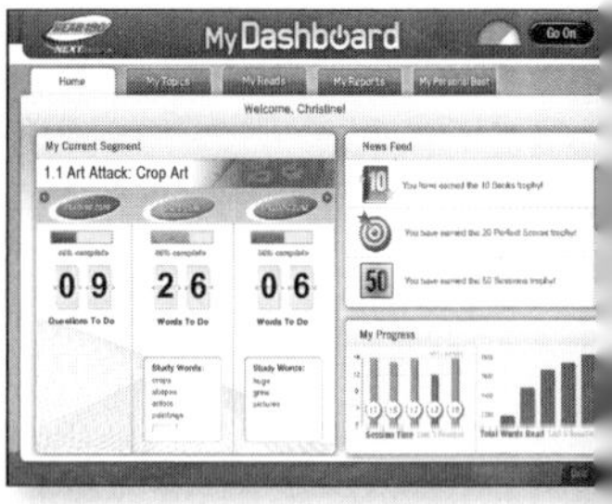

KEY

———— **Teacher**

. . . . **Students**

Teacher Tip

See *Getting Started: Your First Three Weeks With READ 180,* in the Teacher Bookshelf and on the Interactive Teaching System (ITS), for lesson plans to introduce the program.

WEEK 2

Administer the computer-based *SRI* College & Career test.

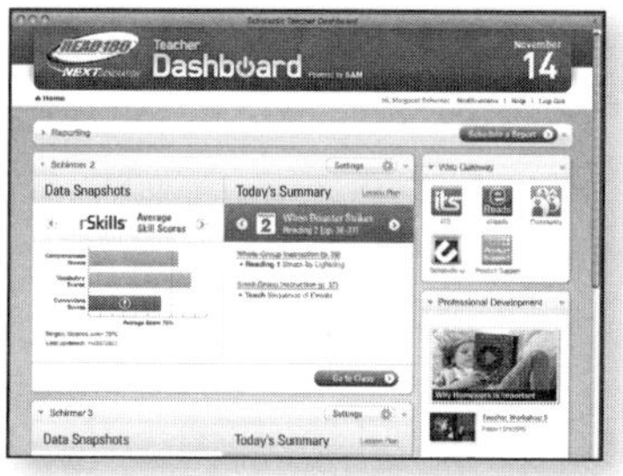

Teach and practice Instructional Routines and rotation procedures.

Run the *SRI* Instructional Planning Report in SAM to form initial groups.

Take the *SRI* College & Career.

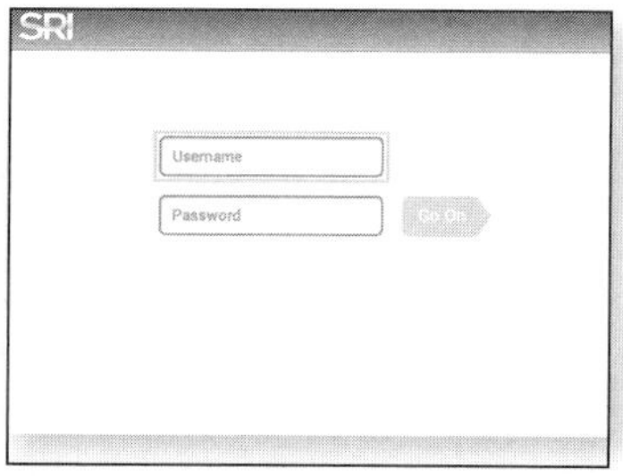

Practice key Instructional Routines and rotation procedures.

Select independent reading books based on Lexile® measures and interests.

WEEK 3

Use the Teacher Dashboard and *rBook Teacher's Edition* to plan and teach daily instruction.

Run the *READ 180* Parent Letter 1 Report in SAM to share students' *SRI* results with families.

Post and review Rotation Chart.

Begin Workshop 1 in the *rBook.*

Begin *READ 180* Topic Software.

Building a Home-to-School Connection

Encourage family involvement in *READ 180* to increase students' motivation and accelerate their reading achievement.

Research Says

A strong base of research evidence demonstrates that student achievement is positively impacted when schools, families, and communities partner to support student learning.
Mapp & Henderson, 2002

Introducing Your Classroom

Parents and caregivers are a critical link in student reading progress. Use these ideas to establish communication with families at the beginning of the year so they feel comfortable contacting you with questions or concerns.

Send Home Welcome Letters Make copies of the Welcome to *READ 180* Next Generation letter (page 238) to introduce your students' families to the program. Attach a copy of Tips for Supporting Reading at Home (page 239) to encourage additional reading practice at home.

Share Baseline Data After administering the first *Scholastic Reading Inventory* College & Career, send home the *READ 180* Parent Report I from SAM to help parents understand their child's baseline reading level. Also share the *SRI* Recommended Reading Report to help parents identify appropriate books for their child at the library or bookstore.

Connect Online Encourage parents to explore the *READ 180* Family Portal at **www.read180.com/familyportal**. This website provides tools in English and Spanish to help caregivers understand what their children are learning in *READ 180* and how they can support their reading progress. Parents can also visit the *READ 180* page on Facebook at **www.facebook.com/read180** to get up-to-date program news and connect with others.

Host a Parent Night Use your school's Open House or Back-to-School Night to introduce your classroom to families. Allow parents to explore the student materials for each small-group rotation.

Teacher Tip

If families have computers at home, consider emailing letters and reminders instead of sending home hard copies. This will allow them to respond more easily.

Collaborating With Families

Use these strategies to maintain contact with families throughout the year, sharing achievements and concerns as they come up.

Send Progress Updates Routinely update parents about their child's reading progress. Make regular phone calls to share good news and student successes. Send home the *READ 180* Parent Report II at the end of each grading period to share student performance data.

Create a Class Website Consider setting up a class website for students to share their reading achievements and for parents to learn what is happening in your classroom. Include the website URL address on any documents that you send home to remind parents to check it out.

Hold Reading Workshops Offer periodic evenings for parents to come into school and discuss how to support reading at home. Parents can share strategies that work in their own homes and learn new ideas from others.

Invite Classroom Guests Invite families to visit your classroom throughout the year to read with students in Modeled and Independent Reading. If any parents have a connection to the current *rBook* Workshop topic, invite them to participate as guest speakers.

Conferencing With Parents

Throughout the year, you may wish to hold one-to-one conferences to speak with parents and caregivers about their child's *READ 180* performance. Consider the focus of your conference as you gather relevant information to share. During some conferences, you may wish to review the student's progress in all small-group rotations, while other times you may want to focus on just one aspect of the student's performance, such as *rBook,* Topic Software, or *rSkills Tests* scores.

Share current report data and student work samples to help families understand their child's progress and how they can help. See page 115 of the *Placement, Assessment, and Reporting Guide* for support with preparing materials to share during parent-teacher conferences.

How to Structure a Parent-Teacher Conference

1. Understand the conference goals prior to sitting down with parents and caregivers. What do you hope to communicate? What can families do to help their child at home? What questions or concerns might they have regarding their child's performance?
2. Gather relevant information and materials to share with the family. Determine which reports and student work samples best demonstrate the topics you want to discuss (see page 115 of the *Placement, Assessment, and Reporting Guide* for suggestions). Remember not to overwhelm the family with too much information.
3. If the parents requested the conference, begin the meeting by allowing them to share their questions and concerns while you listen. Repeat their concerns back to them to make sure you understood them clearly. Then address concerns one at a time.
4. When you begin sharing performance data, start with the positive aspects of the student's work. Give specific examples, and avoid using educational jargon without fully explaining the terms (e.g., *SRI,* rotations, *rBook*).
5. Work with the family to craft a plan to support the student. Set classroom goals and clearly communicate how caregivers can be involved in assisting the student with achieving those goals.
6. End the conference on a positive note, and explain how and when the family will receive updates.

Reflection

One strategy I'll use to build a positive home-to-school connection throughout the year is...

Welcome to *READ 180* Next Generation

Dear Family,

I am excited to announce that our school is implementing *READ 180* Next Generation, an innovative reading intervention program by Scholastic. After careful consideration, your child has been selected to participate in the program in order to support his or her instructional needs.

READ 180 is a research-based program with proven results in raising student reading achievement. *READ 180* uses cutting-edge technology to deliver individualized reading instruction, provide valuable skills practice, and motivate students to become confident readers.

In our *READ 180* class, your child and I will work together to:

- Build essential literacy skills for college and career readiness.
- Bring his or her reading proficiency up to grade level.
- Develop multi-paragraph writing skills.
- Apply reading and writing strategies to other subjects such as social studies, science, and math.
- Show your child that he or she can attain reading success.

READ 180 will challenge your child to work hard. Offer encouragement and provide support at home by visiting the library, setting aside reading time, and discussing the books your child reads.

Thank you in advance for helping us achieve our goals!

Sincerely,

____

READ 180 Teacher

Phone: ______________________________

Email: ______________________________

Resource Links
SAM Keyword: Welcome Letter

Tips for Supporting Reading at Home

Try these ideas to encourage your child to practice reading skills at home.

Encourage Daily Reading

Research shows that reading every day helps children build reading comprehension, fluency, and vocabulary. Consider these suggestions for supporting your child with daily reading:

- **Establish a Routine** Designate a specific time for your child to read a book at his or her level for at least 20 minutes every night. For example, set aside time for reading after dinner or before bedtime.
- **Create a Comfortable Reading Environment** Use pillows, lamps, and comfortable furniture to set up a cozy reading area in your home. Read your own books there to model good reading habits.
- **Incorporate Fast and Fun Reads** Use magazines, newspapers, recipes, TV schedules, and road signs as reading opportunities. Incorporate quick reading whenever and wherever you and your child happen to be.
- **Share Workplace Reading** Bring home materials and documents from your job so your child sees the relevance of reading in the workplace and the long-term importance of becoming a successful reader.
- **Read and Ride** Listen to audiobooks while traveling by car so your child hears modeled fluent reading. Bring a CD or mp3 player with headphones for your child to listen to audiobooks while on a train or plane.
- **Read and Chat** Discuss the books that your child is reading. Ask questions such as: *What was your favorite part? Who were your favorite and least favorite characters? Can you think of another ending?*

Find the Right Books

In *READ 180,* your child has a Lexile—a number that represents his or her reading level based on the Lexile Framework for Reading. Books also have Lexile measures to indicate how difficult they are. By matching your child's Lexile to books with the same Lexile, you can identify reading materials at the right level for your child. Many libraries and bookstores allow you to search for books by Lexile. You can also search for appropriate texts on **www.lexile.com.**

Explore the Online eReads

As part of *READ 180* Next Generation, your child has access to web-based eReads, short nonfiction texts that explore content areas from the *READ 180* Software. Your child can follow these steps to access eReads at home:

1. Type **www.read180.com/ereads** into an Internet browser to access the eReads Zip Code Locator screen.
2. Next to **School Zip Code,** enter your school's zip code: ____________________. Then click **OK.**
3. Select your school from the pull-down menu. Then click **GO.** The **Student Access** screen will appear.
4. Click **GO** under **eReads.**
5. Enter the username and password you use to log into *READ 180* during class.
   Username: ____________________ Password: ____________________
6. Click one of the unlocked eReads Collections on the **Welcome to Your eReads!** screen to begin reading.

Resource Links
SAM Keyword: Reading Tips

Managing Effective Rotations

Use these suggestions to help students transition quickly and quietly between rotations and work productively in each small-group area.

Set Up the Rotations

After Whole-Group Instruction, students break into small groups to work in three rotations: Small-Group Instruction, Instructional Software, and Modeled and Independent Reading. To make the most of students' time in each area, consider the following strategies:

- Explicitly teach procedures and behavioral expectations so students know what to do first when they move to each rotation. In each area, display a poster with rotation procedures for student reference.
- Use a clear signal, such as a timer or clip of music, to indicate when students should begin rotating.
- Laminate a copy of the Rotation Chart (page 241) to display daily groups and rotation order. Use overhead or dry erase markers so you can easily make adjustments.
- Remind students to look at the Rotation Chart at the start of each class, since groups may change often. Check the Groupinator on the Teacher Dashboard to see grouping recommendations.

Practice Rotating

Encourage quiet, quick, calm transitions by explicitly modeling how to move from one rotation area to the next. Follow the recommended steps below to teach students how to rotate. See page 31 of *Getting Started: Your First Three Weeks With READ 180* for additional tips on teaching students to rotate.

1. Point out the three rotation areas in the classroom.
2. Post and explain the Rotation Chart (page 241) so students know their group and rotation order.
3. Share your signal for movement, such as a timer or music clip.
4. Model transitioning from each area to the next. Discuss expectations for walking speed and noise level.
5. Allow each group to practice rotating, one at a time. Then guide all three groups to practice at once.
6. Provide additional practice until all students have mastered rotating quietly and quickly.
7. Periodically revisit your expectations for rotating throughout the school year.

Hold Students Accountable

Encourage productivity during Instructional Software and Modeled and Independent Reading by holding students accountable for independent work. Print copies of the Daily Software Log (page 242) and the Daily Reading Log (page 243) for students to record their daily progress in each rotation. Display a poster-sized copy of the Sentence Starters (SAM Keyword: Sentence Starters) that students can use to complete their logs each day. Check the logs at the start of Small-Group Instruction for immediate accountability and feedback.

Ensure Reading Engagement

Prevent boredom and frustration—and subsequent behavioral disruptions—by supporting students to select engaging books at their level for Modeled and Independent Reading. Distribute the Reader's Survey (SAM Keyword: Survey) to your class at the beginning of the school year. Use the results to help students select Paperbacks and Audiobooks at their *READ 180* Level that you know they will enjoy reading.

READ 180 Rotation Chart

List student names for each small group. Post the completed chart in your classroom so students know their group and rotation order.

Class ____________________________

Group ____________________________

____________ ____________
____________ ____________
____________ ____________
____________ ____________

Rotation Order

1. Instructional Software
2. Modeled and Independent Reading
3. Small-Group Instruction

Group ____________________________

____________ ____________
____________ ____________
____________ ____________
____________ ____________

Rotation Order

1. Modeled and Independent Reading
2. Small-Group Instruction
3. Instructional Software

Group ____________________________

____________ ____________
____________ ____________
____________ ____________
____________ ____________

Rotation Order

1. Small-Group Instruction
2. Instructional Software
3. Modeled and Independent Reading

Resource Links
SAM Keyword: Rotation Chart

Name ______________________________

Start Date ______________ End Date ______________

Segment ______________________________

READ 180 Topic Software Daily Log

▶ Record the work you complete in the *READ 180* Topic Software each day.

Date	Reading Zone Questions To Do	Word Zone Words To Do	Spelling Zone Words To Do	Session Time

Date	Success Zone Completed	Writing Zone Completed

Resource Links
SAM Keyword: Software Log

Name ______________________________

Book Title ______________________________

My Lexile® ______________ Book Lexile® ______________

READ 180 Daily Reading Log

Day	Today's Response	Pages Read		Teacher Initials
		Starting Page	Ending Page	
Monday				
Tuesday				
Wednesday				
Thursday				
Friday				

Resource Links
SAM Keyword: Reading Log

Name: ______________________________

Exit Slips

Write about what you did in *READ 180* today in one of the boxes below.

Today I learned . . .	I am still confused about . . .
I am most excited about . . .	A question I have is . . .

Resource Links
SAM Keyword: Exit Slips

Name: ______________________________

Daily Reflection Journal

Write about what you did during each part of *READ 180* class today.

In **Whole-Group Instruction**, I learned ______________________________

____

In **Small-Group Instruction**, I practiced ______________________________

____

In **Instructional Software**, I worked on ______________________________

____

In **Modeled and Independent Reading**, I read ______________________________

____

The most [interesting/surprising/exciting] thing I did was ______________________________

____

I was [unsure about/confused by] ______________________________

____

Tomorrow, I plan to ______________________________

____

____

____

Resource Links
SAM Keyword: Daily Reflection

Motivating the *READ 180* Student

Try these strategies to motivate your most reluctant students to meet or exceed their goals in *READ 180* and achieve reading success.

Research Says

When students are included in monitoring their own progress, they better understand their growth, gain motivation, and acquire a sense of ownership for learning.

Andrade, 2007/2008; Hupert & Heinze, 2006

Setting Academic Goals

Research shows that students who are motivated intrinsically, or from within, make faster academic progress than those who are not. Students feel more motivated to try their best when they understand what they are working toward. Conference with students regularly throughout the year to define academic goals, share report data, and discuss progress. Print copies of the *READ 180* Goal Setting form (page 247) and guide students to complete it with an action plan for each part of the Instructional Model. Continue to revisit these goals during one-to-one conferences so students can reflect on their own progress.

Self-Monitoring With The Student Dashboard

Encourage students to track their own *READ 180* performance throughout the school year. As they see proof of their reading progress and successes, they will feel motivated to keep working hard to grow as readers. Remind students to spend some time exploring their Dashboard when they log in to the Topic Software each day. The Student Dashboard Home Tab shows progress data for the five Software Learning Zones. Have students use this data to complete the Daily Software Log (page 242) for accountability. Encourage students to examine the News Feed and My Progress areas on the Home Tab to stay up-to-date on their program successes and usage.

The Student Dashboard also includes tabs for My Topics, My Reads, My Reports, and My Personal Best. Students can explore these tabs to review the *READ 180* work they have already done and preview upcoming assignments they still have to complete.

Celebrating Success

Celebrate your students' achievements when they reach their *READ 180* goals or make Lexile growth. Try these tips for celebrating success in your classroom and add any of your own ideas to the list:

- Post student names, individual goals, and successes on bulletin boards.
- Print personalized certificates from SAM. Click **Certificates** in the **Programs** menu at the bottom of a class or student **Profile** screen.
- Share report data with students and families to show growth.
- Send home positive letters to share student progress with families.
- Allow students to choose a special classroom job, activity, or discussion topic.
- Take a field trip to the local library.
- Reward students with bookmarks, journals, pencils, pens, or other treats related to reading and writing.
- ______________________________
- ______________________________

Name: ____________________

READ 180 Goal Setting

Fill in your classroom goals in the ovals. Then write down your action plans.

1. Small-Group Goal

2. Reading Goal

3. Software Goal

To reach my goals I will:

1. ____________________

2. ____________________

3. ____________________

I will know I have made progress toward my goals by:

1. ____________________

2. ____________________

3. ____________________

I will know I have successfully reached my goals when:

1. ____________________

2. ____________________

3. ____________________

Resource Links
SAM Keyword: Goal Setting

Analyzing SAM Reports

Analyze data on class and student reports from the Scholastic Achievement Manager (SAM) to identify next steps for raising reading achievement.

Class Report: ______

First, analyze class data to see how all students are performing relative to each other.

Class:	**Report Time Period:**	
Type/Purpose of Report		
Noteworthy Data	Strengths:	Challenges:
Next Steps		

Student Report: ______

Next, drill down on one student's data to identify individual successes and challenges.

Student:	**Report Time Period:**	
Type/Purpose of Report		
Noteworthy Data	Strengths:	Challenges:
Next Steps		

Resource Links
SAM Keyword: Report Analysis

Identifying SAM Resources

Access downloadable resources on the Scholastic Achievement Manager (SAM) to provide targeted instruction, assign student practice pages, and assess application of *READ 180* skills.

SAM Resources Index

Use the *READ 180* SAM Resources Index to identify downloadable resources that are available on SAM. Download the index from the green Resources tab by entering the SAM Keyword: Keyword Index.

The chart below lists some key resources for getting started with *READ 180* and implementing the program effectively. Download the SAM Resources Index for a complete list of available resources and Keywords.

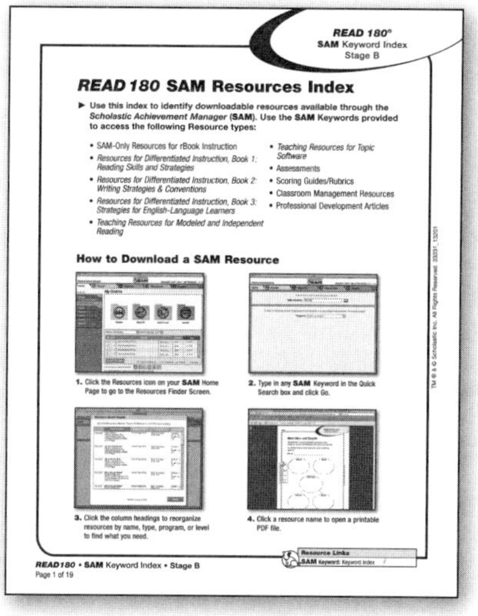
***READ 180*®**
SAM Keyword Index
Stage B

READ 180 SAM Resources Index

▶ Use this index to identify downloadable resources available through the *Scholastic Achievement Manager* (**SAM**). Use the **SAM** Keywords provided to access the following Resource types:

- SAM-Only Resources for rBook Instruction
- *Resources for Differentiated Instruction, Book 1: Reading Skills and Strategies*
- *Resources for Differentiated Instruction, Book 2: Writing Strategies & Conventions*
- *Resources for Differentiated Instruction, Book 3: Strategies for English-Language Learners*
- *Teaching Resources for Modeled and Independent Reading*
- *Teaching Resources for Topic Software*
- Assessments
- Scoring Guides/Rubrics
- Classroom Management Resources
- Professional Development Articles

How to Download a SAM Resource

1. Click the Resources icon on your **SAM** Home Page to go to the Resources Finder Screen.
2. Type in any **SAM** Keyword in the Quick Search box and click Go.
3. Click the column headings to reorganize resources by name, type, program, or level to find what you need.
4. Click a resource name to open a printable PDF file.

Resource Links
SAM Keyword: Keyword Index

TM ® & © Scholastic Inc. All Rights Reserved. 33331_13201

READ 180 • **SAM** Keyword Index • **Stage B**
Page 1 of 19

SAM Keyword: Keyword Index

SAM Resource	SAM Keyword
Classroom Management	
Conferencing With Students	Conference Log
Daily Reading Log	Reading Log
Daily Reflection Journal	Daily Reflection
eReads Reading Log	ER Reading Log
Exit Slips	Exit Slips
Lexile Framework for Reading Map	Lexile Tracking
QuickWrite Response	QuickWrite
rBook Lesson Reflection	Lesson Reflection
READ 180 Classroom Implementation Review	Implementation Review
READ 180 Goal Setting	Goal Setting
READ 180 Grading Form	Grading Form
Reader's Survey	Survey
Rotation Chart	Rotation Chart
Sentence Starters	Sentence Starters
Tips for Supporting Reading at Home	Reading Tips
Topic Software Daily Log	Software Log
Welcome to *READ 180* Next Generation	Welcome Letter

SAM Resource	SAM Keyword
RED Routines	
Routine 1: Academic Vocabulary	Academic Vocabulary
Routine 2: Scaffolded Reading	Scaffolded Reading
Routine 3: Think (Write)-Pair-Share	Think Pair
Routine 4: Idea Wave	Idea Wave
Routine 5: Numbered Heads	Numbered Heads
Routine 6: The Writing Process	Writing Process
Routine 7: Peer Feedback	Peer Feedback
Routine 8: React and Write	React and Write
Routine 9: Summarize	Summarize
Teaching and Assessment Resources	
Academic Vocabulary Chart	Academic Vocabulary
Final Book Projects	Final Projects
RDI Assignment Tracking Log	RDI Tracking
Reading Rate Chart	Rate Chart
Workshop Rubric	Workshop Rubric
Workshop Skills Checklist	Skills Checklist

Glossary of Terms

Understand key components of *READ 180* Next Generation instruction and implementation for raising student reading achievement.

Academic Language The vocabulary and lexical tools that students need for speaking, reading, and writing in a formal academic setting.

Academic Vocabulary High-utility words that students will encounter across content areas but may not be part of everyday speech (e.g., *subsequently*), words related to central concepts (e.g., *democracy*), and content-specific terms (e.g., *metaphor*).

Access Screen The browser-based gateway for accessing all *READ 180* technology components. The Educator Access Screen provides access to SAM and the Teacher and Leadership Dashboards. The Student Access Screen connects to the Topic Software, eReads, *SRI, rSkills Tests,* and *SRC!*

Adaptive Software Software that customizes content and pacing based on student performance to continually assess and target individual needs.

Anchor Videos High-interest videos designed to build students' background knowledge and introduce key vocabulary about a topic before students read.

Anchored Instruction Teaching that builds background knowledge and introduces key vocabulary to help students construct mental models that they need to approach a new text.

Boost and Stretch Scaffolded Support Daily differentiation strategies to scaffold or extend lessons based on student readiness. Click its Scaffolded Support in *rBook Interactive Teacher's Edition* lessons to see Boost and Stretch strategies.

College and Career Readiness The skills and strategies necessary for long-term success in college, career, and beyond, including: broad content knowledge, comprehension of increasingly complex literary and informational texts, argument writing with evidence to support ideas, academic language in speaking and writing, and independent critical thinking.

CheckPoints Regular opportunities in a Workshop to use data to regroup students and provide differentiated support. Each *rBook* Workshop has three CheckPoints: Reading, Writing, and End-of-Workshop.

Data Snapshots A Teacher and Leadership Dashboard feature that pulls key data from SAM to allow you to monitor program implementation and student progress at a glance. There is one Data Snapshot for each technology-based component: *READ 180* Topic Software, *SRI, rSkills Tests*, and *SRC!*

eReads Leveled, Web-based, nonfiction articles related to the Topics that students explore on the *READ 180* Topic Software. Each *READ 180* Stage includes 15 eReads Collections, each with four eReads articles for Level 1–2 and Level 3–4.

Instructional Model The research-based, classroom-proven 90-minute structure for class periods that includes Whole-Group Instruction (20 minutes), three 20-minute rotations—Small-Group Instruction, Instructional Software, Modeled and Independent Reading—and Whole-Group Wrap-Up (10 minutes).

Interactive Teaching System (ITS) An electronic teaching resource that consists of digital versions of the *rBook Teacher's Edition* and other instructional materials. Access ITS through the Teacher Dashboard or by visiting **www.read180.com/its.**

Groupinator A feature of the Teacher Dashboard Class Page that provides recommended student grouping for rotations and lessons for CheckPoints based on data from student software performance.

Leadership Dashboard A comprehensive website for school and district administrators to monitor student performance and *READ 180* implementation results.

Learning Zones The five areas of the *READ 180* Topic Software—Reading, Word, Spelling, Success, and Writing—that provide customized instruction, practice, and assessment related to a reading passage.

Level A student's *READ 180* reading level, assigned based on *SRI* test results. Stage A includes Levels 1–3, and Stages B and C include Levels 1–4.

Lexile A measure from BR ("Beginning Reader") to above 1500L that represents a student's reading level and/or readability of a text, based on the Lexile Framework for Reading.

Lexile Framework for Reading A system for measuring student reading levels and text readability on the same scale. Use the *SRI* to assess students' reading comprehension and determine a Lexile measure (e.g., 500L). Use Lexile measures to match students to independent and instructional reading materials within their Lexile range.

Notifications A Teacher Dashboard feature that allows you to opt in to receive weekly emailed updates on student software performance.

QuickWrites Short prompts that build writing confidence and engage students by asking them to respond to what they have read. Look for QuickWrites in *Teaching Resources for Topic Software* and *Teaching Resources for Modeled and Independent Reading*.

rBook Interactive student worktext organized around nine Workshops to practice reading, vocabulary, writing, and academic language during Whole- and Small-Group Instruction.

***READ 180* Topic Software** The adaptive Software students use daily during the Instructional Software rotation. It offers individualized practice and performance tracking for comprehension, vocabulary, fluency, phonics, spelling, and writing.

RED Routines Instructional and structured engagement routines to use regularly during Whole- and Small-Group Instruction to provide consistent instruction, structure academic discussion, and actively engage students in learning.

Report Scheduler A Teacher Dashboard feature that allows you to schedule when SAM will run a report to deliver to your email inbox.

Resources for Differentiated Instruction (RDI) 1–4 A group of four books with lesson plans, routines, practice pages, and professional development articles to help you target Whole- and Small-Group Instruction to meet individual needs during Workshop CheckPoints.

***rSkills* College & Career** Curriculum-based tests that assess student mastery of skills taught in each *rBook* Workshop. There is one *rSkills Test* for each Workshop, with multiple choice, constructed responses, and an optional extended constructed response prompt.

Scaffolded Instruction Teaching that gives students the support tools, or scaffolds, they need to access a text, participate in discussions, or complete an assignment. Scaffolds include teacher modeling, graphic organizers, and sentence starters.

Scholastic Achievement Manager (SAM) SAM allows teachers and administrators to manage and review student enrollment and performance data and access data-driven resources for customizing instruction.

Scholastic Reading Counts! (SRC!) Computer-based quizzes that allow students to demonstrate understanding of the Paperbacks, Audiobooks, and eReads that they read independently.

***Scholastic Reading Inventory (SRI)* College & Career** Computer-based, adaptive assessment that measures a student's reading level. Students take an *SRI* test once for placement in the *READ 180* Topic Software and three additional times for progress monitoring.

Segment One of four sections that make up a Topic on the *READ 180* Topic Software. Each segment includes activities from five zones: Reading, Word, Spelling, Success, and Writing.

Stretch Text A fourth reading passage for each *rBook* Workshop to "stretch," or extend learning, for students who are ready to read a more complex text related to the Workshop topic. The Stretch Texts are available in *Resources for Differentiated Instruction 1* or on SAM.

Student Dashboard An engaging, motivational feature that students access when they log on to the *READ 180* Topic Software. It allows them to track their own learning and progress throughout the year.

Student Digital Portfolio A SAM feature that allows you to review, evaluate, and store students' writing and fluency recordings from the Topic Software and *rSkills Tests*. Click the purple Portfolio tab in SAM to access the Student Digital Portfolio.

Teacher Dashboard A website that supports you to monitor student performance, plan and group for differentiated instruction, and engage in professional development. Access the Teacher Dashboard at home by visiting **www.read180.com/teacherdashboard.**

Text Complexity A comprehensive representation of text readability that consists of three measures: **quantitative,** or how technically difficult the text is, represented by Lexile; **qualitative,** or how complex the subject matter and language is; and **reader and task,** or the specific expectations for student understanding.

Topic A group of four Topic Software segments that share a common theme. There are 15 total Topics for each Stage of the *READ 180* Topic Software.

Workshop One *rBook* unit of reading, vocabulary, writing, and academic language instruction based on a central topic. Each *READ 180* Stage includes nine *rBook* Workshops for Whole- and Small-Group Instruction, which take four to six weeks to complete.

Bibliography

ACT, Inc. (2006). *Reading between the lines: What the ACT reveals about college readiness in reading.* Iowa City, IA.

Adams, M.J. (2009). The challenge of advanced texts: The interdependence of reading and learning. In E.H. Hiebert (Ed.), *Reading More, Reading Better* (pp. 163–189). New York: Guilford.

Afflerbach, P., Pearson, D.P., & Paris, S.G. (2008). Clarifying differences between reading Skills and Reading strategies. *The Reading Teacher,* 61(5), 364–373.

Andrade, H. (2007/2008). Self-assessment through rubrics. *Educational Leadership,* 65(4), 60–63.

August D., & Shanahan, T. (Eds.) (2006). *Developing Literacy in second-language learners: Report of the National Literacy Panel on Language-Minority Children and Youth.* Mahwah, NJ: Erlbaum.

Avalos, M.A. (2006). No two learners are alike: Learners with linguistic and cultural differences. In J.S. Schumm (Ed.), *Reading assessment and instruction for all learners* (pp. 59–86). New York: Guilford.

Biancarosa, G., & Snow, C.E. (2004). *Reading Next—A vision for action and research in middle and high school literacy: A report from Carnegie Corporation of New York.* Washington, DC: Alliance for Excellent Education.

Bos, C.S., & Vaughn, S. (2002). *Strategies for teaching students with learning and behavior problems* (5th ed.). Boston: Allyn & Bacon.

Bransford, J.D., Brown, A.L., & Cocking, R.R. (Eds.) (2003). *How people learn: Brain, mind, experience, and school.* Washington, DC: National Academy Press.

Carnegie Council on Advancing Adolescent Literacy. (2010). *Time to act: An agenda for advancing adolescent literacy for college and career success.* New York: Carnegie Corporation of New York.

Council of Chief State School Officers & National Governors Association. (2010). *Common Core State Standards for English language arts and literacy in history/social sciences, science, and technical subjects—Appendix A: Research supporting key elements of the standards.*

Daggett, W.R., & Hasselbring, T.S. (2007). What we know about adolescent reading. International Center for Leadership in Education. Retrieved online: http://www.leadered.com/pdf/Adolescent%20Reading%20Whitepaper.pdf.

Duke, N.K. (2010). The real-world reading and writing U.S. children need. *Phi Delta Kappan,* 91(5), 68–71.

Dutro, S., & Kinsella, K. (2010). English language development: Issues and implementation at grades six through twelve. *In Improving education for English learners: Research-based approaches.* Sacramento, CA. CDE Press.

Feldman, K., & Denti, L. (2004). High-access instruction: Practical strategies to increase active learning in diverse classrooms. *Focus on Exceptional Children,* 36(7), 1–12.

Forster, M. (2009). Informative Assessment: Understanding and Guiding Learning. ACER Research Conference.

Hasselbring, T.S., & Goin, L. (2004). Literacy instruction for older struggling readers: What is the role of technology? *Reading and Writing Quarterly,* 20(2), 123–144.

Heo, Y. (2007). The impact of multimedia anchored instruction on the motivation to learn of students with and without learning disabilities placed in inclusive middle school language arts classes (Doctoral dissertation, University of Texas, 2007). Dissertations Abstracts International, 6812A, 5031.

Hirsch, E.D., Jr. (2003, Spring). Reading comprehension requires knowledge—of words and the world: Scientific insights into the fourth-grade slump and the nation's stagnant comprehension scores. *American Educator,* 27(1), 10–45.

Hupert, N., & Heinze, J. (2006). Results in the palms of their hands: Using handheld computers for data-driven decision making in the classroom. In M. van 't Hooft & K. Swan (Eds.), *Ubiquitous computing in education: Invisible technology, visible impact* (pp. 211–229). Mahwah, NJ: Erlbaum.

Jensen, E. (2005). *Teaching With the Brain in Mind.* Alexandria, VA: Association for Supervision and Curriculum Development.

Kamil, M.L., Intrator, S.M., & Kim, H.S. (2000). The effects of other technologies on literacy and literacy learning. In M.L. Kamil, P.B. Mosenthal, P.D. Pearson, & R. Barr, (Eds.), *Handbook of Reading Research* (Vol. III, pp. 771–788). Mahwah, NJ: Erlbaum.

Labov, W. (2006). "Summary Statement on African American Vernacular English." Presented at a briefing on struggling readers. Sacramento, CA.

Mapp, K.L., & Henderson, A.T. (2002). *A new wave of evidence: The impact of school, family, and community connections on student achievement.* Austin, Texas: Southwest Educational Development Laboratory (SEDL), National Center for Family and Community Connections with Schools.

Moats, L.C. (2001). "When Older Kids Can't Read." *Educational Leadership,* 58 (6), 36–40.

National Institute of Child Health and Human Development (NICHD). (2000). *Report of the National Reading Panel. Teaching children to read: An evidence-based assessment of the scientific research literature on reading and its implications for reading instruction: Reports of the subgroups* (NIH Publication No. 00–4754). Washington, DC: US Government Printing Office.

National Institute for Literacy (2007). *What content-area teachers should know about adolescent literacy.* Washington, DC: The National Institute for Literacy, The National Institute for Child Health and Human Development (NICHD), U.S. Department of Education's Office for Vocational and Adult Education.

National Joint Committee on Learning Disabilities (2008). *Adolescent Literacy and Older Students With Learning Disabilities: A Report from the National Joint Committee on Learning Disabilities.*

National Reading Panel (2000). *Teaching Students to read: An evidence-based assessment of the scientific research literature on reading and its implications for reading instruction* (NIH Pub. No. 00–4769). Washington, DC: National Institute of Child Health and Human Development.

Perin, D. (2007). Best practices in teaching writing to adolescents. In S. Graham, C.A. MacArthur, & J. Fitzgerald (Eds.), *Best Practices in writing instruction* (pp. 242–264). New York: Guilford.

Pressley, M., Gaskins, I.W., Solic, K., & Collins, S. (2006). A portrait of benchmark school: How a school produces high achievement in students who previously failed. *Journal of Educational Psychology,* 98(2), 282–306.

Index